Jesus of Nazareth

Jesus of Nazareth

Joshua ben Joseph Biography

CC Martin

To order additional copies of this book, contact:
Xlibris
844-714-8691
www.Xlibris.com
Orders@Xlibris.com
859828

Contents

CHAPTER 1

An Introduction to Set the Stage

THIS IS THE TRUE STORY OF THE HISTORICAL FIGURE THAT WAS born Joshua ben Joseph (Joshua son of Joseph) but has become known throughout the world as Jesus of Nazareth. This book was conceived through the use of spiritual visioning over a period of many years. It was a labor of love for the most influential man ever to walk the Earth. His philosophy of love for God and love for our fellow man is as alive and meaningful today as it was two thousand years ago. This work was dictated by Jesus, Mary, Joseph and many other benevolent and very powerful spirits and angels from the spiritual realms where we all came from, and to where we shall return when this material life is over.

Jesus of Nazareth did not come into this world during an age of spiritual decadence. At the time of his birth, this planet was experiencing a revival of spiritual thinking and religious living that had never been seen before. Evolutionary man's ego was sure enough of its position in relation to the world around him that the projected picture of God could finally begin to change from a god of anger and vengeance to a god of love and mercy. The psychological and spiritual needs of the human species were demanding both interior and exterior changes of great importance by this time. Qualities of mercy and understanding that Moses could not speak of fifteen hundred years previously, now had a willing audience of hundreds of thousands. Not only privately, but in masse, all over the Roman Empire, these yearnings surged up, adding a new impetus and giving a natural new direction to man's relation to God.

It was not by pure chance or coincidence that the Father sent one of his Sons to Earth in the manner that he did, and at the time that he did. The plans had been formulated, and the Son had been ordained in the Heavenly Realms, thousands of Earth years before the birth, to coincide with this moment in history and in this location between the Eastern and Western worlds. The Prophet Melchizedek had told the world through his missionaries two thousand years previously of the coming of a Son of God, and now from the Heavenly Realms he waited and watched patiently for the unfolding of this great drama.

When Jesus appeared on Earth, the world presented the most favorable condition for the arrival of a Son of Heaven than had prevailed for thousands of years or has since prevailed up until this day. In the centuries just before, Greek culture and the Greek language had spread over Occident and near Orient, and the Jews, being a member of the Levantine peoples, by nature part Occidental and part Oriental, were eminently fitted to utilize their cultural and linguistic settings for the effective spread of a new religion to both East and West. These most favorable circumstances were further enhanced by the tolerant political rule of the Mediterranean world by the Romans.

This combination of world influences is well illustrated by the activities of the Apostle Paul, who, being in religious culture a Hebrew, proclaimed the Gospel of a Jewish Messiah in the Greek language, while he himself was a Roman citizen.

Nothing like the civilization of the times of Jesus has been seen in the Levant since those days. European civilization in those days was unified and coordinated under an extraordinary threefold influence:

a) the Roman political and social system
b) the Greek language, culture and philosophy
c) the rapidly spreading influence of Jewish religious and moral teachings throughout all the countries of the Levant, and between both Jew and Gentile.

When Jesus was born, the entire Mediterranean world was a unified empire. Good roads, for the first time in the history of the world, interconnected many of the major cities. The seas had been cleared of pirates, and a great era of trade and travel was rapidly advancing. Europe did not again enjoy another such period of free travel and trade until the Nineteenth Century A.D.

Notwithstanding the internal peace and superficial prosperity of the Greco-Roman world, a majority of the inhabitants of the empire languished in squalor and poverty. A small upper class was very rich, while a miserable and impoverished lower class embraced the common people. There was no happy and prosperous middle class in those days. The middle class had just begun to make its appearance in the Roman merchant society.

The first struggles between the expanding Roman and Parthian states had been concluded in the then recent past, leaving Syria in the hands of the Romans. In the times of Jesus, Palestine and Syria were enjoying a period of prosperity, peace, and extensive commercial intercourse with the lands of both the East and West.

The Jews

The Jews of Palestine were a part of the older Semitic tribes known as the Hebrews. The Hebrew were a part of a much larger Semitic brotherhood which also included the Babylonians, the Phoenicians, the Syrians, the Persians and the more recent enemies of Rome, the Carthaginians. During the lifetime of Jesus of Nazareth, the Jews were the most influential group of the Palestinian Semites. They happened to occupy a peculiarly strategic geographic position in the world as it was at that time ruled and organized for trade by Rome.

Many of the great highways joining the nations of antiquity passed through Palestine, which thus became the meeting place, or crossroads, of three continents. The travel, trade, and armies of Babylon, Assyria, Egypt, Syria, Greece, Parthia, and Rome successively swept over Palestine. From time immemorial, major caravan routes from the orient passed through some part of this region to the few good seaports on the Eastern end of the Mediterranean, where ships carried their cargoes to all the maritime Mediterranean world. More than half of this caravan traffic passed through or near the town of Nazareth in Galilee. It was for this reason that Jesus of Nazareth was sent into this hub of the world to proclaim his gospel here and have it spread to the ends of the world on the backs of the caravan camels and on the sails of the Mediterranean fleets.

At the time of the appearance of Jesus of Nazareth, there were four separate and distinct groups that comprised the Jews of that day. They were the Pharisees, the Sadducees, the Zealots and the Essenes. The Essenes wrote the documents you now call the Dead Sea Scrolls. They were the most progressive and liberal of all of these religio-political groups. They had deep roots in some of the Mystery religions of the Greeks and their philosophy and teachings descended from the religions of Mesopotamia. The Essenes operated in much the same way as any other religio-political group of that day. As a means of supporting themselves and to spread their influence and philosophy, they conducted schools for boys and young men. Women were not allowed in these schools. But the schools were not what they appeared to be. Subterfuge was used as part of their operations. Various initiation tests were applied before a candidate could come close to knowing the true doctrines being fostered by the group.

The schools of these religio-political groups often pretended to be giving an education in certain areas of theology and philosophy. The strangers and students would be kept in its outer group. Only those students selected to carry on the work of the sect would be allowed to know the true doctrines. Most students attended such schools without ever knowing of the inner initiates, and the more important work being carried on beneath the camouflage.

John the Baptizer was initiated into the Essene brotherhood at the request of his parents. He was an Essene in all important ways.

Yet a man who steps forward in such a dramatic way automatically steps out of his group and so did John. The Essenes rejected John when he started preaching the gospel of the kingdom of Heaven.

Records of these sects were often falsified, completely doctored, and false records were often planted to confuse the enemy, either political, as in Rome, or religious, as in the other religious groups.

Religion was politics, and politics was religion. There was no differentiation in those days, just as there is no differentiation to this very day in that part of the world. Religion implied sway and power over the masses. It was the business of the rulers to know in which direction the religious winds blew. Because of the power struggles between these religious groups who all wanted to control the masses of believers, there were deliberate falsifications of fact, then and later into the early centuries of the Christian religion. Some sects even kept false records on purpose as blinds, so that if these were stolen, the robbers would think they had what they were after.

In many cases, false records have been found instead of the real ones. This has caused much confusion in your present-day Christian and Jewish religions because you are looking at ancient records that contradict each other. The Essenes, as well as the other groups, kept one set of records to confuse the Zealots, and another set to confuse the Romans, but they carefully guarded the inner set from which all the facts were made. The Essenes were not as violent as the other groups, but they were just as shrewd.

Think of the language used presently by governments and diplomats. Think of the difference between what your government knows, and what your government tells you. It was no different two thousand years ago. Governments will forever keep their secrets to protect themselves, not to protect you. Words, therefore, are often used to cover up as well as to reveal. Great efforts are taken so that knowledge is kept from a majority and for the benefit of a minority of power-hungry individuals. In Biblical times this was all the truer. Literary devices themselves served as formalized methods of seeming to indulge certain information, while actually offering instead falsified data.

The peoples of the Levant in those days also used many verbal rituals. When speaking publicly or to a group of listeners, no question in those days was answered directly, not by those who were at all literate. To answer a question directly meant that you were simple minded and lacked any appreciation of the questioner's greater intelligence, for he seldom asked a question he really wanted answered. It was highly ritualized behavior, but it was understood in those terms. Jesus became a master of this manner of communication. He also spoke in parables, which were a very popular way of addressing groups of people in those days. He asked questions at the end of each parable not intending to receive a reply but instead to pose a situation to the listener, and at the same time to suggest the correct answer. This method of communication had been developed by the Greeks hundreds of years before the Birth of Jesus and was used most effectively by Socrates, Plato and Aristotle.

Of the material that dates to that period of time, and more specifically the Dead Sea Scrolls, modern man cannot understand how to translate the material properly from many of those records, even when the translations are word for word correct. Scholars today consider whole pages of the Dead Sea Scrolls tremendous put-ons, since whole pages are not true. These were expected exaggerations and embellishments that preceded the giving of information.

All religio-political groups at that time, in one way or another, had such fashions. The records meant life or death if they were discovered at the wrong time. Falsifications were often put in simply to lead any readers astray if the books fell into the wrong hands. Those in the know had nothing to worry about. They could not be misled. To them the information was clear and the distortions obvious. The Dead Sea scrolls are full of such protective distortions.

The scribes in those days used signs as codes. These signs appeared in many guises, sometimes intertwined with signatures. These people were much given to codes. Even the arrangement of the letters upon the pages had their meanings. The weight or thickness of various strokes had meaning in terms of emphasis. There were even certain ways of handling a preceding word, so that the word would be a clue that the next word was false. Only those in the know would recognize this and the others would merrily digest the false information. Some of the falsified records that were set out for the enemy to capture even had poison on the pages of the manuscripts - deadly reading material indeed. If you licked your finger to turn the page, you were dead.

When the persecutions began in Jerusalem after the death of Jesus, the descriptions of important individuals were changed to ensure their safety. Backgrounds were often fictional for the same reason. These were life and death struggles. Most of the men involved in these historic struggles lead double and triple lives. They were known in their village by their birth name, in their brotherhoods by another name and often preached by a third name. In most cases their more mundane identities were never revealed but to a few close associates and family members. When the Christians were being hunted and persecuted by the Romans and the Jews, there were additional safeguards taken, particularly by those who believed they had a responsibility to live long enough to see the new gospel find fertile ground. They began the practice of creating doubles. The Apostle Paul was one who was often seen and heard in various places at once, often in different countries at the same time. He would send out willing followers who claimed to be Paul as a diversion against the enemies while he went elsewhere under a different name to preach the good news without danger of being caught.

The Jewish world at that time was controlled by two philosophies.

On the right were the Pharisees and the Zealots, the high and the narrow. They were very orthodox, punctilious upon the minutest details of the law, intensely patriotic and exclusive. They refused to receive any converts and would not even associate with anyone that was not a born Jew. Their God was not a God of all nations and all peoples but was exclusively for the Jews.

On the left were the Sadducees and the Essenes, the broad and the worldly. They were the Hellenized Jews and did not believe in immortality. These broad Jews were all more or less disposed to mingle with and assimilate with the Greeks and other Hellenized peoples around the Mediterranean. They were mostly converts to Judaism and readily accepted more converts. They were ready to share their God and his promises with all men.

Although Palestine was the home of the Jewish religious culture and birthplace of Christianity, the Jews and Jewish converts were abroad in all the known world at that time, living in many nations and trading throughout the Roman and Parthian states. The Jewish religion, being far more satisfying than the mystery religions of the time, found waves of converts throughout the Roman and Parthian states. The vast majority of peoples that now call themselves Jews, especially the European Jews, are not related to the Jews of Palestine, the so-called tribes of Judah and Israel, or even to any of the earlier tribes that comprised the Hebrews. They are, instead, converts from the poor classes and the slave classes that resulted as waves of poor and downcast humanity looked to that religion for spiritual guidance in the centuries before and after the birth of Jesus.

Greece provided a language and a culture, Rome built the roads and unified an empire, but the Jews, with their more than two hundred synagogues and well-organized religious communities scattered hither and yon throughout the Roman world, provided the cultural centers in which the new gospel of the kingdom of Heaven found initial reception, and from which it subsequently spread to the uttermost parts of the world.

Each Jewish synagogue embraced a fringe of Gentile converts, and it was among this fringe of converts that Paul first made the bulk of his early converts to Christianity. Even the temple in Jerusalem possessed its ornate Court of the Gentile Converts. There was a very close connection between the culture, commerce, and workshop of Jerusalem and Antioch. It was in Antioch, that Paul's disciples were first called "Christians."

The centralization of the Jewish temple worship at Jerusalem constituted both the secret of the survival of their monotheism, and the promise of the nurture and sending forth to the world of the Jewish Messiah. The temple at Jerusalem represented the survival of a religio- cultural concept in the face of the downfall of a succession of Gentile national gods and racial persecutors.

The Jewish people at that time, although under Roman rule, enjoyed a considerable degree of self-government and, remembering the recent heroic exploits of deliverance executed by Judas Maccabee and his immediate successors, were vibrant with the expectation of the appearance of a still greater deliverer, the long-expected Messiah that Melchizedek had spoken of two thousand years previously.

The secret of the survival of the Palestinian tribes, the homeland of the Jews, as a semi-independent state was wrapped up in the foreign policy of the Roman government, which desired to maintain control of the Palestinian highway of travel between Syria and Egypt as well as the western terminals of the caravan routes between the Orient and the Occident. Rome did not wish any power to arise in the Levant, which might curb her future expansion in these regions. The Roman policy of intrigue which pitted Seleucid Syria and Ptolemaic Egypt against each other necessitated fostering Palestine as a separate and independent state.

Roman policy, the degeneration of Egypt, and the progressive weakening of the Seleucids before the rising power of Parthia, explain why it was that for several generations the small and unpowerful tribes in Palestine, including the Jews, were able to maintain their independence against both powers of the Seleucids to the north and the Ptolemies to the south. This fortuitous liberty and independence from the political rule of surrounding and more powerful peoples, was attributed by the Jews to the fact that they were the "Chosen People" of Yahweh. Such an arrogant attitude of racial superiority made it all the more difficult for them to endure Roman rule when it finally fell upon their heads. But even in that sad hour after the death of Jesus of Nazareth, when the Romans arrived to destroy Jerusalem, the Jews refused to face the fact that they would never be a major political power.

The Jews of Jerusalem were unusually apprehensive and suspicious during the times of Jesus because they were then ruled by an outsider, Herod the Idumean, who had seized the Kingship of all of the tribes of Palestine by cleverly ingratiating himself with the Roman emperor. Though Herod was a Hebrew, and professed loyalty to the Hebrew ceremonial observances, he proceeded to build temples for many strange Gods.

The great benefit of this arrangement though, was that the friendly relations between Herod and the Roman rulers made the world safe for Jewish, and later Christian, travel and thus opened the way for increased Jewish/Christian penetration even of distant portions of the Roman empire and of foreign treaty nations, and allowed the dispersion of the new gospel of the kingdom of Heaven. The Hellenized Jews proceeded to win waves of converts from as far away as Spain and the British Isles. Most of those converts later became the first Christians. Herod's reign also contributed much toward the further blending of Hebrew and Hellenistic philosophies.

Herod built the harbor of Caesarea, which further aided in making Palestine the crossroads of the civilized world. After he died, his son Herod Antipas governed Galilee and Perea during Jesus' youth and ministry. Antipas, like his father, was a great builder. He rebuilt many of the cities of Galilee, including the important trade center of Sepphoris.

At this time in the history of Palestine, the Galileans were not regarded with full favor by the Jews of Jerusalem. After the days of Moses, the Semitic peoples of Galilee were counted as one of the Hebrew tribes, but after hundreds of years of internal warfare between the tribe of Israel and the tribe of Judah, and after the enslavement of the tribe of Israel in Ninevah, Capital of Assyria, the Galileans allied themselves with the Philistines and the Syrians, and against the tribe of Judah. For several hundred years they did not associate themselves with Jerusalem, but approximately one hundred years before the birth of Jesus, the army of Jerusalem, under the direction of the Romans, invaded Galilee and converted the population by the sword. Those who refused to adhere to the authority and religion of Jerusalem were put to death. Thus, at the time of the birth of Jesus, the Jews still held all Galileans with contempt and did not consider them as Jews, but rather as Gentile converts, which did not accord them the same privileges as the Jews of Jerusalem.

THE GENTILES

From a moral standpoint at the time Jesus came into the world, there was present in the hearts of the nobler Gentiles abundant soil of natural goodness and human affection in which it was possible for the seed of Christianity to sprout and bring forth an abundant harvest of moral character and spiritual achievement. The Gentile world was then dominated by four great philosophies, all more or less derived from the earlier teachings of Plato and the Greek philosophers. These schools of philosophy were:

A) The Epicureans - this school of thought was dedicated to the pursuit of happiness. The better Epicureans were not given to sensual excesses. At least this doctrine helped to deliver the Romans from a more deadly form of fatalism. It taught that men could do something to improve their terrestrial status. This philosophy effectively combated ignorant superstition.

B) The Stoics - Stoicism was the superior philosophy of the higher classes. The stoics believed that a controlling reason-fate dominated all nature. They taught that the soul of man was divine, that it was imprisoned in the evil body of physical nature. Man's soul achieved liberty by living in harmony with nature, with God. Thus, virtue came to be its own reward. Stoicism ascended to a sublime morality; ideals have never since been transcended by any purely human system of philosophy.

While the Stoics professed to be the 'Offspring of God', they failed to know him and therefore failed to find him. Stoicism remained a philosophy. It never became a religion. Its followers sought to attune their minds to the harmony of the universe, but they failed to envision themselves as the children of a loving Father. The Apostle Paul leaned heavily toward Stoicism when he wrote, "I have learned that in whatsoever state I am, therewith to be content."

C) The Cynics - although the Cynics traced their philosophy to Diogenes of Athens, they derived much of their doctrine from the remnants of the teachings of Melchizedek through the missionaries that had lived and worked in Greece. Cynicism had formerly been more of a religion than a philosophy. At least the Cynics made their religio-philosophy democratic. In the fields and in the marketplaces, they continually preached their doctrine that: man can save himself if he only will. They preached simplicity and virtue and urged men to meet death fearlessly. These wandering Cynic preachers were even patterned after the Melchizedek missionaries of two thousand years previously and did much to prepare the spiritually hungry populace for the later Christian missionaries. Their plan of popular preaching was the pattern and the style of Paul's Epistles. Most of the Cynics, preachers and populace alike, became the first of the Greek Christians.

D) The Skeptics - skepticism proclaimed that knowledge was fallacious, and that conviction and assurance were impossible. It was a purely negative attitude and never became widespread.

These philosophies were semi-religious. They were often invigorating, ethical, and ennobling but were usually above the common people. With the possible exception of cynicism, they were philosophies for the strong and the wise, not religions of salvation for the poor and the weak.

Throughout the preceding ages religion had chiefly been an affair of the tribe or nation. It had not often been a matter of concern to the individual. Gods were tribal or national, not personal. Such religious systems afforded little satisfaction for the spiritual longings of the average person.

In the times of Jesus, the Gentile religions of the Occident included:

1) The Pagan Cults - these were a combination of Hellenic and Latin mythology, patriotism, and tradition.

2) Emperor Worship - this deification of man as the symbol of the state was very seriously resented by the Jews and the early Christians and led directly to the bitter persecutions of both churches by the Roman government.

3) Astrology - this pseudo-science founded in Babylon developed into a religion throughout the Greco-Roman empire. Even in the Twentieth Century man has not been fully delivered from this superstitious belief.

4) The Mystery Religions - upon such a spiritually hungry world a flood of mystery cults had broken, new and strange religions from the Levant, which had enamored the common people and had promised them individual salvation. These religions rapidly became the accepted beliefs of the lower classes of the Greco-Roman world. They did much to prepare the way for the rapid spread of the vastly superior Christian teachings, which presented a majestic concept of God, associated with an intriguing theology for the intelligent and a profound offer of salvation for all, including the ignorant but spiritually hungry average man of those days. Christianity was the first religion which had as its premise, the fact that all mortals are equal in

the eyes of God. King and slave held the same position as children of God, and this profound truth brought the multitudes of poor and suffering into the Christian religion.

The Mystery Religions spelled the end of national beliefs and resulted in the birth of the numerous personal cults. The mysteries were many but were all characterized by:

1) Some mythical legend, a mystery - whence their name. As a rule, this mystery pertained to the story of some God's life and death and return to life, as illustrated by the teachings of Mithraism, which, for a time, were contemporary with, and a competitor of, Paul's rising Cult of Christianity.

2) The mysteries were non-national and interracial. They were personal and fraternal, giving rise to religious brotherhoods and numerous sectarian societies.

3) They were, in their services, characterized by elaborate ceremonies of initiation, baptism and impressive sacraments of worship which included holy water, bread and wine, candles, incense, hooded monks with the top of their heads shaven and statues of the mother of God with the child-god in her arms.

4) No matter what the nature of their ceremonies or the degree of their excesses, these mysteries invariably promised their devotees salvation, deliverance from evil, survival after death, and enduring life in blissful realms beyond this world of sorrow and slavery.

Do not make the mistake of confusing the teachings of Jesus with the teachings of the Mystery Religions. The popularity of the Mystery Religions revealed man's quest for survival, thus portraying a real hunger and thirst for personal religion and individual righteousness. Although the Mysteries failed adequately to satisfy this longing, they did prepare the way for the subsequent Gospel of Jesus of Nazareth, who truly brought to this world the knowledge of the essence of the real loving Father and the brotherhood of all men of the Earth.

The Apostle Paul, in an effort to utilize the widespread adherence to the better types of the Mystery Religions, made many adaptations of the teachings of Jesus, interjecting many of the customs and rituals of the Mystery Religions so as to render Christianity more acceptable to a larger number of prospective converts. Paul borrowed the rituals of bread and wine as body and blood, holy water, candles, incense, statues of the mother and child, mystical birth, atonement, original sin, etc. from the Mystery Religions of his day. This was the first major error by the early Christians, and after the first two hundred years the result was that the Gospel of Jesus of Nazareth was lost to the rituals and customs of the "Mystical" Christian Church. There were no mysteries in the simple gospel and loving ministry of Jesus of Nazareth, but the early church created many mysteries under the pretext of attracting more Jewish and Gentile converts. However great were the distortions by Paul's compromise, the teachings of Jesus of Nazareth attributed to Paul were far superior to the best in the mysteries in that:

A) Paul taught a moral redemption, an ethical salvation. Christianity pointed to a new life and proclaimed a new ideal. Paul refused many of the magical rites and ceremonial enchantments, but later Christian leaders who were still lost in the Mystery Religions managed to interject those mysteries back into the ceremonies and beliefs of the early Christian Church.

B) Christianity presented a religion which grappled with final solutions of the human problem, for it not only offered salvation from sorrow and even from death, but it also promised deliverance from sin followed by the endowment of a righteous character.

C) The Mysteries were built upon myths. Christianity, as Paul preached it, was founded upon a historic fact, the bestowal of Jesus of Nazareth, a Son of God, upon the peoples of Earth.

Morality among the Gentiles of this age was not necessarily related to either philosophy or religion. Outside of Palestine, it not always occurred to people that a priest of religion was supposed to lead a moral life. Jewish religion, and subsequently the teachings of Jesus, and later the evolving Christianity of Paul, were the first European religions to lay one hand upon morals and the other upon ethics, insisting that religionists pay some attention to both.

The Stage is Set

Into such a generation of truth-seeking men, dominated by such incomplete systems of philosophy and perplexed by such complex cults of religion, Jesus of Nazareth was born in Palestine. To this same generation he subsequently gave his gospel of personal religion - that all human beings on the face of the Earth are the children of God.

In the decades just prior to the birth of Jesus, the religious thought of Jerusalem had been tremendously influenced and somewhat modified by Greek cultural teachings and even by Greek philosophy. In the long contest between the views of the Eastern and Western schools of Hebrew thought, Jerusalem and the rest of the Occident, and the Levant in general, had adopted the Western Jewish or modified Hellenistic philosophy.

Five hundred years previously, Babylon had given birth to the gradual development of the Jewish idea of one just God ruling the Earth and bound by a special promise to preserve and bring to honor the Jewish people. The Jewish idea was, and is, a curious combination of theological breadth and intense racial patriotism. The Jews of that time looked for a special savior, a Messiah, who was to come and redeem mankind by the agreeable process of restoring the throne of David and Solomon and bringing the whole known world under the domination of the Jewish heel.

As the political power of the Semitic peoples declined, as Carthage and Tyre fell into darkness, and Spain became a Roman province, the dream of a savior grew and spread wherever the Jews told the story of the coming Messiah. The scattered Phoenicians in Spain and North Africa and throughout the Mediterranean became converts to Judaism because of their persecution and loss of their homeland to the southward moving European tribes who were now the Greeks and Romans. There were Arab Jews throughout the countries of North Africa in those days. They now call themselves Muslims.

There were Turkish Jews in the south of what is now called Russia that were being driven south by the southward expanding European man and displaced from their ancient homelands, all converts to the cult of the Messiah. Judaism became the reconstructed political ideal of many shattered peoples, people who had lost homelands and identities and now wanted a savior to come in a golden chariot by sky to correct all wrongs and give all power to the powerless and return lost homelands. There were converts to Judaism throughout the empires of Rome and Parthia, but mostly from the lower and slave classes. The majority of Jews in those days were peoples who had never been in Judea nor had any blood relation to the Palestinian Jews in and around Jerusalem.

Throughout a history of five hundred years of war and civil commotion after the Jewish return from slavery in Babylon, the Jewish conscience persisted. They remained obstinately monotheistic and would have no other God but their one God, Yahweh. In Rome as in Jerusalem, their beliefs were the same. To the best of his ability the Jew held to his covenant with his God. No graven images could enter Jerusalem. Even the Roman standards with their eagles remained outside the walls of Jerusalem.

During the lifetime of Jesus three languages prevailed in Palestine: the common people spoke some dialect of Aramaic, the priests and rabbis spoke Hebrew, and the educated classes and the better strata of Jews in general spoke Greek. The early translation of the Hebrew scriptures into Greek at Alexandria was greatly responsible for the subsequent predominance of the Greek wing of Jewish culture and theology. The writings of the Christian teachers were soon to appear in the same language. The renaissance of Judaism dates from the Greek translation of the Hebrew scriptures. This was vital influence which later determined the drift of Paul's Christian cult toward the west instead of toward the east.

Though the Hellenized Jewish beliefs were very little influenced by the teachings of the Epicureans, they were very materially affected by the philosophy of Plato and the self-abnegation doctrines of the Stoics. The penetration of both Platonic philosophy and Stoic doctrines is exhibited in the writings by Hebrew authors but attributed to their King Solomon. The Greek Jews brought to the Hebrew scriptures such an allegorical interpretation that they found no difficulty in conforming Hebrew theology with their revered Aristotelian philosophy. But this all led to a disastrous confusion until these problems were taken in hand by Philo of Alexandria, who proceeded to harmonize and systematize Greek philosophy and Hebrew theology into a compact and fairly consistent system of religious belief and practice. It was this later teaching of combined Greek philosophy and Hebrew theology that prevailed in Palestine when Jesus lived and taught, and which Paul utilized as the foundation on which to build his more advanced and enlightened cult of Christianity.

Philo was a great teacher, but he made many errors and inconsistencies in his efforts to combine Greek mystical philosophy and Roman stoic doctrines with the legalistic theology of the Hebrews. Paul recognized and wisely eliminated most of these, but not all, from his Pre-Christian basic theology. Philo led the way for Paul more fully to restore the concept of the Heavenly Trinity, which had long been dormant in Jewish theology. In only one matter did Paul fail to keep pace with Philo or to transcend the teachings of this wealthy and educated Jew of Alexandria, and that was the Doctrine of the Atonement. Philo also vaguely glimpsed the reality and presence of the Divine Spirit more clearly than did Paul. As a basis for his writings and teachings, Philo used the last complete copy of the Egyptian Prophet Amenemope's Book of Wisdom and derived most of his philosophic thought from that book.

Where Paul failed miserably was in his teachings of the Theory of Original Sin, the Doctrines of Hereditary Guilt and Innate Evil, and Redemption therefrom. The majority of that philosophy was Mithraic in origin from the days when Paul was a member of the cult of Mithras, having little in common with Hebrew theology, Philo's philosophy, and even less with the teachings of Jesus of Nazareth. Some parts of Paul's teachings regarding Original Sin and the Atonement were original creations of his own, having no basis in any previous religion or philosophy.

Later teachings, such as the Gospel of John, the last of the narratives of Jesus' Earth life, were addressed to the western peoples rather than to the Jews and present a story in the light of the viewpoint of the later Alexandrian Christians, who were also disciples of the teachings of Philo.

Throughout the whole Mediterranean world, no matter where Jews found themselves living, all kept their hearts centered on their Temple at Jerusalem. As many as two and one half million of these converted Jews living outside of Palestine traveled to Jerusalem for the celebrations of their national religious festivals each year. No matter what the theological or philosophic differences of the Eastern (Babylonian) and Western (Hellenic) Jews, they all agreed on Jerusalem as the center of their religion and in looking forward to the coming of the Messiah.

By the time of the arrival of Jesus of Nazareth, the Orthodox Jews had arrived at a settled concept of their origin, history, and destiny.

They had built up a rigid wall of separation between themselves and the Gentile world. They looked upon all Gentile ways with utter contempt. They worshipped the letter of the law and indulged in a form of self- righteousness based upon the false pride of their descent. They had formed preconceived notions regarding the promised Messiah, and most of these expectations envisioned a messiah who would come as a part of their national and racial history. To the Orthodox Jews of those days Jewish theology was irrevocably settled, forever fixed.

The teachings and practices of Jesus regarding tolerance and kindness, therefore, ran counter to the long-standing attitude of the Jews of Jerusalem toward all other peoples who they considered heathen. For generations the Jews had nourished an attitude toward the outside world which made it impossible for them to accept the Master's teachings about the spiritual brotherhood of man. They were unwilling to share Yahweh on equal terms with the Gentiles and were likewise unwilling to accept as the Messiah one who taught such new and strange doctrines that ran counter to Jewish law.

The Scribes, the Pharisees, and the Priesthood held the Jews in a terrible bondage of ritualism and legalism, a bondage far more real than that of the Roman political rule. The Jews of Jesus' time were not only held in subjugation to "the law" but were equally bound by the slavish demands of their traditions, which involved and invaded every minute detail of personal and social life. These minute regulations of conduct pursued and dominated every loyal

Jew no matter what country he lived in, and it is not strange that these Jews immediately rejected one of their own who presumed to ignore their sacred traditions, and who dared to flout their long-honored regulations of social conduct. They could hardly regard with favor the teachings of one who did not hesitate to clash with dogmas which they regarded as having been ordained by Moses himself. They believed that Moses had given them their law and they would not compromise.

By the time of the birth of Jesus, the spoken interpretation of the law by the recognized teachers, the Rabbis, had become a higher authority than the written law itself. All this made it easier for certain religious leaders of the Jews to sway the people against the acceptance of a new gospel.

These circumstances rendered it impossible for the Jews to act as messengers of the new gospel. The Prophet Jeremiah had written of the "law to be written in men's hearts." Ezekiel had spoken of a "new spirit to live in man's soul," and the Psalmists of Egypt had prayed that God would "create a clean heart within and renew a right spirit." But when the Jewish religion of slavery to law fell victim to the stagnation of tradition, the motion of religious evolution stopped dead in its tracks in Palestine and passed westward to the European peoples.

Thus, it came to pass that a different people were called upon to carry the torch of an advancing theology to the world, a system of teaching embodying the philosophy of the Greeks, the law of the Romans, the morality of the Hebrews, and the Gospel of Spiritual Sanctity and brotherly love formulated by Paul and based on the teachings of Jesus of Nazareth.

The Mediterranean Roman Empire, the Parthian kingdom, and the adjacent peoples of Jesus' time all held crude and primitive ideas regarding the geography of the world, astronomy, health, and disease. Naturally they were amazed by the new and startling pronouncements of the carpenter from Nazareth. Their ideas of spirit possession, good and bad, applied not merely to human beings, but every rock and tree was viewed by many as being spirit possessed. This was an enchanted age, and everybody believed in miracles as commonplace occurrences.

Although the social and economic condition of the Roman state was not of the highest order, the widespread domestic peace and prosperity was fertile ground for the arrival of Jesus. At the time of the birth, the society of the Mediterranean World consisted of five well- defined strata:

a) The Aristocracy - the upper classes with money and official power, the privileged and ruling groups.

b) The Business Groups - the merchant princes and the bankers, the traders, the importers and exporters, the international merchants.

c) The Small Middle Class - although this group was indeed small, it was very influential and provided the moral backbone of the early Christian Church, which encouraged these groups to continue in their various crafts and trades. Among the Jews many of the Pharisees belonged to this class of tradesmen.

d) The Free Common People - this group had little or no social standing. Though proud of their freedom, they were placed at great disadvantage because they were forced to compete with slave labor. The upper classes regarded them disdainfully, allowing that they were useless except for "breeding purposes."

e) The Slaves - about half of the population of the Roman empire were slaves. Many were superior individuals and quickly made their way up among the freemen and among the tradesmen. The majority were either mediocre or very inferior.

Slavery, even of superior peoples, was a characteristic of Roman military conquest. The power of the master over his slaves was unqualified. The early Christian Church actively evangelized, and was largely composed of, the lower classes and these slaves.

Superior slaves often received wages and by saving their earnings were able to purchase their freedom. Many such emancipated slaves rose to high positions in the state, the Christian Church, and the business world. It was just such possibilities that made the early Christian church so tolerant of this modified form of slavery.

There were no widespread social problems in the Roman Empire at this time. The major portion of the populace regarded themselves as belonging to that group into which they chanced to be born. There was always a door open through which talented and able individuals could rise from the lower to the higher strata of Roman society, but the people were generally content with their social rank. They were not class conscious, neither did they look upon these class distinctions as being unjust or wrong.

Out of this world, in the reign of Tiberius Caesar, a great teacher arose who was to proclaim the realization of the righteousness and unchallengeable oneness of God, and of man's moral obligation to God. This was Jesus of Nazareth, the seed rather than the founder of Christianity. John the Baptizer was ordained in Heaven to prepare the way. Jesus was ordained in Heaven to bring forth the message, and Paul was sent to carry on the work of both men. Jesus and John carried out their missions remarkably well, but Paul failed in carrying on the true gospel. In order to form his cult of Christianity, he tried to be all things to all people, and in the process greatly distorted the true message of Jesus. This book is dedicated to the finding, and knowing, of the true teachings of Jesus of Nazareth in his own words.

CHAPTER 2

A Child is Born

JOSEPH, THE FATHER OF JESUS, WAS A HEBREW ALTHOUGH HE carried many non-Hebrew strains which had been added to his ancestral tree from time to time by the female line of his forefathers. He was from the Hebrew tribe known as Galilean, and not from the tribe of Judah therefore he was not considered a Jew. The ancestry of the father of Jesus went back to the earlier lines of inheritance leading to the Sumerians and the earlier Eastern Semites of the times of the great civilizations of Mesopotamia. David and Solomon were not in the direct line of Joseph's ancestry since they were from the tribe of Judah.

Joseph's immediate ancestors were mechanics, builders, carpenters, masons, and smiths. Joseph himself was a carpenter and later became a contractor. His family belonged to a long and illustrious line of common people, accentuated now and then by the appearance of unusual individuals who had distinguished themselves in connection with the evolution of religions on Earth.

Mary, the mother of Jesus, was a descendant of a long line of unique ancestors embracing many of the most remarkable women in the racial history of the Earth. Although Mary was an average woman of her day and generation, possessing a fairly normal temperament, she counted among her ancestors such well known women as Annon, Tamar, Ruth, and Bathsheba. No Hebrew woman of that day had a more illustrious lineage of common progenitors or one extending back to more auspicious beginnings. Mary's ancestry, like Joseph's, was characterized by the predominance of strong but average individuals, augmented now and then by outstanding personalities in the march of civilization and the progressive evolution of religion. Racially considered, it is hardly proper to regard Mary as a Hebrew woman. In culture and religious beliefs, she was Hebrew, but in hereditary endowment she was more of a composite of Syrian, Hittite, Phoenician, Greek and Egyptian. Her racial inheritance was more general than that of Joseph.

Of all couples living in Palestine at the time of the birth of Jesus, Joseph and Mary possessed the most ideal combination of widespread racial connections and superior personality. It was the plan of Jesus to appear on Earth as an average man, that the common people might understand him and receive him.

The lifework of Jesus was really begun by John the Baptizer, his Earth cousin. Zacharias, John's father, was from the tribe of Judah and belonged to the Jewish priesthood, while his mother Elizabeth, was a member of the more prosperous branch of the same large family group to which Mary also belonged. Zacharias and Elizabeth, though they had been married many years, were childless. They lived in the village of Judah a few miles outside of Jerusalem.

It was late in the month of June of the year 8 BC by your current calendar, about three months after the wedding of Joseph and Mary in Nazareth, that a strange happening occurred at the home of Elizabeth in the village of Judah. She saw a pillar of light appear at her doorway.

This pillar was as if made of clouds. There shone a bright light from its middle. Then she heard music of unknown, unimaginable beauty, and saw the cloud gradually dissolve to be replaced by a luminous figure in white. Then a serious, awe inspiring man spoke thus: "While your husband, Zacharias, stands before the altar in Jerusalem, and while the assembled people pray for the coming of a deliverer, I, Gabriel, have come to announce that you will shortly bear a son who shall be the forerunner of that divine teacher that will soon come to this world.

Your son will grow up dedicated to the Father, your God. When he has grown to an adult, he will make your heart happy because he will turn many souls to God. He will proclaim the coming of a son of God to your people and he will proclaim the arrival of the spiritual leader of all peoples of all the Earth. Your kinswoman, Mary, shall be the mother of this child of promise, and I will also appear to her."

This vision greatly frightened Elizabeth. After Gabriel's departure she turned this experience over in her mind, long pondering the sayings of the majestic visitor, but did not speak of the revelation to anyone except her husband until her subsequent visit with Mary in early February the following year.

For five months, however, Elizabeth withheld her secret even from her husband. Upon her disclosure of the story of Gabriel's visit, Zacharias was very skeptical and for weeks doubted the entire experience, only consenting halfheartedly to believe in the visitation when he could no longer question that she was expectant with child.

Zacharias was very much perplexed regarding the prospective motherhood of Elizabeth, but he did not doubt the integrity of his wife, notwithstanding his own advanced age. It was not until about six weeks before John's birth that Zacharias, as the result of an impressive dream where Gabriel spoke to him, became fully convinced that Elizabeth was to become the mother of a son of destiny, one who was to prepare the way for the coming of the Messiah.

John was born in the village of Judah in the last week of March of the year 7 BC counting by your current calendar. Zacharias and Elizabeth rejoiced greatly in the realization that a son had come to them as Gabriel had promised, and when on the eighth day they presented the child at the synagogue for circumcision, they named him John. A nephew of Zacharias departed for Nazareth immediately, carrying the message of Elizabeth to Mary proclaiming that a son had been born to her and that his name was to be John.

From his earliest infancy John was judiciously taught by his parents that he was to grow up to become a spiritual leader and religious teacher. The soil of John's heart was ever responsive to the sowing of such suggestive seeds. Even as a child he was found frequently at the temple during the seasons of his father's service, and he was tremendously impressed with the significance of all that he saw.

Gabriel appeared to Mary in the middle of November of the year 8 BC as she was busily doing her daily chores in her small stone home in Nazareth. That evening, at about sundown, before Joseph had returned home from work, Gabriel appeared to Mary in the same manner as he had appeared to Elizabeth. After she had recovered from her fright, he said, "I have come at the direction of one who is my Master and whom you shall soon love and nurture. To you, Mary, I bring good news when I announce that you have a child within you who has been ordained in Heaven. In due time you will give birth to a son. He shall inaugurate the kingdom of Heaven on Earth and among all men. Speak not of this matter except to your husband, Joseph, and to Elizabeth, your kinswoman, to whom I have already appeared. Elizabeth shall presently bear a son also, who will prepare the way for the message of deliverance which your son shall proclaim with great power and deep conviction to all men. Doubt not my word, Mary, for this home has been chosen as the mortal home of the son of God. My benediction rests upon you, the power of the angels will strengthen you, and the God of all the universe shall overshadow you from this day forward."

Mary pondered this visitation secretly in her heart for many weeks, until she was certain she was with a child, before she dared to disclose these unusual events to her husband. When Joseph heard all about this, although he had great confidence in Mary, he was much troubled and could not sleep for many nights. At first Joseph had deep reservations about the Gabriel visitation. Then when he became convinced that Mary had really heard the voice and saw the form of the divine messenger, he was very confused as he pondered how such things could be. How could the child of common human beings be a child of divine destiny? Joseph considered himself too poor and too common to be chosen for this great honor. Never could Joseph reconcile these conflicting ideas until, after several weeks of thought, both he and Mary reached the conclusion that they had been chosen to become the parents of the Jewish Messiah, though it had hardly been the Jewish concept that the expected deliver was to be of common and poor parents. Upon arriving at this momentous conclusion, Mary hastened to depart for a visit with Elizabeth. She persuaded Joseph to let her journey to the village of Judah, four miles west of Jerusalem, in the hills, to visit Elizabeth. Gabriel had informed each of these mothers-to-be of his appearance to the other. Naturally they were anxious to get together, compare experiences, and talk over the probable futures of their sons. Mary remained with her distant cousin for three weeks. Elizabeth did much to strengthen Mary's faith in the vision of Gabriel, so that she returned home more fully dedicated to the call to mother the child of destiny who she was so soon to present to the world as a helpless babe, an average and normal infant of the realm.

Upon her return from Judah, Mary went to visit her parents, Joachim and Hannah, to tell them that she was with child. She confided to her sister Salome that she thought her son was destined to become a great teacher, but this is all she said to anyone, being mindful of the warning given her by Gabriel.

Joseph did not become reconciled to the idea that he and Mary were to become the parents of an extraordinary child until after he had experienced a very impressive dream. In this dream a brilliant celestial messenger appeared to him and said: "Joseph, I appear to you by command of him who now reigns on high, and I am directed to instruct you concerning the son whom Mary shall soon bear, and who shall become a great light to the world. In him shall be life, and his life shall become the light of all mankind. He shall first come to his own people, but they shall reject him. Thereafter to as many peoples of the world as shall receive him, to them will he reveal that they are the children of God." After this experience Joseph never again doubted Mary's story of Gabriel's visit and of the promise that the unborn child was to become a divine messenger to the world.

In all these visitations, nothing was said about the house of David. Nothing was ever intimated about Jesus becoming a deliverer of the Jews, not even that he was to be the long-expected Messiah. Jesus was not the Messiah that the Jews anticipated, but he was the deliverer of the world. The mission he was sent to accomplish was to deliver a message to all races and all peoples, not to any one group.

Joseph was not of the house of King David. It is true that he did go to Bethlehem to be registered for the Roman census, but that was because several generations earlier, one of Joseph's paternal relatives was an orphan and was adopted by a man named Zadoc, a distant relative of David. Thus was the story created by counting Joseph as of the house of David.

Most of the Messianic prophecies of the Hebrew books were changed and made to apply to Jesus long after his life had been lived on Earth. For centuries the Hebrew prophets had proclaimed the coming of a deliverer because the Prophet Melchizedek had told them of this event to come, but they failed to grasp the message that this coming messiah was to be a spiritual deliverer and not a military conqueror who would occupy the throne of David. They expected the miraculous birth and life of a powerful king who would occupy the throne of David in Jerusalem and proceed to establish the Jews as the rulers of all Palestine, and who would bring all the known world under the domination of the Jews. Many figurative passages found throughout the Hebrew scriptures were subsequently misapplied to the life mission of Jesus. Many Old Testament sayings were so distorted as to appear to fit some episode of the Master's Earth life. This was also true of the many genealogies of both Joseph and Mary which were constructed after the career of Jesus on Earth. Many of these lineages contain some of the Master's ancestry, but on the whole, they are not genuine and may not be depended upon as factual. The early followers of Jesus all too often succumbed to the temptation to make all the olden prophetic utterances appear to find fulfillment in the life of their Master. Jesus himself at one time publicly denied any connection with the house of David. Even the passage, 'And a maiden shall bear a son,' from the days of Melchizedek was changed to read, 'And a virgin shall bear a son.'

Joseph was a mild-mannered man, extremely conscientious, and in every way faithful to the religious conventions and practices of his people. He talked little but thought much. The sorry plight of the Jewish people in those days caused Joseph much sadness. As a youth, among his eight brothers and sisters, he had been more cheerful, but in the early years of married life he was subject to periods of mild spiritual discouragement. These temperamental manifestations were greatly improved just before his untimely death and after the economic condition of his family had been enhanced by his advancement from the rank of carpenter to the role of a prosperous contractor.

Mary's temperament was quite opposite to that of her husband. She was usually cheerful, was very rarely downcast, and possessed an ever-sunny disposition. Mary indulged in free and frequent expression of her emotional feelings and was never observed to be sorrowful until after the sudden death of Joseph. She had hardly recovered from this shock when she had thrust upon her the anxieties and questions aroused by the extraordinary career of her eldest son, which was so rapidly unfolding before her eyes. Throughout all these unusual experiences Mary was composed, courageous, and fairly wise in her relationship with her different and little-understood first-born son and his surviving brothers and sisters.

Jesus derived much of his unusual gentleness and marvelous sympathetic understanding of human nature from his father. He inherited his gift as a great teacher and his tremendous capacity for righteous indignation from his mother. In emotional reactions to his adult-life environment, Jesus was at one time like his father, meditative and worshipful, sometimes characterized by apparent sadness. More often he drove forward in the manner of his mother's optimistic and determined disposition. All in all, Mary's temperament tended to dominate the career of this son of God as he grew up and swung into the momentous strides of his adult life. In some particulars Jesus was a blending of his parents' traits. In other respects, he exhibited the traits of one in contrast with those of the other.

From Joseph, Jesus secured his strict training in the usages of the Jewish ceremonials and his unusual acquaintance with the

Hebrew scriptures. From Mary he derived a broader viewpoint of religious life and a more liberal concept of personal spiritual freedom.

The families of both Joseph and Mary were well educated for their time. Joseph and Mary were educated far above the average for their day and station in life. He was a thinker. She was a planner, expert in adaptation and practical in immediate execution. He had black eyes and medium brown hair. She had brown eyes and light hair, almost blond.

Had Joseph lived longer, he undoubtedly would have become a firm believer in the divine mission of his eldest son. Mary alternated between believing and doubting, being greatly influenced by the position taken by her other children and by her friends and relatives. She was always steadied in her final attitude by the memory of Gabriel's appearance to her immediately after the child was conceived.

Mary was an expert weaver and more than average skilled in most of the household arts of that day. She was a good housekeeper and a superior homemaker. Both Joseph and Mary were good teachers, and they saw to it that their children were well versed in the learning of that day.

When Joseph was a young man, he was employed by Mary's father in the work of building an addition to his house. It was when Mary brought Joseph a cup of water, during a noontime meal, that the courtship of this pair began.

Joseph and Mary were married, in accordance with Jewish custom, at Mary's home near Nazareth when Joseph was twenty-one years old, and Mary was eighteen. This marriage concluded a normal courtship of almost two years duration. Shortly thereafter they moved into their modest little stone home in Nazareth, which had been built by Joseph with the assistance of two of his brothers. The house was located near the foot of the near-by elevated land which so charmingly overlooked the surrounding countryside. In this home, these young and expectant parents had thought to welcome the child of promise, little realizing that this momentous event was to transpire far from home in Bethlehem of Judea.

A large part of Joseph's family eventually became believers in the teachings of Jesus, but very few of Mary's people ever believed in him until after he departed from this world. Joseph's family leaned more toward the spiritual concept of the expected Messiah, but Mary and her family, especially her father, held to the idea of the Messiah as a temporal deliverer and political ruler. Mary's ancestors held to the Western, or Alexandrian, view of Jewish religion and had been prominently identified with the Maccabean movement. Joseph's family held vigorously to the Eastern, or Babylonian, views of the Jewish religion. Mary leaned strongly toward the more liberal and broader Western, or Hellenistic, interpretation of the law and the prophets.

The home of Jesus was not far from the high hill in the vicinity of the northerly part of Nazareth, some distance from the village spring, which was in the Eastern section of town. Jesus' family lived in the outskirts of the city, and this made it all the easier for him subsequently to enjoy frequent strolls in the country and to make trips up to the top of this near-by highland, the highest of all the hills of southern Galilee save the Mount Tabor range to the East and the Hill of Nain, which was about the same height. Their home was located a little to the south and east of the southern promontory of this hill and about midway between the base of this elevation and the road leading out of Nazareth toward Cana. Aside from climbing the hill, Jesus' favorite stroll was to follow a narrow trail winding about the base of the hill in a northeasterly direction to a point where it joined the road to Sepphoris.

The home of Joseph and Mary was a one-room stone structure with a flat roof and an adjoining building for housing the animals. The furniture consisted of a low stone table, Earthenware and stone dishes and pots, a loom, a lamp stand, several small stools, and mats for sleeping on the stone floor. In the back yard, near the animal annex, was the shelter which covered the oven and the mill for grinding grain. It required two people to operate this type of mill, one to grind and another to feed the grain. As a small boy Jesus often fed grain to this mill while his mother turned the grinder.

In later years, as the family grew in size, they would all squat about the enlarged stone table to enjoy their meals, helping themselves from a common dish or pot of food. During the winter when the days were short, at the evening meal the table would be lit by a small, flat clay lamp, which was filled with olive oil. After the birth of Martha, Joseph built an addition to this house, a large room, which was used as a carpenter shop during the day and as a sleeping room for the boys.

In the month of March of the year 8 BC, the month Joseph and Mary were married, Caesar Augustus decreed that all inhabitants of the Roman Empire should be numbered, that a census should be made which could be used for effecting better taxation.

The Jews had always been greatly prejudiced against any attempt to number the people. This, in connection with the serious domestic difficulties of Herod, King of Judea, caused the postponement of the taking of this census in the Jewish kingdom for one year. Throughout all the Roman Empire this census was registered in the year 8 BC, but in the Palestinian kingdom of Herod, it was taken in the year 7 BC, one year later.

It was not necessary for Mary to go to Bethlehem for enrollment since Joseph was authorized to register for his family. But Mary, being an adventurous and aggressive woman, insisted on accompanying him. She feared being left alone and the child being born while Joseph was away. Bethlehem was not far from the town of Judah, therefore, Mary also foresaw a possible pleasurable visit with her kinswoman Elizabeth.

Joseph virtually forbade Mary to accompany him, but it was to no avail. When the food was packed for the trip of three or four days, she prepared double rations and made ready for the journey. Before they actually set forth, Joseph had reconciled to Mary's going along, and they cheerfully departed from Nazareth at the break of day.

Joseph and Mary were poor, and since they had only one beast of burden, Mary, being large with child, rode on the animal with the provisions while Joseph walked, leading the beast. The building and furnishing of a home had been a great drain on Joseph since he also had to contribute to the support of his parents since his father had been recently disabled. Thus, this young Hebrew couple sallied forth from their humble home early on a morning of Mid-August of the year 7 BC on their journey to Bethlehem.

Their first day of travel carried them around the foothills of Mount Gilboa, where they camped for the night by the river Jordan and engaged in many speculations as to what sort of a son would be born to them, Joseph adhering to the concept of a spiritual teacher and Mary holding to the idea of a Jewish Messiah, a king and deliverer of the Jewish people.

Bright and early the next morning, Joseph and Mary were again on their way. They ate their midday meal at the foot of Mount Sartaba, overlooking the Jordan Valley, and journeyed on, making Jericho for the night, where they stopped at an inn on the highway in the outskirts of the city. Following the evening meal and after much discussion with other travelers concerning the oppressiveness of Roman rule, the oppressiveness of King Herod, the census enrollment, and the comparative influence of Jerusalem and Alexandria as centers of Jewish learning and culture, the Nazareth travelers retired for the night's rest. Early the next morning they resumed their journey, reaching Jerusalem before noon. They visited the temple and went on to their destination, arriving at Bethlehem by midafternoon.

The inn was already full for the night, so Joseph sought housing with some distant relatives but every room in Bethlehem was full. On returning to the inn where he had left Mary, he was informed that the caravan stables, hewn out of the side of the rock and situated just below the inn, had been cleared of animals and cleaned up for the use by lodgers. Leaving the donkey in the courtyard, Joseph shouldered their bags of clothing and provisions and, with Mary, descended the stone steps to their lodgings below. They found themselves located in what had been a grain storage room to the front of the stalls and mangers.

Tent curtains had been hung to set up cubicles as makeshift rooms. They counted themselves fortunate to have these lodgings rather than to sleep out in the open.

Joseph wanted to go out and enroll immediately but Mary was weary and considerably distressed so she begged him to remain by her side. All that night Mary was restless so that neither of them slept much. By the break of day, the pangs of childbirth were well in evidence, and by noon of that day, with the help and kind ministrations of women fellow travelers who were also staying in the stables, Mary was delivered of a male child. Jesus of Nazareth was born into the world, was wrapped in the clothes which Mary had brought along for such a possible contingency and laid in a near-by manger.

THE FIRST YEAR

In just the same manner as all human babies before that day and since have come into the world, this promised child was born. On the eighth day, according to the Jewish practice, he was circumcised in the synagogue and formally named Joshua ben Joseph.

The day after the birth of Jesus, Joseph went out and made his enrollment. As he was enrolling, he met a man they had talked with two nights previously at Jericho. Joseph was taken by this acquaintance to a well-to-do friend who had a room at the inn, and who said he would gladly exchange quarters with the Nazareth couple. That afternoon they moved up to the inn, where they lived for almost three weeks until they found lodgings in the home of a distant relative of Joseph.

The second day after the birth of Jesus, Mary sent word to Elizabeth that her child had come and received word in return inviting Joseph up to Jerusalem to talk over all their affairs with Zacharias. The following week, once Mary and the child were able to journey, they went to Jerusalem to confer with Zacharias and Elizabeth. Both Zacharias and Elizabeth had become possessed with the sincere belief that Jesus was indeed to become the Jewish Messiah, and that their son, John, was to be his chief aide, his right-hand man of destiny. Since Mary held these same ideas, it was not difficult to prevail upon Joseph to remain in Bethlehem, the city of David, so that Jesus might grow up to become the successor of David on the throne of all Judea.

Accordingly, they remained in Bethlehem for more than a year and Joseph worked in his carpenter's trade.

At the noontime birth of Jesus, Angels from the Heavenly Realms gathered in the stables around the mother and child and did sing anthems of glory, but these utterances of praise were not seen by human eyes nor heard by human ears. No shepherds nor any other mortal creatures came to pay homage to the babe of Bethlehem until weeks later on the arrival of certain priests from Ur of Mesopotamia, who were sent down from Jerusalem by Zacharias.

These priests from Mesopotamia had been told sometime before by a prophet of their country that he had had a dream in which he was informed that the light of the world was about to appear on Earth as a babe and among the Jews of Palestine. Quickly they went forth, these three priests looking for this light of the world. After many weeks of futile search in Jerusalem, they were about to return to Ur when Zacharias met them and, knowing who they sought, disclosed his belief that Jesus was the object of their quest and sent them on to Bethlehem, where they found the babe and left their gifts with Mary. The baby was almost three weeks old at the time of this visit.

These wise men saw no star to guide them to Bethlehem. The beautiful legend of the Star of Bethlehem originated in this way: Jesus was born on August 21, 7 BC counting by your current calendar. On the previous May 29 there occurred an extraordinary conjunction of Jupiter and Saturn in the constellation of Pisces. It is a remarkable astronomic fact that similar conjunctions occurred on September 29 and December 5 of the same year. Upon the basis of these extraordinary but wholly natural events the well-meaning Christians of succeeding generations constructed the appealing legend of the Star of Bethlehem and the adoring Magi led thereby to the manger, where they beheld and worshipped the newborn babe. Oriental and near-Oriental minds delight in fairy tales, and they are continually spinning such beautiful myths about the lives of their religious leaders and political heroes. In the absence of printing, when human knowledge was passed by word of mouth from one generation to another, it was very easy for myths to become traditions and for traditions eventually to become accepted as facts.

Moses had taught the Jews that every first-born son belongs to the Father, intending that the son should become a priest, or otherwise dedicate his life to the work of the Father as was the custom that originated in Mesopotamia thousands of years before the times of Moses. Succeeding generations of Hebrews and Jews had developed the queer practice of killing the first-born son as a sacrifice in the belief that this is what Moses had commanded. By the time of the birth of Jesus, it had become the practice of the Jews that, instead of killing the child, they would redeem him by the payment of five Shekels to any authorized priest. There was also an ordinance at that time, purported to go back to the times of

Moses, which directed that a mother, after the passing of a certain period of time after birth, should present herself at the temple for purification. This practice originated in the Temple Harlotry rituals of the worship of Ishtar and also had nothing to do with Moses. It was customary to perform both of these ceremonies at the same time.

Accordingly, Joseph and Mary went up to the temple at Jerusalem in person to present Jesus to the priests and effect his redemption and also to make the proper sacrifice to insure Mary's ceremonial purification from the alleged uncleanness of childbirth. In those days there lingered daily around the courts of the temple two remarkable characters, Simeon, a singer, and Anna, a poetess. Simeon was Judean, but Anna was a Galilean. This couple were frequently in each other's company, and both were intimates of the priest Zacharias, who had confided the secret of John and Jesus to them. Both Simeon and Anna longed for the coming of the Messiah, and their confidence in Zacharias led them to believe that Jesus was the expected deliverer of the Jewish people.

Zacharias knew the day Joseph and Mary were expected to appear at the temple with Jesus, and he had prearranged with Simeon and Anna to indicate, by the salute of his upraised hand, which one in the procession of first-born children was Jesus.

For the occasion, Anna had written a poem which Simeon proceeded to sing as soon as Zacharias raised his hand, much to the astonishment of both Joseph and Mary, and all who were assembled in the temple courts. On the way back to Bethlehem, Joseph and Mary were silent - confused and overawed. Mary was much disturbed by the farewell salutation of Anna, the aged poetess, and Joseph was not in harmony with this premature effort to make Jesus out to be the expected Messiah of the Jewish people.

The spies of Herod were very active. They quickly reported to him the happenings at the redemption ceremony, and they also reported the visit of the priests of Ur to Bethlehem to visit the newborn "King of the Jews". Herod summoned the Chaldeans to appear before him. He inquired diligently of these wise men about the new "King of the Jews", but they gave him little satisfaction, explaining that the babe had been born of a woman who had come down to Bethlehem with her husband for the census enrollment. Herod, not being satisfied with this answer, sent them forth with a purse and directed that they should find the child so that he too might come and worship him, since they had declared that his kingdom was to be spiritual, not temporal. But when the wise men did not return, Herod grew angry. As he turned these things over in his mind, his informers scoured the countryside looking for the babe. All they could find was a copy of parts of the Simeon song which had been sung at the redemption ceremonies of Jesus. They had failed to follow Joseph and Mary, and Herod was very angry with them when they could not tell him where the pair had taken the baby. He then dispatched searchers to locate them. Knowing Herod pursued them, Joseph and Mary remained away from Bethlehem. The baby was secretly kept with Joseph's relatives.

Joseph was afraid to seek work because of all this, and their small savings were rapidly disappearing. Even at the time of the purification ceremony at the temple, Joseph deemed himself sufficiently poor to warrant his offering for Mary only two young pigeons as was the custom for poor people to do.

THE SECOND YEAR

After more than a year of searching, Herod's spies had not located Jesus, and because of the suspicion that the babe was still concealed in Bethlehem, Herod prepared an order directing that a systematic search be made of every house in Bethlehem, and that all boy babies under two years of age should be killed. In this manner Herod hoped to make sure that this child who was to become "King of the Jews" would be destroyed. Thus, perished in one day sixteen boy babies in Bethlehem of Judea. Intrigue and murder, even in his own immediate family, were common occurrences at the court of King Herod.

The massacre of these infants took place in the middle of October of the year 6 BC when Jesus was a little over a year old. There were believers in the coming Messiah even among Herod's courtiers, and one of these, learning of the order to slaughter the Bethlehem boy babies, communicated with Zacharias, who in turn dispatched a messenger to Joseph. The night before the massacre Joseph and Mary departed from Bethlehem with the babe for Alexandria in Egypt. In order to avoid attracting attention, they journeyed alone at night to Egypt with Jesus wrapped in blankets. They went to Alexandria on funds provided by Zacharias, and there Joseph worked at his carpenters trade while Mary and Jesus lodged with wealthy relatives of Joseph's family. They resided in Alexandria two full years, not returning to Bethlehem until after the death of Herod.

Due to the uncertainties and anxieties of their stay in Bethlehem, Mary did not wean the baby until they had arrived safely in Alexandria, where the family was able to settle down to a normal life for the first time. They lived with kinsfolk, and Joseph was able to support his family well as he secured work shortly after their arrival. He was first employed as a carpenter for several months and then elevated to the position of foreman of a large group of workmen employed on one of the public buildings then in process of construction. This new experience gave him the idea of becoming a contractor and builder after their return to Nazareth.

All through these early years of Jesus' infancy, Mary maintained one long and constant vigil over her child so that nothing would jeopardize his welfare or in any way interfere with his future mission on Earth. No mother was more devoted to her child. In the home where Jesus lived there were two other children about his age, and among the neighbors there were six others whose ages were sufficiently near his own to make them enjoyable playmates. At first Mary was disposed to keep Jesus close by her side. She feared something might happen to him if he were allowed to play in the garden with the other children, but Joseph, with the assistance of his kinsfolk, was able to convince her that such a course would deprive the young lad of the helpful experience of learning how to adjust himself to children of his own age. Mary, realizing that such a program of undue sheltering and unusual protection might tend to make him self-conscious and somewhat self-centered, finally agreed to permit the child to grow up just like any other child. Though she was obedient to this decision, she made it her business always to be on watch while the little folks were at play around the house or in the garden. Only an affectionate mother can know the burden that Mary carried in her heart for the safety of her son during these years of his infancy end early childhood.

THE THIRD YEAR

Throughout their two years at Alexandria, Jesus enjoyed good health and continued to grow normally. Aside from a few friends and relatives no one was told about Jesus' being a "Child of Promise." One of Joseph's relatives revealed this secret to a few friends in Memphis.

These Egyptians were descendants of the remarkable Pharaoh Ikhnaton. They, with a small group of Alexandrian believers, assembled at the palatial home of Joseph's relative a short time before the return to Palestine to wish the Nazareth family well and to pay their respects to the child. On this occasion the assembled friends presented Jesus with a complete copy of the Greek translation of the Hebrew scriptures then in existence. But this copy of the Jewish writings was not placed in Joseph's hands until both he and Mary had finally, and resolutely declined the invitation of their Memphis and Alexandrian friends to remain in Egypt. These believers insisted that the child of destiny would be able to exert a far greater world influence as a resident of Alexandria than of any place in Palestine.

These persuasions delayed their departure for Palestine for some time after they received the news of Herod's death.

Joseph and Mary finally took leave of Alexandria on a boat belonging to a friend bound for Joppa, arriving at that port late in August of the year 4 BC. Jesus turned three years old while on this boat trip. They went directly to Bethlehem, where they spent the entire month of September in counsel with their friends and relatives concerning whether they should remain there or return to Nazareth.

Mary had never given up the idea that Jesus should grow up in Bethlehem, the city of David. Joseph did not really believe that their son was to become a kingly deliverer. Besides, he knew that he himself was not really a descendant of David, that his being counted among the lineage of David was due to the adoption of one of his distant ancestors into the tribe of Judah and the lineage of David. Mary thought the city of David was the most appropriate place in which the new candidate for David's throne should be reared, but Joseph preferred to take chances with Herod Antipas rather than with his brother Archelaus. He entertained great fears for the child's safety in Bethlehem or in any other city of Judea. He believed that Archelaus would be more likely to pursue the menacing policies of his father, Herod, than would Antipas in Galilee. Besides all these reasons, Joseph was outspoken in his preference for Galilee as a better place in which to rear and educate the child, but it required three weeks to overcome Mary's objections.

By the first of October, Joseph had convinced Mary and all their friends that it was best for them to return to Nazareth. Accordingly, early in October of the year 4 BC, they departed from Bethlehem for Nazareth, going by way of Lydia and Scythopolis. They started out early one Sunday morning, Mary and the child riding on their newly acquired beast of burden, while Joseph and five accompanying kinsmen proceeded on foot. Joseph's relatives refused to permit them to make the trip to Nazareth alone. They feared to go to Galilee via Jerusalem, and the western routes were not altogether safe for two lone travelers with a young child since there were many highway robbers on that route.

On the fourth day the party reached its destination in safety. They arrived unannounced at the Nazareth home, which had been occupied for more than three years by one of Joseph's married brothers, who was indeed surprised to see them. So quietly had they gone about their business that neither the family of Joseph nor that of Mary knew they had even left Alexandria. The next day Joseph's brother moved his family out. Mary, for the first time since Jesus' birth, settled down with her little family to enjoy life in their own home. In less than a week Joseph secured work as a carpenter, and they were ecstatic.

Jesus was about three years and two months old at the time of their return to Nazareth. He had stood all these travels very well and was in excellent health and full of childish glee and excitement at having a home of his own to run about in and to enjoy. But he greatly missed his Alexandrian playmates.

On the way to Nazareth Joseph had persuaded Mary that it would be unwise to spread the word among their Galilean friends and relatives that Jesus was a child of promise. They agreed to refrain from all mention of these matters to anyone. They both remained faithful in keeping this promise.

The next important event in the life of this Nazareth family was the birth of the second child, James, in early April, of the year 3 BC. Jesus was thrilled by the thought of having a baby brother, and he would stand around by the hour just to observe the baby's early activities.

It was midsummer of this same year that Joseph built a small workshop close to the village spring and near the caravan lot. After this he did very little carpenter work by the day. He had as associates two of his brothers and several other mechanics, whom he sent out to work while he remained at the shop making yokes and plows and doing other woodwork. He also did some work in leather and with rope and canvas. Jesus, as he grew up, when not at school, spent his time about equally between helping his mother with home duties and watching his father work at the shop, meanwhile listening to the conversation and gossip of the caravan conductors and passengers from the four corners of the Earth.

THE FOURTH YEAR

In July of this year, one month before Jesus was four years old, an outbreak of malignant intestinal trouble spread over all Nazareth from contact with the caravan travelers. Mary became so alarmed by the danger of Jesus being exposed to this epidemic of disease that she bundled up both her children and fled to the country home of her brother, several miles south of Nazareth on the Megiddo Road near Sarid. They did not return to Nazareth for more than two months.

Jesus greatly enjoyed this, his first experience on a farm.

THE FIFTH YEAR

Jesus was five years old when he was made very happy by the coming of his sister Miriam. In the evening of the day after the birth of Miriam, Jesus had a long talk with his father concerning the manner in which various groups of living things are born into the world as separate individuals. The most valuable part of Jesus' early education was secured from his parents in answer to his thoughtful and searching inquiries. Joseph never failed to do his full duty in taking pains and spending time answering the boy's numerous questions. From the time Jesus was five years old until he was about ten, he was one continuous question mark. While Joseph and Mary could not always answer his questions, they never failed fully to discuss his inquiries and in every other possible way to assist him in his efforts to reach a satisfactory solution to the problem which his alert mind had suggested.

Since returning to Nazareth, theirs had been a busy household, and Joseph had been unusually occupied building his new shop and getting his business started again. So fully occupied he had found no time to build a cradle for James, but this was corrected long before Miriam came, so that she had a very comfortable crib in which to nestle while the family admired her. The child Jesus heartily entered into all these natural and normal home experiences. He greatly enjoyed his little brother and his baby sister and was of great help to Mary in their care.

It was the custom in those days of the Hebrews for the mother to bear the responsibility for a child's training until the fifth birthday, and then, if the child was a boy, to hold the father responsible for the lad's education from that time on. This year, therefore, Mary formally turned Jesus over to Joseph for further education.

Though Joseph now assumed the direct responsibility for Jesus' intellectual and religious education, his mother still interested herself in his home training. She taught him to know and care for the vines and flowers growing around the garden walls which completely surrounded the home plot. She also provided shallow boxes of sand in which Jesus worked out maps and did much of his early practice at writing Aramaic, Greek, and later on, Hebrew, for in time he learned to read, write, and speak, fluently all three languages.

With his mother's help, Jesus early on mastered the Galilean dialect of the Aramaic tongue. Now his father began teaching him Greek. Mary spoke little Greek, but Joseph was a fluent speaker of both Aramaic and Greek. The textbook for the study of the Greek language became the copy of the Hebrew scriptures - a complete version of the law and the prophets, including the psalms - which had been presented to them on leaving Egypt. There were only two complete copies of the scriptures in Greek in all Nazareth, and the possession of one of them by the carpenter's family made Joseph's home a much sought after place and enabled Jesus, as he grew up, to meet an almost endless procession of earnest students and sincere truth seekers. By the end of his fifth year, Jesus had assumed custody of this priceless manuscript, having been told on his sixth birthday that the sacred book had been presented to him by Alexandrian friends and relatives. In a very short time, he learned to read it easily.

THE SIXTH YEAR

The first great shock of Jesus' young life occurred when he was around six and a half years old. It had seemed to the lad that his father and mother knew everything. A mild Earthquake occurred, and the child ran to his father asking the cause for the ground to shake so. It was a complete surprise to him when his father said, "My son, I really do not know what causes the ground to tremble." Thus began the inevitable disillusionment in the course of which

Jesus found out that his earthly parents were not all-wise and all-knowing.

Joseph's first thought was to tell the young lad that the Earth tremor had been caused by God, but a moment's reflection admonished him that such an answer would immediately be provocative of further and still more embarrassing inquiries. Even at an early age it was very difficult to answer Jesus' questions about physical or social phenomena by thoughtlessly telling him that either God or the devil was responsible. In harmony with the prevailing belief of the Jews of those days, Jesus was long willing to accept the doctrine of good spirits and evil spirits as the possible explanation of mental and spiritual phenomena, but he very early became doubtful that such unseen influences were responsible for the physical happenings of the natural world.

In the early summer, before Jesus turned seven years old, Zacharias, Elizabeth and John came to visit in Nazareth. Jesus and John had a happy time during this, their first visit within their memory. Although the visitors could remain only a few days, the parents talked over many things, including the future plans for their sons. While they were thus engaged, the lads played with blocks in the sand and in many other ways enjoyed themselves in true boyish fashion.

Having met John, who came from near Jerusalem and was Judean rather than Galilean, Jesus began to show an unusual interest in the history of the Hebrews, the many tribes that comprised the Hebrews, and to inquire in great detail as to the meaning of the Sabbath rites, the synagogue sermons, and the recurring feasts of commemoration.

During this, his sixth year, Joseph and Mary also began to have trouble with Jesus about his prayers. He insisted on talking to his Heavenly Father much as he would talk to his Earth father. This departure from the more solemn and reverent modes of communication with God was a bit disconcerting to his parents, especially to his mother, but there was no persuading him to change. He would say his prayers in the way taught to him by his parents, after which he insisted on having 'just a little personal talk with my Father in Heaven.'

THE SEVENTH YEAR

During Jesus seventh year Joseph turned the shop in Nazareth over to his brothers and formally entered upon his work as a contractor. Before the year was over, the family income had more than tripled. Never again, until after Joseph's death, did the Nazareth family feel the pinch of poverty. The family grew larger and larger, and they spent much money on extra education and travel, but always Joseph's increasing income kept pace with the growing expenses.

The next few years, Joseph did considerable work at Cana, Bethlehem of Galilee, Magdala, Nain, Sepphoris, Capernaum and Endor, as well as much building in and near Nazareth. As James grew up to be old enough to help his mother with the housework and care of the younger children, Jesus made frequent trips away from home with his father to these surrounding towns and villages. Jesus was a keen observer and gained much practical knowledge from these trips away from home. He was carefully storing up knowledge regarding man and the way he lives on Earth.

The child was now seven years old, the age when Hebrew children were supposed to begin their formal education in the synagogue schools. Accordingly, in August of his seventh year, he entered his eventful school life at Nazareth. Already this lad was a fluent reader, writer, and speaker of two languages, Aramaic and Greek. He was now to acquaint himself with the task of learning to read, write, and speak the Hebrew language. He was truly eager for the new school life which was ahead of him.

For the next three years he attended the elementary school of the Nazareth synagogue. In these three years he studied the basics of the Book of the Law as it was recorded in the Hebrew tongue of the time. For the following three years after this he studied in the advanced school and committed to memory, by the method of repeating aloud, the deeper teachings of the scriptural laws. He graduated from this synagogue school in his thirteenth year and was presented to his parents by the synagogue as an educated son of the commandments, meaning a responsible citizen of the commonwealth, all of which required his attendance at the Passovers in Jerusalem.

In the schools of Nazareth, the students sat on the floor in a semicircle facing their teacher, who also sat on the floor facing his students. The teacher was called a Chazzan, and he was an officer of the synagogue. The teachings began with the Book of Leviticus, followed by the other books of the law, followed by a study of the prophets and the psalms. The Nazareth synagogue at that time possessed a complete copy of the scriptures in Hebrew. Nothing but the scriptures was studied up until the twelfth year.

Jesus quickly mastered the Hebrew language, and when he could not find a traveler journeying through Nazareth to speak

Hebrew with, he would often be found at the synagogue reading the Hebrew scriptures to the assembled faithful who could not read Hebrew.

These synagogue schools had no textbooks, therefore, in the teaching methods used, the Chazzan would utter a statement while the pupils in unison would repeat the statement. Once the students learned to read, they would learn their lessons by reading from the one copy of the scriptures they possessed, and constant repetition.

In addition to the more formal education he was receiving, Jesus began to make contact with human nature from the four corners of the known world as men from many lands passed in and out of his father's repair shop. Palestine was a crossroads to the great civilizations of the time. As he grew older, he mingled freely with the caravans as they rested near the spring. Being a fluent speaker of Greek, he had little trouble in conversing with the majority of the caravan travelers and conductors.

Galilee, and especially Nazareth, was a caravan route and crossroads of travel for the great caravans from the four corners of the world, and the people here were considered converted Gentiles by the Jews of Jerusalem. At the same time, it was known as a center of liberal interpretation of Jewish traditional law, a fact which further alienated the rabbinical teachers of Jerusalem from the teachers of Nazareth.

In Galilee the Jews mingled freely with the Gentiles unlike their practice in Judea where the Jews shunned the Gentiles. Of all the cities of Galilee, the Jews of Nazareth were most liberal in their interpretation of the social restrictions based on the fears of contamination as a result of contact with the Gentiles. These conditions gave rise to the common saying in Jerusalem of those days, 'Will anything good ever come out of Galilee.'

Jesus received his moral training and spiritual culture chiefly in his own home. He received much of his intellectual and theological education from the Chazzan. But his real education, the preparing of the mind and heart for the actual test of dealing with the problems of life - he received by mingling with his fellow men. It was this close association with his fellow man, young and old, Jews and Gentiles, who afforded him the opportunity to know the human race. Jesus was highly educated in that he thoroughly understood men and loved them dearly.

Throughout his years at the synagogue school, he was a brilliant student, possessing a great advantage since he was conversant with three languages. The Nazareth Chazzan, on the occasion of graduation from school, remarked to Joseph that he feared he had learned more from Jesus than he had been able to teach the lad.

Throughout his course of study, Jesus learned much and derived great inspiration from the Sabbath Sermons in the synagogue. It was customary to ask distinguished visitors, stopping over the Sabbath in Nazareth, to address the synagogue. In those early years in Nazareth, he heard many great thinkers of the entire Hebrew world expound their views, and especially many who were hardly orthodox Jews since the synagogue of Nazareth was an advanced and liberal center of Hebrew thought and culture.

When entering school at seven years, it was customary for the pupils to choose their birthday text, a sort of golden rule to guide them throughout their years as students. The text which Jesus chose was from the Prophet Isaiah: "The spirit of God is upon me, for the Father has anointed me. He has sent me to bring good news to the meek, to bind up the brokenhearted, to proclaim liberty to the captives, and to set the spiritual prisoners free."

Nazareth, in those days, was one of twenty-four priest centers, or parishes, of the Jewish nation, but the Galilean priests were more liberal in the interpretation of the traditional laws than were the Judean priests and scribes. At Nazareth they were also more liberal regarding the observance of the Sabbath. It was, therefore, the custom for Joseph to take Jesus out for walks on Sabbath afternoons. One of their favorite hikes was to climb the high hill near their home, from which they could obtain a panoramic view of all of Galilee. To the northwest, on a clear day they could see the long ridge of Mount Carmel running down to the sea. Many times, as they rested on this hilltop, Jesus heard his father relate the story of the Prophet Elijah, one of the first of that long line of Hebrew Prophets, who denounced King Ahab and exposed the Baal worshipping rabbis. To the north Mount Hermon raised its snowy peak in majestic splendor and monopolized the skyline, almost 3,000 feet of the upper slopes glistening white with year-round snow. Far to the east they could faintly see the Jordan Valley and far beyond lay the rocky hills of Moab. Also, to the south and the east, when the sun shone upon their marble walls, they could see the Greco-Roman cities of the Decapolis, with their amphitheaters and pretentious temples. When they lingered until the setting sun, they could make out, to the west, the sailing vessels on the distant Mediterranean.

From four directions, Jesus could observe the caravan trains as they wound their way in and out of Nazareth. To the south he could overlook the broad and fertile plain country of Esdraelon, stretching off toward Mount Gilboa and Samaria.

When they did not climb the heights to view the distant landscape, they strolled through the countryside and studied nature in her various moods in accordance with the seasons. Jesus' earliest training, aside from that of the home, had to do with a reverent and sympathetic contact with the beauty of nature.

THE EIGHTH YEAR

By the time Jesus was eight years old, he was known to all the mothers and young women of Nazareth, who had met him and talked with him at the spring, which was not far from his home, and which was one of the social centers of contact and gossip for the entire town. In his eighth year Jesus also learned to milk the family cow and care for the other animals. He also learned to make cheese and weave. By the time he was ten, he was an expert loom operator. Around this time, he and a neighbor boy named Jacob, became friends of a potter who worked down by the flowing spring. As they watched Nathan's fingers mold the clay on the potter's wheel, many times they both determined they were going to be potters when they grew up. Nathan was very fond of both of these bright beautiful young lads, and often gave them clay to practice with. He sought to stimulate their creative imaginations by suggesting competitive efforts in modeling various objects and animals.

In his eighth year, Jesus met a teacher of mathematics from Damascus, and learning some new techniques of numbers, he spent much time on mathematics for several years. He developed a keen sense of numbers, distances, and proportions.

Jesus enjoyed his brother James very much and by the end of this year had begun to teach him the alphabet. It was in this year also that he made arrangements to exchange dairy products for lessons on the harp. He had an unusual liking for anything musical. Later on, he did much to promote an interest in vocal music among his youthful associates. By the time he was eleven years of age, he was a skillful harpist and greatly enjoyed entertaining both family and friends with his extraordinary interpretations and able improvisations.

All was not smooth sailing in these formative years. Both at home and at school, Jesus persisted in asking many embarrassing questions concerning both science and religion, particularly regarding geography and astronomy. He was especially insistent on finding out why there was a dry season and a rainy season in Palestine. Repeatedly he sought the explanation for the great difference between the temperatures of Nazareth and the Jordan Valley. He simply never ceased to ask such intelligent but perplexing questions.

His third brother, Simon, was born in April of this year, 2 AD. In February of this year, Nahor, one of the Chazzans in a Jerusalem Academy of the rabbis, came to Nazareth to observe Jesus, having been on a similar mission to the home of Zacharias near Jerusalem. He came to Nazareth at the instigation of Zacharias. While at first he was somewhat shocked by Jesus' frankness and unconventional manner of relating himself to things religious, he attributed it to the remoteness of Galilee from the centers of Jewish learning and culture and advised Joseph and Mary to allow him to take Jesus back with him to Jerusalem, where he could have the advantages of education and training at the center of Jewish culture. Mary was half persuaded to consent since she was convinced he was to become the Messiah, the Jewish deliverer. Joseph hesitated since he was equally persuaded that Jesus was to grow up to become a man of destiny, but what that destiny would prove to be, he was profoundly uncertain. He never really doubted that his son was to fulfill some great mission on Earth. The more he thought about Nahor's advice, the more he questioned the wisdom of the proposed journey to Jerusalem.

Because of this difference of opinion between Joseph and Mary, Nahor requested permission to lay the whole matter before Jesus. Jesus listened attentively, talked with Joseph, Mary, and a neighbor, Jacob, a stonemason whose son was Jesus' favorite playmate. Two days later, Jesus reported that since there was such a difference of opinion among his parents and advisers, and since he did not feel competent to assume the responsibility for such a decision, not feeling strongly one way or the other, in view of the whole situation, he had decided to "talk with my father in Heaven." While he was not perfectly sure about the answer that he had been given, he rather felt he should remain at home with his father and mother adding that they who love him so much should be able to do more for him and guide him more safely than strangers who can only view his body and observe his mind but can hardly truly know him. They all marveled at this answer and Nahor went on his way back to Jerusalem. It was many years before the subject of Jesus' going away from home again came up for consideration.

The Ninth Year

The most serious trouble to come up at school occurred in late winter of this year when Jesus dared to challenge the Chazzan regarding the teaching that all images, pictures, and drawings were idolatrous in nature. Jesus delighted in drawing landscapes as well as in modeling a great variety of objects in potter's clay.

Everything of that sort was strictly forbidden by Jewish law, but up to this time he had managed to disarm his parents' objection to such an extent that they had permitted him to continue in these activities.

But trouble was stirred up at school when one of the pupils discovered young Jesus drawing a charcoal picture of the teacher on the floor of the schoolroom. There it was, plain as day, and the elders were called immediately and had viewed it before the committee went to call on Joseph to demand that something be done to suppress the lawlessness of his eldest son. Though this was not the first-time complaints had come to Joseph and Mary about the doings of their versatile and aggressive child, this was the most serious of all the accusations which had thus far been lodged against him. Jesus listened to the indictment of his artistic efforts for some time, being seated on a large stone just outside the back door. He resented their blaming his father for his alleged misdeeds. So, in he marched, fearlessly confronting his accusers. The elders were thrown into disarray. Some were inclined to view the episode humorously, while one or two seemed to think the boy was sacrilegious if not blasphemous. Joseph was perplexed and Mary was indignant.

But Jesus insisted on being heard. After he had his say and courageously defended his viewpoint, with consummate self-control, he announced that he would abide by the decision of his father in this as in all other matters controversial. The committee of elders departed in silence.

Mary endeavored to influence Joseph to permit Jesus to model in clay at home, provided he promised not to carry on any of the questionable activities at school, but Joseph felt impelled to rule that the Rabbinical interpretation of the second commandment should prevail. Thus, Jesus no more drew or modeled the likeness of anything from that day as long as he lived in his father's house. But he was unconvinced of the wrong of what he had done, and to give up such a favorite pastime constituted one of the great trials of his young life.

In the latter part of June of this year, Jesus and Joseph first climbed up to the summit of Mount Tabor. It was a clear day, and the view was magnificent. It seemed to this nine-year old lad that he had really gazed upon the entire world except for India, Africa, and Rome.

THE TENTH YEAR

Jesus' second sister, Martha, was born in September of this year, just after Jesus turned ten. Three weeks after the arrival of Martha, Joseph, who was home for a while, started the building of an addition to their house, a combined workshop and bedroom. A small workbench was built for Jesus, and for the first time he possessed tools of his own. At odd times for many years, he worked at this bench and became highly expert in the making of yokes.

This winter and the next were the coldest in Nazareth for many decades. Jesus had seen snow on the mountains, and several times it had fallen in Nazareth, remaining on the ground only a short time, but not until this winter had he seen ice. The fact that water could be seen as a solid, a liquid, and a vapor caused the lad to think a great deal about the physical world and its creation.

The climate of Nazareth was not usually severe. January was the coldest month with the temperature averaging around 50 degrees F. During July and August, the hottest months, the temperature would vary from 75 to 90 degrees F. From the mountains to the Jordan and the Dead Sea Valley, the climate of Palestine ranged from the frigid to the torrid.

Even during the warmest summer months, a cool sea breeze usually blew from the west from 10 a.m. to 10 p.m. but every now and then terrific hot winds from the eastern desert would blow across all of Palestine. These hot blasts usually came in February and March, near the end of the rainy season. In those days the rain fell in refreshing showers from November to April, but it did not rain steadily. There were only two seasons in Palestine, summer and winter, the dry and rainy seasons. In January the flowers began to bloom, and by the end of April the whole of the land was one vast flower garden.

In May of this year, on his uncle's farm, Jesus for the first time helped with the harvest of the grain. Before he was thirteen, he had managed to find out something about practically everything that men and women worked at around Nazareth except metal working, and he spent several months in a smith's shop when older, after the death of his father, to learn the art of metal working.

When work and caravan travel were slow, Jesus made many trips with his father on pleasure or business to nearby Cana, Endor, and Nain. Even as a lad he frequently visited Sepphoris, only a little over three miles from Nazareth. This was the capital of Galilee and one of the residences of Herod Antipas.

Jesus continued to grow physically, intellectually, socially, and spiritually. His trips away from home did much to give him a better and more generous understanding of his own family, and by this time even his parents were beginning to learn from him as well as to teach him. Jesus was an original thinker and a skillful teacher, even in his youth. He was in constant collision with the so-called "oral law"', but he always sought to adapt himself to the practices of his family. He got along fairly well with the children of his age, but he often grew discouraged with their slow acting minds. Before he was ten years old, he had become the leader of a group of seven lads who formed themselves into a society for promoting the acquirements of manhood, physical, intellectual, and religious. Among these boys Jesus succeeded in introducing many new games and various improved methods of physical recreation.

It was in the month of July of his 10th year when Jesus, while strolling through the countryside with his father, first gave expression to feelings and ideas which indicated that he was becoming self- conscious of the unusual nature of his life mission. Joseph listened attentively to the momentous words of his son but made few comments. He volunteered no information. The next day Jesus had a similar but longer talk with his mother.

Mary likewise listened to the pronouncements of the lad, but neither did she volunteer any information. It was almost two years before Jesus again spoke to his parents concerning this increasing revelation within his own consciousness regarding the nature of his personality and the character of his mission on Earth.

He entered the advanced school of the synagogue in August. At school he was constantly creating trouble with the questions he persisted in asking. Increasingly he kept all Nazareth in more or less of a hubbub. His parents were reluctant to forbid his asking these uneasy questions, and his chief teacher was greatly intrigued by the lads' curiosity, insight, and hunger for knowledge.

Jesus' playmates saw nothing supernatural in his conduct. In most ways he was just like themselves. His interest in study was somewhat above average but not wholly unusual. He did ask more questions at school than the others.

His most unusual and outstanding trait was his unwillingness to fight for his rights. Since he was such a well-developed lad for his age, it seemed strange to his playfellows that he refused to defend himself even from injustice or when subjected to personal abuse. He did not suffer much on account of this though, because of his friendship with Jacob, the son of a stonemason, who was a year older. Jacob was a great admirer of Jesus and made it his business to see that no one was permitted to impose upon Jesus because of his refusal to fight physically. Several times, older and uncouth youths attacked Jesus, relying on the knowledge that he would not defend himself, but they always suffered swift retribution at the hands of his self-appointed guardian and ever-ready defender, Jacob.

Jesus was the generally accepted leader of the Nazareth lads who stood for the higher ideals of their day and generation. He was really loved by his youthful associates, not only because he was fair, but also because he possessed a rare and understanding sympathy that exhibited love and bordered on discreet compassion.

THE ELEVENTH YEAR

This year he began to show a marked preference for the company of older people. He delighted in talking over things cultural, educational, social, economic, political, and religious with older minds, and his depth of reasoning and keenness of observation so charmed his adult associates that they were always more than willing to visit with him. Until he became responsible for the support of the home, his parents were constantly seeking to influence him to associate with those of his own age, or more nearly his age, rather than with older and better-informed individuals for whom he showed such a preference.

Later this year he went on a fishing expedition for the very first time with his uncle. They were gone for two months along the Sea of Galilee and were very successful. He enjoyed this so much that before reaching manhood, he had become an expert fisherman.

His physical development continued well. He was an advanced and privileged pupil at school. He got along fairly well at home with his younger brothers and sisters, having the advantage of being three- and one-half years older than the oldest of the other children. He was well thought of in Nazareth except by the parents of some of the duller children, who often spoke of Jesus as being a bit too smart and lacking in proper humility. He manifested a growing tendency to direct the play activities of his youthful associates into more serious and thoughtful channels. He was a born teacher and simply could not refrain from so functioning, even when supposedly engaged in play.

Joseph early began to instruct Jesus in the diverse means of gaining a livelihood, explaining the advantages of agriculture over industry and trade. Galilee was a more beautiful and prosperous district than Judea, and it cost only about one fourth as much to live there as in Jerusalem and Judea. It was a province of agricultural villages and thriving industrial cities, containing more than two hundred towns of over five thousand population and thirty of over fifteen thousand.

While on his first trip with his father to observe the fishing industry on the Lake of Galilee, Jesus had just about made up his mind to become a fisherman. A close association with his father's vocation later on influenced him to become a carpenter, while still later a combination of influences led him to the final choice of becoming a religious teacher of a new order.

Throughout his 11th year the lad continued to make trips away from home with his father, but he also frequently visited his uncle's farm and occasionally went over to Magdala to engage in fishing with the uncle who made his headquarters near that city. Joseph and Mary were often tempted to show some special favoritism for Jesus, or otherwise to betray their knowledge that he was a child of promise, a son of destiny, but both of his parents were extraordinarily wise in all these matters. The few times they did in any manner exhibit any preference for him, even in the slightest degree, the lad was quick to refuse all such special consideration.

Young Jesus spent a great deal of time at the caravan supply shop, and by conversing with the travelers from all parts of the world, he acquired a store of information about international affairs that was amazing, considering his age. This was the last year in which he enjoyed much free play and youthful joyousness. From this time on difficulties and responsibilities rapidly multiplied in the life of this boy.

In the middle of May of this year the lad accompanied his father on a business trip to Scythopolis, the chief Greek city of the Decapolis, the ancient Hebrew city of Beth-Shean. On the way Joseph recounted much of the olden history of King Saul, the Philistines, and the subsequent events of the Hebrews' turbulent history. Jesus was tremendously impressed with the clean appearance and well-ordered arrangement of this so-called heathen city. He marveled at the open-air theater and admired the beautiful marble temple dedicated to the worship of the heathen gods. Joseph was much disturbed by the lad's enthusiasm and sought to counteract these favorable impressions by extolling the beauty and grandeur of the Jewish temple at Jerusalem. Jesus had often gazed curiously upon this magnificent Greek city from the hill of Nazareth and had many times inquired about its extensive public works and ornate buildings, but his father had always sought to avoid answering these questions. Now they were face to face with the beauties of this Gentile city, and Joseph could not gracefully ignore Jesus' questions.

Just at this time the annual competitive games and public demonstrations of physical prowess between the Greek cities of the Decapolis were in progress at the Scythopolis amphitheater, and Jesus was insistent that his father take him to see the games, and he was so insistent that Joseph hesitated to deny him. The boy was thrilled with the games and entered most heartily into the spirit of the demonstrations of physical development and athletic skill. Joseph was inexpressibly shocked to observe his son's enthusiasm as he beheld these exhibitions of heathen pride.

After the games were finished, Joseph received the surprise of his life when he heard Jesus express his approval of them and suggest that it would be good for the young men of Nazareth if they could be thus benefited by wholesome outdoor physical activities. Joseph talked earnestly and long with Jesus concerning the evil nature of such practices, but he well knew that the lad was unconvinced.

The only time in their life together that Jesus ever saw his father angry was on this trip. That night in their room at the inn, in the course of their discussions, the boy suggested that they go back home and work for the building of an amphitheater at Nazareth. When Joseph heard his son express such un-Jewish sentiments, he forgot his usual calm demeanor and, seizing Jesus by the shoulder, angrily said: "My son, never again let me hear you give utterance to such an evil thought as long as you live." Jesus was startled by his father's display of emotion. He had never before been made to feel the personal sting of his father's indignation and was astonished and shocked beyond expression. He only replied: "Very well, my father, it shall be so." Never again did the boy even in the slightest manner allude to the games and other athletic activities of the Greeks as long as his father lived.

In mid-June, Jude was born. Complications attended the birth of this, the seventh child. Mary was so very ill for several weeks that Joseph remained at home. Jesus was very much occupied with errands for his father and with many duties occasioned by his mother's illness. Never again did this boy find it possible to return to the childlike attitude of his earlier years. From the time of his mother's illness - just before he was 11 years old, he was compelled to assume the responsibilities of the first-born son and to do this one or two full years before these burdens would normally have fallen on his shoulders.

The Chazzan spent one evening each week with Jesus, helping him to master the Hebrew Scriptures. He was greatly interested in the progress of his promising pupil, therefore he was willing to assist him in many ways. This Jewish teacher exerted a great influence upon this growing mind, but he was never able to comprehend why Jesus was so indifferent to all his suggestions regarding the prospects of going to Jerusalem to continue his education under the learned rabbis.

Years later, Jesus saw the Greek amphitheater at Jerusalem and realized how hateful such things were from the Jewish point of view.

Nevertheless, throughout his life he endeavored to introduce the idea of wholesome recreation into his personal plans and, as far as Jewish practice would permit, into the later program of regular activities for his twelve Apostles.

By the end of his eleventh year Jesus was a vigorous, well-developed, moderately humorous, and fairly lighthearted youth, but from this year on he was more and more given to profound meditation and serious contemplation. He was much given to thinking about how he was to carry out his obligations to his family and at the same time be obedient to the call of his mission to the world. Already he had conceived that his ministry was not to be limited to the Jews or even to the Palestinian peoples.

THE TWELFTH YEAR

The Twelfth year was an eventful year for this young lad. He continued to make progress at school and was inexhaustible in his study of nature, while increasingly he carried on his study of the methods whereby men make a living. He began doing regular work in the home carpenter shop and was permitted to manage his own earnings, a very unusual arrangement in a Jewish home of those days. This year he also learned the wisdom of keeping such matters a secret in the family. He was becoming conscious of the way in which he had caused trouble in the village, and henceforth he became increasingly discreet in concealing everything which might cause him to be regarded as different from his fellows.

Throughout this year he experienced many moments of uncertainty, if not actual doubt, regarding the nature of his mission. His developing human mind did not yet fully grasp the reality of his dual nature. The fact that he had a single personality rendered it difficult for his consciousness to recognize the double origin of the factors which comprised the nature of his personality.

From this time on he became more successful in getting along with his brothers and sisters. He was increasingly tactful, always compassionate and considerate of their welfare and happiness, and enjoyed good relations with them up to the beginning of his public ministry.

It was a trying experience for Joseph and Mary to undertake the rearing of this unprecedented combination of divinity and humanity, and they deserve great credit for so faithfully and successfully discharging their parental responsibilities. Increasingly, Jesus' parents realized that there was something superhuman resident within this son, but they never even faintly dreamed that this son of promise was indeed a Son of God, ordained in Heaven. Joseph and Mary lived and died without ever realizing that their son was a Son of God incarnate in mortal flesh.

This year Jesus paid more attention than ever to music, and he continued to teach the home school for his brothers and sisters. It was at about this time that the lad became keenly conscious of the difference between the viewpoints of Joseph and Mary regarding the nature of his mission. He pondered much over his parent's differing opinions, often hearing their discussions when they thought he was sound asleep. More and more he inclined to the view of his father, so that his mother was destined to be hurt by the realization that her son was gradually rejecting her guidance in matters having to do with his life and career. As the years passed, this breach of understanding widened. Less and less did Mary comprehend the significance of Jesus' mission, and increasingly was this good mother hurt by the failure of her favorite son to fulfill her expectations.

Joseph developed a growing belief in the spiritual nature of Jesus' mission. It is unfortunate that he did not live to see the fulfillment of his concept of Jesus' mission on Earth.

During his last year at school, when he was twelve years old, Jesus argued with his father about the Jewish custom of touching the bit of parchment nailed upon the doorpost each time on going into, or coming out of, the house and then kissing the finger that touched the parchment. As a part of this ritual, it was customary to say: "The

Father shall preserve our going out and our coming in, from this time forth and even forevermore." Joseph and Mary had repeatedly instructed Jesus as to the reasons for not making images or drawing pictures, explaining that such creations might be used for idolatrous purposes. Though Jesus failed fully to grasp their beliefs against images and pictures, he possessed a high concept of consistency and therefore pointed out to his father the essentially idolatrous nature of this habitual obedience to the doorpost parchment. Joseph removed the parchment from the door after this incident.

As the years passed, Jesus did much to modify the practice of religious forms in their home, such as the family prayers and other customs. It was possible to do many such things at Nazareth, for its synagogue was under the influence of a liberal school of rabbis.

Throughout this and the two following years Jesus suffered great mental distress as the result of his constant effort to adjust his personal views of religious practices and social customs to the established beliefs of his parents. He was bothered by the conflict between the urge to be loyal to his own convictions and his dutiful submission to his parents.

His greatest conflict was between two very high commands which were uppermost in his youthful mind. The one was: "Be loyal to your highest convictions of truth and righteousness." The other was: "Honor your father and your mother." However, he never shirked the responsibility of making the necessary adjustments between these views of loyalty to one's personal convictions and duty toward one's family, and he achieved the satisfaction of the blending of personal convictions and family obligations into a masterful concept of family solidarity based upon loyalty, fairness, tolerance, and love.

The Thirteenth Year

In his thirteenth year, the lad of Nazareth passed from boyhood to the beginning of young manhood. His voice began to change, and other features of mind and body gave evidence of the oncoming status of manhood.

In early January of this year, his baby brother Amos, was born. Jude was not yet two years of age, and the baby sister, Ruth, was yet to come. Jesus had a sizable family of small children left to his watch care when his father met his accidental death the following year.

It was the following month, February, that Jesus became humanly assured that he was destined to perform a mission on Earth for the enlightenment of man and the revelation of God. Momentous decisions, coupled with far-reaching plans, were formulating in the mind of this youth, who was, to outward appearances, an average lad of Nazareth. The Angels in Heaven looked on with fascination and amazement as all this began to unfold in the thinking and acting of the adolescent carpenter's son.

In March, Jesus graduated from the course of training in the local school connected with the Nazareth synagogue. This was a great day in the life of any ambitious Hebrew family, the day when the first-born son was pronounced a son of the commandments and the ransomed first born of God, a child of the Most High and servant of the Father of all the Earth.

Joseph came home from his work at Sepphoris, where he was in charge of the work crews in a new public building, to be present on this happy occasion. Jesus' teacher confidently believed that his alert and diligent pupil was destined to some outstanding career, some distinguished mission. The elders, notwithstanding all their trouble with Jesus' nonconformist tendencies, were very proud of the lad and had already begun laying plans which would enable him to go to Jerusalem to continue his education in the renowned Hebrew academies.

As Jesus heard these plans discussed from time to time, he became increasingly sure that he would never go to Jerusalem to study with the rabbis. But he little dreamed of the tragedy, so soon to occur, which would ensure the abandonment of all such plans by causing him to assume the responsibility for the support and direction of a large family, presently to consist of five brothers and three sisters as well as his mother and himself. Jesus had a larger and longer experience rearing this family than was accorded to Joseph, his father. He did measure up to the standard which he subsequently set for himself: to become a wise, patient, understanding, and effective teacher and eldest brother to this family so suddenly sorrow-stricken and so unexpectedly bereaved.

Jesus, having now reached the threshold of young manhood and having been formally graduated from the synagogue schools, was qualified to proceed to Jerusalem with his parents to participate with them in the celebration of his first Passover. A considerable company of over 100 persons made ready to depart from Nazareth early one April morning for Jerusalem. They journeyed south toward Samaria, but on reaching Jezreel, they turned east, going around Mount Gilboa into the Jordan Valley in order to avoid passing through Samaria.

Joseph and his family would have enjoyed going down through Samaria by way of Jacob's Well and Bethel, but since the Jews disliked dealing with the Samaritans, they decided to go with their neighbors by way of the Jordan Valley. Joseph did not share their feelings since his work crews consisted of many Samaritans as well as Jews and other Hebrews.

By this time, the much-dreaded Archelaus had been deposed, and they had little to fear in taking Jesus to Jerusalem. Twelve years had passed since the first Herod had sought to destroy the babe of Bethlehem, and no one would now think of associating that affair with this obscure lad from Galilee.

Before reaching the Jezreel junction, they passed the ancient village of Shunem, and Jesus heard again about the most beautiful maiden of all the Hebrews who once lived there and also about the wonderful works Elisha performed there. In passing by Jezreel, Jesus' parents recounted the doings of Ahab and Jezebel and the exploits of Jehu. In passing around Mount Gilboa, they talked much about the death of Saul on the slopes of this mountain, the doings of King David, and the associations of this historic spot.

As they rounded the base of Gilboa, the pilgrims could see the Greek city of Scythopolis. They gazed upon the marble structures from a distance but avoided going near the Gentile city lest they so defile themselves that they could not participate in the forthcoming solemn and sacred ceremonies of the Passover at Jerusalem. Mary could not understand why neither Joseph nor Jesus would speak of Scythopolis. She did not know about their controversy of the previous year as they had never revealed this episode to her.

The road now led immediately down into the tropical Jordan Valley, and soon Jesus was to have exposed to his wondering gaze the crooked and ever winding Jordan with its glistening and rippling waters as it flowed down toward the Dead Sea. They laid aside their outer garments as they journeyed south in this tropical valley, enjoying the luxurious fields of grain and the beautiful oleanders laden with their pink blossoms, while massive snow-capped Mount Hermon stood far to the north, in majesty looking down on the valley. A little over three hours' travel from Scythopolis they came upon a bubbling spring, and here they camped for the night, out under the starlit heavens.

On their second day's journey they passed by where the Jabbok, from the east, flows into the Jordan and looking east up this river valley, they recounted the days of Gideon, when their ancestors, the Midianites, poured into this region to overrun the land. Toward the end of the second day's journey, they camped near the base of the highest mountain overlooking the Jordan valley, Mount Sartaba, whose summit was occupied by the fortress where Herod had imprisoned one of his wives and buried his two murdered sons.

The third day they passed by two villages which had been recently built by Herod and noted their superior architecture and their beautiful palm gardens. By nightfall they reached Jericho, where they remained until the morning. That evening Joseph, Mary, and Jesus walked a mile and a half to the site of the ancient Jericho, where Joshua, for whom Jesus was named, had performed his renowned exploits according to Hebrew stories.

By the fourth and last day of their journey, the road was a continuous procession of pilgrims. They now began to climb the hills leading up to Jerusalem. As they neared the top, they could look across the Jordan to the mountains beyond and south over the sluggish waters of the Dead Sea. About halfway up to Jerusalem, Jesus gained his first view of the Mount of Olives, and Joseph pointed out to him that the holy city lay just beyond this ridge, and the lad's heartbeat fast with joyous anticipation of soon beholding the city.

On the eastern slopes of Mt. Olivet, they paused for a rest at the border of a little village called Bethany. The hospitable villagers poured forth to minister to the pilgrims, and it happened that Joseph and his family had stopped near the house of a man named Simon, who had three children about the same age as Jesus, Mary, Martha and Lazarus. They invited the Nazareth family in for refreshment, and a lifelong friendship started between the two families. Many times, afterwards in his eventful life, Jesus stopped in this home.

They pressed on, soon standing on the brink of Mt. Olivet, and Jesus saw for the first time the holy city, the pretentious palaces, and the inspiring temple. At no time in his life did Jesus ever experience such a purely human thrill as that which at this time so completely enthralled him as he stood there on this April afternoon on the Mount of Olives, taking in his first view of Jerusalem. In later years, on this very same spot, he would stand and weep over the city which was about to reject and murder yet another prophet, the last and the greatest of the Heavenly teachers.

They hurried on to Jerusalem. It was now Thursday afternoon.

On reaching the city, they journeyed past the temple, and never had Jesus beheld such throngs of human beings. He meditated deeply on how these Jews had assembled here from the uttermost parts of the known world.

Soon they reached the place prearranged for their accommodation during the Passover week, the large home of a well-to- do relative of Mary's, one who knew something of the early history of both John and Jesus, through Zacharias. The following day, the day of preparation, they made ready for the appropriate celebration of the Passover Sabbath.

While all Jerusalem was a stir in preparation for the Passover, Joseph found time to take his son around to visit the academy where it had been arranged for him to resume his education two years later, as soon as he reached the required age of fifteen. Joseph was truly puzzled when he observed how little interest Jesus showed in all these carefully laid plans.

Jesus was profoundly impressed by the temple and all the associated services and other activities. For the first time since he was four years old, he was too preoccupied with his own meditations to ask many questions. He did, however, ask his father several embarrassing questions as to why the Heavenly Father required the slaughter of so many innocent and helpless animals. His father well knew from the expression on the lad's face that his answers and attempts at explanation were unsatisfactory to his deep-thinking and keen-reasoning son.

On the day before the Passover Sabbath, flood tides of spiritual illumination swept through the mortal mind of Jesus and filled his human heart to overflowing with affectionate pity for the spiritually blind and morally ignorant multitudes assembled for the celebration of the ancient Passover commemoration. This was one of the most extraordinary days that the Son of God spent in the flesh. During the night, for the first time in his Earth life, there appeared to him an Angel from Heaven who said: "The hour has come. It is time that you begin to be about your Father's business."

No incident in all of Jesus' Earth career was more engaging, more humanly thrilling, than his first remembered visit to Jerusalem. He was especially stimulated by the experience of attending the temple discussions by himself, and it long stood out in his memory as the great event of his later childhood and early youth. This was his first opportunity to enjoy a few days of independent living, the exhilaration of going and coming without restraint and restrictions. This brief period of undirected living, during the week following Passover, was the first complete freedom from responsibility he had ever enjoyed. It was many years subsequent to this before he again had a period of freedom from all sense of responsibility, even for a short time.

Women seldom went to the Passover feast at Jerusalem. They were not required to be present, and in fact were not permitted within the innermost temple but were instead required to view from the Women's Gallery. When his mother decided to go, many other Nazareth women were led to make the journey, so that the Passover company contained the largest number of women, in proportion to men, ever to go up to the Passover from Nazareth. It was customary to chant a Psalm on the way to Jerusalem, so this group chanted the One Hundred and Thirtieth Psalm all the way to Jerusalem.

From the time they left Nazareth until they reached the summit of the Mount of Olives, Jesus had experienced one long stress of expectant anticipation. All through a joyful childhood he had reverently heard of Jerusalem and its temple. From the Mount of Olives and from the outside, on closer inspection, the temple had been all and more than Jesus had expected. But when he once entered it's sacred portals, utter disillusionment began.

In company with his parents Jesus passed through the temple precincts on his way to join that group of new sons of the law who were about to be consecrated as citizens. He was a little disappointed by the general demeanor of the temple throngs, but the first great shock of the day came when his mother left them on her way to the Women's Gallery. It had never occurred to Jesus that his mother was not allowed to accompany him to the consecration ceremony. He was thoroughly indignant that she was made to suffer from such unjust discrimination. While he strongly resented this, aside from a few remarks of protest to his father, he said nothing more about it. But he thought much, and thought deeply, as his questions to the Scribes and Teachers a week later proved out.

He passed through the consecration rituals but was disappointed by their perfunctory and routine natures. He missed that personal interest which characterized the ceremonies of the synagogue at Nazareth. He then returned to greet his mother and prepared to accompany his father on his first trip about the temple and its various courts, galleries, and corridors. The temple precincts could accommodate over two hundred thousand worshippers at one time, and while the vastness of these buildings greatly impressed his mind, he was more intrigued by the contemplation of the spiritual significance of the temple ceremonies and their associated worship.

Though many of the temple rituals very touchingly impressed his sense of the beautiful and the symbolic, he was always disappointed by the explanation of the real meanings of these ceremonies which his parents would offer in answer to his many searching inquiries. Jesus simply would not accept explanations of worship and religious devotion which involved belief in the wrath of God or the anger of the Almighty. In further discussion of these questions, after the conclusion of the temple visit, when his father became mildly insistent that he acknowledge acceptance of the

Orthodox Jewish beliefs, Jesus turned suddenly upon his parents and, looking appealingly into the eyes of his father, said: "My father, it cannot be true that our Father in Heaven can so regard his erring children on Earth. The Heavenly Father cannot love his children less than you love me. I know that no matter what unwise thing I might do, you would never pour out your wrath upon me nor vent your anger against me. If you, my Earth father, possess such human reflections of the divine, how much more must the Heavenly Father be filled with goodness and overflowing with love and mercy for us all. I refuse to believe that my Father in Heaven is capable of venting his anger unmercilessly on us, his children."

Everywhere Jesus went throughout the temple courts, he was shocked and sickened by the irreverence which he observed. He deemed the conduct of the temple throngs to be inconsistent with their presence in his Father's house. But he received the shock of his young life when his father escorted him into the Court of the Gentile converts with its noisy jargon, loud talking and cursing, mingled indiscriminately with the bleating of sheep and the babble of noises which betrayed the presence of the money-changers and the vendors of sacrificial animals and other commercial commodities.

But most of all was his sense of propriety outraged by the sight of the frivolous women of the King's Court, otherwise known as Temple Harlots, parading about within this precinct of the temple, just such painted women as he had so recently seen when on a visit to Sepphoris. This profanation of the temple fully aroused all his youthful indignation, and he did not hesitate to express himself freely to Joseph.

Jesus admired the sentiment and service of the temple, but he was shocked by the spiritual ugliness which he beheld on the faces of so many of the unthinking worshipers.

They now passed down to the Priests' Court beneath the rock ledge in front of the temple, where the altar stood, to observe the killing of the droves of sacrificial animals and the washing away of the blood from the hands of the officiating priests at the bronze fountain. The blood covered pavement, the gory hands of the priests, and the screams of thousands of lambs as they were slaughtered were more than this nature-loving lad could stand. The terrible sight sickened the boy. He clutched his father's arm and begged to be taken away. They walked back through the Court of the Gentiles, and even the coarse laughter and profane jesting which he heard there before were a relief from the sights he had just beheld in the inner temple.

Joseph saw how his son had been sickened at the sights of the temple rites and wisely led him around to view the 'Gate Beautiful', the artistic gate made of Corinthian bronze. But Jesus had had enough for his first visit at the temple. They returned to the upper court for Mary and walked about in the open air and away from the crowds for an hour, viewing the Asmonean Palace, the stately home of Herod, and the tower of the Roman guards. During this stroll Joseph explained to Jesus that only the inhabitants of Jerusalem were permitted to witness the daily sacrifices in the temple, and that the people from Galilee, like all other Jews, were allowed only three times a year to participate in the temple worship: at the Passover, at the Feast of Pentecost, and at the Feast of Tabernacles. Only the Jews of Jerusalem considered themselves holy enough to participate daily in the temple ceremonies. Afterward they went to their lodgings and got ready for the celebration of Passover.

Five Nazareth families were guests of the family of Simon of Bethany in the celebration of this Passover meal. Simon purchased the paschal lamb from the temple for his company. It was the slaughter of these lambs in the temple in such enormous numbers that had so affected Jesus on his temple visit. They planned to eat the Passover with Mary's relatives, but Jesus persuaded his parents to accept the invitation to go to Bethany.

That night they assembled for the Passover rites, eating the roasted lamb with unleavened bread and bitter herbs. Jesus, being a new son of the covenant, was asked to recount the origin of the Passover, and this he did, but he somewhat disconcerted his parents by the inclusion of numerous remarks mildly reflecting the impressions made on his youthful but thoughtful mind by the things which he had so recently seen and heard. This evening was the beginning of the seven- day ceremonies of the Feast of the Passover.

Even at this early date, though he said nothing about such matters to his parents, Jesus had begun to turn over in his mind the propriety of celebrating the Passover without the slaughtered lamb. He felt assured in his own mind that his Father in Heaven was not pleased with this spectacle of sacrificial offerings, and as the years passed, he became increasingly determined someday to establish the celebration of a bloodless Passover.

Jesus slept very little that night. His rest was greatly disturbed by revolting dreams of the slaughter and suffering of the animals. His mind was distraught, and his heart torn by the inconsistencies and absurdities of the theology of the whole Jewish ceremonial system.

His parents likewise slept little. They were greatly disturbed by the events of the day just ended. They were completely upset in their own hearts by the lad's strange and determined attitude. Mary became nervously agitated during the evening, but Joseph remained calm, though he was equally puzzled. Both of them feared to talk frankly with the lad about these problems, though Jesus would gladly have talked with his parents if they had dared to encourage him.

The next day's services at the temple were more acceptable to Jesus and did much to relieve the unpleasant memories of the previous day. The following morning young Lazarus took Jesus in hand, and they began a systematic exploration of Jerusalem and its environs.

Before the day was over, Jesus discovered the various places about the temple where teaching conferences were in progress. Aside from a few visits to the Holy of Holies to gaze in wonder as to what really was behind the veil of separation, he spent most of his time about the temple at these teaching conferences.

Throughout the Passover week, Jesus kept his place among the new sons of the commandment, and this meant that he must seat himself outside the rail which segregated all persons who were not full citizens. Being thus made conscious of his youth, he refrained from asking the many questions which surged back and forth in his mind. At least he refrained until the Passover celebration had ended and these restrictions on the newly consecrated youths were lifted.

On Wednesday of the Passover Week, Jesus was permitted to go home with Lazarus to spend the night at Bethany. This evening, Lazarus, Martha, and Mary heard Jesus discuss things temporal and eternal, human and divine, and from that night on they all three loved him as if he had been their own brother.

Many times, during the Passover week, his parents would find Jesus sitting off by himself with his youthful head in his hands, profoundly thinking over all that he had seen. They had never seen him behaved like this, and not knowing how much he was confused in mind and troubled in spirit by the experience through which he was passing, they were sorely perplexed. They did not know what to do. They welcomed the passing of the days of the Passover week and longed to have their strangely acting son safely back in Nazareth.

Day by day Jesus was thinking through his problems. By the end of the week, he had made many adjustments. When the time came to return to Nazareth, his youthful mind was still swarming with perplexities and beset by a host of unanswered questions and unsolved problems.

Before Joseph and Mary left Jerusalem, they made definite arrangements for Jesus to return when he reached the age of fifteen to begin his long course of study in one of the best-known academies of the rabbis. Jesus accompanied his parents and teacher on their visits to the school, but they were all distressed to observe how indifferent he seemed to all they said and did. Mary was deeply pained at his reactions to the Jerusalem visit, and Joseph was profoundly perplexed at the lad's strange remarks and unusual conduct.

After all, Passover week had been a great event in Jesus' life. he had enjoyed the opportunity of meeting scores of boys his own age, fellow candidates for the consecration, and he utilized such contacts as a means of learning how people lived in Mesopotamia,

Turkestan, and Parthia, as well as in the far-western provinces of Rome and other parts of the known world. He was already fairly conversant with the way in which the youth of Egypt and other regions near Palestine grew up.

There were thousands of young people in Jerusalem at this time, and the Nazareth lad personally met, and more or less extensively interviewed, more than one hundred and fifty. He was particularly interested in those who hailed from the far eastern and the remote western countries. As a result of these contacts the lad began to entertain a desire to travel about the world for the purpose of learning how the various groups of his fellow men toiled for their livelihood.

It had been agreed that the Nazareth party would gather in the region of the temple at midmorning on the first day of the week after the Passover festival had ended to begin their journey back home.

While his parents awaited the assembly of their fellow travelers, Jesus went into the temple to listen to the discussions. Presently the company prepared to depart, the men going in one group and the women in another as was their custom in journeying to and from the Jerusalem festivals. Jesus had gone up to Jerusalem in company with his mother and the women. Being now a young man of the consecration, he was supposed to journey back to Nazareth in company with his father and the men. As the Nazareth party moved on toward Bethany, Jesus was completely absorbed in the discussion in the temple and was entirely unmindful of the passing of the time for the departure of his parents.

He did not realize that he had been left behind until the conferences adjourned at noontime.

The Nazareth travelers did not miss Jesus because Mary thought he journeyed with the men, while Joseph thought he traveled with the women since he had gone up to Jerusalem with the women, leading Mary's donkey. They did not discover his absence until they reached Jericho and prepared to stay for the night. After making inquiry of the last of the party to reach Jericho and learning that none of them had seen their son, they spent a sleepless night, turning over in their minds what might have happened to him, recounting many of his unusual reactions to the events of Passover week, and mildly chiding each other for not seeing to it that he was in the group before they left Jerusalem.

In the meantime, Jesus had remained in the temple throughout the afternoon, listening to the discussions and enjoying the quieter atmosphere, the great crowds of Passover week having about disappeared. At the conclusion of the afternoon discussions, in none of which Jesus participated, he decided to go to Bethany rather than to the house of Mary's relatives, arriving just as Simon's family made ready to partake of their evening meal. The three youngsters were overjoyed to greet Jesus, and he remained in Simon's house for the night. He visited very little during the evening, spending most of the time alone in the garden meditating.

Early next day, Jesus was up and on his way to the temple. On the brow of Mt. Olivet, he paused and wept over the sight his eyes beheld - a spiritually decadent people enslaved by traditions and living under the surveillance of the Roman occupation legions. Midmorning found him in the temple with his mind made up to take part in the discussions. Meanwhile, Joseph and Mary also had arisen at the early dawn with the intention of retracing their steps to Jerusalem.

First, they hurried to the house of Mary's relatives, where they had lodged as a family during the Passover week, but no one there had seen Jesus. After searching all day and finding no trace of him, they returned to their relatives for the night.

At the second conference, Jesus felt bold enough to ask questions, and in a very amazing way he participated in the temple discussions, but always in a manner consistent with his youth. Sometimes his pointed questions were somewhat embarrassing to the learned teachers of the Jewish law, but he evidenced such a spirit of candid fairness, coupled with an evident hunger for knowledge, that the majority of the temple teachers were disposed to treat him with every consideration.

But when he presumed to question the justice of putting to death a drunken Gentile who had wandered away from the Court of the Gentiles and unintentionally entered the forbidden and reputedly sacred precincts of the temple, one of the more intolerant teachers grew impatient with the lad's implied criticisms and, glowering down upon him, asked how old he was. Jesus replied, "Thirteen years lacking more than four months." "Then", remarked the now irate teacher, "why are you here, since you are not of age as a son of the law?" When Jesus explained that he had received consecration during the Passover, and that he was a finished student at the Nazareth schools, the teachers derisively replied in unison, "We might have known. He is from Nazareth of Galilee." But the leader insisted that Jesus was not to be blamed if the rulers of the synagogue at Nazareth had graduated him, technically, when he was twelve instead of thirteen. Notwithstanding that several of his detractors got up and left, it was ruled that the lad might continue undisturbed as a pupil of the temple discussions.

When this, his second day in the temple, was finished, again he went to Bethany for the night. Again, he went out in the garden to meditate and pray. It was apparent that his mind was concerned with the contemplation of weighty problems.

Jesus' third day with the scribes and teachers in the temple witnessed the gathering of many spectators who, having heard of this youth from Galilee, came to enjoy the experience of seeing a lad confuse the old wise men of the law. Simon also came down from Bethany to see what the boy was up to. Throughout this day, Joseph and Mary continued their anxious search for Jesus, even going several times into the temple but never thinking to scrutinize the several discussion groups, although they once came almost within hearing distance of his fascinating voice.

Before the day had ended, the entire attention of the chief discussion group of the temple had become focused upon the questions being asked by young Jesus. Among his many questions were:

1. What really exists in the Holy of Holies behind the veil?
2. Why should women in Jerusalem be segregated from the male temple worshippers?
3. If God is a Father who loves his children, why all this slaughter of animals to gain divine favor? Has the teaching of Moses been misunderstood?
4. Since the temple is supposedly dedicated to the worship of the Father in Heaven, why do you permit the presence of those who engage in barter and trade?
5. Is the expected Messiah to become a temporal prince to sit on the throne of David, or is he to function as the light of life in the establishment of a spiritual kingdom?

All day through, those who listened marveled at these questions, and none was more astonished than Simon. For more than four hours this Nazareth youth plied the Jewish teachers with thought provoking and heart-searching questions. He made few comments on the remarks of his elders. He conveyed his teaching by the questions he would ask. By the deft and subtle phrasing of a question he would challenge their teaching and, at the same time, suggest his own beliefs. In the manner of his asking a question there was an appealing combination of sagacity and humor which endeared him even to those who resented his youthfulness. He was always eminently fair and considerate in asking these penetrating questions. On this eventful afternoon in the temple, he exhibited that same reluctance to take unfair advantage of an opponent which characterized his entire subsequent public ministry. As a youth, and later on as a man, he seemed to be utterly free from all egotistical desire to win an argument merely to experience logical triumph over his fellows, being interested in just one thing, to proclaim everlasting truth and thus effect a fuller revelation of the Eternal God.

When the day was over, Simon and Jesus walked together back to Bethany. For most of the distance both the man and the boy were silent. Again, Jesus paused on the brow of Olivet, but as he viewed the city and its temple, he did not weep this time. He only bowed his head in silence.

After the evening meal at Bethany, he again declined to join the merry circle but instead went to the garden, where he meditated long into the night, vainly endeavoring to think out some definite plan of approach to the problem of his lifework and to decide how best he might labor to reveal to his spiritually blinded countrymen a more beautiful concept of the Heavenly Father and to set them free from their terrible bondage to law, ritual, ceremonial, and musty traditions. But the clear light did not come yet to this truth-seeking lad.

Jesus was strangely unmindful of his earthly parents, even at breakfast when Lazarus' mother remarked that his parents must be about home by that time. Jesus did not seem to comprehend that they would be somewhat worried about his having lingered behind.

On the fourth day again, he journeyed to the temple, but he did not pause to meditate at the brow of Olivet. In the course of the morning's discussions much time was devoted to the law and the prophets. The teachers were astonished that Jesus was so familiar with the Scriptures, in Hebrew as well as Greek. But they were amazed not so much by his knowledge of scriptures as by his youth.

At the afternoon conference they had hardly begun to answer his question relating to the purpose of prayer when the leader invited the lad to come forward and state his own views regarding prayer and worship.

The evening before, Jesus' parents had heard about this strange youth who so deftly sparred with the interpreters of the law, but it had not occurred to them that this lad was their son. They had about decided to journey out to the home of Zacharias as they thought Jesus might have gone to see Elizabeth and John. Thinking Zacharias might perhaps be at the temple, they stopped there on their way to the city of Judah. As they strolled through the courts of the temple they were utterly amazed when they recognized the voice of the missing lad and beheld him seated among the temple teachers.

Joseph was speechless, but Mary gave vent to her long pent-up fear and anxiety when, rushing up to the lad, now standing to greet his astonished parents, she said: "My child, why have you treated us like this? It is now more than three days that your father and I have searched for you sorrowing. Whatever possessed you to desert us?" It was a tense moment. All eyes were turned on Jesus to hear what he would say. His father looked reprovingly at him but said nothing.

Jesus was supposed to be a young man by now. He had finished the regular schooling of a child, had been recognized as a son of the law, and had received consecration as a citizen. Yet his mother more than mildly chided him before all the people assembled, right in the midst of the most serious and sublime effort of his young life, thus bringing to an inglorious conclusion one of the greatest opportunities he ever had to function as a teacher of truth, a preacher of righteousness and a revealer of the loving character of his Father in Heaven.

But the lad was equal to the occasion. After a startled moment's thought, Jesus answered his mother, saying: "Why is it that you have looked for me, my parents? Would you not expect to find me in my Father's house since the time has come when I should dedicate my life to my Father's work?"

Everyone was astonished at the lad's manner of speaking.

Silently they all withdrew and left him standing alone with his parents. Presently the young man relieved the embarrassment of all three when he quietly said: "Come, my parents, no one has done other than that which he thought best. Our Father in Heaven has ordained these things. Let us depart for home."

In silence they started out, arriving at Jericho for the night. only once did they pause, and that on the brow of Olivet, when the lad raised his walking staff aloft and, quivering from head to foot under the surging of intense emotion, said: "O Jerusalem, Jerusalem, and the people thereof, what slaves you are, subservient to the Roman yoke and victims of your own backward traditions, but I will return someday to cleanse your temple and deliver my people from this bondage."

On the three-day journey to Nazareth, Jesus said little. Neither did his parents say much in his presence. They were truly at a loss to understand the conduct of their son, but they did treasure in their hearts his sayings, even though they could not fully comprehend their meanings.

On reaching home, Jesus made a brief statement to his parents, assuring them of his affection and implying that they need not fear he would again give any occasion for their suffering anxiety because of his conduct. He concluded this momentous statement by saying: "While I must follow the will of my Father in Heaven, I will also be obedient to my father and mother on Earth."

Though Jesus, in his mind, would many times refuse to consent to the well-intentioned but misguided efforts of his parents to dictate the course of his thinking or to establish the plan of his work on Earth, still, in every manner consistent with his dedication to the doing of his Heavenly Father's will, he did most gracefully conform to the desires of his earthly father and to the customs of his mortal family. Even when he could not consent, he would do everything possible to conform. He was an artist in the matter of adjusting his dedication to duty to his obligations of family loyalty and social service.

Joseph was puzzled, but Mary, as she reflected on these experiences, gained comfort, eventually viewing his utterance on Olivet as prophetic of the Messianic mission of her son as the deliverer of the Jews. She set to work with renewed energy to mold his thoughts into patriotic and nationalistic channels and enlisted the efforts of her brother, Jesus' favorite uncle. In every other way did the mother of Jesus address herself to the task of preparing her son to assume the leadership of those who would restore the throne of David and forever cast off the Gentile yoke of political bondage.

THE FOURTEENTH YEAR

Of all of Jesus' years on Earth as a mortal being, the fourteenth and fifteenth years were the most difficult and crucial. These two years, after he began to be self-conscious of divinity and destiny, were the most trying of his remarkable life on Earth. It is this period of two years which should be called the great test, the real temptation of Jesus. No human youth, in passing through the early confusions and adjustment problems of adolescence, has ever experienced a more crucial testing than that which Jesus had to pass through during his transition from boyhood to young manhood.

This important period in his youthful development began with the conclusion of the Jerusalem visit and with his return to Nazareth. At first Mary was happy with the thought that she had her boy back once more, that Jesus had returned home to be a dutiful son, not that he was ever anything else, and that he would henceforth be more responsive to her plans for his future. But she would not long bask in this warm glow of maternal delusion. Very soon she was to be more completely disillusioned. More and more the boy was in the company of his father. Less and less did he come to her with his problems, while increasingly both his parents failed to comprehend his frequent alternation between the affairs of this world and the contemplation of his relation to his Father's business. Frankly, they did not understand him, but they did truly love him.

As he grew older, Jesus' pity and love for the Jewish people deepened, but with the passing years, there developed in his mind a growing resentment towards the politically appointed priests. Jesus had great respect for the sincere Pharisees and the honest scribes, but he held the hypocritical Pharisees and the dishonest theologians in great contempt. He looked with disdain upon all those religious leaders who were not sincere. When he scrutinized the sad leadership of the Jews, he was sometimes tempted to look with favor on the possibility of his becoming the Messiah of Jewish expectation, not for the annihilation of the Roman Legions, but for the annihilation of the corrupt Jewish priests and politicians. He never yielded to that overwhelming lifelong temptation.

The story of his exploits among the wise men of the temple in Jerusalem was gratifying to all of Nazareth, especially to his former teachers in the synagogue school. For a time, his praise was on everybody's lips. All the village recounted his childhood wisdom and praiseworthy conduct and predicted that he was destined to become a great leader. They thought that at last a really great teacher was to come out of Nazareth in Galilee. They all looked forward to the time when he would be fifteen years of age so that he might be permitted regularly to read the scriptures in the synagogue on the Sabbath day.

By the time of his 14th year, he had become a very good yoke maker and worked very well with both canvas and leather. He was also rapidly developing into an expert carpenter and cabinetmaker. The summer of this year, he made frequent trips to the top of the hill to the northwest of Nazareth for prayer and meditation. He was gradually becoming more self-conscious of the nature of his purpose for being on Earth.

This hill, a little more than 100 years previously had been the high place of Baal, and now it was the site of the tomb of Simeon, a reputed holy man of the Hebrews. From the summit of this hill of Simeon, Jesus looked out over Nazareth and the surrounding countryside. He would gaze upon Megiddo and recall the story of the Egyptian army winning a great victory in Asia, and how, later on, this same army defeated the Judean King Josiah. Not far away he could look upon Taanach, where Deborah and Barak defeated Sisera. In the distance he could view the hills of Dothan, where Joseph's brothers sold him into slavery according to Hebrew stories. Then he would shift his gaze over to Ebal and Gerizim and recall the traditions of Abraham, Jacob, and Abimelech. Thus, he recalled and thought over in his mind the historic and traditional events of his father Joseph's Hebrew people.

He continued to carry on his advanced courses of reading under the synagogue teachers, and he also continued with the home education of his brothers and sisters as they grew up to suitable ages.

In August, for the lad's fourteenth birthday, his father Joseph arranged to set aside the income from his Nazareth and Capernaum properties to pay for Jesus long course of study at Jerusalem. It was planned that he should go to Jerusalem in August of the following year when he would turn fifteen years of age.

By the beginning of this year, both Joseph and Mary began to have frequent doubts about the destiny of their son. He was indeed a brilliant and lovable child, but he was so difficult to understand, so hard to fathom, and again, nothing extraordinary or miraculous ever happened. Scores of times had his proud mother stood in breathless anticipation, expecting to see her son engage in some superhuman or miraculous performance, but always were her hopes dashed down in cruel disappointment. All this was discouraging, even disheartening. The devout people of those days truly believed that prophets and men of promise always demonstrated their calling and established their divine authority by performing miracles and working wonders. But Jesus did none of these things. The confusion of his parents steadily increased as they contemplated his future.

The improved economic condition of the Nazareth family was reflected in many ways around the home and especially in the increased number of smooth white boards which were used as writing slates by Jesus and his brothers and sisters. Jesus was also permitted to resume his music lessons. He was very fond of playing the harp.

Throughout this year it can truly be said that Jesus grew in favor with man and with God. The prospects of the family seemed very good. The future was bright.

All did go exceedingly well, until that fateful day at the end of September when a runner from Sepphoris brought home the tragic news that Joseph had been severely injured by the falling of a derrick while at work at the Governor's residence. The messenger from Sepphoris had stopped at the shop on the way to Joseph's home, informing Jesus of his father's accident, and they went together to the house to break the sad news to Mary. Jesus desired to go immediately to his father, but Mary insisted that she must hurry to his side. She directed that James, then ten years of age, should accompany her to Sepphoris while Jesus remained home with the younger children until she should return, since she did not know how seriously Joseph had been injured. Joseph died before Mary arrived. They brought him back to Nazareth, and the following day he was laid to rest by the side of his forefathers.

Just as prospects for the future looked so bright and the future looked so secure, the cruel hand of fate struck the head of this Nazareth household. The affairs of this home were disrupted permanently, and the plans for Jesus and his future education in Jerusalem were dashed. This carpenter lad, barely fourteen years of age, awakened to the realization that he had not only to fulfill the commission of his Heavenly Father to reveal the Divine Truth on Earth, but that his young human nature must now also shoulder the responsibility of caring for his widowed mother and seven brothers and sisters - and one more on the way. This lad of Nazareth now became the sole support and comfort of his bereaved family. Thus was permitted an occurrence of the natural order of events on Earth which would force this young man of destiny so early to assume these heavy but highly educational and disciplinary responsibilities attendant upon becoming the head of a human family, of becoming father to his own brothers and sister, of supporting and protecting his mother, of functioning as guardian of his father's home, the only home he was to know while on this world.

Jesus cheerfully accepted the responsibilities so suddenly thrust upon him, and he carried them faithfully to the end. At least one great problem and anticipated difficulty in his life had been tragically solved.

He would not have to go to Jerusalem to study under the rabbis. From that day forward, he was ever willing to learn from even the humblest of little children, but it will remain forever true that he never derived authority to teach truth from human sources.

Still, he knew nothing of the Gabriel visits to his mother and father before his birth. He did not learn of this until he met John at the Jordan River at the beginning of his public ministry.

From this day forward, this young carpenter from Nazareth increasingly measured every institution of society and every usage of religion by the unvarying test: What does it do for the human soul? Does it bring God to man? Does it bring man to God? While he did not neglect the recreational and social aspects of life, more and more of his time was devoted to just two things: the care of his family and the preparation of himself to do the will of his Heavenly Father.

This year the neighbors began the custom of dropping by often, especially during the long winter evenings to hear Jesus play the harp since he had become quite an accomplished player. They loved to listen to his stories also, since he was a very good storyteller. He would also read to them from the Greek scriptures that had been given to him at Alexandria when he left as a child.

The economic affairs of the family continued to run smoothly for a short time. Joseph had left plenty of money available on his death. Jesus early demonstrated the possession of keen business judgment and financial sagacity. He was liberal but frugal. He was saving but generous. He proved to be a wise and efficient administrator of his father's estate.

In spite of all that Jesus and the Nazareth neighbors could do to bring cheer into the home, Mary and the children were overcast with sadness. Joseph had been a loving husband and father, and they all missed him. It seemed so tragic to think that he died before they could speak to him or hear his farewell blessing.

THE FIFTEENTH & SIXTEENTH YEARS

By the middle of his fifteenth year, Jesus had taken a firm grasp upon the management of his family's affairs. Before this year had passed, their savings had about disappeared, and they were face to face with the necessity of disposing of one of the Nazareth houses which Joseph and his neighbor Jacob owned in partnership.

In mid-April of the year 9 AD by your current calendar, Ruth, the baby of the family, was born, and to the best of his ability Jesus endeavored to take the place of his father in comforting and ministering to his mother during this trying and peculiarly sad ordeal. For almost a score of years no father could have loved and nurtured his daughter any more affectionately and faithfully than Jesus cared for little Ruth.

He was an equally good father to all the other members of his family.

During this year Jesus first formulated the prayer which he subsequently taught to his Apostles, and which to many has become known as "The Father's Prayer". It was an evolution of the family altar. They had many forms of praise and several formal prayers. After his father's death, Jesus tried to teach the older children to express themselves individually in prayer, much as he so enjoyed doing, but they could not grasp his thought and would invariably fall back upon their memorized prayer forms. It was in this effort to stimulate his older brothers and sisters to say individual prayers that Jesus would endeavor to lead them along by suggestive phrases, and presently, without intention on his part, it developed that they were all using a form of prayer which was largely built up from these suggestive lines which Jesus had taught them.

At last Jesus gave up the idea of having each member of the family formulate spontaneous prayers, and one evening in October he sat down by the little squat lamp on the low stone table, and, on a piece of smooth cedar board with a piece of charcoal he wrote out the prayer which became from that time on the standard family petition and which you now known as The Father's Prayer.

This year Jesus was much troubled with confused thinking.

Family responsibility had removed all thought of immediately carrying out any plan for responding to the Jerusalem visitation directing him to do his Father's business. Jesus reasoned that the watch care of his earthly father's family must take priority over all other duties.

In the course of this year Jesus found a passage in the Book of Enoch which influenced him in the later adoption of the term "Son of Man" as a designation for his mission on Earth. He had thoroughly considered the idea of the Jewish Messiah and was firmly convinced that he was not to be that Messiah. He longed to help his father's people, but he never expected to lead Jewish armies in overthrowing the foreign domination of Palestine by the Roman Army. He knew he would never sit on the throne of David in Jerusalem. Neither did he believe that his mission was that of a spiritual deliverer or moral teacher solely to the Jewish people. In no conceivable manner, therefore, could his life mission be the fulfillment of the intense longings and supposed Messianic prophesies of the Hebrew scriptures. At least, not as the Jews understood these predictions of the prophets. Likewise, he was certain he was never to appear as the Son of Man pictured by the Prophet Daniel.

But when the time came for him to go forth as a world teacher, what would he call himself? What claim should he make concerning his mission? By what name would he be called by the people who would become believers in his teachings?

While turning all these problems over in his mind, he found in the synagogue library at Nazareth, among the apocalyptic books which he had been studying, this manuscript called The Book of Enoch.

Though he was certain that it had not been written by Enoch, it proved very intriguing to him, and he read and reread it many times. There was one passage which particularly impressed him, a passage in which this term, Son of Man, appeared. The writer of this so-called Book of Enoch went on to tell about this Son of Man, describing the work he would do on Earth and explaining that this Son of Man, before coming down on this Earth to bring salvation to mankind, had walked through the courts of Heavenly glory with his Father, the Father of all, that he had turned his back upon all this grandeur and glory to come down to Earth to proclaim salvation to needy mortals. As Jesus read these passages, well understanding that much of the Eastern mysticism which had become mixed with these teachings was erroneous, he responded in his heart and recognized in his mind that of all the Messianic predictions of the Hebrew scriptures and of all the theories about the Jewish deliverer, none was so near the truth as this story tucked away in this only partially accredited Book of Enoch. He then and there decided to adopt as his inaugural title Son of Man. This title he carried until he subsequently began his public work and took the title of Son of God. Jesus had an unerring ability for the recognition of truth, and truth he never hesitated to embrace, no matter from what source it appeared to emanate.

By this time, he had quite thoroughly settled many things about his forthcoming work for the world, but he said nothing of these matters to his mother, who still held stoutly to the idea of his being the Jewish Messiah.

The great confusion of Jesus' younger days now arose. Having settled something about the nature of his mission on Earth to be about his Father's business - to show forth his Father's loving nature to all mankind - he began to ponder anew the many statements in the scriptures referring to the coming of a national deliverer, a Jewish teacher or king. To what event did these prophecies refer? Was not he a Jew, or was he? Was he, or was he not, of the house of David? His mother said he was. His father had ruled that he was not. He decided he was not. But had the prophets confused the nature and mission of the Messiah?

After all, could it be possible that his mother was right? In most matters, when differences of opinion had arisen in the past, she had been right. If he were a new teacher and not the Messiah, then how should he recognize the Jewish Messiah if such a one should appear in Jerusalem during the time of his Earth mission. Further, what should be his relation to this Jewish Messiah? What would be his relation, after embarking on his life mission, to his family, to the Jewish commonwealth and religion, to the Roman Empire, to the Gentiles and their religions? Each of these momentous problems this young Galilean turned over in his mind and seriously pondered while he continued to work at the carpenter's bench, laboriously making a living for himself, his mother, and eight other hungry mouths.

Before the end of this year, Mary saw the family funds diminishing. She turned the sale of doves over to James. Presently they bought a second cow, and with the aid of Miriam they began the sale of milk to their Nazareth neighbors.

His profound periods of meditation, his frequent journeys to the hilltop for prayer on the Sabbath, and the many strange ideas which Jesus advanced from time to time, thoroughly alarmed his mother.

Sometimes she thought the lad was beside himself, and then she would steady her fears, remembering that he was, after all, a child of promise and in some manner different from other youths.

But Jesus was learning to not speak of all his thoughts, not to present all his ideas to the world, not even to his own mother. From this year on, Jesus' disclosures about what was going on in his mind steadily diminished. He talked less about those things which an average person could not grasp, and which would lead to his being regarded as peculiar or different from ordinary folks. To all appearances he became commonplace and conventional, though he did long for someone who could understand his problems. He craved a trustworthy and confidential friend, but his problems were too complex for his human associates to comprehend. The uniqueness of the situation compelled him to bear his burdens alone.

With the coming of his fifteenth birthday, Jesus could officially occupy the synagogue pulpit on the Sabbath day. Many times before, in the absence of speakers, young Jesus had been asked to read the scriptures, but now the day had come when, according to law, he could conduct the service. Therefore, on the first Sabbath after his fifteenth birthday, the Chazzan arranged for Jesus to conduct the morning service of the synagogue. When all the faithful in Nazareth had assembled, the young man, having made his selection of Scriptures, stood up and began to read:

"The spirit of the Father is upon me, for the Father has anointed me. He has sent me to bring good news to the meek, to bind up the brokenhearted, to proclaim liberty to the captives, to set the spiritual prisoners free, to proclaim the year of God's favor and the day of our God's reckoning, to comfort all mourners, and to give them beauty for ashes, the oil of joy in the place of mourning, and a song of praise instead of the spirit of sorrow, that they may be called trees of righteousness, the plantings of the Father, in whom he may be glorified. Seek good and not evil that you may live, and so the Father, the God of Heaven and Earth, shall be with you until the end of time. Hate evil and love good. Establish judgment in the gate. Wash your souls.

Make yourselves clean. Put away the evil of your doings from before his eyes. Cease to do evil and learn to do good. Seek justice. Relieve the oppressed. Defend the fatherless and plead for the widow.

How shall I come before the Father, to bow myself before the Father of all the Earth? Shall I come before him with burnt offerings or with calves a year old? Will the Father be pleased with thousands of rams, ten thousands of sheep to slaughter, or with rivers of oil? Shall I give my first-born son for my transgressions, the fruit of my body for the sins of my soul? No! For the Father has showed us 0 Brothers, what is good. The Father only requires of you to do justly, love mercy, and walk humbly with your Father in Heaven?

To whom, then, will you compare God who sits upon the circle of the Earth? Lift up your eyes and behold him who has created all the world, who brings forth the Heavenly host and calls them all by their names. He does all these things by the greatness of his might, and because he is strong in power. He gives power to the weak, and to those who are weary he gives them strength to persevere. He says to all people: Fear not, for I am with you. be not dismayed, for I am your god. I will strengthen you and I will help you. Yes, I will uphold you with the right hand of my righteousness, for I am the Father, your God. I will hold your right hand, saying to you, fear not, for I will help you.

'You are my witnesses, says the Father, and my servants who I have chosen that all may know and believe me and understand that I am eternal. I am the Father, and beside me there is no other.'

When he had read these words, he sat down, and the people went out of the temple silently to their homes, pondering over the words which he had so graciously read to them. Never had his townspeople seen him so magnificently solemn. Never had they heard his voice so earnest and so sincere. Never had they observed him so manly and decisive, so authoritative.

This Sabbath afternoon Jesus climbed the Nazareth hill with James. When they returned home, he wrote out the Ten Commandments in Greek on two smooth boards in charcoal.

Subsequently Martha colored and decorated these boards, and for a very long time they hung on the wall over James' small workbench.

Gradually Jesus and his family returned to the simple life of their earlier years. Their clothes and even their food became simpler. They had plenty of milk, butter, and cheese. In season they enjoyed the produce of their garden, but each passing month necessitated the practice of greater frugality. Their breakfast was very plain. They saved their best food for the evening meal. However, lack of wealth did not imply social inferiority.

Already had this youth almost encompassed the comprehension of how men lived in his day. How well he understood life in the home, field, and workshop as shown by his subsequent teachings, which reveal his intimate contact with all phases of human experience.

The Nazareth Chazzan continued to cling to the belief that Jesus was to become a great teacher, probably the successor of the renowned Gamaliel of Jerusalem.

All of Jesus' plans for a career were thwarted. The future did not look bright as matters now developed. But he did not falter. He was not discouraged. He lived on, day by day, doing well the present duty and faithfully discharging the immediate responsibilities of his station in life.

The pay of a common day laboring carpenter was slowly diminishing. The next year they found it difficult to pay the civil taxes, not to mention the synagogue taxes and the temple tax of one-half Shekel. During this year the tax collector tried to squeeze extra revenue out of Jesus, even threatening to take his harp.

Fearing that the copy of the Greek scriptures that had been given to him on leaving Alexandria as a child might be confiscated by the tax collectors, Jesus, on his fifteenth birthday, presented it to the Nazareth synagogue library as his gift of maturity.

This year, Jesus and Mary went over to Sepphoris to receive the decision of Herod regarding an amount of money due Joseph at the time of his accidental death. They had hoped for the receipt of a considerable sum of money, but the treasurer at Sepporis had offered them a paltry amount. Joseph's brothers had taken an appeal directly to Herod himself, and now Jesus stood in the palace and heard Herod decree that his father had nothing due him at the time of his death. For such an unjust decision Jesus never again trusted Herod Antipas.

Years later he would refer to Herod as "that fox."

The work at the carpenter's bench during this and subsequent years deprived Jesus of any continued opportunity of mingling with the caravan passengers. The family supply shop had already been taken over by his uncle, and Jesus worked completely in the home shop, where he was near to help Mary with the family. About this time, he began sending James up to the camel lot to gather information about world events, and thus he sought to keep in touch with the news of the day. As he grew up to manhood, he passed through all those conflicts and confusions which the average young persons of previous and subsequent ages have undergone. The rigorous experience of supporting his family was a sure safeguard against his having much time for idle meditation or the indulgence of mystic tendencies.

This was the year that Jesus rented a large piece of land just to the north of their home, which was divided up as a family garden plot. Each of the older children had an individual garden, and they entered into keen competition in their agricultural efforts. Their eldest brother spent some time with them in the garden each day during the season of vegetable cultivation. As Jesus worked with his younger brothers and sisters in the garden, many times he entertained the wish that they could move to a farm out in the country where they could enjoy the liberty and freedom of an unhampered life. But they did not find themselves growing up in the country. Jesus, being a thoroughly practical youth as well as an idealist, intelligently and vigorously attacked his problem just as he found it and did everything within his power to adjust himself and his family to the realities of their situation and to adapt their condition to the highest possible satisfaction of their individual and collective longings.

At one time Jesus had hoped that he might be able to gather up sufficient means, provided they could collect the considerable sum of money due his father for work on Herod's palace, to warrant undertaking the purchase of a small farm. He had really given serious thought to this plan of moving his family out into the country. But when Herod refused to pay them any of the funds due Joseph, they gave up the ambition of owning a home in the country. As it was, they contrived to enjoy much of the experience of farm life since they now had three cows, four sheep, a flock of chickens, a donkey, and a dog, in addition to doves. Even the little tots had their regular duties to perform in the well-regulated scheme of management which characterized the home life of this Nazareth family.

With the close of his fifteenth year, Jesus completed the journey of that dangerous and difficult period in human existence, that time of transition between the more complacent years of childhood and approaching manhood with its increased responsibilities and opportunities for the development of a noble character. The growth period for mind and body had ended, and now began the real career of this young man of Nazareth.

As Jesus entered upon his adolescent years, he found himself the head and sole supporter of a large family. Within a very few years after his father's death all their property was gone. As time passed, he became increasingly conscious of his pre-existence, and at the same time began more fully to realize that he was present on Earth and in the flesh for the express purpose of revealing his Heavenly Father to mortal man.

No adolescent youth who has lived, or ever will live, in this world, has had, or ever will have, more weighty problems to resolve or more intricate difficulties to untangle. No youth of Earth will ever be called upon to pass through more testing conflicts or more trying situations than Jesus himself endured during those difficult years from fifteen to twenty.

This Son of God passed through infancy and experienced an uneventful childhood. Then he emerged from that testing and trying transition stage between childhood and young manhood - and became the adolescent Jesus.

His 16th year, he reached his full physical growth. He was a virile and comely youth. He became increasingly sober and serious, but he was kind and sympathetic. His eyes were kind but searching. His smile was always engaging and reassuring. His voice was musical but authoritative. His greeting was cordial but unaffected. Always, even in the most commonplace of contacts, there seemed to be evidence of the touch of a twofold nature, the human and the divine. He always displayed this combination of the sympathizing friend and the authoritative teacher. These personality traits began early to become manifest, even in these adolescent years.

This physically strong and robust youth also acquired the full growth of his human intellect, not the full experience of human thinking but the fullness of capacity for such intellectual development. He possessed a healthy and well-proportioned body, a keen and analytical mind, and kind and sympathetic disposition, a somewhat fluctuating but aggressive temperament, all of which were becoming organized into a strong, striking, and attractive personality.

As time went on, it became more difficult for his mother and his brothers and sisters to understand him. They stumbled over his sayings and misinterpreted his doings. They were all unable to comprehend their eldest brother's life because their mother had given them to understand that he was destined to become the deliverer of the Jewish people. After they had received these suggestions from Mary they were thoroughly confused when Jesus would make frank denials of all such ideas and intentions.

This year, Simon started school, and they were compelled to sell another house. James now took charge of the teaching of his three sisters, two of whom were old enough to begin serious study. As soon as Ruth grew up, she was taken charge by Miriam and Martha.

Ordinarily the girls of Jewish families received little education, but Jesus maintained that girls should go to school the same as boys, and since the synagogue school would not allow them, there was nothing to do but conduct a home school especially for them.

Throughout this year Jesus was closely confined to the workbench. Fortunately, he had plenty of work. His work was of such a superior grade that he was never idle no matter how slack work might be in that region. At times he had so much to do that James would help him. The work did not pay much, but there was always more than he could do.

By the end of this year, he had just about made up his mind that he would, after rearing his family and seeing them married, enter publicly upon his work as a teacher of truth and as a revealer of the Heavenly Father to the world. He knew he was not to become the expected Jewish Messiah, and he concluded that it was next to useless to discuss these matters with his mother. He decided to allow her to entertain whatever ideas she might choose since all he had said in the past had made little or no impression upon her and he recalled that his father had never been able to say anything that would change her mind. From this year on he talked less and less with his mother, or anyone else, about these problems. His was such a peculiar mission that no one living on Earth could give him advice concerning its prosecution.

He was a real father to the family. He spent every possible hour with the youngsters, and they truly loved him. His mother grieved to see him work so hard. She sorrowed that he was toiling day after day at the carpenter's bench earning a living for the family instead of being at Jerusalem studying with the rabbis. While there was much about her son that Mary could not understand, she did love him, and she most thoroughly appreciated the willing manner in which he shouldered the responsibility of the home.

THE SEVENTEENTH YEAR

In his 17th year, there was considerable agitation in Palestine, especially at Jerusalem and in Judea, in favor of rebellion against the payment of taxes to Rome. There was coming into existence a strong nationalist party, soon to be called the Zealots. The Zealots, unlike the Pharisees, were not willing to await the coming of the Messiah. They proposed to bring things to a head immediately through political revolt.

A group of organizers from Jerusalem arrived in Galilee and were making good headway until they reached Nazareth. When they came to see Jesus, he listened carefully to them and asked many questions but refused to join the party. He declined fully to disclose his reasons for not enlisting, and his refusal had the effect of keeping out many of his youthful fellows in Nazareth.

Mary did her best to induce him to enlist, but she could not budge him. She went so far as to suggest that his refusal to support the nationalist cause at her request was insubordination, a violation of his pledge made upon their return from Jerusalem that he would, from that day forth, be subject to the will of his parents. In answer to this insinuation, Jesus laid a kindly hand on her shoulder and, looking directly into her eyes, said: "My mother, how could you?" Mary withdrew her statement immediately.

One of Jesus' uncles had already joined this group, subsequently becoming an officer in the Galilean division. For several years thereafter there was something of an estrangement between Jesus and his uncle because of Jesus' refusal to join the party.

Trouble began to brew in Nazareth. Jesus' attitude in these matters had resulted in creating a division among the youths of the city. About half had joined the nationalist organization, and the other half began the formation of an opposing group of more moderate patriots, expecting Jesus to assume the leadership. They were amazed when he refused the honor offered him, pleading as an excuse his heavy family responsibility, which they all understood. But the situation was still further complicated when a wealthy Jew named Isaac came forward agreeing to support Jesus' family if he would lay down his tools and assume leadership of the Nazareth Zealots organization.

Jesus, then scarcely seventeen years of age, was confronted with one of the most delicate and difficult situations of his early life.

Patriotic issues, especially when complicated by tax-gathering foreign oppressors, are always difficult for spiritual leaders to relate themselves to, and it was doubly so in this case since the Jewish religion was at the core of all this agitating against Rome.

Jesus' position was made more difficult because his mother and uncle, and even his younger brother James, all urged him to join the nationalist Zealot cause. All the better Galileans of Nazareth had enlisted, and those young men who had not joined the movement would all enlist the moment Jesus changed his mind. He had but one wise counselor in all of Nazareth, his old teacher, the Chazzan, who counseled him about his reply to the citizens' committee of Nazareth when they came to ask for his answer to the public appeal which had been made. In all Jesus' young life this was the very first time he had consciously resorted to public strategy. Up until this time, he had always depended upon a frank statement of truth to clarify the situation, but now he could not declare the full truth. He could not suggest that he was more than a man. He could not disclose his knowledge of the mission which awaited his reaching riper manhood. Despite these limitations his religious convictions and national loyalty were directly challenged. His family was in a turmoil, his youthful friends in division, and the entire Jewish contingent of the town in a quandary. How innocent he had been of all intention to make trouble of any kind, much less a disturbance of this sort.

Something had to be done. He must state his position, and this he did bravely and diplomatically to the satisfaction of many, but not all.

He adhered to the terms of his original plea, maintaining that his first duty was to his family, that a widowed mother and eight brothers and sisters needed something more than mere money could buy, the physical necessities of life, that they were entitled to a father's love, watch care and guidance, and that he could not in clear conscience release himself from the obligation which a cruel accident had thrust upon him.

He paid compliment to his mother and eldest brother for being willing to release him but reiterated that loyalty to a dead father forbade his leaving the family no matter how much money was forthcoming for their material support, making his dramatic statement: "Money cannot love". In the course of this address Jesus made several veiled references to his life mission but explained that, regardless of whether or not it might be inconsistent with the military idea, along with everything else in his life, it had been given up in order that he might be able to discharge faithfully his obligation to his family.

Everyone in Nazareth well knew he was a good father to his family, and this was a matter so near the heart of every noble Galilean that Jesus' plea found an appreciative response in the hearts of many of his hearers. Some of those who were not thus minded were disarmed by a subsequent speech made by James, which, while not on the program, was delivered at this time. That very day the Chazzan had rehearsed James in his speech, but that was their secret.

James stated that he was sure Jesus would help to liberate his people if he were only old enough to assume responsibility for the family, and that, if they would only consent to allow Jesus to remain with the family, to be the father and teacher, then they would have not just one leader from Joseph's family, but presently, five loyal nationalists, for there are five of us boys to grow up and come forth from the brother-father's guidance to serve the nation. Thus, the lad brought forth to a fairly happy ending a very tense and threatening situation.

The crisis for the time being was over, but never was this incident forgotten in Nazareth. The agitation persisted. Never again was Jesus in universal favor. The division of sentiment was never fully overcome. This, augmented by other and subsequent occurrences, was one of the chief reasons why Jesus moved to Capernaum in later years.

Henceforth Nazareth maintained a divided sentiment regarding the Son of God.

James graduated from the synagogue school this year and began full-time work at home in the carpenter shop. He had become a clever worker with tools and now took over the making of yokes and plows while Jesus began to do more house finishing and expert cabinet work.

This year Jesus made great progress in the organization of his mind. Gradually he was bringing his divine and human natures together, and he accomplished all this organization of intellect by the force of his own decisions. So far, nothing supernatural had occurred in this young man's career except the visit of an Angel, who once appeared to him during the night in Jerusalem in his thirteenth year.

The Eighteenth Year

In the course of his 18th year all the family property, except the home and garden, was disposed of. The last piece of Capernaum property was sold. The proceeds were used for taxes, to buy some new tools for James, and to make a payment on the old family supply and repair shop near the caravan lot, which Jesus now proposed to buy back since James was old enough to work at the house shop and help Mary around the house. With the financial pressure thus eased for the time being, Jesus decided to take James to the Passover. They went up to Jerusalem a day early, to be alone, going by way of Samaria. They walked, and Jesus told James about the historic places en route as his father had taught him on a similar journey five years earlier.

In passing through Samaria, they saw many strange sights. On this journey they talked over many of their problems, personal, family, and national. James was a very religious type of lad, and while he did not fully agree with his mother regarding the little he knew of the plans concerning Jesus' lifework, he did look forward to the time when he would be able to assume responsibility for the family so that Jesus could begin his mission. He was very appreciative of Jesus' taking him up to the Passover, and they talked over the future more fully than ever before.

Jesus did much thinking as they journeyed through Samaria, particularly at Bethel, and when drinking from Jacob's Well. He and his brother discussed the traditions of Abraham, Isaac, and Jacob. He did much to prepare James for what he was about to witness in Jerusalem, thus seeking to lessen the shock he himself had experienced on his first visit to the temple. But James was not so sensitive to some of these sights. He commented on the heartless manner in which most of the priests performed their duties but, on the whole, greatly enjoyed this trip to Jerusalem.

They went to Bethany for the Passover supper. Simon had already been laid to rest with his fathers, and so Jesus presided over this household as the head of the Passover family.

After the Passover supper Mary sat down to talk with James while Martha, Lazarus, and Jesus talked together far into the night in the garden around the fire. The next day they attended the temple services, and James was received into the commonwealth. That morning, as they paused on the brow of Olivet to view the temple, while James exclaimed in wonder, Jesus gazed on Jerusalem in silence.

James could not comprehend his brother's demeanor. That night they again, returned to Bethany and would have departed for home the next day, but James was insistent on their going back to visit the temple, explaining that he wanted to hear the teachers. While this was true, secretly in his heart he wanted to hear Jesus participate in the discussions, as he had heard his mother talk about. Accordingly, they went to the temple and heard the discussions, but Jesus asked no questions. It all seemed insignificant to this awakening mind of man and God - he could only pity them in their ignorance and darkness.

James was greatly disappointed that Jesus said nothing. To his inquiries Jesus made one reply: "My hour has not yet come."

The next day they journeyed home by way of Jericho and the Jordan Valley, and Jesus recounted many things along the way, including his former trip over this road when he was thirteen years old.

Upon returning to Nazareth, Jesus began work in the old family repair shop by the spring and was greatly cheered by being able to meet so many people each day from all parts of the country and surrounding districts. Jesus truly loved people- just common folks. Each month he made his payments to the shop and, with James' help, continued to provide for the family.

Several times a year, when visitors were not present to do the readings, Jesus continued to read the Sabbath scriptures at the synagogue and many times offered comments on the lesson, but usually he so selected the passages that comment was unnecessary. He was skillful, so arranging the order of the reading of the various passages that one would illuminate the other. He never failed, weather permitting, to take his brothers and sisters out on Sabbath afternoons for their nature walks.

Around this time the Chazzan inaugurated a young men's club for philosophic discussion which met at the homes of different members and often at his own home, and Jesus became a prominent member of this group. By this means he was able to regain some of the local prestige which he had lost at the time of the recent nationalistic controversies.

His social life, while restricted, was not wholly neglected. He had many warm friends and real admirers among both the young men and the young women of Nazareth.

THE NINETEENTH YEAR

In September, Elizabeth and John came to visit the Nazareth family. John, having now lost his father, intended to return to the Judean hills to engage in agriculture and sheep raising unless Jesus advised him to remain in Nazareth to take up carpentry or some other line of work. They did not know that the Nazareth family was practically penniless. The more Mary and Elizabeth talked about their sons, the more they became convinced that it would be good for the two young men to work together and see more of each other.

Jesus and John had many talks together. They talked over some very intimate and personal matters. When they had finished this visit, they decided not to see each other again until they would meet in their public service after the Heavenly Father should call them both to their work. John was tremendously impressed by what he saw at Nazareth, and persuaded that he should return home and labor for the support of his mother. He became convinced that he was to be a part of Jesus' life mission, but he saw that Jesus was to occupy many years with the rearing of his family. He was much more content to return to his home and settle down to care for their little farm and to minister to the needs of his mother. Never again did John and Jesus see each other until that day by the Jordan when the Son of Man presented himself for baptism.

In December of this year, death for the second time struck the family. Little Amos, the youngest of the boys, died after a week of illness with a high fever. After passing through this time of sorrow with her first-born son as her only support, Mary at last and in the fullest sense recognized Jesus as the real head of the family. He was truly a worthy head.

For four years now their standard of living had steadily declined. Year by year they felt the pinch of increasing poverty. By the close of this year, they faced one of the most difficult experiences of all their uphill struggles. James had not yet begun to earn much, and the expenses of a funeral on top of everything else staggered them. But Jesus would only say to his anxious and grieving mother: "Mother Mary, sorrow will not help us. We are all doing our best, and your smile, perhaps, might even inspire us to do better. Day by day we are strengthened for these tasks by our hope of better days ahead." His sturdy and practical optimism was truly contagious. All the children lived in an atmosphere of anticipation of better times and better things.

This hopeful courage contributed mightily to the development of strong and noble characters, in spite of the depressiveness of their poverty.

Jesus possessed the ability effectively to mobilize all his powers of mind, soul, and body on the task immediately at hand. He could concentrate his deep-thinking mind on the problem which he wished to solve, and this, in connection with his untiring patience, enabled him serenely to endure the trials of a difficult mortal existence - to live as if he were seeing Him who is invisible.

By the time of his 19th year, Jesus and Mary were getting along much better. She regarded him less as a son, and more of a father to her other children. Each day's life swarmed with practical and immediate difficulties. Less frequently they spoke of his lifework, for, as time passed, all their thoughts were mutually devoted to the support and upbringing of their family of four boys and three girls.

By the beginning of this year Jesus had fully won his Mother to the acceptance of his methods of child training - the positive injunction to do good in the place of the older Jewish method of forbidding to do evil. In his home and throughout his public-teaching career Jesus invariably employed the positive form of encouragement. Always and everywhere did he say: "You shall do this. You ought to do that." Never did he employ the negative mode of teaching derived from the ancient taboos. He refrained from placing emphasis on evil by forbidding it, while he exalted the good by commanding its performance. Prayer time in this household was the occasion for discussing anything and everything relating to the welfare of the family.

Jesus began wise discipline upon his brothers and sisters at such an early age that little or no punishment was ever required to secure their prompt and wholehearted obedience. The only exception was Jude, upon whom on various occasions Jesus found it necessary to impose penalties for his infractions of the rules of the home. On three occasions when it was deemed wise to punish Jude for self-confessed and deliberate violations of the family rules of conduct, his punishment was fixed by the unanimous decree of the older children and was agreed to by Jude himself before it was inflicted.

While Jesus was most methodical and systematic in everything he did, there was also in all his administrative rulings a refreshing elasticity of interpretation and an individuality of adaptation that greatly impressed all the children with the spirit of justice which actuated their father-brother. He never arbitrarily disciplined his brothers and sisters, and such uniform fairness and personal consideration greatly endeared Jesus to all his family.

James and Simon grew up trying to follow Jesus' model of placating their bellicose and sometimes irate playmates by persuasion and nonresistance, and they were fairly successful. But Joseph and Jude, while agreeing to such teachings at home, made haste to defend themselves when attacked by their comrades. In particular was Jude guilty of violating the spirit of these teachings. But nonresistance was not a rule of the family. No penalty was attached to the violation of personal teachings.

In general, all of the children, particularly the girls, would consult Jesus about their childhood troubles and confide in him just as they would have in an affectionate father.

James was growing up to be a well-balanced and even-tempered youth, but he was not so spiritually inclined as Jesus. He was a much better student than Joseph, who, while a faithful worker, was even less spiritually minded. Joseph was a plodder and not up to the intellectual level of the other children. Simon was a well-meaning boy but too much of a dreamer. He was slow in getting settled down in life and was the cause of considerable anxiety to Jesus and Mary. but he was always a good and well-intentioned lad. Jude was a firebrand. He had the highest of ideals, but he was unstable in temperament. He had all of his mother's determination and aggressiveness, but he lacked much of her sense of proportion and discretion.

Miriam was a well-balanced and level-headed daughter with a keen appreciation of things noble and spiritual. Martha was slow in thought and action but a very dependable and efficient child. Baby Ruth was the sunshine of the home. Though thoughtless of speech, she was very sincere of heart. She just about worshipped her big brother, Jesus. But they did not spoil her. She was a beautiful child but not quite so comely as Miriam, who was not only the belle of the family, but also of the entire of Nazareth.

As time passed, Jesus did much to liberalize and modify the family teachings and practices related to Sabbath observance and many other phases of religion, and to all these changes Mary gave hearty assent. By this time Jesus had become the unquestioned head of the house.

This year Jude started school, and it was necessary for Jesus to sell his harp in order to pay these expenses. Thus disappeared the last of his recreational pleasures. He much loved to play the harp when tired in mind and weary in body, but he comforted himself with the thought that at least the harp was safe from the tax collector.

Although Jesus was very poor during these years, his social standing in Nazareth was in no way impaired. He was one of the foremost young men of the city and very highly regarded by most of the young women. Since Jesus was such a splendid specimen of robust and intellectual manhood, and considering his reputation as a spiritual leader, Rebecca, the eldest daughter of Ezra, a wealthy merchant and trader of Nazareth, discovered that she was slowly falling in love with this son of Joseph. She first confided her affections to Miriam. Miriam went to Mary immediately and told her of Rebecca's affection for Jesus. Mary became intensely interested. Was she about to lose her eldest son? Who would replace him as the head of the household? Would troubles never cease? Then she paused to contemplate what effect marriage would have upon Jesus' future career. Not often, but at least sometimes, she recalled the fact that Jesus was a child of promise.

After she and Miriam had talked this matter over, they decided to make an effort to stop it by going directly to Rebecca, laying the whole story before her, and honestly telling her about their belief that Jesus was a son of destiny, that he was to become a great religious leader and perhaps even the Messiah.

Rebecca listened intently. She was thrilled with the recital and more than ever determined to cast her lot with this man of her choice and to share his career of leadership. She thought that such a man would all the more need a faithful and efficient wife. She interpreted Mary's efforts to dissuade her as a natural reaction to the dread of losing the head and sole support of her family, but knowing that her father approved of her attraction for the carpenter's son, she rightly reckoned that he would gladly supply the family with sufficient income fully to compensate for the loss of Jesus' earnings. When her father agreed to such a plan, Rebecca had further conferences with Mary and Miriam, and when she failed to win their support, she went directly to Jesus. This she did with the co-operation of her father, who invited Jesus to their home for the celebration of Rebecca's seventeenth birthday.

Jesus listened attentively and sympathetically to the recital of these things, first by the father, then by Rebecca herself. Then he made a courteous reply to the effect that no amount of money could take the place of his obligation personally to rear his father's family, to fulfill the most sacred of all human trusts loyalty to one's own flesh and blood.

Rebecca's father was deeply touched by Jesus' words of family devotion and retired from the discussion. His only remark to Mary, his wife, was: "We can't have him for a son. He is too noble for us."

Then began the eventful talk with Rebecca. Thus far in his life, Jesus had made little distinction in his association with boys and girls, with young men and young women. His mind had been altogether too much occupied with the pressing problems of practical earthly affairs. and the intriguing contemplation of his eventual career ever to have given serious consideration to the consummation of personal love in a human marriage. But now he was face to face with another of those problems which every average human being must confront and decide.

After listening attentively, he sincerely thanked Rebecca for her expressed admiration, adding that it would cheer him and comfort him all the days of his life. He explained that he was not free to enter into relations with any woman other than those of simple brotherly caring and pure friendship. He made it clear that his first and paramount duty was the rearing of his father's family, that he could not consider marriage until that was accomplished.

Rebecca was heartbroken. She refused to be comforted and pressed her father to leave Nazareth forever. He finally consented to move his family to Sepphoris. In later years, to the many men who sought her hand in marriage, she had only one answer: "I await the man I love". She lived for only one purpose - to await the hour when the greatest man who ever lived would begin his career as a teacher of living truth. She followed him devotedly through his eventful years of public labor and was present that day when he rode triumphantly into Jerusalem. She also stood among the other women by the side of Mary on that fateful and tragic afternoon when the Son of God hung on that wooden cross.

The Twentieth Year

In his 20th year, the story of Rebecca's love for Jesus was whispered around Nazareth and later on at Capernaum. In the years to follow many women loved Jesus even as men loved him, but never again did he have to reject the personal attentions of another woman's devotion. From this time on, human affection for Jesus took more of the nature of worshipful and adoring regard. Both men and women loved him devotedly and for what he was, not with any tinge of self-satisfaction or desire for affectionate possession. But for many years, whenever the story of Jesus' human personality was told, the devotion of Rebecca was remembered.

Miriam, knowing fully all the details of the events regarding Rebecca, and seeing how her brother had forsaken the love of a beautiful maiden came to realize how dedicated Jesus was to his mission and grew to idealize him and to love him with a very touching and profound affection.

Although they could hardly afford it, Jesus had a strange longing to go up to Jerusalem for the Passover this year. His mother, knowing of his recent experience with Rebecca, wisely urged him to make the journey. He was not conscious of it, but what he most wanted was an opportunity to talk with Lazarus and to visit Martha and Mary.

Next to his own family he loved these three most of all.

In making this trip to Jerusalem, he went by way of Megiddo, Antipatris, and Lydia, in part covering the same route traversed when he was brought back to Nazareth on the return from Egypt. He spent four days going up to the Passover and thought much about the past events which had transpired in and around Megiddo, the international battlefield of Palestine.

Jesus passed on through Jerusalem, only pausing to look upon the temple and the gathering throngs of visitors. He had a strange and increasing aversion to this Herod-built temple with its politically appointed priesthood. He wanted most of all to see Lazarus, Martha, and Mary. Lazarus was the same age as Jesus and now head of the house. By the time of this visit Lazarus' mother had also been laid to rest. Martha was a little over one year older than Jesus, while Mary was two years younger. Jesus was the idol of all three of them.

On this visit occurred one of those periodic outbreaks of rebellion against tradition, the expression of resentment for those ceremonial practices which Jesus deemed misrepresentative of his Father in Heaven. Not knowing Jesus was coming, Lazarus did not buy a paschal lamb, but had arranged to celebrate the Passover with friends in an adjoining village down the Jericho road. Jesus now proposed that they celebrate the feast where they were, at Lazarus' house. Lazarus said they did not have the paschal lamb to celebrate with. At this, Jesus entered upon a prolonged and convincing dissertation to the effect that the Father in Heaven was not really concerned with such childlike and meaningless rituals. After solemn and fervent prayer, they rose, and Jesus said: "Let the childlike and darkened minds of the Jewish people serve their God as Moses directed. Let us who have seen the light of life no longer approach our Father by the darkness of death. Let us be free in the knowledge of the truth of our Father's eternal love."

That evening around sundown, these four sat down and partook of the first Passover feast ever to be celebrated by devout

Jews without the paschal lamb. The unleavened bread and the wine had been made ready for this Passover, and these emblems, which Jesus termed the bread of life and the water of life, he served to his companions, and they ate in solemn conformity with the teachings just discussed. It was his custom to engage in this sacramental ritual whenever he paid subsequent visits to Bethany. When he returned home, he told all this to his mother. She was shocked at first but came gradually to see his viewpoint. Nevertheless, she was greatly relieved when Jesus assured her that he did not intend to introduce this new idea of the Passover in their family. At home with the children he continued, year by year, to eat the Passover according to the laws of Moses.

It was during this year, his 20th, that Mary had a long talk with Jesus about marriage. She asked him if he would entertain the idea of marriage if he did not have family responsibility. Jesus explained to her that, since immediate duty forbade his marriage, he had given the subject little thought. He expressed himself doubting that he would ever enter the marriage state. He said that all such things must await the time when: "my father's work must begin." Having settled already in his mind that he was not to become the father of children in the flesh, he gave very little thought to the subject of human marriage.

This year he began anew the task of further weaving his mortal and divine natures into a simple and effective human individuality. He continued to grow in moral status and spiritual understanding.

Although all their Nazareth property except for their home was now gone, this year they received a little financial help from the sale of a half interest in a piece of property in Capernaum that Joseph had bought together with a boat builder named Zebedee.

Joseph graduated at the synagogue school this year and prepared to begin work at the small bench in the home carpenter shop. Although the estate of their father was exhausted, there were prospects that they would successfully fight off poverty since three of them were now regularly at work.

Jesus was rapidly becoming a man, not just a young man but an adult. He had learned well to bear responsibility. He knew how to carry on in the face of disappointment. He had stood bravely when his plans were defeated, and his purposes temporarily derailed. He had learned how to be fair and just even in the face of injustice. He had learned well how to adjust his ideals of spiritual living to the practical demands of earthly existence. He had learned how to plan for the achievement of a higher and distant goal of idealism while he worked earnestly for the achievement of a nearer and immediate goal of necessity. He had steadily acquired the art of adjusting his aspirations to the commonplace demands of the human occasion. He slowly learned how to live the Heavenly life while he continued on with earthly existence. More and more he depended upon the ultimate guidance of his Heavenly Father while he assumed the fatherly role of guiding and directing the children of his Earth family. He became experienced in the skill of wresting victory from the very jaws of defeat.

He learned how to transform the difficulties of time into the triumphs of eternity.

As the years passed, this young man of Nazareth continued to experience life as it is lived in mortal flesh on the worlds of time and space. He lived a full, representative, and replete life on Earth. He left this world ripe in the experience which a son of Heaven must pass through during the short and strenuous years of life in the flesh.

As a child he accumulated a vast body of knowledge. As a youth, he sorted, classified, and correlated this information. Now as a man of the realm he began to organize these mental possessions preparatory to utilization in his subsequent teaching, ministry, and service on behalf of his fellow mortals.

Born into the world a babe of the realm, he lived his childhood life and passed through the successive stages of youth and young manhood. Now he stood on the threshold of full manhood, rich in the experience of human living, replete in the understanding of human nature, and full of sympathy for the frailties of human nature. He was becoming an expert in the divine art of revealing his Father to all ages and stages of mortals.

THE TWENTY-FIRST YEAR

In his 21st year, as a full-grown man - an adult of the realm - he prepared to continue his main mission of revealing God to men and leading men to God. His physical appearance at this age of adulthood and until death was as follows: He was tall for the men of his time and well-proportioned, being 5 feet 8 inches tall and weighing 170 pounds. He had an air of severity in his countenance which at once attracted the love and reverence of those around him. His hair was the color of new wine, a dark reddish tint, and fell to the shoulders where it curled. His hair parted in two upon the forehead in the manner of the men of Nazareth. His forehead was flat and fair, his face without blemish or defect, and adorned with a graceful expression. His nose and mouth were very well proportioned, his beard thick and the same color as his hair. His eyes were gray and extremely lively. He was very straight in stature, with large hands and long straight fingers. His arms were beautifully proportioned from the long years he spent working with wood. In his censures he was powerful, but in his encouragement and instructions, he was amiable and courteous. There was something wonderfully charming in this face, with a mixture of gravity. He was never seen to laugh but was observed to weep at times when he saw injustice and persecution. He talked little but with great quality. He was indeed a beautiful specimen of a human being. Some even thought he was the handsomest man in all the world.

With his arrival at adult years, Jesus began the task of completing the experience of mastering life as a mortal man. He entered upon this task fully realizing his dual nature. But he had already effectively combined these two natures into one Jesus of Nazareth.

Joshua Ben Joseph knew full well that he was a man, a mortal man, conceived and born of a woman. This is why he selected the first of his titles, Son of Man. He obtained knowledge, gained experience, and combined these into wisdom, just as do all other mortals of the realm. Until after his baptism he availed himself of no supernatural powers. He employed no agency that was not a part of his human endowment as the son of Joseph and Mary.

As to the attributes of his pre-human existence in the Heavenly realms, he left behind all those gifts. Prior to the beginning of his public work his knowledge of men and events was wholly self-limited. He was a true man among men.

The Nazareth carpenter now fully understood the work before him, but he chose to live his human life in the channel of its natural flow. In some of these matters he is indeed an example to his mortal brothers. He lived his mortal life just as all others in the human family lived theirs. It benefited him in every respect to be as human as his brothers.

Of his human nature he was never in doubt. It was self-evident and always present in his consciousness. But of his divine nature there was always room for doubt and conjecture, at least this was true right up to the event of his baptism. The self-realization of divinity was a slow and, from the human standpoint, natural evolutionary revelation. This revelation and self-realization of divinity began in Jerusalem when he was not quite thirteen years old with the first supernatural occurrence of his human existence. This experience of realizing his divine nature was completed at the time of his second supernatural experience while in the flesh, the episode of his baptism by John in the Jordan, which marked the beginning of his public career of ministry and teaching.

Between these two celestial visitations, one in his thirteenth year and the other at his baptism, there occurred nothing supernatural or superhuman in the life of this incarnate Son of Heaven. He never once used the powers at his disposal, nor did he utilize the guidance of celestial personalities, aside from that of his guardian Angel, in the living of his human life up to the day of his baptism by John.

Always, even after his emergence into the larger life on Earth, Jesus was submissively subject to the will of his Father in Heaven.

After his baptism he thought nothing of permitting his sincere believers and grateful followers to worship him. Even while he wrestled with poverty and toiled with his hands to provide the necessities of life for his family, his awareness that he was a Son of God was growing. A profound suspense pervaded the Heavenly Realms throughout these years. All celestial eyes were continuously focused on Earth, and on Palestine with breathless anticipation.

This year he went up to Jerusalem with Joseph to celebrate Passover. Having taken James to the temple for consecration, he deemed it his duty to take Joseph also. Jesus never exhibited any degree of partiality in dealing with his family. He went with Joseph to Jerusalem by the usual Jordan Valley route, but he returned to Nazareth by the East Jordan way, which led through Amathus. Going down the Jordan, Jesus narrated Jewish history to Joseph and on the return trip told him about the experiences of the reputed Tribes of Ruben, Gad, and Gilead that Hebrew traditions said had dwelt in these regions east of the river.

Joseph asked Jesus many leading questions concerning his life mission, but to most of these inquiries Jesus would only reply, "My hour has not yet come." However, in these intimate discussions many words were dropped which Joseph remembered during the stirring events of subsequent years. Jesus, with Joseph, spent this Passover with his three friends at Bethany, as was his custom when in Jerusalem attending these festival commemorations.

THE TWENTY SECOND YEAR

This year was one of several years during which Jesus' brothers and sisters were facing the trials and tribulations peculiar to the problems and readjustments of adolescence. Jesus now had brothers and sisters ranging in age from seven to eighteen, and he was kept busy helping them to adjust themselves to the new awakenings of their intellectual and emotional lives. He had thus to grapple with the problems of adolescence as they became manifest in the lives of his younger brothers and sisters.

This year Simon graduated from the synagogue school and began work with Jesus' old boyhood playmate and ever-ready defender, Jacob, the son of the stonemason. As a result of several family conferences, it was decided that it was unwise for all the boys to take up carpentry. They decided that by diversifying their trades they would be prepared to take contracts for putting up entire buildings. They had not all been gainfully employed since three of them had been working as full-time carpenters.

Jesus continued this year at house finishing and cabinetwork but spent most of his time at the caravan repair shop. James was beginning to alternate with him in attendance at the shop. The latter part of this year, when carpenter work was slow, Jesus left James in charge of the repair shop, and Joseph at the home bench while he went over to Sepporis to work with a metal smith. He worked six months with metals and acquired considerable skill at the anvil.

Before taking up his new employment at Sepphoris, Jesus held one of his periodic family conferences and solemnly installed James, then just past eighteen years old, as acting head of the family. He promised his brother hearty support and full cooperation, and he exacted formal promises of obedience to James from each member of the family. From this day James assumed full financial responsibility for the family, and Jesus made his weekly contributory payments to his brother. Never again did Jesus take the home reins out of James' hands. While working at

Sepphoris he could have walked home every night, if necessary, but he intentionally remained away. His true motive was to train James and Joseph in the bearing of the family responsibility. He had begun the slow process of weaning his family from dependence on him. Each Sabbath Jesus returned to Nazareth, and sometimes during the week when occasion required, to observe the working of the new plan, to give advice and offer helpful suggestions.

Living much of the time in Sepphoris for six months afforded Jesus a new opportunity to become better acquainted with the Gentile viewpoint of life. He worked with Gentiles, lived with Gentiles, and in every possible manner he made a close and painstaking study of their habits of living and of the Gentile mind.

The moral standards of this home city of Herod Antipas were so far below those of even the caravan city of Nazareth that after six months at Sepphoris, Jesus would find excuses for returning to Nazareth. The group he worked for became engaged in public construction work in both Sepphoris and the new city of Tiberius.

Jesus was disinclined to have anything to do with any work of employment under the supervision of Herod Antipas. There were still other reasons which made it wise, in the opinion of Jesus, for him to go back to Nazareth. When he returned to the repair shop, he did not again assume the personal direction of family affairs. He worked in association with James at the shop and as far as possible permitted him to continue oversight of the home. James' management of family expenditures and his administration of the home budget were undisturbed.

It was by just such wise and thoughtful planning that Jesus prepared the way for his eventual withdrawal from active participation in the affairs of his family. When James had had two years' experience as acting head of the family - and two full years before he was married - Joseph was placed in charge of the household funds and entrusted with the general management of the home.

THE TWENTY-THIRD YEAR

This year the financial pressure was slightly relaxed with four of the children at work. Miriam earned a good salary by the sale of milk and butter. Martha had become an expert weaver. The purchase price of the repair shop was over one third of the cost. The situation was such that Jesus stopped work for three weeks to take Simon to Jerusalem for the Passover. This was the longest period away from daily work he had enjoyed since the death of his father.

They journeyed to Jerusalem by way of the Decapolis and through Pella, Gerasa, Philadelphia, Heshbon, and Jericho. They returned to Nazareth by the coast route, touching Lydia, Joppa, Caesarea, then around Mount Carmel to Ptolemais and on to Nazareth. This trip fairly well-acquainted Jesus with the whole of Palestine north of the Jerusalem district.

At Philadelphia Jesus and Simon became acquainted with a merchant from Damascus who developed such a great liking for the Nazareth pair that he insisted they stop with him at his Jerusalem headquarters. While Simon attended the temple, Jesus spent much of his time talking with this well-educated and much traveled man of world affairs. This merchant owned over four thousand caravan camels. He had interests all over the Roman world and was now on his way to Rome. He proposed that Jesus come to Damascus to enter his oriental import business, but Jesus explained that he did not feel justified in going so far away from his family just then. But on the way back home he thought much about the distant cities and the more remote countries of the Far West and the Far East, countries he had so frequently heard spoken of by the caravan passengers and conductors.

Simon greatly enjoyed his visit to Jerusalem. He was duly received into the commonwealth at the Passover consecration of the new sons of the commandment. While Simon attended the Passover ceremonies, Jesus mingled with the throngs of visitors and engaged in many interesting personal conferences with numerous Gentile converts.

Perhaps the most notable of all these contacts was the one with a young Greek named Stephen. This young man was on his first visit to Jerusalem and chanced to meet Jesus on Thursday afternoon of Passover week. While they both strolled about viewing the Asmonean Palace, Jesus began the casual conversation that resulted in their becoming interested in each other, and which led to a four-hour discussion of the way of life and the true God and his worship. Stephen was tremendously impressed with what Jesus said. He never forgot his words.

This was the same Stephen who, in later years, became a believer in the teachings of Jesus, and whose boldness in preaching this early gospel resulted in his being stoned to death by irate Jews. Some of Stephen's extraordinary boldness in proclaiming his view of the new gospel was the direct result of this earlier interview with Jesus. But Stephen never even faintly surmised that the Galilean friend he had talked with some fifteen years previously was the very same person whom he later proclaimed the world's savior, and for whom he was so soon to die, thus becoming the first martyr of the newly emerging Christian religion. When Stephen yielded up his life as the price of his attack upon the Jewish temple and its corrupt priests, there stood and watched a man named Saul, a Roman citizen from Tarsus. When Saul saw how this Greek could die for his faith, there were aroused in his heart those emotions which eventually led him to embrace the cause for which Stephen had died. Later on, he became the aggressive and indomitable Paul, the philosopher and founder of the Christian religion.

On the Sunday after Passover week Simon and Jesus started on their way back to Nazareth. Simon never forgot what Jesus taught him on this trip. He had always loved Jesus, now he felt that he had begun to really know his father-brother. They had many heart-to-heart talks as they journeyed through the country and prepared their meals by the wayside. They arrived home on Thursday afternoon, and Simon kept the family up late that night, relating his experiences.

Mary was very upset by Simon's report that Jesus spent most of the time in Jerusalem visiting with the strangers, especially those from the far countries. Jesus' family never could comprehend his great interest in people, his urge to visit with them, to learn about their way of living, and to find out what they were thinking about.

More and more the Nazareth family became engrossed with their immediate and human problems. Not often was mention made of the future mission of Jesus, and very seldom did he speak of his future career. His mother rarely thought about his being a child of promise.

She was slowly giving up the idea that Jesus was to fulfill any divine mission on Earth, yet at times her faith was revived when she paused to recall the visit by Gabriel before this child was born.

The last four months of this year Jesus spent in Damascus as the guest of the merchant whom he first met at Philadelphia when on his way to Jerusalem. A representative of this merchant had sought out Jesus when passing through Nazareth and escorted him to Damascus. This Syrian merchant that had embraced the Jewish religion proposed to devote an extraordinary sum of money to the establishment of a school of religious philosophy at Damascus. He planned to create a center of learning which would outrival Alexandria. He proposed that Jesus should immediately begin a long tour of the world's educational centers preparatory to becoming the head of this new project. This was one of the greatest temptations that Jesus ever faced in the course of his human career.

Presently this merchant brought before Jesus a group of twelve merchants and bankers who agreed to support this newly projected school. Jesus manifested deep interest in the proposed school, and even helped them plan for its organization, but always expressed the fear that his other and unstated but prior obligations would prevent his accepting the direction of such a pretentious enterprise. His benefactor was persistent, and he profitably employed Jesus at his home doing some translating while he, his wife, and their sons and daughters sought to prevail upon Jesus to accept the teaching honor. But he would not consent. He well knew that his mission on Earth was not to be supported by institutions of learning. He knew that he must not obligate himself in the least to be directed by the councils of men, no matter how well-intentioned.

He who had already been rejected by the Jerusalem religious leaders, even after he had demonstrated his leadership and knowledge, was recognized and hailed as a master teacher by the businessmen and bankers of Damascus, and all this when he was an obscure and unknown carpenter from Nazareth.

He never spoke about this offer to his family, and the end of this year found him back in Nazareth going about his daily duties just as if he had never been tempted by the flattering propositions of his Damascus friends. Never did these men of Damascus ever associate the later citizen of Capernaum who turned all Jewry upside down, with the former carpenter of Nazareth who had dared to refuse the honor which their combined wealth might have procured.

Jesus cleverly and intentionally detached various episodes of his life so that they never became, in the eyes of the world, associated together as the doings of a single individual. Many times, in subsequent years he listened to the recital of the story of the strange Galilean who declined the opportunity of founding a school in Damascus to compete with Alexandria.

One purpose which Jesus had in mind, when he sought to segregate certain features of his earthly experience, was to prevent the building up of such a versatile and spectacular career as would cause subsequent generations to venerate the teacher instead of obeying the truth which he had lived and taught. Jesus did not want to build up such a human record of achievement as would attract attention away from his teachings. Very early he recognized that his followers would be tempted to formulate a religion about him which might become a competitor of the Gospel of the kingdom that he intended to proclaim to the world. Accordingly, he consistently sought to suppress everything during his eventful career which he thought might be made to serve this natural human tendency to exalt the teacher instead of proclaiming his teachings. Little did he imagine that it would take only a very few years after his death before human nature would exalt the teacher and forget the truths which he tried to teach the world.

This same motive also explains why he permitted himself to be known by different titles during various stages of his diversified life on Earth. Again, he did not want to bring any undue influence to bear upon his family or others, which would lead them to believe in him against their honest convictions. He always refused to take undue or unfair advantage of the human mind. He did not want men to believe in him unless their hearts were responsive to the spiritual realities revealed in his teachings.

By the end of this year the Nazareth home was running fairly smoothly. The children were growing up, and Mary was becoming accustomed to Jesus' being away from home. He continued to turn over his earnings to James for the support of the family, retaining only a small portion for his immediate personal expenses.

As the years passed, it became more difficult to realize that this man was a Son of God on Earth. He seemed to become quite an individual of the realm, just another man among men. But it had been ordained by the Father that the life of Jesus should unfold in just this very manner.

THE TWENTY-FOURTH YEAR

This was Jesus' first year of comparative freedom from family responsibility. James was very successful in managing the home with Jesus' help in counsel and finances. The week following the Passover of this year a young man came up from Alexandria to Nazareth to arrange for a meeting between Jesus and a group of Alexandrian Jews at a point on the Palestinian coast. This conference was set for the middle of June, and Jesus went over to Caesarea to meet with five prominent Jews of Alexandria, who sought to establish him as the religious leader of their city. They offered as an inducement, the beginning position of assistant to the Chazzan in their main synagogue.

The spokesman for this committee explained to Jesus that Alexandria was destined to become the headquarters of Jewish culture for the entire world, and that the Hellenic trend of Jewish affairs had outdistanced the Babylonian school of thought. They reminded Jesus of the ominous rumblings of rebellion in Jerusalem and throughout Palestine and assured him that any uprising of the Palestinian peoples would be equivalent to national suicide, that the iron hand of Rome would crush the rebellion in months and Jerusalem would be destroyed, the temple demolished, and not one stone left standing.

Jesus listened to all they had to say, thanked them for their confidence, but declined to go to Alexandria, saying to them: "My hour has not yet come." They were totally perplexed by his apparent indifference to the honor they had sought to confer upon him. Before taking leave of Jesus, they presented him with a purse in token of the esteem of his Alexandrian friends and in compensation for the time and expense of coming over to Caesarea to confer with them. But he likewise refused their money, saying: "The house of Joseph has never received alms, and we cannot eat another's bread as long as I have strong arms and my brothers can labor."

His friends from Egypt set sail for home, and in subsequent years, when they heard rumors of the Capernaum boat builder who was creating such a commotion in Palestine, few of them suspected that he was the babe of Bethlehem who had grown up among them in Alexandria, and the same strange-acting Galilean who had so unceremoniously declined the invitation to become a great teacher in Alexandria.

The remainder of this year was the most uneventful six months of his whole career. He enjoyed this temporary respite from the usual problems to solve and difficulties to surmount. He communed much with his Father in Heaven and made tremendous progress in the mastery of his human mind.

But human affairs in the worlds of time and space do not run smoothly for very long. In December, James had a private talk with Jesus, explaining that he was in love with Esta, a young woman of Nazareth, and that they would sometime like to be married if it could be arranged. He called attention to the fact that Joseph would soon be eighteen years old, and that it would be a good experience for him to have a chance to serve as the acting head of the family. Jesus gave consent for James' marriage two years later, provided he had, during the intervening time, properly trained Joseph to assume direction of the home.

Now things began to happen. Marriage was in the air. James' success in gaining Jesus' agreement to his marriage emboldened Miriam to approach him with her plans. Jacob, the younger stone mason, onetime self-appointed champion of Jesus, now business associate of James and Joseph, had long sought to gain Miriam's hand in marriage. After Miriam had laid her plans before Jesus, he directed that Jacob should come to him making formal request for her and promised his blessing for the marriage just as soon as she felt that Martha was competent to assume her duties as eldest daughter.

At home, he continued to teach the evening school three times a week, read the scriptures often in the synagogue on the Sabbath, visited with his mother, taught the children, and in general conducted himself as a worthy and respected citizen of Nazareth.

The Twenty Fifth Year

This year began with the Nazareth family all in good health and witnessed the finishing of the regular schooling of all the children with the exception of Ruth.

Jesus had become one of the most robust and refined specimens of manhood to appear on Earth. His physical development was superb.

His mind was active, keen, and penetrating - compared with the average mentality of his contemporaries. It had developed gigantic proportions, and his spirit was indeed humanly divine.

The family finances were in the best condition since the depletion of Joseph's estate. The final payments had been made to the caravan repair shop. They owed no man and for the first time in years had some funds ahead. This being the case, and since he had taken his other brothers to Jerusalem for their first Passover ceremonies, Jesus decided to accompany Jude, who had just graduated from the synagogue school, on his first visit to the temple.

They went up to Jerusalem and returned by the same route, the Jordan Valley, as Jesus feared trouble if he took his young brother through Samaria. Already at Nazareth Jude had gotten into slight trouble several times because of his hasty disposition, coupled with his strong patriotic sentiments.

They arrived at Jerusalem in due time and were on their way for a first visit to the temple, the very sight of which had stirred and thrilled Jude to the very depths of his soul, when they chanced to meet Lazarus of Bethany. While Jesus talked with Lazarus and sought to arrange for their joint celebration of the Passover, Jude started up real trouble for them all. Close at hand stood a Roman guard who made some improper remarks regarding a Jewish girl who was passing by.

Jude raged with fiery indignation and was not slow in expressing his resentment of such an impropriety directly to, and within hearing of, the soldier. At that time the Roman Legionnaires were very sensitive to anything bordering on Jewish disrespect, so the guard promptly placed Jude under arrest. This was too much for the young patriot, and before Jesus could caution him by a warning glance, he had delivered a loud denunciation of pent-up anti-Roman feelings, all of which only made a bad matter worse. Jude, with Jesus by his side, was taken at once to the military prison.

Jesus endeavored to obtain either an immediate hearing for Jude or else his release in time for the Passover celebration that evening, but he failed in these attempts. Since the next day was a Holy Convocation in Jerusalem, even the Romans would not presume to hear charges against a Jew. Accordingly, Jude remained in confinement until the morning of the second day after his arrest, and Jesus stayed at the prison with him. They were not present in the temple at the ceremony of receiving the sons of the law into full citizenship. Jude did not pass through this formal ceremony for several years, until he was next in Jerusalem at a Passover and in connection with his propaganda work on behalf of the Zealots, the patriotic organization to which he belonged and in which he was very active.

The morning following their second day in prison Jesus appeared before the military magistrate on behalf of Jude. By making apologies for his brother's youth and by a further explanatory, but judicious, statement with reference to the provocative nature of the episode which had led up to the arrest of his brother, Jesus so handled the case that the magistrate expressed the opinion that the young Jew might have had some possible excuse for his violent outburst. After warning Jude not to allow himself again to be guilty of such rashness, he said to Jesus in dismissing them: "You had better keep your eye on the lad. He is liable to make a lot of trouble for all of you." The Roman judge spoke the truth. Jude did make considerable trouble for Jesus in later years, and always was the trouble of this same nature - clashes with the civil authorities because of his thoughtless and unwise patriotic outbursts.

Jesus and Jude walked over to Bethany for the night to explain why they had failed to keep their appointment for the Passover supper and set out for Nazareth the following day. Jesus did not tell the family about his young brother's arrest at Jerusalem, but he had a long talk with Jude about this episode several weeks after their return. After this talk with Jesus, Jude himself told the family. He never forgot the patience and forbearance his brother manifested throughout this entire trying experience.

This was the last Passover Jesus ever attended with any member of his own family. Increasingly he was to become separated from his own flesh and blood.

This year his moments of deep meditation were often broken into by Ruth and her playmates. Always was Jesus ready to postpone the contemplation of his future work for the world so that he might share in the childish joy and youthful gladness of these youngsters, who never tired of listening to Jesus relate the experiences of his various trips to Jerusalem. They also greatly enjoyed his stories about animals and nature.

The children were always welcome at the repair shop. Jesus provided sand, blocks, and stones by the side of the shop, and groups of youngsters flocked there to amuse themselves. When they tired of their play, the braver ones would peek into the shop, and if its keeper was not busy, they would make bold to go in and say: "Uncle Joshua, come out and tell us a big story." Then they would lead him out by tugging at his hands until he was seated on the favorite rock by the corner of the shop, with the children on the ground in a semicircle before him. How the little folks did enjoy their Uncle Joshua. They were learning to laugh, and to laugh heartily. It was customary for one or two of the smallest of the children to climb upon his knees and sit there, looking in wonderment at his expressive features as he told his stories. The children loved Jesus, and Jesus loved the children.

It was difficult for his friends to comprehend the range of his intellectual activities, how he could so suddenly and so completely swing from the profound discussion of politics, philosophy, or religion to the lighthearted and joyous playfulness of these tots of from five to ten years of age. As his own brothers and sisters grew up, as he gained more leisure, and before the grandchildren arrived, he paid a great deal of attention to these little ones. But he did not live on Earth long enough to enjoy the grandchildren very much.

The Twenty Sixth Year

As this year began, Jesus became strongly conscious that he possessed a wide range of potential power. But he was likewise fully persuaded that this power was not to be employed by his personality as a human, at least not until his hour should come.

At this time, he thought much but said little about the relation of himself to his Father in Heaven. The conclusion of all this thinking was expressed once in his prayer on the hilltop, when he prayed: "Regardless of who I am and what power I may or may not possess, I always have been, and always will be, subject to the will of my Father." Yet, as this man walked around Nazareth to and from his work, it was literally true that in him were hidden all the treasures of wisdom and knowledge.

All this year the family affairs ran smoothly except for Jude. For years James had had trouble with his youngest brother, who was not inclined to settle down to work nor was he to be depended upon for his share of the home expenses. While he would live at home, he was not conscientious about earning his share of the family upkeep.

Jesus was a man of peace, and continuously was he embarrassed by Jude's belligerent exploits and numerous patriotic outbursts.

James and Joseph were in favor of casting him out, but Jesus would not consent. When their patience would be severely tried, Jesus would only counsel: "Be patient. Be wise in your counsel and eloquent in your lives, that your young brother may first know the better way and then be constrained to follow you into it." The wise and loving counsel of Jesus prevented a break in the family. They remained together. But Jude never was brought to his sober senses until after his marriage.

Mary seldom spoke of Jesus' future mission. Whenever this subject was referred to, Jesus only replied: "My hour has not yet come." Jesus had just about completed the difficult task of weaning his family from dependence on the immediate presence of his personality. He was rapidly preparing for the day when he could consistently leave this Nazareth home to begin the more active prelude to his real ministry for men.

This year Jesus enjoyed more than usual leisure, and he devoted much time to training James in the management of the repair shop and Joseph in the direction of home affairs. Mary sensed that he was getting ready to leave them. She had just about given up the thought that Jesus was the Messiah. She could not understand him. She simply could not fathom her first born son.

Jesus spent a great deal of time this year with the individual members of his family. He would take them for long and frequent strolls up the hill and through the countryside. Before harvest he took Jude to the farmer uncle south of Nazareth, but Jude did not remain long after the harvest. He ran away, and Simon later found him with the fishermen at the lake. When Simon brought him back home, Jesus talked things over with the runaway lad, and since he wanted to be a fisherman, went over to Magdala with him and put him in the care of a relative who was a fisherman. Jude worked fairly well and regularly from that time on until his marriage. He continued as a fisherman after his marriage.

At last, the day had come when all Jesus' brothers had chosen, and were established in, their lifework. The stage was being set for Jesus' departure from home.

In November a double wedding occurred. James and Esta, and Miriam and Jacob were married. It was truly a joyous occasion. Even Mary was happy once more except every now and then when she realized that Jesus was preparing to go away. She suffered under the burden of great uncertainty. if Jesus would only sit down and talk it all over freely with her as he had done when he was a boy, but he was consistently uncommunicative. He was profoundly silent about the future.

James and his bride, Esta, moved into a neat little home on the west side of town, a gift from her father. While James continued his support of his mother's home, his quota was cut in half because of his marriage. Joseph was formally installed by Jesus as head of the family. Jude was now very faithfully sending his share of funds home each month. The weddings of James and Miriam had a very beneficial influence on Jude, and when he left for the fishing grounds, the day after the double wedding, he assured Joseph that he could depend on him to do his duty and more if needed. He kept this promise.

Miriam moved in next door to Mary in the home of Jacob.

Jacob's father had been laid to rest with his forefathers. Martha took Miriam's place in the home, and the new organization was working smoothly before the year ended.

The day after this double wedding Jesus held an important conference with James. He told James, confidentially, that he was preparing to leave home. He presented full title to the repair shop to James, formally and solemnly abdicated as head of Joseph's house, and established his brother James as head and protector of the house. He drew up, and they both signed, a secret compact in which it was stipulated that, in return for the gift of the repair shop, James would henceforth assume full financial responsibility for the family, thus releasing Jesus from all further obligations in these matters. After the contract was signed, after the budget was so arranged that the actual expenses of the family would be met without any contribution from Jesus, he said to James: "But, my son, I will continue to send you something each month until my hour shall come. What I send shall be used by you as the occasion demands. Apply my funds to family necessities or pleasures as you see fit. Use them in case of sickness or apply them to meet the unexpected emergencies which may befall on any individual member of the family."

Thus did Jesus make ready to enter upon the second phase of his adult life before the public entrance upon his Father's work. Jesus had fully and finally separated himself from the management of the domestic affairs of his Nazareth family. He continued, right up to the event of his baptism, to contribute to the family finances and to take a keen personal interest in the spiritual welfare of every one of his brothers and sisters. Always was he ready to do everything humanly possible for the comfort and happiness of his widowed mother.

He had by now made every preparation for detaching himself permanently from the Nazareth home. This was not easy for him to do. He naturally loved his people. He loved his family, and this natural affection had been tremendously augmented by his extraordinary devotion to them.

All the family had slowly awakened to the realization that Jesus was making ready to leave them. The sadness of the anticipated separation was only tempered by this graduated method of preparing them for the announcement of his intended departure. For more than four years they saw that he was planning for this eventual separation.

THE TWENTY SEVENTH YEAR

In January of this year, on a cold rainy Sunday morning, Jesus took leave of his family, explaining that he was going over to Tiberias and then on a visit to other cities around the Sea of Galilee. Thus, he left them, never again to be a regular member of the household.

He spent one week at Tiberius, the new city which was soon to succeed Sepphoris as the capital of Galilee. Finding little to interest him, he passed on successively through Magdala and Bethsaida to Capernaum, where he stopped to pay a visit to his father's friend Zebedee. Zebedee was a boat builder, and his sons were fishermen. Jesus was an expert in both designing and building. He was a master at working with wood, and Zebedee had long known of the skill of this Nazareth craftsman. For a long time, Zebedee had contemplated making improved boats. He now laid his plans before Jesus and invited the visiting carpenter to join him in the enterprise, and Jesus readily consented.

Jesus worked with Zebedee only a little more than one year, but during that time he created a new style of boat and established entirely new methods of boat making. By superior techniques and greatly improved methods of steaming the boards, Jesus and Zebedee began to build boats of a very superior type, craft which were far safer for sailing the lake then were the older types. For several years Zebedee had more work, turning out these new-style boats, than his small establishment could handle. In less than five years practically all the craft on the lake had been built in the shop of Zebedee at Capernaum.

Jesus became well known to the Galilean fishermen as the designer of the new boats.

Zebedee was a moderately well-off man. His boat building shops were on the lake to the south of Capernaum, and his home was situated down the lake shore near the fishing headquarters of Bethsaida. Jesus lived in the home of Zebedee during the year he remained at Capernaum. He had long worked alone in the world, without a father, and thus greatly enjoyed this period of working with a father-partner.

Zebedee's wife, Salome, was a relative of Annas, onetime high priest of Jerusalem and still the most influential of the Sadduccean group, having been deposed only eight years previously. Salome became a great admirer of Jesus. She loved him as she loved her own sons, James, John and David. Her four daughters looked upon Jesus as their elder brother. Jesus often went out fishing with James, John and David, and they learned that he was an experienced fisherman as well as an expert boat builder.

All this year Jesus sent money each month to his brother James. He returned to Nazareth in October to attend Martha's wedding, and he was not again in Nazareth for over two years, when he returned shortly before the double wedding of Simon and Jude.

Throughout this year, Jesus built boats and continued to observe how men lived on Earth. Frequently he would go down to visit the caravan station, Capernaum being on the direct travel route from Damascus to the south. Capernaum was a strong Roman military post, and the garrison's commanding officer was a Roman convert to Judaism. The Jews considered him a devout man. This officer belonged to a wealthy Roman family, and he took it upon himself to build a beautiful synagogue in Capernaum, which had been presented to the Jews a short time before Jesus came to live with Zebedee. Jesus conducted the services in this new synagogue more than half the time this year, and some of the caravan people who chanced to attend remembered him as the carpenter from Nazareth.

When it came to the payment of taxes, Jesus registered himself as a skilled craftsman of Capernaum. From this day on to the end of his Earth life he was known as a resident of Capernaum. He never claimed any other legal residence, although he did, for various reasons, permit others to assign his residence to Damascus, Bethany, Nazareth and even Alexandria.

At the Capernaum synagogue he found many new books in the library chests, and he spent at least five evenings a week at intense study. One evening he devoted to social life with the older folks, and one evening he spent with the young people. There was something gracious and inspiring about the personality of Jesus which invariably attracted young people. He always made them feel at ease in his presence. Perhaps his great secret in getting along with them consisted in the twofold fact that he was always interested in what they were doing, while he seldom offered them advice unless they asked for it.

The Zebedee family almost worshipped Jesus. They never failed to attend the conferences of questions and answers which he conducted each evening after supper before he departed for the synagogue to study. The youthful neighbors also came in frequently to attend these after supper meetings. To these little gatherings Jesus gave varied and advanced instruction, just as advanced as they were capable of understanding. He talked quite freely with them, expressing his ideas and ideals about politics, sociology, science, and philosophy, but never presumed to speak with authoritative finality except when discussing religion - the relation of man to God.

Once a week, Jesus held a meeting with the entire household, shop, and shore helpers, for Zebedee had many employees. It was among these workers that Jesus was first called: "The Master." They all loved him. He enjoyed his labors with Zebedee in Capernaum, but he missed the children playing out by the side of the Nazareth carpenter shop.

Of the sons of Zebedee, James was the most interested in Jesus as a teacher of philosophy. John cared most for his religious teaching and opinions. David respected him as a mechanic but took little interest in his religious views or philosophic teachings.

Frequently Jude came over on the Sabbath to hear Jesus talk in the synagogue and would stay to visit with him. The more Jude saw of his eldest brother, the more he became convinced that Jesus was a truly great man.

This was the last year of Jesus' settled life. Never again did Jesus spend a whole year in one place or at one undertaking. The days of his Earth pilgrimage were rapidly approaching. Periods of intense activity were not far in the future, but there were now about to intervene between his simple but intensely active life of the past and his still more intense and strenuous public ministry, a few years of extensive travel and highly diversified personal activity. His training as a man of the realm had to be completed before he could enter upon his career of teaching and preaching.

THE TWENTY EIGHTH YEAR

In March of this year, Jesus took leave of Zebedee and of Capernaum. He asked for a small sum of money to defray his expenses to Jerusalem. While working with Zebedee he had drawn only small sums of money, which each month he would send to the family at Nazareth. One month Joseph would come down to Capernaum for the money. The next month Jude would come down. Jude's fishing headquarters was only a few miles south of Capernaum.

When Jesus took leave of Zebedee's family, he agreed to remain in Jerusalem until Passover time, and they all promised to be present for that event. They even arranged to celebrate the Passover supper together. They all sorrowed when Jesus left them, especially the daughters of Zebedee.

Before leaving Capernaum, Jesus had a long talk with his new-found friend and close companion, John Zebedee. He told John that he contemplated traveling extensively until: "my hour has come". He asked John to act in his stead in the matter of sending some money to his family in Nazareth each month until the funds due him should be exhausted. John made him this promise: "My brother, go about your business, do your work in the world. I will act for you in this or any other matter, and I will watch over your family even as I would foster my own mother and care for my own brothers and sisters. I will disburse your funds, which my father holds as you have directed and as they may be needed, and when your money has been expended, if I do not receive more from you, and if your mother is in need, then will I share my own earnings with her. Go your way in peace. I will act in your stead in all these matters."

After Jesus had departed for Jerusalem, John consulted with his father, Zebedee, regarding the money due Jesus, and he was surprised that it was such a large sum. As Jesus had left the matter so entirely in their hands, they agreed that it would be the better plan to invest these funds in property and use the income for assisting the family at Nazareth. Since Zebedee knew of a little house in Capernaum which carried a mortgage and was for sale, he directed John to buy this house with Jesus' money and hold the title in trust for his friend. John did as his father advised him. For two years the rent of this house was applied to the mortgage and was augmented by a certain large fund which Jesus presently sent up to John to be used as needed by the family.

These two sums of money almost equaled the amount of the obligation. Zebedee supplied the difference, so that John paid up the remainder of the mortgage. In this way, Jesus became the owner of a house in Capernaum, but he never knew about it.

When the family at Nazareth heard that Jesus had departed from Capernaum, they believed the time had come for them to get along without any further help from him. James remembered his contract with Jesus, and with the help of his brothers, forthwith assumed full responsibility for the care of the family.

Back in Jerusalem, for almost two months Jesus spent the greater part of his time listening to the temple discussions with occasional visits to the various schools of the rabbis. Most of the Sabbath days he spent in Bethany.

Jesus had carried with him to Jerusalem a letter from Salome, Zebedee's wife, introducing him to the former high priest, Annas.

Annas spent much time with him, personally asking him to visit the many academies of the Jerusalem religious teachers. While Jesus thoroughly inspected these schools and carefully observed their methods of teaching, he never so much as asked a single question in public. Although Annas looked upon Jesus as a great man, he was puzzled as to how to advise him. He recognized the foolishness of suggesting that he enter any of the schools of Jerusalem as a student, and yet he well knew Jesus would never be accorded the status of a regular teacher since he had never been trained in these schools.

Presently, the time of Passover drew near, and along with the throngs from every quarter arrived at Jerusalem from Capernaum, Zebedee and his entire family. They all stopped at the spacious home of Annas, where they celebrated Passover as one happy family.

Before the end of this Passover week, by pure chance, Jesus met a wealthy traveler and his son, a young man about seventeen years of age. These travelers were from India and were on their way to visit Rome and other points on the Mediterranean. They had arrived in Jerusalem to look for an interpreter for the two of them and also as a tutor for the son as they journeyed. The father liked Jesus immediately and insisted that he joins them on this trip throughout the Mediterranean. Jesus told them about his family and that it was hardly fair to go away for almost two years, during which time they might find themselves in need. The traveler from the orient proposed to advance to Jesus the wages of one year so that he could entrust such funds to his friends for the safeguarding of his family. On this arrangement, Jesus agreed to make the trip. He turned over this large sum of money to John, the son of Zebedee, and it was this sum that John subsequently applied to the purchase of the property in Capernaum. Jesus took Zebedee fully into his confidence regarding this Mediterranean journey, but he requested that he tell no man, not even his own flesh and blood, and Zebedee never did disclose his knowledge of Jesus' whereabouts during this long period of almost two years. Before Jesus' return from this trip, the family at Nazareth had just about given him up as dead. Only the assurances of Zebedee, who went up to Nazareth with his son John on several occasions, kept hope alive in Mary's heart.

During this time, the Nazareth family got along very well. Jude had considerably increased his quota and kept up this extra contribution until he was married. Notwithstanding that they required little assistance, it was the practice of John Zebedee to take presents each month to Mary and Ruth, as Jesus had instructed him.

THE MEDITERRANEAN TOUR

The tour of the Roman world consumed most of the twenty-eighth and the entire twenty-ninth year of Jesus' life on Earth. The three travelers left Jerusalem on a Sunday morning, in the month of April, 22 AD They followed a preplanned schedule around the Mediterranean, and finally departed company in the city of Charax on the Persian Gulf in mid-December of the year 23 AD.

From Jerusalem they went to Caesarea by way of Joppa. At Caesarea they took a boat for Alexandria. From Alexandria they sailed for Lasea in Crete. From Crete they sailed for Carthage, touching Cyrene. At Carthage they took a boat for Naples, stopping at Malta, Syracuse, and Messina. From Naples they went to Capua, then they traveled by the Appian Way to Rome.

After their stay in Rome, they went overland to Tarentum, where they set sail for Athens in Greece, stopping at Nicopolis and Corinth.

From Athens they went to Ephesus by way of Troas. From Ephesus they sailed for Cyprus, putting in at Rhodes on the way. They spent considerable time visiting and resting on Cyprus and then sailed for Antioch in Syria. From Antioch they journeyed south to Sidon and then went over to Damascus. From there they traveled by caravan to Mesopotamia, passing through Thapsacus and Larissa. They spent some time in Babylon, visited Ur and other ancient places along the river, and then went to Susa. From Susa they journeyed to Charax, from where the father and son departed for India, and Jesus returned to Palestine.

Throughout this tour of the Roman world, for many reasons, Jesus was known as the Damascus Scribe. At Corinth and other stops on the return trip he was known as the Jewish tutor.

This was an eventful period in his life. While on this journey he made many contacts with his fellow men, but this experience is a phase of his life which he never revealed to any member of his family nor to any of the Apostles. Jesus lived out his life in the flesh and departed from this world without anyone other than Zebedee knowing that he had made this extensive trip. Some of his friends thought he had returned to Damascus. Others thought he had gone to India. His own family inclined to the belief that he was in Alexandria, since they knew that he had once been invited to go there for the purpose of becoming an assistant Chazzan.

During the time and through the experiences of this tour of the Roman world, Jesus practically completed his educational contact with the diversified peoples of the world of his day and generation. By the time of his return to Nazareth, through the medium of this travel training he had just about learned how man lived and created out his existence on Earth.

The real purpose of his trip around the Mediterranean basin was to know man. He came very close to hundreds of humans on this journey. He met and loved all manner of men, rich and poor, high and low, black and white, educated and uneducated, cultured and uncultured, animalistic and spiritual, religious and irreligious, moral and immoral.

On this Mediterranean journey Jesus made great advances in his human task of mastering the material and mortal mind. By the end of this tour Jesus virtually knew, with all human certainty that he was a Son of God. His spirit more and more were able to bring up in his human mind shadowy memories of his Heavenly experiences in association with his Divine Father.

To the on looking Angels in the Heavenly realms, this Mediterranean trip was the most enthralling of all Jesus' Earth experiences, at least of all his career right up to the event of his death. This was the fascinating period of his personal ministry among men in contrast with the soon-following epoch of public ministry. This unique episode was all the more engrossing because he was at this time still the carpenter of Nazareth, the boat builder of Capernaum and the Scribe of Damascus. He was still the Son of Man. He had not yet achieved the complete mastery of his human mind. The purely human religious experience - the personal spiritual growth - of the son of man almost reached the apex of achievement during this, the twenty-ninth year of his life.

Throughout these years, while he did not appear to engage in so many moments of formal communion with his Father in Heaven, he perfected increasingly effective methods of personal communication with the spirit presence of his Father. He lived a real life, a full life, and a truly normal, natural, and average life in the flesh. He experienced the equivalent of the entire sum and substance of the living of a life of a human being in a material world of time and space.

The Son of Man experienced those wide ranges of human emotion which reach from superb joy to profound sorrow. He was a child of joy and a being of rare good humor. Likewise, was he a man of sorrows and acquainted with grief. In a spiritual sense, he did live through mortal life from the bottom to the top, beginning to the end. From a material point of view, he might appear to have escaped living through both social extremes of human existence, but intellectually he became wholly familiar with the entire and complete experience of mankind.

CHAPTER 3

John the Baptizer

J OHN THE BAPTIZER WAS BORN ON MARCH 25, OF THE YEAR 7 BC by your modern calendar just as Gabriel had foretold Elizabeth in June of the previous year. For five months, Elizabeth had kept Gabriel's visitation secret. When she finally told her husband, Zacharias, he was greatly troubled, and believed her story only after he had an unusual dream about six weeks before the birth of John. Except for the visit of Gabriel to Elizabeth, and the dream of Zacharias where Gabriel appeared to him, there was nothing unusual or supernatural connected with the birth of John.

On the eighth day he was circumcised according to the Jewish custom. He grew up as an ordinary child, day by day and year by year, in the small village known in those days as the town of Judah, about four miles west of Jerusalem.

The most eventful occurrence in John's early childhood was the visit, in company with his parents, to Jesus and the Nazareth family. This visit occurred in the month of June, of the year 1 BC of your time, when he was a little over six years old.

After their return from Nazareth John's parents began the systematic education of the lad. There was no synagogue school in this little village. However, as he was a priest, Zacharias was well educated, and Elizabeth was far better educated than the average Judean woman.

Since John was an only child, they spent a great deal of time on his mental and spiritual training. Zacharias had only short periods of service at the temple in Jerusalem, so he devoted much of his time to teaching his son.

Zacharias and Elizabeth had a small farm on which they raised sheep. They hardly made a living on this land, but for their main income Zacharias received a regular allowance from the temple funds dedicated to the priesthood.

John had no school from which to graduate at the age of fourteen, but his parents had selected this as the appropriate year for him to take the formal vows of the Essene Brotherhood, an ancient brotherhood of holy men whose roots went back to the days of the Salem Missionaries. Accordingly, Zacharias and Elizabeth took their son to Engedi, down by the Dead Sea. This was the southern headquarters of the Essene brotherhood, and there the lad was duly and solemnly inducted into this order for life. After these ceremonies and the making of the vows to abstain from all intoxicating drinks, to let the hair grow, and to refrain from touching the dead, the family proceeded to Jerusalem, where, before the temple, John completed the making of the offerings which were required of those taking the vows of the Essenes.

John took the same life vows that had been administered to another illustrious Essene, Samuel the Prophet. A life Essene was looked upon as a sanctified and holy personality. The Jews regarded an Essene with almost the respect and veneration accorded the High Priests of Jerusalem.

John returned home from Jerusalem to tend his father's sheep and grew up to be a strong man with a noble character.

When he was sixteen, John became greatly impressed with Elijah, the prophet of Mount Carmel, whom he had just read a great deal about. He decided to adopt the dress of that old prophet. From that day on John always wore a hairy garment with a leather girdle. At sixteen, he was more than six feet tall and almost full grown. With his flowing hair and peculiar mode of dress he was indeed a picturesque youth. His parents expected great things from their only son.

Zacharias died in July of the year 12 AD, when John was just past eighteen years old. This was a time of great embarrassment to John since the Essene vow forbade contact with the dead, even in one's own family. Although John had endeavored to comply with the restrictions of his vow regarding contamination by the dead, he was not able to comply fully with the requirements of the Essene order.

Therefore, after his father's burial he went to Jerusalem, where, in the Essene Court, he offered the sacrifices required for his cleansing.

In September of this year Elizabeth and John made a journey to Nazareth to visit Mary and Jesus. John had just about made up his mind to launch out in his lifework, but he was admonished, not only by Jesus' words but also by his example, to return home, take care of his mother, and await the coming of the Father's hour. After bidding Jesus and Mary good-bye at the end of this enjoyable visit, John did not again see Jesus until they met at the event of the baptism in the Jordan River.

John and Elizabeth returned to their home and began to lay plans for the future. Since John refused to accept the priest's allowance due him from the temple funds, by the end of two years they had lost everything. They decided to go south with the sheep herd.

Accordingly, the summer that John was twenty years of age they moved to Hebron. In the so-called wilderness of Judea, John tended his sheep along a brook that was a tributary to a larger stream which entered the Dead Sea at Engedi. The Engedi colony included not only Essenes of lifelong consecration but numerous other ascetic herdsmen who congregated in this region with their herds and fraternized with the Essene brotherhood. The Engedi colony supported themselves by sheep raising and from gifts wealthy Jews made to the Essene brotherhood.

As time passed, John returned less often to Hebron, while he made more frequent visits to Engedi. He was so entirely different from the majority of the Essenes that he found it very difficult fully to fraternize with the brotherhood. He was very fond of Abner though, the acknowledged leader and head of the Engedi colony of Essenes.

Along the valley of this little brook John built a dozen stone shelters and night corrals, consisting of piled-up stones, where he could watch over and safeguard his herds of sheep and goats. John's life as a shepherd afforded him a great deal of time for thought. He talked much with Ezda, an orphan lad of Beth-Zur, whom he had adopted, and who cared for the herds when John made trips to Hebron to see his mother and to sell sheep, as well as when he went down to Engedi for Sabbath services. John and the lad lived very simply, subsisting on mutton, goat's milk, wild honey, and the edible locusts of that region. This, their regular diet, was supplemented by provisions brought from Hebron and Engedi from time to time.

Elizabeth kept John informed about Palestinian and world affairs, and his conviction grew deeper and deeper that the time was fast approaching when the old order was to end. He knew he was to become the herald of the approach of a new age, the kingdom of Heaven. This rugged shepherd was very partial to the writings of the Prophet Daniel. He read a thousand times Daniel's description of the great image, which Zacharias had told him represented the history of the great kingdoms of the world, beginning with Babylon, then Persia, Greece, and finally Rome. John perceived that already was Rome divided into Syria, Egypt, Palestine, and other provinces. Then he further read: "In the days of these kings shall the God of Heaven set up a kingdom which shall never be destroyed. This kingdom shall not be left to other people but shall break in pieces and consume all these kingdoms, and it shall stand forever. There was given him dominion and glory and a kingdom that all peoples, nations, and languages should serve him. His dominion is an everlasting dominion, which shall not pass away, and his kingdom never shall be destroyed. The kingdom and dominion and the greatness of the kingdom under the whole Heaven shall be given to the people of the Son of the Most High, whose kingdom is an everlasting kingdom, and all dominions shall serve and obey him."

John was never able to completely rise above the confusion produced by what he had heard from his parents concerning Jesus and by these passages which he read in the scriptures. In Daniel he read: "I saw in the night visions, and beheld, one like the Son of Man came with the clouds of Heaven, and there was given him dominion and glory and a kingdom." But these words of the prophet did not harmonize with what his parents had taught him. Neither did his talk with Jesus, at the time of their visit when he was eighteen years old, correspond with these statements of the scriptures. Notwithstanding this confusion, throughout all of the perplexity, his mother assured him that his distant cousin, Joshua Ben Joseph, was the true Messiah, that he had come to sit on the throne of David, and that he, John, was to become his advance herald and chief support.

From all John heard of the vice and wickedness of Rome and the dissoluteness and moral barrenness of the empire, from what he knew of the evil doings of Herod Antipas and the high priests of Judea, he wholeheartedly believed that the end of the age was imminent. It seemed to this rugged and noble child of nature that the world was ripe for the end of the age of man and the dawn of the new and divine age - the kingdom of Heaven. The feeling grew in John's heart that he was to be the last of the old prophets and the first of the new. He fairly vibrated with the mounting impulse to go forth and proclaim to all men: "Repent, get right with God. Get ready for the end. Prepare yourselves for the appearance of the new and eternal order of Earth affairs, the kingdom of Heaven.:

In mid-August of the year 22 AD, when John was twenty-eight years old, his mother suddenly died. Elizabeth's friends, knowing of the Essene restrictions regarding contact with the dead, even in one's own family, made all arrangements for the burial of Elizabeth before sending for John. When he received word of the death of his mother, he directed Ezda to drive his herds to Engedi and he started for Hebron.

On returning to Engedi from his mother's funeral, he presented his flocks to the brotherhood and for a season detached himself from the outside world while he fasted and prayed. John knew only of the old methods of approach to divinity. He knew only of the records of the prophets such as Elijah, Samuel, and Daniel. Elijah was his ideal as a prophet. Elijah was the first of the Hebrew teachers to be regarded as a prophet, and John truly believed that he was to be the last of this long and illustrious line of the messengers of Heaven.

For two and a half years, John lived at Engedi, and he persuaded most of the Essene brotherhood there that the end of the age of man was at hand, that the kingdom of Heaven was about to appear. But he erred in his early teachings in that his teachings were all based on the Jewish idea and concept of the Messiah as the promised deliverer of the Jewish nation from the domination of their Gentile rulers.

Throughout this period John read much in the sacred writings which he found at the Engedi home of the Essenes. He was especially impressed by Isaiah and by Malachi, the last of the prophets up to that time. He read and reread the last five chapters of Isaiah, and he believed these prophecies. Then he would read in Malachi: "Behold, I will send you Elijah the prophet before the coming of the great and dreadful day of the Father. He shall turn the hearts of the fathers toward the children and the hearts of the children toward their father, lest I come and smite the Earth with a curse." It was only this promise of Malachi that Elijah would return that deterred John from going forth to preach about the coming kingdom and to encourage his fellow Jews to flee from the wrath to come. John was ripe for the proclamation of the message of the coming kingdom, but this expectation of the coming of Elijah held him back for more than two years. He knew he was not Elijah. What did Malachi mean? Was the prophecy literal or figurative? How could he know the truth? He finally dared to think that, since the first of the prophets was called Elijah, the last should be known, eventually, by the same name. He believed for a season that he was the Prophet Elijah come back to fulfill a mission. Nevertheless, he had doubts, doubts sufficient to prevent his ever calling himself Elijah.

It was the influence of Elijah that caused John to adopt his methods of direct and blunt assault upon the sins and vices of the Jews of his day. He sought to dress like Elijah, and he endeavored to talk like Elijah. In every outward aspect he was like the old prophet. He was just such a stalwart and picturesque child of nature, just such a fearless and daring teacher of righteousness. John was not illiterate, but neither was he educated. He knew well the Jewish sacred writings, but he was hardly cultured. He was a clear thinker, a powerful speaker, and a fiery denunciator. He was hardly an example to his age, but he was an eloquent rebuke to the Jewish leaders of his day.

At last, he came up with the method of proclaiming the new age, the kingdom of God. He settled that he was to proclaim the arrival of the Messiah. He swept aside all doubts and departed from Engedi one day in March, 25 AD, to begin his short but brilliant career as a public preacher.

In order to understand John's message, you must understand the status of the Jews at the time John appeared on a stage. For almost one hundred years all Palestine had been in a quandary. They were at a loss to explain their continuous subjugation to Gentile overlords. They asked themselves: "Did not Moses teach that righteousness is always rewarded with prosperity and power? Are we not God's chosen people? Why is the throne of David desolate and vacant?" In light of the doctrines, they attributed to Moses and the sayings of the prophets, the Jews found it difficult to explain their long-continued national subjugation.

Around one hundred years before the birth of Jesus and John, a new school of religious teachers had arisen in Palestine, these were the Apocalyptists. These new teachers evolved a system of belief that accounted for the sufferings and humiliation of the Jews on the ground that they were paying the penalty for the nation's sins. These preachers fell back onto the well-known reasons assigned to explain the Babylonian and other captivities of former times. The Apocalyptists taught that Jews should take heart, the days of their affliction were almost over. The discipline of God's chosen people was about finished. God's patience with the Gentile foreigners was about exhausted. The end of Roman rule was coming to an end, along with the end of the world. These new teachers leaned heavily on the predictions of the Prophet Daniel, and they consistently taught that creation was about to pass into its final stage. The kingdoms of this world were about to become the kingdom of God. To the Jewish mind of that day this was the meaning of that phrase - the kingdom of Heaven - which runs throughout the teachings of both Jesus and John. To the Jews of Palestine the phrase, kingdom of Heaven, had but one meaning, an absolutely righteous state in which God (through the Messiah) would come to rule the nations of Earth in perfection of power just as he ruled in Heaven, "Your will be done on Earth as it is in Heaven." Implicit within this theory was that the Messiah was to be a Jewish king who would rule the world and thereby bring the entire known world beneath the Jewish heel.

In the days of John all Jews were expectantly asking: "How soon will the kingdom come?" There was a general feeling that the end of the rule of the Gentile nations was drawing near. There was present throughout all Jewry a lively hope and a keen expectation that the consummation of the desire of the ages would occur during the lifetime of that generation.

While the Jews differed greatly in their ideas of the nature of the coming kingdom, they were alike in their belief that the event was impending, near at hand, even at the door. Many who read the Hebrew scriptures literally looked expectantly for a new king in Palestine, for a regenerated Jewish nation delivered from its enemies and presided over by the successor of King David, the Messiah who would quickly be acknowledged as the rightful and righteous ruler of all the world.

Another, though smaller group of devout Jews, the Essenes, held a vastly different view of this kingdom of God. They taught that the coming kingdom was not of this world, that the world was approaching its certain end, and that a new Heaven and a new Earth were to usher in the establishment of the kingdom of God, that this kingdom was to be an everlasting dominion, that sin was to be ended, and that the citizens of the new kingdom were to become immortal in their enjoyment of this endless bliss.

All were agreed that some drastic purging or purifying action would precede the establishment of the new kingdom on Earth. The Literalists taught that a world-wide war would ensue which would destroy all unbelievers, while the faithful would sweep on to universal and eternal victory, while the Spiritualists taught that the kingdom would be ushered in by the great judgment of God which would relegate the unrighteous to their well-deserved judgment of punishment and final destruction, while at the same time elevating the believing Jews to high seats of honor and authority with the Messiah, who would rule over the redeemed nations in God's name. This latter group even believed that some God-fearing Gentiles might be admitted to the fellowship of the new kingdom.

Some of the Jews held to the opinion that God might possibly establish this new kingdom by direct and divine intervention, but the vast majority believed that he would interpose some representative intermediary, the Messiah. That was the only meaning the term Messiah had in the minds of the Jews of the generation of John and Jesus. Messiah did not refer to one who merely taught God's will or proclaimed the necessity for righteous living. To all such holy persons the Jews gave the title of Prophet. The Messiah was to be more than a Prophet. The Messiah was to bring in the new kingdom, the kingdom of God. No one who failed to do this could be the Messiah in the eyes of the Jews.

Who would this Messiah be? Again the Jews differed. The older ones clung to the Doctrine of the Son of David. The newer taught that, since the new kingdom was a Heavenly kingdom, the new ruler might also be a divine personality, one who had long sat at God's right hand in Heaven. Strange as it may appear, those who conceived of the ruler of the new kingdom looked upon him not as a human Messiah, not as a mere man, but as the Son of God, a heavenly prince, long held in waiting thus to assume the rulership of the Earth made new. Such was the religious background of the Jewish world when John went forth proclaiming: "Repent, for the kingdom of Heaven is at hand."

It becomes apparent, therefore, that John's announcement of the coming kingdom had at least half a dozen different meanings in the minds of those who listened to his impassioned preaching. But no matter what significance they attached to the phrases which John stated, each of these various groups of Jewish-kingdom expectants was intrigued by the proclamations of this sincere, enthusiastic, rough-and- ready preacher of righteousness and repentance, who so solemnly preached to his hearers to flee from the wrath to come.

Early in the month of March, of the year 25 AD by your current calendar, John journeyed around the western coast of the Dead Sea and up the River Jordan to the Jericho ford. Crossing over to the other side of the river, he established himself near the entrance to the ford and began to preach to the people who passed by on their way back and forth across the river. This was the most frequented of all the Jordan crossings.

It was apparent to all who heard John that he was more than a preacher. The great majority of those who listened to this strange man who had come out of the Judean wilderness went away believing that they had heard the voice of a prophet. No wonder the souls of these weary and expectant Jews were deeply stirred by such a phenomenon. Never in all Jewish history had the devout

Jews so longed for consolation, or more ardently anticipated the restoration of the throne of their King David. Never in all of Hebrew history could John's message that the kingdom of Heaven is at hand, have made such a deep and universal appeal as at the very time he so mysteriously appeared on the banks of this southern crossing of the Jordan.

He came from the herdsmen like Amos. He was dressed like Elijah, and he thundered his admonitions and poured forth his warnings to the Jews just as Elijah had done. This strange preacher created a mighty stir throughout all Palestine as the travelers carried abroad the news of his preaching along the Jordan.

There was still another feature about the work of this preacher, he baptized every one of his believers in the Jordan River for the remission of sins. Although baptism was already an ancient ceremony among the Jews and the Gentiles, they had never seen it employed as John now made use of it. It had long been the practice of the Jews to baptize Gentile converts into the fellowship of the outer court of the temple, but never had the Jews themselves been asked to submit to baptism for the remission of sins. Only fifteen months elapsed between the time John began to preach and baptize, and his arrest and imprisonment at the orders of Herod Antipas, but in this short time he baptized considerably over one hundred thousand Jews and Gentiles. These were the people who first began calling John: "The Baptizer."

John preached four months at the Bethany ford before starting north up the Jordan. Tens of thousands of listeners, some curious but many earnest and serious, came to hear him from all parts of Judea, Perea and Samaria. Some even came all the way from Galilee just to hear John.

In May of this same year, while John preached at Bethany ford, the Priests and Levites sent a delegation out from Jericho to inquire of John whether he claimed to be the Messiah, and by whose authority he preached. John answered them by saying: "Go tell your masters that you have heard the voice of one crying in the wilderness, and saying, make ready the way of the Father, make straight a highway for our God. Every valley shall be filled, and every mountain and hill shall be brought low. The uneven ground shall become a plain, while the rough places shall become a smooth valley. All flesh shall see the salvation of God."

John was a heroic but tactless preacher. One day when he was preaching and baptizing on the west bank of the Jordan, a group of Pharisees and Sadducees came forward and presented themselves for baptism. Before leading them down into the water, John addressed them as a group and said: "Who warned you to flee as snakes before the fire, from the wrath to come? I will baptize you, but I warn you to bring forth fruit worthy of sincere repentance. Even now the ax is laid to the very roots of the trees. Every tree that does not bring forth good fruit will be cut down and cast into the fire."

John conducted classes for his disciples, in the course of which he instructed them in the details of their new life and tried to answer their many questions. He counseled the teachers to instruct in the spirit as well as the letter of the law. He instructed the rich to feed the poor. To the tax gatherers he said: "Extort no more than that which is assigned you." To the soldiers he said: "Do no violence and exact nothing wrongfully. Be content with your wages." While to all he declared: "Make ready for the end of this age. The kingdom of Heaven is at hand."

John still had many confused ideas about the coming kingdom and its king. The longer he preached the more confused he became. But never did this intellectual confusion concerning the nature of the coming kingdom lessen his conviction of the certainty of the kingdom's immediate appearance. In mind John was confused, but in spirit he never was. He had no doubts about the coming of the kingdom, but he was far from certain whether Jesus was to be the ruler of that kingdom. As long as John held to the idea of the restoration of the throne of David, the teachings of his parents that Jesus, born in the City of David, was to be the long-expected deliverer seemed consistent. But at those times when he leaned more toward the doctrine of a spiritual kingdom and the end of the temporal age on Earth, he was sorely in doubt as to the part Jesus would play in such events. Sometimes he questioned everything, but not for long. He really wished he might talk it all over with his cousin, but that was contrary to their expressed agreement.

As John journeyed north, he thought much about Jesus. He paused at more than a dozen places as he traveled up the Jordan. It was during this time that he first made reference to another one who was to come after me, when a spectator asked him if he was the Messiah. John answered: "There will come after me one who is greater than I, whose sandal straps I am not worthy to stoop down and tie. I baptize you with water, but he will baptize you with the Holy Spirit."

In response to the questions of his disciples John continued to expand his teachings, from day to day adding more that was helpful and comforting compared with his early and cryptic message to repent and be baptized. By this time throngs were arriving from

Galilee and Decapolis. Scores of earnest believers lingered with their adored teacher day after day.

By December of that year, John reached the neighborhood of Pella in his journey up the Jordan River. His fame had now extended throughout all of Palestine, and his work had become the chief topic of conversation in all the towns around the Sea of Galilee. Jesus had spoken favorably and often of John's message, and this had caused many from Capernaum to join John's cult of repentance and baptism. James and John, the fishermen sons of Zebedee had gone down in December, soon after John took up his preaching position near Pella and had offered themselves for baptism. They went to see John once a week and brought back to Jesus fresh, first-hand reports of the evangelist's work.

Jesus' brothers, James and Jude, had talked about going down to John for baptism. Now that Jude had come over to Capernaum for the Sabbath services, both he and James, after listening to Jesus' discourse in the synagogue, decided to take counsel with him concerning their plans. This was on a Saturday night in mid-January of the year 26 AD. Jesus requested that they postpone the discussion until the following day, when he would give them his answer. Jesus slept very little that night, being in close communion with his Father in Heaven. He had arranged to have noontime lunch with his brothers and to advise them concerning baptism by John. That Sunday morning Jesus was working as usual in the boat shop. James and Jude arrived with the lunch and were waiting in the lumber room for him, as it was not yet time for the midday break and they knew that Jesus was very regular about such matters.

Just before the noon rest, Jesus laid down his tools, removed his work apron, and announced to the three workmen in the room with him: "My hour has come." He went out to his brothers James and Jude, repeating to them: "The hour of my Father has now come. Let us go to John." The brothers were astonished and did not quite understand what this meant, but they started immediately for Pella with Jesus, eating their lunch as they journeyed. They rested for the night in the Jordan Valley and arrived on the scene of John's baptizing about noon of the next day.

John had just begun baptizing the candidates for the day. Scores of repentant were standing in line awaiting their turn when Jesus and his two brothers appeared and took up their positions in this line of earnest men and women who had become believers in John's preaching of the coming kingdom. John had been asking the sons of Zebedee about the whereabouts of Jesus. He had heard of Jesus' remarks concerning his preaching, and he was day by day expecting to see him arrive on the scene, but he had not expected to greet him in the line of baptism candidates.

As he was engrossed with the details of rapidly baptizing such a large number of believers, John did not look up to see Jesus until he stood directly in front of him. When John recognized Jesus, he stopped the ceremonies immediately while he greeted his cousin and asked: "But why do you come down into the water to greet me?" Jesus answered him: "To subject myself to your baptism." Then John replied: "But I have need to be baptized by you. Why do you come to me?" Jesus reached close to John and whispered in his ear: "Bear with me. It is important to set this example for my brothers standing here with me.

This is the sign that the people may know that my hour has come." There was a tone of finality and authority in Jesus' voice such that John made no more protests.

John trembled with emotions as he made ready to baptize Jesus of Nazareth in the Jordan River. Thus did John baptize the Son of God just after noon on Monday, January 24, 26 AD. When John had baptized Jesus and his two brothers, he dismissed the others for the day, announcing that he would resume baptisms at noon the next day.

The people started departing, but the four men stood in the river talking. All of a sudden, an apparition, as if a bright cloud, hovered above the head of Jesus for just a moment and everyone within hearing heard a voice say: "This is my son in whom I am well pleased." A great change came over the countenance of Jesus, and coming up out of the water in silence he took leave of them, going toward the hills to the East. No man saw Jesus again for forty days.

John followed Jesus a sufficient distance to tell him the story of Gabriel's visit to his mother. He had heard it so many times from his mother's lips. He allowed Jesus to continue on his way after he had said: "Now I know of a certainty that you are the deliverer." Jesus made no reply but continued to walk.

When John returned to his followers, who now numbered some thirty men, he found them in earnest conference, discussing what had just happened in connection with Jesus' baptism. They were all the more astonished when John now made known to them the story of the Gabriel visitation to Mary before Jesus was born, and also that Jesus spoke no word to him in denial even after he had told him about this. This group of thirty or more talked long into the starlit night. They wondered where Jesus had gone, and when they would see him again.

After the experience of this day John's preaching took on new and definite notes of proclamation concerning the coming kingdom and the expected Messiah. It was a tense time, these forty days of waiting for the return of Jesus. But John continued to preach with great power, and his disciples began to preach to the overflowing throngs which gathered around John at the Jordan River. In the course of these forty days of waiting, many rumors spread around the countryside and even to Tiberias and Jerusalem. Thousands came over to see the new attraction in John's camp, the reputed Messiah, but Jesus was not to be seen. When the disciples of John asserted that the strange man of God had gone to the hills, many doubted the entire story.

About three weeks after Jesus had left them, there arrived on the scene at Pella a new deputation from the priests and Pharisees at Jerusalem. They asked John directly if he was Elijah or the prophet that Moses promised. When John answered: "I am not", they then asked him if he was the Messiah. John again replied: "I am not." Then these men from the temple of Jerusalem asked John: "If you are not Elijah, nor the Prophet, nor the Messiah, then why do you baptize the people and create all this stir?" John replied: "It should be for those who have heard me and received my baptism to say who I am, but I declare to you that, while I baptize with water, there is one among us now who will baptize you with the Holy Spirit." The entourage finally departed in utter exasperation.

These forty days were the most difficult for John and his followers. What was to be the relation of John to Jesus? A hundred questions came up, all with no ready answers. Politics and selfishness began to make their appearance. Intense discussions grew up around the various ideas and concepts of the Messiah. Would he become a military leader and assume the throne of David? Would he smite the Roman armies, or would he come to establish a spiritual kingdom?

John decided, along with the minority, that Jesus had come to establish the kingdom of Heaven, although he was not altogether clear in his own mind as to just what was to comprise this mission of the establishment of the kingdom of Heaven.

These were strenuous days in John's experience, and he prayed for the return of Jesus. Some of John's disciples organized scouting parties to go in search of Jesus, but John forbade, saying: "Our time is in the hands of our Father in Heaven. He will direct us as he is directing his chosen son."

It was early on the morning of the Sabbath, February 23, that the company of John, engaged in eating their morning meal, looked up toward the north and saw Jesus coming to them. As he approached them, John stood upon a large rock and, with his thunderous voice, said: "Behold the Son of God, the deliverer of the world. This is he of whom I have spoken. For this cause have I come out of the wilderness to preach repentance and to baptize with water, proclaiming that the kingdom of Heaven is at hand. Now comes one who shall baptize you with the Holy Spirit. I beheld the Divine Spirit descending upon this man, and I heard the voice of God declare that this is his son in whom he is well pleased."

Jesus bade them return to their food while he sat down to eat with John. His brothers, James and Jude, were no longer with John. They had already returned to Capernaum.

Early next morning Jesus took leave of John and his disciples, heading for Galilee. He gave them no word as to when they would again see him. To John's inquiries about his own preaching and mission Jesus only said: "My Father will guide you now and, in the future, as he has in the past." These two great men separated that morning with a warm embrace on the banks of the Jordan River, never to see each other again in their mortal lifetimes.

Since Jesus had gone north into Galilee, John felt compelled to head south again along the Jordan River retracing the steps from where he came. Accordingly, John and his disciples began their journey south. About one quarter of John's immediate followers had, in the meantime departed for Galilee in quest of Jesus. There was sadness and confusion about John. He never again preached as he had before baptizing Jesus. He felt that the responsibility of the coming kingdom was no longer on his shoulders. He felt that his work was almost finished. He was disconsolate and lonely, but he preached on, baptizing as he went.

Near the village of Adam, John camped for several weeks. It was at this place that he made the verbal attack on Herod Antipas for unlawfully taking the wife of another man. By June of this year, 26 AD, John was back at the Bethany ford of the Jordan, where he had begun his preaching of the coming kingdom more than a year previously. In the weeks following the baptism of Jesus the character of John's preaching gradually changed into a proclamation of mercy for the common people, while he denounced with renewed vengeance the corrupt political and religious leaders of the Jews.

Herod Antipas, in whose territory John had been preaching, became alarmed that John might start a rebellion. Herod also resented John's public criticisms of his domestic affairs. In view of all this, Herod decided to put John in prison. Accordingly, early in the morning of June 12th, before the multitudes had arrived to hear the preaching and witness the baptizing, Herod's palace guard placed John under arrest. As weeks passed and he was not released, his disciples scattered over all Palestine, many of them going into Galilee to join the followers of Jesus.

John had a very bitter and lonely experience in prison. Few of his followers were allowed to see him. He longed to see Jesus but had to be content with hearing of his work through those of his followers who had become believers in the Son of God. He was often tempted to doubt Jesus and his divine mission. If Jesus were the Messiah, why did he do nothing to deliver him from this unbearable imprisonment? For more than a year and a half this rugged man of God's outdoors languished in that despicable prison. This experience was a great test of his faith in, and loyalty to, Jesus. Indeed, this whole experience was a great test of John's faith even in God. Many times, he was tempted to doubt even the genuineness of his own mission and experience.

After he had been in prison several months, a group of his followers came to him and, after relating the public activities of Jesus, said: "So you see, teacher, Jesus prospers and receives all who come to him. He even feasts with publicans and sinners. You preached courageously to him, and yet he does nothing to affect your deliverance." But John answered his followers: "This man can do nothing unless it has been given him by our Father in Heaven. You well remember that I said that I am not the Messiah, but I am one sent on before to prepare the way for him. I performed the mission that I was sent to do. He who has the bride is the bridegroom, but the friend of the bridegroom who stands nearby and hears him rejoices greatly because of the bridegrooms' voice. My joy is therefore fulfilled. He must increase while I decrease. I am of this Earth and have declared my message. Jesus of Nazareth has come down to the Earth from Heaven and is above us all. This Son of God has descended from God, and the words of God he will declare to you. For the Father in Heaven gives not the spirit by measure to his own son. The Father loves his son and will presently put all things in the hands of this son. He who believes in the son believes in the Father and has eternal life. These words which I speak are true and abiding."

The followers were amazed at John's pronouncements, so much so that they departed in silence. John was also very agitated, for he perceived that he had uttered a prophecy. Never again did he wholly doubt the mission and divinity of Jesus. But it was a sore disappointment to John that Jesus sent him no word, that he did not come to visit him, and that he exercised none of his great power to deliver him from prison. But Jesus knew all about this. He had great love for John, but being now cognizant of his divine nature and knowing fully the great things in preparation for John when he departed from this world and also knowing that John's work on Earth was finished, he restrained himself from interfering in the natural path of the great preacher-prophet's career.

This long suspense in prison was humanly unbearable. Just a few days before his death John again sent trusted messengers to Jesus, inquiring: "Is my work finished? Why do I languish in prison? Are you truly the Messiah, or shall we look for another?" When these two disciples gave this message to Jesus, the Son of God replied: "Go back to John and tell him that I have not forgotten him, but to suffer me also this, for it becomes us to fulfill all righteousness. Tell John what you have seen and heard, that the poor have good tidings preached to them, and finally, tell the beloved herald of my Earth mission that he shall be abundantly blessed in the age to come if he finds no occasion to doubt and stumble over me." This was the last word John received from Jesus. This message greatly comforted him and did much to stabilize his faith and prepare him for the tragic end of his life that followed very shortly after this message was received.

Since John was working in Southern Perea when arrested, he had been taken immediately to the prison of the fortress of Machaerus, where he was incarcerated until his execution. Herod ruled over Perea as well as Galilee, and he maintained residence at this time at both Julius and Machaerus in Perea. In Galilee the official residence had been moved from Sepphoris to the new capital at Tiberias.

Herod feared to release John lest he instigate rebellion. He feared to put him to death lest the multitude riot in the capital, for thousands of Pereans believed that John was a holy man, a prophet. Therefore, Herod kept the Essene preacher in prison, not knowing what else to do with him. Several times John had been called before Herod, but never would he agree either to leave the domains of Herod or to refrain from all public activities if he were released. This new agitation concerning Jesus of Nazareth, which was steadily increasing, admonished Herod that it was no time to turn John loose. Besides, John was also a victim of the intense and bitter hatred of Herodias, Herod's unlawful wife.

On numerous occasions Herod had John brought to him and together they sat and talked about the kingdom of Heaven, and while sometimes seriously impressed with his message, Herod was afraid to release him from prison.

Since much building was still going on at Tiberias, Herod spent considerable time at his Perean residences, and he was partial to the fortress of Machaerus. It was a matter of several years before all the public buildings and the official residence at Tiberias would be fully completed.

In celebration of his birthday Herod gave a great feast in the Machaerian Palace for his chief officers and other men high in the councils of the government of Galilee and Perea. Since Herodias had failed to bring about John's death by direct appeal to Herod, she now set herself to the task of having John put to death by cunning planning.

In the course of the evening's festivities and entertainment, Herodias presented her daughter to dance before the banqueters. Herod was very pleased with the damsel's performance, called her before him and said: "You are charming. I am very pleased with you. Ask me on this my birthday for whatever you desire, and I will give it to you, even to half of my kingdom." Herod did all this while well under the influence of much wine. The young lady drew aside and inquired of her mother what she should ask of Herod. Herodias said: "Go to Herod and ask for the head of John the Baptizer." The young woman, returning to the banquet table, said to Herod: "I request the head of John the Baptizer be delivered to me on a platter."

Herod was filled with fear and sorrow, but because of his oath and because of all those who sat at his dinner table, he would not deny the request. Herod Antipas sent a soldier from his palace guard to bring the head of John. So was John that night beheaded in the prison, the soldier bringing the head of the prophet on a platter and presenting it to the young woman at the rear of the banquet hall. The damsel gave the platter to her mother. When John's followers heard of this, they came to the prison for his body, and after laying it in a tomb, they went and told Jesus.

CHAPTER 4

The Twelve Apostles

I T IS AN ELOQUENT TESTIMONY TO THE CHARM AND righteousness of Jesus that, although he repeatedly dashed to pieces the hopes of his Apostles and tore to shreds their every ambition for personal exaltation, only one deserted him.

The Apostles learned from Jesus about the kingdom of Heaven, and Jesus learned much from them about the kingdom of men, human nature as it evolved on Earth. These twelve men represented many different types of human temperament, and they had not been made alike by schooling. Most of these Galilean fishermen were Jews by the sword. They were of Gentile blood whose families had been forcibly converted by the sword in the First Century BC when all of the Gentile population of Galilee was converted.

Do not make the mistake of regarding the Apostles as being altogether ignorant and unlearned, although they were fishermen. All of them, except the Alpheus twins, were graduates of the synagogue schools, having been thoroughly trained in the Hebrew scriptures and in much of the current knowledge of that day. Seven were graduates of the Capernaum synagogue schools, and there were no better schools in all of Galilee.

Andrew, the First Chosen

Andrew, chairman of the Apostles, was born in Capernaum. He was the oldest child in a family of five, himself, his brother Simon, and three sisters. His father had been a partner of Zebedee in the fishing business at Bethsaida, the fishing harbor of Capernaum. When he became an Apostle, Andrew was unmarried but made his home with his married brother, Simon Peter. Both were fishermen and partners of James and John, the sons of Zebedee.

In the year he was chosen as an Apostle, Andrew was 33 years old. He sprang from an excellent line of ancestors and was the ablest man of the twelve. Excepting oratory, he was the equal of his associates in almost every imaginable ability. Jesus never gave Andrew a nickname, a fraternal designation. But even as the Apostles soon began to call Jesus, Master, they also designated Andrew by a term equivalent of, Chief.

Andrew was a good organizer but a better administrator. He was one of the inner circle of three Apostles, but his appointment by Jesus as the head of the Apostolic group made it necessary for him to remain on duty with his brothers while the other three enjoyed very close communion with the master. to the very end Andrew remained Dean of the Apostles.

Although Andrew was never an effective preacher, he was an efficient personal worker, being the pioneer missionary of the kingdom in that, as the first chosen Apostle, he immediately brought to Jesus his brother, Simon, who subsequently became one of the greatest preachers of the kingdom. Andrew was the chief supporter of Jesus' policy of utilizing the program of personal work as a means of training the twelve as messengers of the kingdom.

Whether Jesus privately taught the Apostles or preached to the multitude, Andrew was usually conversant with what was going on. He was an understanding executive and an efficient administrator. He rendered a prompt decision on every matter brought to his notice unless he deemed the problem one beyond the domain of his authority, in which event he would take it straight to Jesus.

Andrew and Peter were very unlike in character and temperament, but it must be recorded everlastingly to their credit that they got along together splendidly. Andrew was never jealous of Peter's oratorical ability. Not often will an older brother of Andrew's type be observed exerting such a profound influence over a younger and talented brother. Andrew and Peter never seemed to be in the least jealous of each other's abilities or achievements. Late one evening of the celebration of Pentecost, when, largely through the energetic and inspiring preaching of Peter, two thousand souls became the followers of Jesus, Andrew said to his brother: "I could not do that, but I am glad I have a brother who can." To which Peter replied: "But for your bringing me to the Master and for your steadfastness in keeping me with him, I should not have been here to do this." Andrew and Peter were the exceptions to the rule, proving that even brothers can live together peaceably and work together effectively.

After Pentecost, Peter was famous, but it never bothered Andrew to spend the rest of his life being introduced as Simon Peter's brother.

Of all the Apostles, Andrew was the best judge of men. He knew that trouble was brewing in the heart of Judas Iscariot even when none of the others suspected that anything was wrong with their treasurer.

But he told none of them his fears. Andrew's great service to the kingdom was in advising Peter, James, and John concerning the choice of the first missionaries who were sent out to proclaim the gospel, and also in counseling these early leaders about the organization of the administrative affairs of the kingdom. Andrew had a great gift for discovering the hidden resources and latent talents of young people.

Very soon after the departure of Jesus, Andrew began the writing of a personal record of many of the sayings and doings of his departed master. After Andrew's death other copies of this private record were made and circulated freely among the early teachers of the Christian Church. These informal notes of Andrew's were subsequently edited, amended, altered, and added to until they made up a fairly consecutive narrative of the Master's life on Earth. But they were all lost to history, the last of these altered and amended copies was destroyed by fire at Alexandria, Egypt in the middle of the Second Century.

Andrew was a man of clear insight, logical thought, and firm decision, whose great strength of character consisted in his superb stability. His temperamental handicap was his lack of enthusiasm. He, many times failed to encourage his associates by judicious commendation. This reluctance to praise the worthy accomplishments of his friends grew out of his dislike of flattery and insincerity. Andrew was one of those all-round, even-tempered, self-made, and successful men of modest affairs.

Every one of the Apostles loved Jesus, but it remains true that each of the twelve was drawn toward him because of some certain trait of personality which made a special appeal to the individual Apostle.

Andrew admired Jesus because of his consistent sincerity, his unaffected dignity. when men once knew Jesus, they were possessed with the urge to share him with their friends. They really wanted all the world to know him.

When the later persecutions finally scattered the Apostles from Jerusalem, Andrew journeyed through Armenia, Asia Minor, and Macedonia and, after bringing many thousands into the kingdom, he was finally apprehended and crucified in Patrae in Achaia. It was two full days before this robust man died on the cross, and throughout these tragic hours he never complained of the pain or the torture but instead he continued to proclaim the glad tidings of the salvation of the kingdom of Heaven to all who were within hearing distance of the cross he hung on.

SIMON PETER

When Simon joined the Apostles, he was thirty years of age. He was married, had three children, and lived at Bethsaida, near Capernaum. His brother, Andrew, and his wife's mother lived with him. Both Peter and Andrew were fishing partners of the sons of Zebedee.

The Master had known Simon for some time before Andrew presented him as the second of the Apostles. When Jesus gave Simon the name Peter, he did it with a smile. It was to be a sort of nickname. Simon was well known to all his friends as an erratic and impulsive fellow. Later on, Jesus did attach a new and significant meaning to this lightly bestowed nickname.

Simon Peter was a man of impulse, an optimist. He had grown up permitting himself freely to indulge strong feelings. He was constantly getting into difficulties because he persisted in speaking without thinking. This sort of thoughtlessness also made incessant trouble for all of his friends and associates and was the cause of his receiving many mild rebukes from the Master. The only reason Peter did not get into more trouble because of his thoughtless speaking was that he very early learned to talk over many of his plans and schemes with his older brother, Andrew, before he ventured to make public proposals.

Peter was a born speaker, eloquent and dramatic. He was also a natural and inspirational leader of men, a quick thinker but not a deep reasoner. He asked many questions, more than all the Apostles put together, and while the majority of these questions were good and relevant, many of them were thoughtless and foolish. Peter did not have a deep mind, but he knew his mind fairly well. He was therefore a man of quick decision and sudden action. while others talked at their astonishment at seeing Jesus on the beach, Peter jumped in and swam ashore to meet the Master.

The trait which Peter most admired in Jesus was his wonderful tenderness. Peter never grew weary of contemplating Jesus' forbearance. He never forgot the lesson about forgiving the wrongdoer, not only seven times but seventy times and seven. He thought much about these impressions of the Master's forgiving character during those dark and dismal days immediately following his thoughtless and unintended denial of Jesus in the High Priest's courtyard.

Peter was distressingly vacillating. He would suddenly swing from one extreme to the other. First, he refused to let Jesus wash his feet and then, on hearing the Master's reply, begged to be washed all over. But, after all, Jesus knew that Peter's faults were of the head and not of the heart. He was one of the most inexplicable combinations of courage and cowardice that ever lived on Earth. His great strength of character was loyalty and friendship. Peter really and truly loved Jesus. Yet despite this towering strength of devotion, he was so unstable and inconstant that he permitted a servant girl to tease him into denying his Master. Peter could withstand persecution and any other form of direct assault, but he withered and shrank before ridicule. He was a brave soldier when facing a frontal attack, but he was a fear- cringing coward when surprised with an assault from the rear.

Peter was the first of Jesus' Apostles to come forward to defend the work of Philip among the Samaritans and Paul among the Gentiles. Yet later on at Antioch he reversed himself when confronted by ridiculing Judaizers, temporarily withdrawing from the Gentiles only to bring down upon his head the fearless wrath of Paul.

He was the first one of the Apostles to make wholehearted confession of Jesus' combined humanity and divinity, and the first to deny him. Peter was not so much of a dreamer, but he disliked descending from the clouds of ecstasy and the enthusiasm of dramatic indulgence to the plain and matter-of-fact-world of reality.

In following Jesus, literally and figuratively, he was either leading the procession or else trailing behind. But he was the outstanding preacher of the twelve. He did more than any other one man, aside from Paul, to establish the kingdom and send its messengers to the four corners of the Earth in one generation.

After his rash denials of the Master, he found himself again. With Andrew's sympathetic and understanding guidance he again led the way back to the fish nets while the Apostles waited to find out what was to happen after the crucifixion. When he was fully assured that Jesus had forgiven him and knew he had been received back into the Master's fold, the fires of the kingdom burned so brightly within his soul that he became a great and saving light to thousands who sat in darkness.

After leaving Jerusalem, and before Paul became the leading spirit among the Gentile Christian Churches, Peter traveled extensively, visiting all the churches from Babylon to Corinth. He even visited and ministered to many of the churches which had been raised up by Paul.

Although Peter and Paul differed much in temperament and education, even in theology, they worked together harmoniously for the uplifting of the churches during their later years.

A touch of Peter's style and teaching is shown in the sermons partially recorded by Luke and in the Gospel of Mark. His vigorous style was better shown in his letter known as the First Epistle of Peter. At least this was true before it was subsequently altered by a disciple of Paul.

Peter persisted in making the mistake of trying to convince the Jews that Jesus was, after all, really and truly the Jewish Messiah.

Right up to the day of his death, Peter continued to suffer great confusion in his mind between the concepts of Jesus as the Jewish Messiah, Christ as the world's redeemer, and the Son of God as the revelation of God, the loving Father of all mankind.

Peter's wife was a very able woman. For years she labored acceptably as a member of the Women's Corps, and when Peter was driven out of Jerusalem, she accompanied him upon all his journeys to the churches as well as on all his missionary excursions. The day her illustrious husband yielded up his life, she was thrown to the wild beasts in the arena at Rome.

Thus, this man Peter, an intimate of Jesus, one of the inner circle, went forth from Jerusalem proclaiming the glad tidings of the kingdom with power and glory until the fullness of his ministry had been accomplished. He regarded himself as the recipient of high honors when his captors informed him that he must die as his Master had died, on the cross. Thus was Simon Peter crucified in Rome.

JAMES ZEBEDEE

James, the older of the two Apostle sons of Zebedee, whom Jesus nicknamed "Sons of Thunder", was thirty years old when he became an Apostle. He was married, had four children, and lived near his parents on the outskirts of Capernaum. He was a fisherman, plying his trade in company with his younger brother John and in association with Andrew and Simon. James and his brother, John, enjoyed the advantage of having known Jesus longer than any of the other Apostles.

The able Apostle was a temperamental contradiction. He seemed to possess two natures, both of which were the result of strong feelings. He was particularly impassioned when his indignation was once fully aroused. He had a fiery temper when once it was adequately provoked, but when the storm was over, he was always first to justify and excuse his anger under the pretense that it was wholly an outward show of righteous indignation. Except for these periodic upheavals of wrath, James' personality was much like that of Andrew. He did not have Andrew's discretion or insight into human nature, but he was a much better public speaker. Next to Peter, James was the best public orator among the twelve.

Though James was in no way moody, he could be quiet and withdrawn one day and a very good talker and storyteller the next. He usually talked freely with Jesus, but among the twelve, for days at a time he was the silent man. His one great weakness was these spells of unaccountable silence.

The outstanding feature of James' personality was his ability to see all sides of a proposition. Of all the twelve, he came the nearest to grasping the real importance and significance of Jesus' teachings. Like the rest, he too, was slow at first to comprehend the Master's meaning, but once they had finished their training, he had acquired a superior concept of Jesus' message. James was able to understand a wide range of human nature. He got along well with the versatile Andrew, the impetuous Peter, and his self-contained brother John.

Though James and John had their troubles trying to work together, it was inspiring to observe how well they got along. They did not succeed quite so well as Andrew and Peter, but they did much better than would ordinarily be expected of two brothers, especially such headstrong and determined brothers. But strange as it may seem, these two sons of Zebedee were much more tolerant of each other than they were of strangers. They had great affection for one another. They had always been happy playmates. It was these Sons of Thunder who wanted to call fire down from Heaven to destroy the Samaritans who presumed to show disrespect for their Master. But the untimely death of James greatly modified the powerful temperament of his younger brother John.

The characteristic of Jesus which James most admired was the Master's sympathetic affection. Jesus' understanding interest in the small and the great, the rich and the poor, made a great appeal to him.

James was a well-balanced thinker and planner. Along with Andrew, he was one of the more level-headed of the Apostolic group. He was a vigorous individual but was never in a hurry. He was an excellent balance wheel for Peter.

He was modest and undramatic, a daily server, an unpretentious worker, seeking no special reward when he once grasped something of the real meaning of the kingdom. Even in the story about the mother of James and John, who asked that her sons be granted places on the right hand and the left hand of Jesus, it should be remembered that it was the mother who made this request. When they signified that they were ready to assume such responsibilities, it should be recognized that they understood the dangers accompanying the Master's supposed revolt against the Roman power, and that they were also willing to pay the price. When Jesus asked if they were ready to drink the cup, they replied that they were. It was literally true, that James did drink the cup with the Master, since he was the first of the Apostles to experience martyrdom, being early put to death by beheading with a sword by Herod Agrippa. James was thus the first of the twelve to sacrifice his life upon the new battleground of the kingdom. Herod Agrippa feared James above all the other Apostles. He was indeed often quiet and silent, but he was brave and determined when his convictions were aroused and challenged.

James lived his life to the full, and when the end came, he bore himself with such grace and fortitude that even his accuser and informer, who attended his trial and execution, was so touched that he rushed away from the scene of James' death to join the Apostles of Jesus.

JOHN ZEBEDEE

When he became an Apostle, John was twenty-four years old and was the youngest of the twelve. He was unmarried and lived with his parents in Bethsaida. He was a fisherman and worked with his older brother James in partnership with Andrew and Peter. Both before and after becoming an Apostle, John functioned as the personal agent of Jesus in dealing with the Master's family, and he continued to bear this responsibility as long as Mary, the mother of Jesus, lived.

Since John was the youngest of the twelve and so closely associated with Jesus in his family affairs, he was very dear to the Master, but it cannot be truthfully said that he was "the disciple whom Jesus loved." You would hardly suspect such a magnanimous personality as Jesus to be guilty of showing favoritism, of loving one of his Apostles more than the others. The fact that John was one of the three personal aides of Jesus lent further color to this mistaken idea, not to mention that John, along with his brother, had known Jesus longer than the others.

Peter, James, and John were assigned as personal aides to Jesus soon after they became Apostles. Shortly after the selection of the twelve, and at the time when Jesus appointed Andrew to act as director of the group, he said to Andrew: "Now I desire that you assign two or three of your associates to be with me and to remain by my side, to comfort me and to minister to my daily needs." Andrew thought best to select for this special duty the next three first-chosen Apostles. He would have liked to volunteer for such a blessed service himself, but the Master had already given him his commission. So, he immediately directed that Peter, James, and John attach themselves to Jesus.

John Zebedee had many lovely traits of character, but one which was not so lovely was his uncontrolled but usually well-concealed conceit. His long association with Jesus made many and great changes in his character. This conceit was greatly lessened, but after growing old and becoming rather senile, this self-esteem reappeared to a certain extent, so that, when engaged in directing Nathan in the writing of the Gospel which now bears his name, the aged Apostle did not hesitate repeatedly to refer to himself as the: "disciple whom Jesus loved." In view of the fact that John came nearer to being the chum of Jesus than any other Earth mortal, that he was his chosen personal representative in so many matters, it is not strange that he should have come to regard himself as the disciple whom Jesus loved since he most certainly knew he was the disciple whom Jesus so frequently trusted.

The strongest trait in John's character was his dependability. He was prompt and courageous, faithful and devoted. His greatest weakness was this characteristic conceit. He was the youngest member of his father's family and the youngest of the Apostolic Group. Perhaps he was just a bit spoiled. Maybe he had been humored slightly too much. But the John of later years was a very different type of person than the self-admiring and arbitrary young man who joined the ranks of the Apostles when he was twenty-four.

The characteristics that John appreciated most in the Master were his love and unselfishness. These traits made such an impression on him that his whole subsequent life became dominated by the sentiment of love and brotherly devotion. He talked about love and wrote about love. This Son of Thunder became The Apostle of Love. At Ephesus, when the aged leader was no longer able to stand in the pulpit and preach but had to be carried to church in a chair, and when at the close of the service he was asked to say a few words to the believers, for years his only utterance was: "My little children, love one another."

John was a man of few words except when his temper was aroused. He thought much but said little. As he grew older, his temper became more subdued, better controlled, but he never overcame his reluctance to talk. He never fully mastered this inclination to be silent. But he was gifted with a remarkable and creative imagination.

There was another side to John that one would not expect to find in this quiet and introspective type. He was somewhat bigoted and unjustifiably intolerant. In this respect he and James were much alike - they both wanted to call down fire from Heaven on the heads of the disrespectful Samaritans. When John encountered some strangers teaching in Jesus' name, he promptly forbade them. But he was not the only one of the twelve who was tainted with this kind of self-esteem and superiority consciousness.

John's life was tremendously influenced by the sight of Jesus' going about without a home as he knew how faithfully he had made provision for the care of his mother and family. John also deeply sympathized with Jesus because of his family's failure to understand him, being aware that they were gradually withdrawing from him. This entire situation, together with Jesus' ever deferring his slightest wish to the will of the Father in Heaven and his daily life of implicit trust, made such a profound impression on John that it produced marked and permanent changes in his character, changes which manifested themselves throughout his entire subsequent life.

John had a cool and daring courage which few of the other Apostles possessed. He was the one Apostle who followed right along with Jesus the night of his arrest and dared to accompany his Master into the very jaws of death. He was present and near at hand right up to the last earthly hour and was found faithfully carrying out his trust with regard to Jesus' mother and ready to receive such additional instructions as might be given during the last moments of the Master's mortal existence. One thing is certain, John was thoroughly dependable. John usually sat on Jesus' right hand when the twelve sat down to eat. He was the first of the twelve really and fully to believe in the resurrection, and he was the first to recognize the Master when he came to them on the seashore after his resurrection.

John was very closely allied with Peter in the early activities of the Christian movement, becoming one of the chief supporters of the Jerusalem church. He was the right-hand support of Peter on the day of Pentecost.

Several years after the martyrdom of James, John married his brother's widow. The last twenty years of his life he was cared for by a loving granddaughter.

John was in prison several times and was banished to the Isle of Patmos for a period of four years until another Emperor came to power in Rome. Had John not been tactful and shrewd, he would undoubtedly have been killed as was his more outspoken brother James. As the years passed, John, together with James, the brother of Jesus, learned to practice wise conciliation when they appeared before the civil magistrates. They found that a soft answer turns away wrath. They also learned that it was easier to represent the church as a spiritual brotherhood devoted to the social service of mankind rather than as the kingdom of Heaven. They taught about loving service rather than about ruling power, kingdom and kings.

When in temporary exile on Patmos, John wrote the Book of Revelations, which you now have in greatly changed and distorted form. This book contains the surviving fragments of a great revelation, large portions of which were lost, other portions of which were removed, subsequent to John's writing. It is preserved in only fragmentary and changed form and is totally without merit at this point in time.

John traveled much, labored incessantly, and after becoming leader of the Asia churches, settled down at Ephesus. He directed his associate and companion, Nathan, in the writing of the so-called: "Gospel according to John" at Ephesus, when he was ninety-one years old. Of all the twelve Apostles, John eventually became the outstanding theologian. He died a natural death at Ephesus in AD 103 when he was one hundred and one years of age.

Philip the Curious

Philip was the fifth Apostle to be chosen, being called when Jesus and his first four Apostles were on their way from John's rendezvous on the Jordan to Cana of Galilee. Since he lived at Bethsaida, Philip had for some time known of Jesus, but it had not occurred to him that Jesus was a really great man until that day in the Jordan Valley when he said: "Come and follow me." Philip was also somewhat influenced by the fact that Andrew, Peter, James and John had accepted Jesus as the Messiah.

Philip was twenty-seven years of age when he joined the Apostles. He had recently been married, but he had no children at this time. The nickname which the Apostles gave him signified "Curiosity". Philip was always wanting to be shown. He never seemed to see very far into any proposition. He was not necessarily dull, but he lacked imagination. This lack of imagination was the great weakness of his character. He was a commonplace and matter-of-fact individual.

When the Apostles were organized for service, Philip was made steward. It was his duty to see that they were at all times supplied with provisions. He was a good steward. His strongest characteristic was his methodical thoroughness. He was both mathematical and systematic.

Philip came from a family of seven, three boys and four girls. He was next to the oldest, and after the resurrection he baptized his entire family into the kingdom. Philip's people were fisher folk. His father was a very able man, a deep thinker, but his mother was of a very mediocre family. Philip was not a man who could be expected to do big things, but he was a man who could do little things in a big way, do them well and acceptably. Only a few times in four years did he fail to have food on hand to satisfy the needs of all. Even the many emergency demands attendant upon the life they lived seldom found him unprepared. The commissary department of the Apostolic family was intelligently and efficiently managed.

The strong point about Philip was his methodical reliability. The weak point in his make-up was his utter lack of imagination, the absence of the ability to put two and two together to obtain four. He was almost entirely lacking in certain types of imagination. He was the typical every day and commonplace average man. There were a great many such men and women among the multitudes who came to hear Jesus teach and preach, and they obtained great comfort from observing one just like themselves elevated to an honored position in the councils of the Master. They obtained courage from the fact that one like themselves had already found a high place in the affairs of the kingdom. Jesus learned much about the way some human minds function as he so patiently listened to Philip's foolish questions and so many times complied with his steward's request to be shown.

The one quality about Jesus which Philip so continuously admired was the Master's unfailing generosity. Never could Philip find anything in Jesus which was small, or stingy, and he worshipped this ever-present and unfailing unselfishness.

There was little about Philip's personality that was impressive.

He was often spoken of as: "Philip of Bethsaida, the town where Andrew and Peter live." He was almost without perceptive vision. He was unable to grasp the dramatic possibilities of a given situation. He was also greatly lacking in spiritual insight. He would not hesitate to interrupt Jesus in the midst of one of the Master's most profound lessons to ask an apparently foolish question. But Jesus never reprimanded him for such thoughtlessness. He was patient with him and considerate of his inability to grasp the deeper meanings of the teachings. Jesus well knew that, if he once rebuked Philip for asking these annoying questions, he would not only wound this honest soul, but such a reprimand would so hurt Philip that he would never again feel free to ask questions. Jesus knew that in this world there were many thousands and tens of thousands of similar slow-thinking mortals, and he wanted to encourage them all to look to him and always to feel free to come to him with their questions and problems. After all, Jesus was really more interested in Philip's foolish questions than in the sermon he might be preaching. Jesus was greatly interested in men, all kinds of men.

The Apostolic steward was not a good public speaker, but he was a very persuasive and successful personal worker. He was not easily discouraged. He was a plodder and very tenacious in anything he undertook. He had that great and rare gift of saying: "come." When his first convert, Nathaniel, wanted to argue about the merits of Jesus of Nazareth, Philip's effective reply was: "Come and see." He was not a dogmatic preacher who encouraged his hearers to go do this and do that. He met all situations as they arose in his work with: "Come. Come with me, I will show you the way." That is always an effective technique in all forms and phases of teaching. Even parents may learn from Philip the better way of saying to their children not: "Go do this and go do that", but rather: "Come with me while I show and share with you the better way."

The inability of Philip to adapt himself to a new situation was well shown when the Greeks came to him at Jerusalem, saying: "Sir, we desire to see Jesus of Nazareth." Philip would have said to any Jew asking such a question: "Come." But these men were foreigners, and Philip could remember no instruction from his superiors regarding such matters. So, the only thing he could think to do was to consult the Chief of Staff, Andrew, and then they both escorted the inquiring Greeks to Jesus. Likewise, when he went into Samaria preaching and baptizing believers, as he had been instructed by his Master, he refrained from laying hands on his converts in token of their having received the Spirit of Truth. This was done by Peter and John, who presently came down from Jerusalem to observe his work on behalf of the mother church.

Philip went through the trying times of the Master's death, participated in the reorganization of the twelve, and was the first to go forth to win souls for the kingdom outside of the immediate Jewish ranks, being most successful in his work for the Samaritans and in all his subsequent labors in behalf of the gospel.

Philip's wife, who was a strong member of the Women's Corps, became actively associated with her husband in his evangelistic work after their flight from the Jerusalem persecutions. His wife was a fearless woman. She stood at the foot of Philip's cross encouraging him to proclaim the glad tidings even to his murderers, and when his strength failed, she began the recital of the story of salvation by faith in the Heavenly Father. She was silenced only when the irate Jews rushed upon her and stoned her to death. Their eldest daughter, Leah, continued their work, and became the renowned Prophetess of Hierapolis.

Philip, the onetime steward of the twelve, was a mighty man in the kingdom, winning souls wherever he went. He was finally crucified for his faith and buried at Hierapolis.

HONEST NATHANIEL

Nathaniel, the sixth and last of the Apostles to be chosen by the Master himself, was brought to Jesus by his friend Philip. He had been associated in several business enterprises with Philip and, with him, was on the way down to see John the Baptizer when they encountered Jesus.

When Nathaniel joined the Apostles, he was twenty-five years old and was the next to the youngest of the group. He was the youngest of a family of seven, was unmarried, and the only support of aged and infirm parents, with whom he lived in Cana. His brothers and sisters were either married or deceased, and none lived there. Nathaniel and Judas Iscariot were the two best educated men among the twelve.

Nathaniel had planned on becoming a merchant.

Jesus did not give Nathaniel a nickname, but the twelve soon began to speak of him in terms that signified honesty and sincerity.

He was without guile. This was his great virtue. He was both honest and sincere. The weakness of his character was his pride. He was very proud of his family, his city, his reputation, and his nation, all of which is commendable if it is not carried too far. But Nathaniel was inclined to go to extremes with his personal prejudices. He was disposed to prejudge individuals in accordance with his personal opinions. He was not slow to ask the question, even before he had met Jesus: "Can anything good ever come out of Nazareth?" But Nathaniel was not obstinate, even if he was proud. He was quick to reverse himself the moment he looked into the Master's eyes.

In many respects, Nathaniel was the odd genius of the twelve. He was an apostolic philosopher and dreamer, but he was a very practical sort of dreamer. He alternated between seasons of profound philosophy and periods of rare and droll humor. When in the proper mood, he was probably the best storyteller among the twelve. Jesus greatly enjoyed hearing Nathaniel's stories on things both serious and frivolous.

Nathaniel progressively took Jesus and the kingdom more seriously, but never did he take himself seriously.

The Apostles all loved and respected Nathaniel, and he got along with them splendidly, except for Judas Iscariot. Judas did not think Nathaniel took his Apostleship sufficiently seriously and once went secretly to Jesus and complained about him. Jesus said to him: "Judas, watch carefully your steps. Do not give yourself undue importance as an Apostle. Who of us is competent to judge his brother? It is not the Father's will that his children should participate in only the serious things of life. Let me repeat, I have come that my mortal brothers may have joy, gladness, and life more abundantly. Go then, Judas, and do well that which may be required of you to do but leave Nathaniel, your brother, to give account of himself to God." The memory of this, with that of many similar experiences, long lived in the self-deceiving heart of Judas Iscariot.

Many times when Jesus was away on the mountain with Peter, James, and John, and things were becoming tense and tangled among the Apostles, when even Andrew was in doubt about what to say to his disconsolate brothers, Nathaniel would relieve the tension by a bit of philosophy or a flash of good humor.

Nathaniel's duty was to look after the families of the twelve. He was often absent from the apostolic councils. When he heard that sickness or anything out of the ordinary had happened to one of the families, he lost no time in getting to that home. The twelve rested securely in the knowledge that their families' welfare was safe in the hands of Nathaniel.

Nathaniel most revered Jesus for his tolerance. He never grew weary of contemplating the broadmindedness and generous sympathy of the Son of God. Nathaniel's father, Bartholomew, died shortly after Pentecost. He loved his father so much that he changed his name to Bartholomew. This Apostle then went into Mesopotamia, and then into India proclaiming the glad tidings of the kingdom and baptizing believers. His brothers never knew what became of their onetime philosopher, poet, and humorist. He also became a great man in the kingdom and did much to spread his Master's teachings, even though he did not participate in the organization of the subsequent Christian Church. Nathaniel died of old age in India.

Matthew Levi

Matthew, the seventh Apostle, was chosen by Andrew. Matthew belonged to a family of tax gatherers, or publicans, but was himself a customs collector in Capernaum, where he lived. He was thirty-one years old, married and had four children. He was a man of moderate wealth, the only one of any means belonging to the Apostolic Corps. He was a good businessman, a good social mixer, and was gifted with the ability to make friends and to get along smoothly with a great variety of people.

Andrew appointed Matthew the financial representative of the Apostles. He was the fiscal agent and publicity spokesman for the Apostolic organization. He was a keen judge of human nature and a very efficient propagandist. His is a personality difficult to visualize, but he was a very earnest disciple and an increasing believer in the mission of Jesus and in the certainty of the kingdom. Jesus never gave Matthew a nickname, but his fellows commonly referred to him as the: "Money-getter."

Matthew's strong point was his wholehearted devotion to the cause. That he, a publican, had been taken in by Jesus and his Apostles, was the cause for overwhelming gratitude on the part of the former revenue collector. However, it required some time for the rest of the Apostles, especially Simon Zelotes and Judas Iscariot, to become reconciled to the publican's presence in their midst. Matthew's weakness was his shortsighted and materialistic viewpoint of life. But in all these matter he made great progress as the months went by. He also had to be absent from many of the most precious times of instruction as it was his duty to keep the treasury replenished.

It was the Master's forgiving disposition which Matthew most appreciated. He would never cease to recount that faith only was necessary in the business of finding God. He always liked to speak of the kingdom as: "this business of finding God."

Though Matthew was a man with a past, he gave an excellent account of himself, and as time went on, his associates became proud of the publican's performances. He was one of the Apostles who made extensive notes on the sayings of Jesus, and these notes were used as the basis of Isador's subsequent narrative of the sayings and doings of Jesus, which have become known as the Gospel According to Matthew.

The great and useful life of Matthew, the businessman and customs collector of Capernaum, has been the means of leading thousands upon thousands of other businessmen, public officials, and politicians, through the subsequent ages, to hear that engaging voice of the master saying: "Come and follow me." Matthew really was a shrewd politician, but he was intensely loyal to Jesus and devoted to the task of seeing that the messengers of the coming kingdom were adequately financed.

The presence of Matthew among the twelve was the means of keeping the doors of the kingdom wide open to many downhearted and outcast souls who had regarded themselves as long since outside the bounds of religious acceptability. Outcast and despairing men and women flocked to hear Jesus, and he never turned a single one away.

Matthew received freely tendered offerings from believing disciples and the immediate audience of the Master's teachings, but he never openly solicited funds from the multitudes. He did all his financial work in a quiet and personal way and raised most of the money among the wealthier class of interested believers. He gave practically the whole of his modest fortune to the work of the Master and his Apostles, but they never knew of this generosity, except for Jesus, who knew all about it. Matthew hesitated openly to contribute to the Apostolic funds for fear that Jesus and his associates might regard his money as being tainted. So, he gave much in the names of other believers. During the earlier months, when Matthew knew his presence among them was more or less of a trial, he was strongly tempted to let them know that his funds often supplied them with their daily bread, but he never yielded to this temptation. When evidence of the dislike of the publican would surface, Matthew would burn to reveal to them his generosity, but always he managed to keep quiet.

When the funds for the week were short of the estimated requirements, Matthew would often draw heavily upon his own personal resources. Sometimes when he became greatly interested in Jesus' teaching, he preferred to remain and hear the instructions, even though he knew he must personally make up for his failure to solicit the necessary funds. But Matthew always wished that Jesus might know that much of the money came from his own pocket. Little did he realize that the Master knew all about it. The Apostles all died without ever knowing that Matthew was their greatest benefactor. Matthew had given so much of his own wealth to the Apostolic Corps and their families, that when he went forth to proclaim the gospel of the kingdom after the beginning of the persecutions, he was practically penniless.

When the persecutions caused the believers to leave Jerusalem, Matthew journeyed north, preaching the gospel of the kingdom and baptizing believers. He was lost to the knowledge of his former apostolic associates, but on he went, preaching and baptizing through Syria, Cappadocia, Galatia, Bithynia and Thrace. It was in Thrace, at Lysimachia, that disbelieving Jews conspired with the Roman soldiers to cause his death. This regenerated publican died triumphant in the faith of a salvation he had so surely learned from the teachings of the Master during his recent life on Earth.

THOMAS DIDYMUS

Thomas was the eighth Apostle and was chosen by Philip. In later times he became known as: "Doubting Thomas," but his fellows hardly looked upon him as a chronic doubter. True, his was a logical, skeptical type of mind, but he had a form of courageous loyalty which forbade those who knew him intimately to regard him as a skeptic.

When Thomas joined the Apostles, he was twenty-nine years old, was married, and had four children. Formerly he had been a carpenter and stone mason, but later he had become a fisherman and resided at Tarichea, situated on the west bank of the Jordan where it flows out of the Sea of Galilee. He was regarded as the leading citizen of this little village. He had very little education, but he possessed a keen, reasoning mind and was the son of excellent parents, who lived at Tiberias.

Thomas had the one truly analytical mind of the twelve. He was the real scientist of the Apostolic group.

The early home life of Thomas had been unfortunate. His parents were not altogether happy in their married life, and this was reflected in Thomas' adult experience. He grew up having a very disagreeable and quarrelsome disposition. Even his wife was glad to see him join the Apostles. She was relieved by the thought that her pessimistic husband would be away from home most of the time. Thomas also had a streak of suspicion which made it very difficult to get along peaceably with him. Peter was very much upset by Thomas at first, complaining to his brother, Andrew, that Thomas was: "mean, ugly, and always suspicious of everyone." But the better his associates knew Thomas, the more they liked him. They found he was superbly honest and unflinchingly loyal. He was perfectly sincere and unquestionably truthful, but he was a natural-born faultfinder and had grown up to become a real pessimist. His analytical mind had become cursed with suspicion. He was rapidly losing faith in his fellow man when he became associated with the twelve and thus came in contact with the noble character of Jesus. This association with the Master began at once to transform Thomas' whole disposition and to effect great changes in his mental reactions to his fellow men.

Thomas' great strength was his fine analytical mind coupled with his unflinching courage, when he had once made up his mind. His great weakness was his suspicious doubting, which he never fully overcame throughout his whole lifetime in the flesh.

In the organization of the twelve, Thomas was assigned to arrange and manage the itinerary, and he was an able director of the work and movements of the Apostolic Corps. He was a good executive, an excellent businessman, but he was handicapped by his many moods. He was one man one day and another man the next. He was inclined toward melancholic brooding when he joined the Apostles but contact with Jesus and the Apostles largely cured him of this fault.

Jesus enjoyed Thomas very much and had many long, personal talks with him. His presence among the Apostles was a great comfort to all honest doubters and encouraged many troubled minds to come into the kingdom, even if they could not wholly understand everything about the spiritual and philosophic teachings of Jesus. Thomas' membership in the twelve was a standing declaration that Jesus loved even the honest doubters.

The other Apostles held Jesus in reverence because of some special and outstanding trait of his replete personality, but Thomas revered his Master because of his well-balanced character. Increasingly Thomas admired and honored one who was so lovingly merciful yet so just and fair; so firm but never obstinate; so calm but never indifferent; so helpful and so sympathetic but never meddlesome or dictatorial; so strong but at the same time so gentle; so positive but never rough or rude; so tender but never vacillating; so pure and innocent but at the same time so virile, aggressive, and forceful; so truly courageous but never rash or foolhardy; such a lover of nature but so free from all tendency to revere nature; so humorous and so playful, but so free from frivolity. It was this matchless symmetry of personality that so charmed Thomas. He probably enjoyed the highest intellectual understanding and personality appreciation of Jesus of any of the twelve.

In the councils of the twelve, Thomas was always cautious, following a policy of safety first, but if his conservatism was voted down or overruled, he was always the first fearlessly to move out in execution of the program decided upon. Again and again, he would stand out against some project as being foolhardy and presumptuous. He would debate to the bitter end, but when

Andrew would put the proposition to a vote, and after the twelve would elect to do that which he had so strenuously opposed, Thomas was the first to say, "Let's go." He was a good loser. He did not hold grudges nor nurse wounded feelings.

Many times, he opposes letting Jesus expose himself to danger, but when the Master would decide to take such risks, it was always Thomas who rallied the Apostles with his courageous words: "Come on my brothers, let us go and die with him."

Thomas was in some respects just like Philip. He also wanted "to be shown," but his outward expressions of doubt were based on entirely different intellectual operations. Thomas was analytical, not merely skeptical. As far as personal physical courage was concerned, he was one of the bravest among the twelve.

Thomas had some very bad days. He was depressed and downcast at times. The loss of his twin sister when he was nine years old had caused him much youthful sorrow and had added to his temperamental problems of later life. When Thomas would become depressed, sometimes it was Nathaniel who helped him to recover, sometimes Peter, and frequently one of the Alpheus twins. When he was most depressed, unfortunately he always tried to avoid coming in direct contact with Jesus. But the Master knew all about this and had an understanding sympathy for his Apostle when he was thus afflicted with depression and harassed by doubts.

Sometimes Thomas would get permission from Andrew to go off by himself for a day or two. But he soon learned that such a course was not wise. He early found that it was best, when he was in depression, to stick close to his work and to remain near his associates. But no matter what happened in his emotional life, he kept right on being an Apostle. When the time came to move forward, it was always Thomas who said: "Let's go."

Thomas is a great example of a human being who has doubts, faces them, and wins. He had a great mind. He was no carping critic. He was a logical thinker. He was the acid test of Jesus and his fellow Apostles. If Jesus and his work had not been genuine, it could not have held a man like Thomas from the start to the finish. He had a keen and sure sense of fact. At the first appearance of fraud or deception, Thomas would have walked away from them all. Scientists may not fully understand all about Jesus and his work on Earth, but there lived and worked with the Master and his human associates a man whose mind was that of a true scientist, Thomas Didymus, and he wholeheartedly believed in Jesus of Nazareth.

Thomas had a difficult time during the days of the trial and crucifixion. He was for a time in the depths of despair and depression, but he rallied his courage, stuck to the Apostles, and was present with them to welcome Jesus on the Sea of Galilee. For a while he gave in to his doubting depression but eventually renewed his faith and courage. He gave wise counsel to the Apostles after Pentecost and, when persecutions scattered the believers, went to Cyprus, Crete, the North African coast, and Sicily, preaching the glad tidings of the kingdom and baptizing believers. Thomas continued preaching and baptizing until he was apprehended by soldiers of the Roman government and was put to death in Malta. Just a few weeks before his death he had begun the writing of the life and teachings of Jesus.

James and Judas Alpheus

James and Judas, the twin sons of Alpheus, fishermen living near Kheresa, were the ninth and tenth Apostles and were chosen by James and John Zebedee. They were twenty-six years old and married.

James had three children, and Judas had two.

There is not much to say about these two common fishermen.

They loved their master, and he loved them also, but they never interrupted his teachings with questions. They understood very little about the philosophical discussions or the theological debates of their fellow Apostles, but they rejoiced to find themselves numbered among such a group of mighty men. These two men were almost identical in personal appearance, mental characteristics, and extent of spiritual perception. What may be said of one should be recorded of the other.

Andrew assigned them to the work of policing the multitudes. They were the chief ushers of the preaching hours, and the general servants and errand runners for the twelve. They helped Philip with the supplies, they carried money to the families for Nathaniel, and always they were ready to lend a helping hand to any of the others no matter what the need.

The multitudes of common people were greatly encouraged to find two like themselves honored with places among the Apostles. By their very acceptance as Apostles these mediocre twins were the means of bringing many weak believers into the kingdom. The common people also liked the idea of being directed and managed by official ushers who were common people just like themselves.

James and Judas were also known by some as Thaddeus and Lebbeus. They had neither strong points nor weak points.

The nicknames given them by the others were good natured designations meaning: "Mediocre." They were the: "least of all the Apostles." They knew it and were cheerful about it.

James Alpheus especially loved Jesus because of the Master's simplicity. These twins could not comprehend the mind of Jesus, but they did grasp the sympathetic bond between themselves and the heart of their Master. Their minds were not of a high order, but they had a real experience in their spiritual natures. They believed in Jesus. They were Sons of God and fellows in the kingdom.

Judas Alpheus was drawn to the Master because of his genuine humility. Such humility linked with such personal dignity made a great appeal to Judas. The fact that Jesus would always ask that his miraculous acts be kept confidential made a great impression on this simple child of nature.

These twins were good natured, mild-mannered helpers, and everybody loved them. The Master welcomed these young men of one talent to positions of honor on his personal staff in the kingdom because there were millions of other such simple and fear-controlled souls in the world whom he likewise wished to welcome into active and believing fellowship with himself and his outpoured Spirit of Truth. Jesus did not look down upon littleness, only upon evilness. James and Judas were little, but they were also good and faithful. They were simple, but they were also big-hearted, kind and generous.

How gratefully proud were these humble men on that day when the Master refused to accept a certain rich man as an evangelist unless he would sell his goods and help the poor. When the people heard this and saw the twins among his counselors, they knew for sure that the Master did not favor one man over another. Only a divine institution, the kingdom of Heaven, could have ever been built upon such a mediocre human foundation.

The twins served faithfully until the end, until the dark days of trial, crucifixion, and despair. They never lost their faith in Jesus, and they were the first to believe in his resurrection. But they could not comprehend the establishment of the kingdom. Soon after their Master was crucified, they returned to their families and their fishing nets.

Their work was done. They did not have the ability to go on in the more complex battles of the kingdom. But they lived and died conscious of having been honored and blessed with four years of close and personal association with the Son of God.

SIMON THE ZEALOT

Simon Zelotes, the eleventh Apostle, was chosen by Simon Peter.

He was an able man of good ancestry and lived with his family at Capernaum. He was twenty-eight years old when he was called. He was a fiery agitator and was also a man who spoke much without thinking. He had been a merchant in Capernaum before he turned his entire attention to the patriotic organization of the Zealots.

Simon was put in charge of the rest and relaxation of the Apostolic group, and he became a very efficient organizer of the play and recreational life of the twelve. Simon's strength was his inspirational loyalty. When the Apostles found a man or woman who floundered in indecision about entering the kingdom, they would send for Simon. It usually required only about fifteen minutes for this enthusiastic advocate of salvation through faith in God to settle all doubts and remove all indecision, to see a new soul born into the: "liberty of faith and the joy of salvation."

Simon's great weakness was his material-mindedness. He could not quickly change himself from a Jewish national to a spiritually minded internationalist. Four years was too short a time in which to make such an intellectual and emotional transformation, but the Master was always patient with him.

The one thing about Jesus which Simon so much admired was the Master's calmness, his assurance, poise, and inexplicable composure.

Although Simon was a rabid revolutionist, a fearless firebrand of agitation, he gradually subdued his fiery nature until he became a powerful and effective preacher of: "peace on Earth and good will among all men." Simon was a great debater. He loved to argue. When it came to dealing with the legalistic minds of the educated Jews, or the intellectual quibbling of the Greeks, the task was always assigned to Simon.

He was a rebel by nature and an iconoclast by training, but Jesus won him for the higher concepts of the kingdom of Heaven. He had always identified himself with the party of protest, but he now joined the party of progress, unlimited and eternal progression of spirit and truth. Simon was a man of intense loyalties and warm personal devotions, and he did profoundly love Jesus.

Jesus was not afraid to identify himself with businessmen, laboring men, optimists, pessimists, philosophers, skeptics, publicans, politicians, or patriotic zealots.

The Master had many private talks with Simon, but he never fully succeeded in making an internationalist out of this ardent Jewish nationalist. Jesus often told Simon that it was proper to want to see the social, economic, and political orders improved, but he would always add: "That is not the business of the kingdom of Heaven. We must be dedicated to the doing of the Father's will. Our business is to be ambassadors of a spiritual government on high, and we must not immediately concern ourselves with anything but the representation of the will and character of the Divine Father who stands at the head of the government whose credentials we bear." It was all very difficult for Simon to comprehend, but gradually he began to grasp something of the meaning of the Master's teachings.

After the dispersion because of the Jerusalem persecutions, Simon went into temporary retirement. He was literally crushed. As a nationalist patriot he had surrendered to Jesus' teachings. Now all was lost. He was in despair, but in a few years, he rallied his hopes and went forth to proclaim the gospel of the kingdom.

He went to Alexandria and, after working up the Nile, penetrated into the heart of Africa, everywhere preaching the Gospel of Jesus and baptizing believers. Thus, he labored until he was an old and feeble man. He died and was buried in the heart of Africa.

Judas Iscariot

Judas Iscariot, the twelfth Apostle to be called, was chosen by Nathaniel and was the only real Jew of the twelve. He was born in Kerioth, a small town in Southern Judea. When he was a lad, his parents moved to Jericho, where he lived and had been employed in his father's various business enterprises until he became interested in the preaching and work of John the Baptizer. Judas' parents were Sadducees, and when their son joined John's disciples, they disowned him.

When Nathaniel met Judas at Tarichea, he was seeking employment with a fish-drying enterprise at the lower end of the Sea of Galilee. He was thirty years old and unmarried. He was probably the best educated man among the twelve. Judas had no outstanding trait of personal strength, though he had many outwardly appearing traits of culture and habits of training. He was a good thinker but not always a truly honest thinker. Judas did not really understand himself. He was not really sincere in dealing with himself.

Andrew appointed Judas treasurer of the twelve, a position which he was eminently qualified to hold, and up to the time of the betrayal of his master he discharged the responsibilities of his office honestly, faithfully, and most efficiently.

There was no special trait about Jesus which Judas admired above the generally attractive and exquisitely charming personality of the Master. Judas was never able to rise above his Judean prejudices against his Galilean associates. He would even criticize in his mind many things about Jesus. The Master whom eleven of the Apostles looked upon as the perfect man, as the: "One altogether lovely and the chief among ten thousand," this self-satisfied Judean often dared to criticize in his own heart. He really entertained the notion that Jesus was timid and somewhat afraid to assert his complete power and authority.

Judas was a good businessman. It required tact, ability, and patience, as well as painstaking devotion, to manage the financial affairs of such an idealist as Jesus, to say nothing of wrestling with the haphazard business methods of some of his Apostles. Judas really was a great executive and a farseeing and able financier. He was a stickler for the organization. None of the twelve ever criticized Judas. As far as they could see, Judas was a matchless treasurer, a learned man, a loyal Apostle, and in every sense of the word a great success. The Apostles all loved Judas. He was really one of them. He believed in Jesus, but never really loved the Master with a whole heart. The case of Judas illustrates the truthfulness of that saying: "There is a way that seems right to a man, but the path ends in death." It is completely possible to fall victim to the peaceful deception of the paths of sin and death. Be assured that Judas was always financially loyal to his Master and his fellow Apostles. Money was not the motive for the betrayal.

Judas was the only son of unwise parents. When very young, he was pampered and petted. He was a spoiled child. As he grew up, he had exaggerated ideas about his self-importance. He was a very poor loser. He had loose and distorted ideas about fairness. He was given to the indulgence of hate and suspicion. He was an expert at misinterpretation of the words and acts of his friends. All through his life Judas had cultivated the habit of getting even with those whom he thought had mistreated him. His sense of values and loyalty was defective.

To Jesus, Judas was a faith adventure. From the beginning the Master fully understood the weakness of this Apostle and well knew that dangers of admitting him to the brotherhood. But it is the nature of the Sons of God to give every mortal creature a full and equal chance for salvation and survival in the worlds of space and time. Jesus wanted the mortals of this world to know that, when doubts exist as to the sincerity and wholeheartedness of a mortals devotion to the kingdom, it is the invariable practice of the Father in Heaven to receive the doubtful candidate. The doorway to eternal life is wide open to all. There are no restrictions or qualifications except for the faith of the one who wants to enter.

This is just the reason why Jesus permitted Judas to go on to the very end, always doing everything possible to transform and save this weak and confused Apostle. But when light is not honestly received and lived up to, it tends to become darkness within the soul. Judas grew intellectually regarding Jesus' teachings about the kingdom, but he did not make progress in the acquisition of spiritual character as did the other Apostles. He failed to make satisfactory personal progress in spiritual experience.

Judas became increasingly a brooder over personal disappointments, and finally he became a victim of resentment. His feelings had many times been hurt, and he grew unreasonably suspicious of his best friends, even of the Master. Presently he became obsessed with the idea of getting even, anything to avenge himself, even betrayal of his associates and the Master.

These wicked and dangerous ideas did not take definite shape until the day when a grateful woman opened an expensive box of oil and poured it on Jesus' feet. This seemed wasteful to Judas, and when his public protest was so sweepingly disallowed by Jesus right there in the hearing of all, it was too much for Judas. That event was the final act that he could tolerate, and, at that moment, he determined the mobilization of all the accumulated hate, hurt, malice, prejudice, jealousy, and revenge of a lifetime. He made up his mind to get even with someone. He crystallized all the evil of his nature upon the one innocent person in all the sordid drama of his unfortunate life just because Jesus happened to be the chief actor in the episode which marked his passing from the progressive kingdom of light into that self- chosen domain of darkness.

The Master many times, both privately and publicly, had warned Judas that he was slipping, but divine warnings are usually useless in dealing with embittered human nature. Jesus did everything possible, consistent with man's moral freedom, to prevent Judas' choosing to go the wrong way. The great test finally came. The son of resentment failed. He yielded to the sour and sordid dictates of a proud and vengeful mind, a mind of exaggerated self-importance, and swiftly plunged himself into confusion, despair, and depravity.

Judas then entered into the shameful intrigue to betray his Master and quickly carried the dark scheme into effect. During the working of his anger-conceived plans of traitorous betrayal, he experienced moments of regret and shame, and in these sane moments he faintheartedly conceived, as a defense in his own mind, the idea that Jesus might possibly exert his immense powers and save himself at the last moment.

When the wicked and awful business was over, this renegade mortal, who thought lightly of selling his friend for thirty pieces of silver to satisfy his long-nursed craving for revenge, rushed out and committed the final act in the drama of fleeing from the realities of life - he committed suicide.

The eleven Apostles were horrified, stunned. Jesus regarded the betrayer only with pity. The celestial world has found it difficult to forgive Judas. His name is infamous throughout the Heavenly Realms just as it is on Earth.

CHAPTER 5

Sermon on the Mount

THE SERMON ON THE MOUNT, ONE OF THE MOST BEAUTIFUL and inspiring of all of the teachings of Jesus, was the ordination sermon for his twelve Apostles, to tell them what their life work would be for the rest of their earthly existence as he prepared to send them out into the world two by two to teach in all the villages of Palestine.

One bright morning in the springtime after he had been teaching them for some time, and at a time when he thought they were ready to go out into the world, he gathered them all together and told them that the time had come for him to instruct them on what their lifework would be for the rest of their earthly existence. He sat them down on the ground in a circle and began to address them. Here is his message restated in modern words.

"The new kingdom which my Father in Heaven is about to set up in the hearts of his children on Earth is to be an everlasting dominion. There shall be no end to his rule in the hearts of those who desire to do his divine work. I say to you that my Father is not the God of Jew or Gentile. He is the God of all who come from East and West, North and South, of all lands and all peoples.

The power of his kingdom shall consist, not in the strength of armies nor in the might of riches, but rather in the glory of the divine spirit that has come to teach the minds and rule the hearts of the citizens of this Heavenly kingdom, the sons and daughters of God. This is the brotherhood of love where righteousness reigns, and whose battle cry shall forever be: Peace on Earth, goodwill towards all men. The kingdom which you are soon to go forth proclaiming, is the desire of the good men of all ages, the hope of all the Earth, and the fulfillment of the wise promises of many prophets throughout the ages.

But for you my twelve precious men, and for those who will follow in your footsteps into this kingdom, there is a severe test. Faith alone will pass you through the portals, but you must also bring forth the fruits of my Father's spirit if you are to continue to ascend in the progressive life of the divine spirit. Not everyone who says, 'Father, Father' will enter the kingdom of Heaven, but rather they who do the will of my Father who is in Heaven.

Your message from this day forward must be: Seek first the kingdom of God and his righteousness, and in finding these, all other things essential to eternal survival shall be secured there. I want to make it clear to you that this kingdom of my Father will not come with an outward show of power or with unseemly demonstration. You are not to go forth proclaiming that the kingdom is here, or that the kingdom is there. The kingdom of which you shall preach from now on is God is within you.

Whosoever of you seeks to become great in my Father's service shall become a minister to all, and whosoever seeks to become first among you, let him become the server of his brothers. So shall this kingdom progress in this world until it shall break down every barrier and bring all men to know my Father and believe in the saving truth which I have come to declare. Even now, the kingdom of God is at hand.

This humble gathering which your eyes behold, this small beginning of twelve common men, shall multiply and grow until eventually the whole of the Earth shall be filled with the praise of my Father. It will not be so much by the words that you will speak as by the lives that you must lead that men will come to know that you have been with me and have learned of my Father's kingdom. I will lay no grievous burdens on your mind, but I am about to put on your souls the solemn responsibility of representing me in the world when I leave to return to my Father's kingdom."

Jesus then had the Apostles kneel in a circle around him. He touched each one on the head and blessed him. Then he extended his hands and prayed:" My Father in Heaven, I bring to you these humble men, my messengers. From among your children on Earth I have chosen these twelve to go forth to represent me as I came forth to represent you on Earth. Love them and be with them as you have loved me and been with me. Give these men wisdom as I place all the affairs of your kingdom in their hands. I thank you Father for these men, and I commit them to your safe keeping while I go on to finish the work which you have given me."

After many minutes of prayer and reflection, the Apostles each in turn stood up and hugged Jesus. None said a word. They were overcome with so much love. They all knew at that very moment that the kingdom of Heaven had been placed in the hands of men of the Earth.

Now Jesus sat them down around him once more and began his sermon: "Now that you are ambassadors of my Father's kingdom, you have become a class of men separate and distinct from all other men on Earth. You are not now as men among men but as the enlightened citizens of another and Heavenly realm living among the ignorant creatures of this backward and dark world. It is not enough that you live as you were before this hour, but from now on you must live as those who have tasted the glories of a better life and have been sent back to Earth as ambassadors of the king of that new and better world. Of the teacher, more is expected than of the pupil. Of the master, more is expected than of the servant. Of the citizens of a Heavenly kingdom, more is expected than of the citizens of this world. Some of the things I will say to you will seem hard, but you have elected to represent me in the world even as I now represent the Father. As my representatives on Earth, you will be obligated to abide by those teachings and practices which are reflective of my ideals of mortal living in this world."

"I send you forth to proclaim liberty to the spiritual captives, joy to those in the bondage of fear, and to heal the sick in accordance with the will of my Father in Heaven. When you find my brothers in distress, speak encouragingly to them saying:

> Happy are the poor in spirit, the humble, for theirs
> are the treasures of the kingdom of Heaven.
> Happy are they who hunger and thirst for
> righteousness, for they shall be filled.

Happy are the meek, for they shall inherit the Earth. Happy are the pure in heart, for they shall see God. Happy are they who mourn, for they shall be comforted.

Happy are they who weep, for they shall receive the spirit of rejoicing. Happy are the merciful, for they shall obtain mercy.

Happy are the peacemakers, for they shall be called the sons of God. Happy are they who are persecuted for righteousness' sake, for theirs is the kingdom of Heaven. Happy are you when men shall revile you and persecute you and shall say all manner of evil against you falsely.

Rejoice and be exceedingly glad, for great is your reward in Heaven." "My brothers, as I send you forth into the world, you shall be the salt of the Earth, salt with a saving flavor. If this salt has lost its flavor, wherewith shall the Earth be salted?

You must be the light of the world. A city set upon a hill cannot be hidden. Neither do men light a candle and put it under a basket, but on a candlestick for all to see. It gives light to all who are in the house. Let your light so shine before men that they may see your good works and be led to glorify your Father in Heaven.

I am sending you into the world to represent me and to act as ambassadors of my Fathers' kingdom. As you go forth to proclaim the good news, put your trust in the Father whose messengers you are. Do not forcibly resist injustice. Put not your trust in the arm of the flesh. If your neighbor strikes you on the right cheek, turn to him the other also. Be willing to suffer injustice rather than to go to law among you or your brothers. In kindness and with mercy minister to all who are in distress and in need.

Love your enemies. Do good to those who hate you. Bless those who curse you. Pray for those who spitefully use you. Whatsoever you believe that I would do for my brothers, do you also for my brothers.

Your Father in Heaven makes the sunshine on evil as well as on good. He sends rain on the just as well as on the unjust. You are the sons of God, even more, you are now the ambassadors of God, therefore be merciful to all your brothers, even as God is merciful to all, good and evil alike.

You are commissioned to save men, not to judge them. At the end of your earthly life, you all expect God to be merciful on your souls, therefore do I entrust you during your mortal life to be merciful to all of your brothers in the flesh. Make not the mistake of trying to pluck a splinter out of your brothers' eye when there is a log in yours. First remove the log from your eye, then you will be able to see much better to remove the splinter from your brothers' eye.

Understand truth clearly. Live the righteous life fearlessly, and so shall you be my Apostles and my Fathers' ambassadors. You have heard me say, 'If the blind lead the blind, they shall both fall into the pit'. If you want to guide others into the kingdom, you must walk in the clear light of living truth. In all the business of the kingdom, I request that you show just judgment and keen wisdom.

I warn you against false prophets who will come to you in sheep's clothing, while on the inside they are like ravening wolves. By their fruits you shall know them. Do men gather grapes from thorns or figs from thistles? Every good tree brings forth good fruit, but the bad tree brings forth bad fruit. A good tree cannot bear bad fruit, neither can a bad tree bear good fruit. In gaining an entrance into the kingdom of Heaven, it is the motive that counts. My Father looks into the hearts of men and judges by their inner longings and their sincere intentions.

On the day of judgment in the kingdom of Heaven, many will come to me and say, 'Did we not prophesy in your name and by your name do many things?' But I will say to them, 'I never knew you.

Depart from me you who are false teachers. You never had faith in my Father. You only used his name for your own grandiose schemes of selfishness.' Everyone who hears my message and sincerely executes his commission to represent me before men even as I have represented my Father to you, shall find an abundant entrance into my Father's kingdom. Now go into the world and minister and love your brothers as I have loved you and as my Father has loved us all."

This beautiful Sermon on the Mount was Jesus' ordination charge to the twelve Apostles. It was the Master's personal commission to each one of them to go out and preach the gospel and represent him in the world of men even as he was so eloquently representing his Father in Heaven.

The universal meanings that Jesus had taught the Apostles, and which he reiterated in this sermon, were as follows:

1. You are the salt of the Earth.

    In Jesus' time, salt was precious. It was even used for money. Salt not only flavors food, but it also preserves it. It serves best by being used or spent. If you are to serve God, you must give of yourself unselfishly.

2. By their fruits you shall know them.

   Personality is basically changeless. What changes is the moral character. Moral worth cannot be derived from mere repression, obeying the injunction: "Thou shall not." Fear and shame are very poor motivations for religious living. Religion is valid only when it reveals that God is our Father and that we are all brothers. The major error of religions throughout history has been negativism. Strong characters are not derived from not doing wrong, they are derived from doing right. There is a world of difference. Unselfishness is the badge of human greatness. The highest levels of spiritual growth are reached by worship, and by service to others. The happy and effective person is motivated, not by the fear of doing wrong, but by the love and joy of doing right, true spirituality.

3. You are the light of the world.

   While light dispels darkness, it can also be so blinding as to confuse and frustrate. We are reminded to let our light so shine that our fellow brothers will be guided into new and Godly paths of elevated living, but our light should so shine as not to attract attention to ourselves, but to God. Even one's vocation can be utilized as an effective reflector for the spreading of this light of life.

4. Happy are the poor in spirit, the humble.

   To a child, happiness is the satisfaction of immediate pleasure cravings. The adult is willing to sow seeds of self-denial in order to reap subsequent harvests of happiness.

In Jesus' time and since, happiness has all too often been associated with the idea of the possession of wealth. In the story of the Pharisee and the Publican praying in the temple, the one felt rich in spirit - egotistical. The other felt poor in spirit - humble. One was self-sufficient. The other was teachable and truth-seeking. The poor in spirit seek for goals of spiritual wealth, for God. Such seekers after truth do not have to wait for rewards in the distant future. They are rewarded now. They find the kingdom of Heaven within their very own hearts, and they experience such happiness now, and come to understand when Jesus said, "The kingdom of Heaven is here and now."

5. Happy are they who hunger and thirst for righteousness, for they shall be filled.

Only those who feel poor in spirit will ever hunger for God. Only the humble seek divine strength and crave spiritual power. But it is most dangerous to knowingly engage in spiritual fasting in order to improve one's appetite for spiritual endowment. Physical fasting becomes dangerous after four or five days. one is apt to lose all desire for food. So, it is in spiritual fasting. You are in danger of losing your appetite for spirituality. Prolonged fasting, either physical or spiritual, tends to destroy hunger. A life in grace is a pleasure, not a duty.

Jesus' love was a dynamic love, fatherly and brotherly. It was not the negative or, thou-shalt-not, type of righteousness. How can you ever hunger for something that is negative?

6. Happy are the meek, for they shall inherit the Earth. Meekness has no relation to fear. It is rather an attitude of man co- operating with God: "Your will be done". It embraces patience and forbearance and is motivated by an unshakable faith in a benevolent and friendly universe. It masters all temptations to rebel against God. Jesus was the ideal meek man in that he never lost sight of the philosophy he came to teach, "Your will be done, Father."

7. Happy are the pure in heart, for they shall see God.

Spiritual purity is not a negative quality. It lacks suspicion and revenge. In discussing purity, Jesus did not intend to deal with human sexual attitudes. He referred to that faith which man should have in his fellow man, that faith which a parent has in his child, and which enables man to love his fellows even as a father would love them. A father's love needs not pamper. It does not condone evil. Fatherly love has a single purpose, and it always looks for the best in its children. That is the attitude of a true parent.

To see God means to find true spiritual insight. When you come to know the Father, you become confident in the assurance of being a son of God, and you can increasingly love all of your brothers in the flesh, not only as a brother, brotherly love, but also as a father, with fatherly affection.

It is easy to teach this to a child. Children are naturally trustful, and parents should see to it that they do not lose that simple faith. In dealing with children, avoid all deception and refrain from suggesting suspicion. Wisely help them choose their heroes and select their lifework.

8. Happy are they who mourn, for they shall be comforted. Common sense would never suggest that happiness could be derived from mourning. Jesus did not refer to outward or ostentatious mourning. He referred to an emotional state-of-mind of tenderheartedness. It is a great error to teach boys and young men that it is unmanly to show tenderness or otherwise to give evidence of emotional feeling or physical suffering. Sympathy is a worthy attribute of the male as well as the female. It is not necessary to be tough and callous to be manly. This is the wrong way to create courageous men.

The world's greatest men have not been afraid to mourn. Being sensitive and caring of human needs creates genuine and lasting happiness, while such kindly attitudes safeguard the soul from the destructive influences of anger, hate, and suspicion.

9. Happy are the merciful for they shall obtain mercy.

Mercy here denotes the height and depth and breadth of the truest friendship - loving kindness. Mercy sometimes may be passive, but here it is active and dynamic. A loving parent experiences little difficulty in forgiving his child. In an unspoiled child, the urge to relieve suffering is natural.

10. Happy are the peacemakers, they shall be called the sons of God.

The Jews of Jesus' time were longing for military deliverance, not for peacemakers. But Jesus' peace is not of the pacifist and negative kind. In the face of trials and persecutions he said, "My peace I leave with you. Let not your heart be troubled, neither let it be afraid". This is the peace that prevents ruinous conflicts. Personal peace creates strong personalities. Social peace prevents fear, greed, and anger.

Political peace prevents race antagonisms, national suspicions, and war. Peacemaking is the cure of distrust and suspicion.

Children can easily be taught to become peacemakers. They enjoy team activities. They like to play together. Jesus once said, "Whosoever shall save his life shall lose it, but whosoever shall lose his life shall find it." Go and find your peace with all your brothers.

11. Happy are they who are persecuted for righteousness' sake, for theirs is the kingdom of Heaven.

So often, persecution follows peace. But young people and brave adults never shun difficulty or danger. Jesus said:"Greater love has no man than to lay down his life for his friends." A fatherly love can freely do all these things - things that brotherly love can hardly encompass. Progress has always been the final harvest of persecution.

These beautiful beatitudes of the Sermon on the Mount are based on faith, hope and love. Fatherly love delights in returning good for evil, and in doing good in retaliation for injustice. Take these truths that Jesus taught to the Apostles and to the masses and apply them to your daily life and you will soon come to realize what perfect wisdom love is.

CHAPTER 6

The Public Ministry

J ESUS BEGAN HIS PUBLIC WORK AT THE HEIGHT OF THE POPULAR
interest in John's preaching and at a time when the Jewish
people of Palestine were eagerly looking for the appearance of the
Messiah. There was a great contrast between John and Jesus. John
was an eager and earnest worker, but Jesus was a calm and happy
laborer. Only a few times in his entire life was Jesus ever in a hurry.
Jesus came as a comforting consolation to the world. To those who
came to know him, he became somewhat of an example. John was
hardly a comfort or an example.

He preached about the Heavenly realms but never quite
discovered the joy of it. Though Jesus often spoke of John as the
greatest of the prophets of the old order, he also stated that the
least of those who saw the great light of the new way and entered
Heaven thereby was indeed greater than John.

When John preached about the coming of the new covenant,
the burden of his message was: repent, flee from the wrath to

come. When Jesus began to preach about the new covenant, there was some admonition to repent from wrongdoing, but such a message was always followed by the gospel, the good message of the joy and liberty of the new way of life and the living the righteous way in harmony with nature and with all men.

The Jews of those days entertained many ideas about the expected deliverer, and each of these different schools of messianic teaching was able to point to statements in the Hebrew Scriptures as proof of the correctness of their beliefs. In a general way, the Jews regarded their national history as beginning with Abraham and culminating in the Messiah and the new age of the kingdom of God. In earlier times they had envisioned this deliverer as The Servant of the Father, then as The Son of Man. In later times, some even went so far as to refer to the Messiah as the Son of God. No matter whether he was called the Seed of Abraham or The Son of David, all were agreed that he was to be the Messiah, the Anointed One. Thus did the concept evolve from the Servant of the Father to the Son of David, Son of Man, and then to the Son of God.

In the days of John and Jesus, the more learned Jews had developed an idea of the coming Messiah as the perfected and representative Jew, combining in himself as the "Servant of the Father" the threefold characteristics of prophet, priest, and king.

The Jews devoutly believed that, just as Moses had delivered their fathers from Egyptian bondage by miraculous wonders, so would the coming Messiah deliver the Jewish people from Roman domination by even greater miracles of power and marvels of racial triumph. The rabbis had gathered together almost five hundred passages from the Scriptures which, in spite of their apparent contradictions, they proclaimed were prophecies of the coming Messiah. In the midst of all these details of time, technique, and function, they completely lost sight of the personality of the promised Messiah. They were looking for a restoration of Jewish national glory - Judea's nationalistic exaltation rather than for the spiritual salvation of the world. It therefore became evident that Jesus of Nazareth could never have satisfied this materialistic Messiah concept of the Jewish mind of those days. Many of their Messianic predictions, had they but viewed these prophetic utterances in a different light, would have very naturally prepared their minds for the recognition of Jesus as the terminator of one age and the beginner of a new and enlightened era of mercy and salvation for all nations.

The Jews had been brought up to believe in the Doctrine of the Shekinah. But this symbol of the divine presence was not to be seen in the temples. They believed that the coming of the Messiah would affect its restoration. They held confusing ideas about racial sin and the supposed evil nature of man. Some religious sects within the Jews taught that Adam's sin had cursed the human race, and that the Messiah would remove this curse and restore man to divine favor.

Others taught that God, in creating man, had put into his being both good and evil natures, that when he observed the outworking of this arrangement, he was greatly disappointed, and that he repented that he had thus made man. Those who taught this believed that the Messiah was to come in order to redeem man from this inherent evil nature.

The majority of the Jews of those days believed that they continued to languish under Roman rule because of their national sins and because of the half-heartedness of the Gentile converts. To these Jews, the entire Jewish nation had not wholeheartedly repented, therefore the Messiah delayed his coming into the world. There was much talk about repentance. This was the reason for the strong and immediate attraction to John's preaching: repent and be baptized, for the kingdom of Heaven is at hand. The kingdom of Heaven could mean only one thing to any devout Jew of that day: the coming of the Messiah.

There was one feature of the arrival of Jesus which was utterly foreign to the Jewish concept of the Messiah, and that was the union of the two natures, the human and the divine. The Jews had variously conceived of the Messiah as perfected human, superhuman, and even as divine, but they never entertained the concept of the union of the human and the divine. This was also the great stumbling block of Jesus' early disciples. They easily grasped the human concept of the Messiah as the Son of David, as presented by the earlier prophets. They understood the superhuman idea posed by Daniel and some of the later prophets of the Son of Man concept. They even understood the concept of the Son of God as depicted by the author of the Book of Enoch and by certain of his contemporaries. But never had they for a single moment entertained the concept of the union in one Earth personality of the two natures, the human and the divine. The incarnation of the Son of God in the form of a human of the Earth had not been revealed beforehand by any great prophet. It was revealed only in Jesus. The world knew nothing of such things until the Son of God was made flesh and lived among the mortals of the realm.

Jesus was baptized at the very height of John's preaching when Palestine was aflame with the expectancy of his message, "The kingdom of God is at hand." When all Jewry was engaged in serious and solemn self-examination. The Jewish sense of racial solidarity was very profound. The Jews not only believed that the sins of the father might afflict his children, but they firmly believed also that the sins of one Jew could curse the nation. Accordingly, not all who submitted to John's baptism regarded themselves as being guilty of the specific sins which John denounced. Many devout souls were baptized by John for the good of Judea. They feared that some sin of ignorance on their part might delay the coming of the Messiah. They felt that they belonged to a guilty and sin-cursed nation, therefore they presented themselves for baptism so that they might manifest fruits of racial penitence.

When Jesus of Nazareth went down into the Jordan to be baptized, he was a mortal of the realm who had reached the pinnacle of human evolutionary development in all matters related to the conquest of his human mind and to communication with the divine spirit within him. He stood in the Jordan that day a perfected mortal of an evolutionary world of time and space. Perfect synchrony and full communication had become established between his mortal mind and the spirit that dwelled within him, the divine gift of his Father in Heaven. Just such a spirit dwells in all normal beings living on Earth.

The ceremony of the baptism was the final act of his purely human life on Earth. He entered the river as the Son of Man, and emerged as the Son of God, ready to do the will of his Father in Heaven. This day of baptism ended the purely human life of

Jesus. The Divine Son found his Father, the Universal Father acknowledged his incarnated son, and they spoke one to the other.

When Jesus was baptized, he repented of no misdeeds. He made no confession of sin. His was the baptism of consecration to the performance of the will of the Heavenly Father. At his baptism he heard the unmistakable call of his Father, the final summons to be about his Father's business, and he went away into private seclusion for forty days to think over these manifold developments.

Jesus was thirty-one and a half years old when he was baptized. While the writings of Luke say that Jesus was baptized in the Fifteenth year of the reign of Tiberius Caesar, which would be AD 29 since Augustus died in AD 14, it should be remembered that Tiberius was Co- Emperor with Augustus for two and one half years before the death of Augustus, having had coins struck in his honor in October of the year AD 11. The Fifteenth year of his actual rule was, therefore, this very year of AD 26, that of Jesus' baptism. This was also the year that Pontius Pilate began his rule as Governor of Judea.

After his baptism he entered upon the forty days of adjusting himself to the changed relationships of the world and the universe occasioned by the development of his spirit. During this isolation in the Perean Hills he decided upon the policy to be pursued and the methods to be employed in the new and changed phase of Earth life which he was about to inaugurate.

Jesus did not go into the wilderness for the purpose of fasting, nor for the affliction of his soul. He was not an ascetic, and he forever spoke against all such notions regarding this approach to God. His reasons for seeking this solitude were entirely different from those of Moses and Elijah, and even John the Baptizer.

Jesus was then wholly self-conscious concerning his relation to the universe of his mortal birth and also to the Heavenly realms. He now fully recalled his ministry, and the counsel given to him by his Heavenly brother, Immanuel, when Jesus decided to enter upon the journey of a mortal of the realm on Earth. He now clearly and fully comprehended all these far-flung relationships, and he desired to be away for a season of quiet meditation so that he could think out the plans and decide on the procedures for the carrying out of his public ministry on behalf of this world.

Day by day, up in the hills, Jesus formulated his plans for the remainder of his earthly experience. He first decided not to teach contemporaneously with John. He planned to remain in comparative retirement and private ministry until the work of John achieved its purpose, or until John was suddenly stopped by imprisonment. Jesus well knew that John's fearless and tactless preaching would presently arouse the fears and anger of the Jewish rulers, and that they would soon put an end to his preaching. In view of John's precarious situation, Jesus began definitely to plan his program of public labors on behalf of all people of this world.

The first thing Jesus did, after thinking through the general plan of coordinating his program with John's movement, was to review in his mind the instructions of Immanuel. Carefully he thought over the advice given him concerning his methods of teaching, and that he was to leave no permanent writing behind. Never again did Jesus write on anything except sand. On his next visit to Nazareth, much to the sorrow of his brother Joseph, Jesus destroyed all of his writings that were preserved on the boards around the carpenter shop, and which hung upon the walls of the old home. Jesus pondered well Immanuel's advice pertaining to his economic, social, and political attitude toward the world as he should find it.

Jesus did not fast during this forty days' isolation. The longest period he went without food was his first two days in the hills when he was so engrossed with his thinking that he forgot all about eating. But on the third day he went in search of food. Neither was he tempted during this time by any evil spirits or rebel personalities in this world or from any other world.

These forty days were the occasion of the final union between the human mind and the divine mind, or rather it should be stated that this was the first real functioning of these two minds as one mind. The results of this momentous season of meditation demonstrated conclusively that the divine mind had triumphantly and spiritually dominated the human intellect. The mind of man became the mind of God. Although the will of the mind of man is ever present, always will a spiritualized human mind say: "Not my will but yours be done, Father."

This was the very first time in the history of Earth that a human being born of the realm was able to achieve the tremendous task of subordinating his human mind, his soul and his ego, to the will of his divine mind. This fact, and this act, is within the ability of each and every human being on the face of this Earth, but since the time that Jesus achieved this, no one human being has ever been able to reach this pinnacle, although many have tried, and many have come joyously close to it.

The events of this time were not the fantastic visions of a starved and weakened mind, neither were they confused symbolisms which afterward gained record as the: "Temptations of Jesus in the wilderness." Rather was this a season for thinking over the whole eventful and varied future career of his Earth life and for the careful laying of those plans for further ministry which would best serve this world. During these days of meditation, Jesus pondered the whole span of human existence on Earth.

The Angel Gabriel accompanied Jesus during these entire forty days, and they held many wonderful conversations about the entire spectrum of living the life of a human being and carrying on a mission of divine proportions. Gabriel reminded Jesus that there were two ways in which he might manifest himself to the world in case he should choose to stay on Earth for some time. These two methods of world ministry that Gabriel suggested were:

1) Jesus' Own Way - the way that might seem most pleasant and profitable from the standpoint of the immediate needs of this world and the present edification of his own universe.

2) The Father's Way - setting the example of an ideal of human life as visualized by the Heavenly Host in the spiritual realms.

It was thus made clear to Jesus by Gabriel that there were two ways in which he could order the remainder of his Earth life. Each of these ways had something to be said in its favor as it might be regarded in the light of the immediate situation. It was also indicated to Jesus that it would afford his heavenly brother, Immanuel, great joy and satisfaction if he, Jesus, should see fit to finish up his Earth career of incarnation as he had so nobly begun it, always subject to the Father's will. During the days of this isolation Jesus promised himself he would go back to the world to finish his Earth career, and that in a situation involving any two ways he would always choose the Father's will. He lived out the remainder of his Earth life always true to that conviction. Even to the bitter end he invariably subordinated his sovereign will to that of his Heavenly Father.

The forty days in the mountain wilderness were not a period of great temptations but were instead a period of great decisions. During these days of lone communion with himself and Angel Gabriel, he arrived, one by one, at the great decisions which were to control his policies and conduct for the remainder of his Earth career.

Subsequently the tradition of a great temptation became attached to this period of isolation through confusion with the fragmentary narratives of the Mount Hermon struggles, and further because it was the custom in Palestine to have all great prophets and human leaders begin their public careers by undergoing these supposed seasons of fasting and prayer. It had always been Jesus' practice, when facing any new or serious decisions, to withdraw for communion with his own spirit that he might seek to know the will of his Father in Heaven.

In all this planning for the remainder of his Earth life, Jesus was always torn in his human heart by two opposing courses of conduct:

1) he entertained a strong desire to win his people, and the whole world, to believe in him and to accept his new spiritual teachings. He well knew their confused ideas concerning the coming Messiah and desired to correct their beliefs.

2) to live and work as he knew his Father would approve, and to continue in the establishment of the new spirituality, to reveal the Father and show forth his divine character of love.

Throughout these eventful days Jesus lived in an ancient rock cavern, a shelter in the side of the hills near a village sometime called Beit Adis. He drank from the small spring which came from the side of the hill near this rock shelter.

THE PUBLIC TEACHINGS

Before Jesus preached his memorable Sermon on the kingdom of God, the very first outward effort of his public ministry, he read from the Scriptures these passages: "You shall be to me a kingdom of priests, a holy people. Yahweh is our judge. Yahweh is our lawgiver. Yahweh is our king. He will save us. Yahweh is my king and my God. He is a great king over all the Earth. Loving kindness is upon Israel in this kingdom. Blessed be the glory of the Father for he is our king."

The following teachings are directly from Jesus and have all been restated in modern terminology.

TEACHING ON THE KINGDOM OF GOD

Jesus: "I have come to announce the beginning of the Fathers' rule. This new religion shall include the worshipping souls of Jews and Gentiles alike, rich and poor, free and bond, for my Father does not favor some over others. His love and his mercy are for all.

My Father in Heaven has sent his spirit to dwell within the minds of all men, and when I shall have finished my work on Earth, likewise shall I pour the Spirit of Truth upon all peoples of all lands. The Spirit of my Father and the Spirit of Truth shall establish you in the coming religion of spiritual understanding and divine righteousness. My kingdom is not of this world. The Son of God shall not lead forth armies in battle for the establishment of a throne of power or a kingdom of worldly glory. When my spirituality has unfolded, you shall come to know the Son of God as the Prince of Peace, the revealer of the everlasting Father in Heaven. The children of this world fight for the establishment and enlargement of the kingdoms of this world, but my disciples shall enter the graces of Heaven by their moral decisions and by their spiritual victories. Once they have entered the Father's realm, they shall find joy, righteousness, and eternal life.

Those who first seek to enter this new realm, thus beginning the journey of striving for a nobility of character like that of my Father, shall very soon possess all else that is needful. But I say to you in all sincerity: unless you seek entrance into the Heavenly realms with the faith and trust of a little child, you shall not gain admission.

Do not be deceived by those who come saying to you here is the place or there is the place, for my Father's realm is not comprised of things visible and material. This realm is even now among you, for where the Spirit of God teaches and leads the soul of man, there in reality is the Heavenly realm. This place of God is righteousness, peace, and joy in the Holy Spirit.

In my Father's kingdom there shall be neither Jew nor Gentile, only those who seek perfection through service to their brothers, for I tell you truthfully that he who wants to be great in my Father's realm must first become the server of all. If you are willing to serve your fellows, you shall sit down with me in my kingdom, even as I, by serving in the guise of a human being, shall presently sit down with my Father in his Heavenly realm.

This new religion is like a seed growing in the good soil of a field. It will not reach full fruit quickly. There is an interval of time between the establishment of the religion in the soul of man and that hour when the religion ripens into the full fruit of everlasting righteousness and eternal salvation.

This new way which I declare to you is not a reign of power and material plenty. The Father's realm is not a matter of meat and drink but rather a life of progressive development and increasing joy in the service of my Father in Heaven. Has not my Father said of his children of the world, 'It is my will that they should eventually be perfect, even as I am perfect.'

I have come to preach the good news of the new way. I have not come to add to the heavy burdens of those who want to enter this realm. I have come to teach the new and better way, and those who are able to enter the coming realm shall enjoy the divine rest that it will offer.

Whatever it shall cost you in the things of your world, no matter what price you must pay to enter the kingdom of Heaven, you shall receive many times more joy and spiritual progress in this world, and in the age to come when this material life is over.

Your entrance into the Father's realm does not need to wait upon marching armies, upon overturned kingdoms of this world, or upon the breaking of captive yokes. The Heavenly realm is here and now, and all who enter shall find abundant liberty and joyous salvation.

This realm is an everlasting dominion. Those who enter the new way shall ascend to my Father. They will certainly reach the right hand of his glory in paradise. All who enter the new realm shall become the Sons of God. I have not come to call on the would-be righteous, but instead to call on the sinners, and on those who hunger and thirst for the joy and love of divine perfection.

John came to you preaching of the need for repentance to prepare you to enter the new way. Now I come to you proclaiming that faith, the gift of God, is the price you need to pay to enter into the kingdom of Heaven. If you believe that my Father loves you with an infinite love, then you are already in the kingdom of God."

Teaching at the Temple

The first Passover after the beginning of his public ministry found Jesus and his disciples preaching outside of the temple to the throngs that arrived for the Passover celebration. This was the message that Jesus and the disciples preached on this occasion:

1. The kingdom of Heaven is at hand.
2. By faith in the Fatherhood of God you may enter the kingdom of Heaven, thus becoming the Sons of God.
3. Love is the rule of living within the Heavenly realms, devotion to God while loving your neighbor as you love yourself.
4. Obedience to the will of the Father; yielding the fruits of the spirit in one's personal life, is the law of the new way.

The multitudes that came from all over the Roman world to celebrate Passover heard this wonderful message and thousands of them rejoiced in its enlightened teaching. The chief priests and rulers of the Jews became very much concerned about Jesus and his Apostles and debated among themselves what to do about them.

Besides teaching in and around the temple, Jesus and his Apostles, as well as other believers, engaged in much personal work among the Passover throngs all over Jerusalem. These Passover men and women subsequently carried the news of Jesus' Gospel from Jerusalem to the uttermost parts of the Roman empire and also to the East. This was the beginning of the spread of the Gospel of the kingdom to the outside world. No longer was the work of Jesus confined to Palestine and to the Jews.

TEACHING ABOUT YAHWEH

A wealthy trader from Crete, traveling through Palestine, heard Jesus speak publicly one day and asked him, "But teacher, Moses and the prophets of old taught us that Yahweh is a jealous God, a God of great wrath and fierce anger. The prophets said he hates evildoers and takes vengeance on those who do not obey his laws. You and your disciples come teaching that God is a kind and compassionate Father who so loves all men, even sinners, that he would welcome them into this new kingdom of Heaven, which you proclaim is so near at hand.

What am I supposed to believe?"

Jesus replied: "You have well stated the teachings of the olden prophets who taught the children of their generation in accordance with the light of their day. Our Father in Heaven is changeless.

But the concept of his nature has enlarged and grown from the beginning of time to the days of Moses down through the times of Amos and even to the generation of the prophet Isaiah. Now have I come to reveal the Father in new glory and to show forth his love and mercy to all men of this world. As the gospel of this new religion spreads over the world with its message of good cheer and good will to all men, new and better relations will develop among the families of all nations. As time passes, parents and their children will love each other more, and this will bring about a better understanding of the love that the Father in Heaven has for his children on Earth. Remember, that a good and true father not only loves his family as a whole, as a family, but he also truly loves and affectionately cares for each individual member of the family. So, it is with my Father in Heaven.

You, being a father of many, know well the truth of my words.

You love all of your children as a human father on Earth, therefore you must now accept the truth of the love of the Heavenly Father for you, not just for all the children of the world, but for you as an individual.

When your children are very young and immature, and you have to chastise them for misbehaving, they may believe that their father does not love them very much and is angry and filled with resentful wrath. Their immaturity cannot penetrate beyond the punishment to see their father's farseeing and corrective affection. But when these same children become grown-up men and women, it would be foolish for them to cling to these earlier and misconceived notions regarding their father. As men and women, they should now understand their father's love for them in all these early disciplines.

Shouldn't mankind then, as the centuries pass, learn to better understand the true nature and loving character of the Father in Heaven? Have you learned anything from successive generations of spiritual illumination if you persist in viewing God as Moses and the prophets saw him? I say to you, under the bright light of this very hour, you should see the Father as none of those who have gone before ever saw him. Thus, seeing him now as a loving and merciful Father, you should celebrate entering the new world where such a wonderful Father rules, and you should seek to have his will of love dominate your life from this day forward."

TEACHINGS TO FLAVIUS

Flavius, a wealthy Greek converted to Judaism, was talking with Jesus one day. Flavius was a great lover of the beauty in art and sculpture. The house where he lived when in Jerusalem was a beautiful building. This home was exquisitely adorned with priceless treasures which he had gathered here and there on his world travels. When he first thought of inviting Jesus to his home, he feared that the Master might take offense at the sight of these sculptures which the Jews considered unholy images. But Flavius was greatly surprised when Jesus entered his home and, instead of rebuking him for having these supposedly idolatrous objects scattered about the house, manifested great interest in the entire collection and asked many appreciative questions about each object as Flavius escorted him from room to room, showing him all of his favorite statues.

The Master sensed that his host was bewildered at his friendly attitude toward art. When they had finished the survey of the entire collection, Jesus said: "Because you appreciate the beauty of things created by my Father and fashioned by the artistic hands of man, why should you expect to be rebuked? Because Moses at one time sought to combat idolatry and the worship of false gods, why should all men frown upon the reproduction of grace and beauty? I say to you Flavius, the followers of Moses have misunderstood him, and today they make false gods of even his prohibitions of images and the likeness of things in Heaven and on Earth. But even if Moses had taught such restrictions to the darkened minds of those days, what has that to do with this day when the Father in Heaven is revealed as the Universal Spirit over all of creation? Flavius, I declare to you that in the coming life they shall no longer teach: 'Do not worship this and do not worship that.' No longer shall men concern themselves with commands to refrain from this and take care not to do that, but rather all will be concerned with only one duty. This duty of man will be comprised of two great privileges, sincere worship of the Infinite Creator, the Father in Heaven, and loving service bestowed upon one's fellow man. Once you progress to the point that you love your neighbor as you love yourself, then you will know that you are a Son of God and that you have discovered the kingdom of Heaven.

In those dark ages when my Father was not well understood, Moses was justified in his attempts to curtail idolatry, but in the coming age the Father will be revealed in the life of the son. This new revelation of God will make it forever unnecessary to confuse the Creator Father with idols of stone or images of gold and silver. From this day forth, intelligent men can enjoy the treasures of art without confusing such material appreciation of beauty with the worship and service of the Father in Heaven, the God of all things and all people."

Flavius believed all that Jesus taught him that evening over dinner. The next day he went to Bethany beyond the Jordan and was baptized by the disciples of John. This he did because the Apostles of Jesus did not yet baptize believers. When Flavius returned to Jerusalem, he made a great feast for Jesus and invited sixty of his friends. After this dinner, many of these guests also became believers in the message of the coming religion.

TEACHINGS ON THE CONCEPTS OF GOD

One night, around the campfire, the twelve Apostles and others present asked Jesus many questions about the Father in Heaven. The Master's answers to these questions can best be presented by the following summary in modern phraseology:

The Master proceeded to instruct the Apostles about the evolution of the concept of God throughout the course of the development of the Hebrew peoples. He called attention to the following phases in the growth of the idea of God:

1. Yahweh: the God of the Sinai clans. This was the primitive concept of God which Moses taught as the Father God of the Hebrews. The Father in Heaven never fails to accept the sincere worship of his children on Earth, no matter how crude their concept of God or by what name they symbolize his divine nature.
2. The Most High: this concept of the Father in Heaven was proclaimed by Melchizedek to Abraham and was carried

far from Salem by those who subsequently believed in this enlarged and expanded idea of God. Abraham and his brother had left Ur because of the establishment of sun worship, and they became believers in Melchizedek's teachings of El Elyon, the Most High God. Theirs was a composite concept of God, consisting of a blending of their older Mesopotamian ideas with the Doctrine of the Most High.

3. El Shaddai: many of the Hebrews worshipped El Shaddai, the Egyptian concept of the God of Heaven, which they learned about during their captivity in the land of the Nile. Over the centuries, all three of these concepts, Yahweh, The Most High, and El Shaddai, became joined together to form the doctrine of the Creator God, the Father God of the Hebrews.

4. Elohim: since the times of Melchizedek the teachings of the Trinity of Heaven had persisted. Scriptures stated that in the beginning the Gods had created the Heavens and the Earth. By the time those records were made, the Trinity Concept of three Gods in one had already found acceptance in the religion of the forefathers of the Hebrews.

5. Ultimate Yahweh: by the times of Isaiah the common beliefs about God had expanded into the concept of a Universal Creator who was simultaneously all-powerful and all-merciful. This evolving and enlarged concept of the Father virtually replaced all previous ideas of God in the religion of the Hebrews.

6. The Father in Heaven: Jesus said "Now we come to know God as our Father in Heaven. Our teachings must provide

a religion where the believer is a son of God. That is the good news of the Gospel of the kingdom of Heaven. The revelation of the nature of God will continue to enlarge and brighten throughout the endless ages to come.

At all times and during all ages the true worship of any human being, as concerns individual spiritual progress, is recognized by the spirit as homage given to the Father in Heaven."

Never before had the Apostles been so shocked as they were upon hearing these teachings of the growth and development of the concept of God in the Hebrew minds of previous generations. As they sat before Jesus in silent bewilderment, the Master continued: "You would have known these truths had you read the scriptures. Have you not read in Samuel where it says: 'And the anger of the Father was kindled against Israel, so much so that he moved David against them, saying, go and number Israel and Judah.' This was not strange because in the days of Samuel the children of Abraham really believed that Yahweh created both good and evil. But when a later writer narrated these events, subsequent to the enlargement of the Jewish concept of the nature of God, he did not dare attribute evil to Yahweh. Therefore, he said: 'And Satan stood up against Israel and provoked David to number Israel.' Can you see how the Scriptures clearly show the concept of the nature of God continuing to grow from one generation to another?"

"When the Palestinian tribes came out of Egypt in the days before the enlarged revelation of Yahweh, they had ten commandments which served as their laws right up to the times when they were encamped below Mount Sinai. These ten commandments of the Hebrews were:

1. You shall worship no other God, for Yahweh is a jealous God.
2. You shall not make molten gods.
3. You shall keep the feast of the unleavened bread.
4. Of all the males of men and cattle, the first born belongs to Yahweh.
5. Six days you may work, but on the seventh you shall rest.
6. You must observe the feast of the first fruits and the feast of harvests.
7. You shall not offer a blood sacrifice with leavened bread.
8. The sacrifice of the feast of Passover shall not be left until morning.
9. The first of the fruits of the ground you shall bring to the house of Yahweh.
10. You shall not boil a young goat in its mother's milk.

Then, in the midst of the thunder and fire of the erupting Mount Sinai, Moses taught them the new ten commandments, which you must all agree are much more worthy utterances to accompany the enlarging Yahweh concept of God. Did you ever take notice that these commandments were twice recorded in the scriptures? In the first case, deliverance from Egypt is assigned as the reason for Sabbath keeping, while in a later record the advancing religious beliefs of our forefathers demanded that this be changed to the recognition of the fact of Creation as the reason for Sabbath observance.

If you follow further through the Scriptures you will see that, in the greater spiritual enlightenment of Isaiah's day, these ten negative commandments were changed into the great and positive law of love, the injunction to love God, and your neighbor as yourself. It is this law of love for God and for your fellow man that I also declare to you as constituting the whole duty of man."

TEACHING ON ASSURANCE

The next time that Jesus and his Apostles were in Jerusalem, one of the great sermons which Jesus preached in the temple at Jerusalem was in answer to a question asked by one of his listeners, a man from Damascus. The man asked Jesus: "But teacher, how shall we know for sure that you were sent by God, and that we may truly enter into this religion which you and your disciples declare is near at hand?"

Jesus replied to the following, paraphrased in modern words: "As regards my message and the teachings of my disciples, you should judge them by their fruits. If we proclaim to you the truths of the spirit, the spirit will acknowledge in your heart that our message is genuine.

Concerning the Heavenly realm and your assurance of acceptance by the Father, let me ask what Father among you who is a worthy and kindhearted Father would keep his son in anxiety or suspense regarding his status in the family or his place of security in the affections of his Father's heart? Do you Earth fathers take pleasure in torturing your children with uncertainty about their place of abiding love in your human hearts? No. Neither does your Father in Heaven leave his children in doubtful uncertainty as to their position in the new religion.

If you receive God as your Father, then indeed and in truth you are the sons of God. If you are sons, then you are secure in the position and standing of all that concerns divine sonship. If you believe my words, then you must believe in the Heavenly citizen who sent me, and by thus believing in the Father, you have established your status as a Heavenly citizen. If you follow the will of the Father in Heaven, you shall never fail in reaching the eternal life in the Divine kingdom.

The divine spirit that dwells within you shall bear witness that we are truly the children of God. If you are the sons of God, then you have been born of the spirit of God. Whosoever has been born of the spirit has the power to overcome all doubt, and this is the victory that overcomes all uncertainty.

The Prophet Isaiah once said, speaking of our times: 'When the spirit is once poured upon us from on high, then shall the work of righteousness become peace, quietness, and assurance forever.' To all who truly believe this gospel, I will become the door for their reception into the eternal mercies and the everlasting life of my Father's realm.

You, then, who hear this message and believe this gospel of the new way are the sons of God, and you already have life everlasting. The evidence to all the world that you have been born of the spirit will be that you sincerely love one another."

The throng of listeners remained many hours with Jesus, asking him questions and listening attentively to his comforting answers. Even the Apostles were emboldened by Jesus' teaching to preach the new gospel with more power and assurance. This experience in Jerusalem was a great inspiration to the twelve. It was their first contact with such enormous crowds, and they learned many valuable lessons which proved of great assistance in their later work.

Teachings in Samaria

After the enormously successful first preaching tour at Jerusalem during the Passover, Jesus and his disciples decided to exit Judea due to the increasing hostility and opposition by the priests and religious leaders of Jerusalem. They traveled north into Samaria, preaching at each village they came to. They attracted great crowds, and people came from many distant places to hear the new gospel of the kingdom of Heaven.

The group finally arrived at the Greek cities of Archelais and Phasaelis on the banks of the Jordan River, where they had their very first experience preaching to an audience comprised almost entirely of Gentiles, Greeks, Romans and Syrians. Very few Jews lived in Samaria, especially in these two Greek towns. In teaching to these Roman citizens, the Apostles encountered new difficulties in the proclamation of the message of the coming religion, and they met with new objections to the teachings of Jesus. At one of the many evening conferences with his Apostles, Jesus listened attentively to these objections to the Gospel of the kingdom as the twelve repeated their experiences with the subjects of their personal labors.

Afterward, Philip asked a question of Jesus which was typical of the frustrations they were all having. Philip asked: "Master, these Greeks and Romans make light of our message, saying that such teachings are fit for only weaklings and slaves. They assert that their religions are superior to our teachings because they inspire the development of a strong, robust, and aggressive character. They tell us that we would convert all men into enfeebled specimens of passive no resisters who would soon perish from the face of the

Earth. They like you, Master, and freely admit that your teaching is heavenly and ideal, but they will not take us seriously. They say that your religion is not of this world, that men cannot live as you teach. Now, Master, what shall we say to these Gentiles?"

Jesus responded, "I have come into this world to do the will of my Father and to reveal his loving character to all mankind. That, my brothers, is my mission. This one mission I will perform regardless of the misunderstanding of my teachings by Jews or Gentiles of this day or of another generation. But you should not overlook the fact that even divine love has its severe disciplines. A Father's love for his son often times makes the father to restrain the unwise acts of his thoughtless youngsters. The child does not always comprehend the wise and loving motives of the father's restraining discipline. But I declare to you that my Father in Heaven does rule the universe by the compelling power of his love. Love is the greatest of all spiritual forces. Truth is liberating, but love is the ultimate relationship. No matter what blunders your fellow men make in their personal management of today, in an age to come the gospel which I declare to you will rule this very world. The ultimate goal of human progress is the recognition of the Fatherhood of God and the loving Brotherhood of Man.

But who told you that my Gospel was intended only for slaves and weaklings? Do you, my chosen Apostles, resemble weaklings? Did John look like a weakling? Do you observe that I am enslaved by fear? It is true that the poor and oppressed of this generation have the gospel preached to them. This is because the religions of this world have neglected the poor and oppressed, but my Father does not favor one man over another. Besides, the poor of this day have been the first to heed the call to repentance of their backward ways and acceptance of sonship with my Father. The gospel of the kingdom is to be preached to all men, Jew and Gentile, Greek and Roman, rich and poor, free and bond, and equally to young and old, male and female.

Because my Father is a God of love, and delights in the practice of mercy, do not entertain the idea that the service of the new way is to be one of monotonous ease. The Heavenly journey is the ultimate adventure of all time, the rugged achievement of eternal life. Your service to the new religion will call for all the courageous manhood that you and your co-workers can muster. Many of you will be put to death for your loyalty to the Gospel of this kingdom. It is easy to die in the line of physical battle when your courage is strengthened by the presence of your fighting comrades, but it requires a higher and more profound form of human courage and devotion calmly and all alone to lay down your life for the love of a truth enshrined in your mortal heart.

Today, the unbelievers may taunt you for preaching a gospel of nonresistance and for living lives of nonviolence, but you are the first volunteers of a long line of sincere believers in the Gospel of this kingdom who will astonish all mankind by their heroic devotion to these teachings. No armies of the world have ever displayed more courage and bravery than will be portrayed by you and your loyal successors who shall go forth to all the world proclaiming the good news - the Fatherhood of God and the brotherhood of men. The courage of the flesh is the lowest form of bravery. Mental bravery is a higher type of human courage, but the highest courage that man can exhibit is unswerving loyalty to spiritual goals. Such courage constitutes the heroism of the man who knows God and loves him. You are all God-fearing men. You are in truth the personal associates of the Son of God."

Seldom did the Master speak to his Apostles with evident strong feelings, but this was one of those few occasions when he spoke with extreme earnestness, accompanied by marked emotion. The result upon the public preaching and personal ministry of the Apostles was immediate. From that very day their message took on a new note of courageous dominance. The twelve continued to acquire the spirit of positive aggression in the new gospel of the kingdom. From this day forward they did not preoccupy themselves so much with the preaching of the negative virtues and the passive injunctions of their Master's many-sided teachings.

Teachings on Self-Mastery

The Master was a perfect specimen of human self-control.

When he was criticized, he criticized not. When he suffered, he uttered no threats against his tormentors. When he was denounced by his enemies, he simply committed himself to the judgment of his Father in Heaven.

One evening around the campfire, Andrew asked Jesus: "Master, should we practice self-denial as John taught us, or are we supposed to strive for the self-control of your teachings? Where do your teachings differ from those of John?" Jesus answered in this way, "John indeed taught you the way of righteousness in accordance with the light that he saw. His was the religion of self-examination and self-denial. But I come with a new message for you of self-forgetfulness and self-control. My teachings show you the way of life as revealed to me by my Father in Heaven."

Truthfully, I say to you that he who rules his own self is greater than he who captures a city. Self-mastery is the measure of a man's moral nature and the indicator of his spiritual development. In the old order you fasted and prayed. Now you are taught to believe and rejoice. In the Father's realm you are to become new creatures. Old things are to pass away. In my teachings, I show you how all things are to become new. If you truly believe my teachings in your heart, by your love for one another you are to convince the world that you have passed from bondage into liberty, and from death into life everlasting.

In your old ways you sought to suppress, obey, and conform to the rules and laws of living. In the new way, first you are transformed by the Spirit of Truth and thereby strengthened in your inner soul by the constant spiritual renewing of your mind, and then you will be endowed with the power of the perfect will of God. Do not forget that God's spirit actually dwells within you. If then, this spirit dwells within you, then you no longer have to be slaves of the flesh, but instead the free and liberated sons of the spirit. The new law of the spirit will endow you with the liberty of mastery over self in the place of the old law of the fear of self-bondage and the slavery of self-denial.

In times past, when you have done evil, you blamed your acts on the influence of an evil spirit, when in truth you have been led astray by your very own natural tendencies. Did not the Prophet Jeremiah long ago tell your forefathers that the human heart is deceitful above all things and sometimes even desperately wicked? How easy it is for you to become self-deceived and thereby fall into foolish fears, diverse lusts, enslaving pleasures, malice, envy, and even vengeful hatred.

Salvation will come to you by the reawakening of your spirit and not by the self-righteous deeds of the flesh. You are justified by faith and strengthened by grace, not by fear and the self-denial of the flesh, although the Father's children who have been born of the spirit are always masters of the self and all that pertains to the desires of the flesh. When you come to know that you have been saved by faith, you will have real peace with God. All who follow in the way of this Heavenly peace are destined to be sanctified to the eternal service of God. From this day forth, it is not your duty but rather your privilege to cleanse yourselves from all evils of mind and body while you seek for perfection in the love of God.

Your station as a Son of God is grounded in faith, and you are to remain unmoved by fear. Your joy must be born of trust in the divine word, and you shall not be led to doubt the Father's love and mercy. It is the very goodness of God that leads men into true and genuine repentance. Fear will not lead you to repentance. The secret to the mastery of self is entwined with your faith in the spirit that dwells within you, which forever works by love. Even this saving faith you did not develop by yourselves. It is also the gift of the Father to you, the son. If you are indeed the children of this living faith, then you are no longer the slaves of self but rather the triumphant masters of yourselves, the liberated sons of God.

If, then, my children, you are born of the spirit, you will be forever delivered from the bondage of a life of self-denial over the desires of the flesh, and you will be translated into the joyous life of the spirit, where you will spontaneously show forth the fruits of the spirit in your daily lives. The fruits of the spirit are the essence of the highest type of ennobling self-control, even the heights of earthly moral achievement, true mastery of the self."

Teachings on Prayer and Worship

While in Samaria during one preaching tour, and camped at the base of Mount Gerazim, Jesus taught many great truths to his disciples and to the assembled masses. Of particular interest was this teaching regarding worship, paraphrased into modern terminology:

"True religion is the worshipful action by an individual soul in its relationship with the Creator Father. Organized religion is man's attempt to socialize the worship of many individuals.

Worship, the contemplation of the spiritual things of the universe, must alternate with service to your fellow man. Work should alternate with play. Religion should be balanced by humor. Profound philosophy should be relieved by rhythmic poetry. The strain of living should be relaxed by the restfulness of worship. The feelings of insecurity arising from the fear of isolation in the universe should be countered by faith in the Father and by the contemplation of his goodness."

"Prayer is designed to make man less thinking but more feeling. It is not designed to increase knowledge but rather to expand insight. Worship is intended to anticipate a better life ahead and then to reflect these new awakenings back onto the life which now is. Prayer is spiritually sustaining, but worship is divinely creative.

Worship is the technique of looking to the one for the inspiration of the many. Worship is the yardstick which measures the extent of the soul's detachment from the material world, and its simultaneous and secure attachment to God.

Prayer is self-reminding; worship is self-forgetting. Worship is effortless attention, true and ideal soul rest, a form of restful spiritual exercise.

Worship is the act of a part identifying itself with the whole, the finite identifying itself with the infinite, the son identifying himself with the Father, time in the act of striking step with eternity. Worship is a son's personal communion with the Father."

Although the Apostles grasped only a few of these teachings at the camp, and their generation of men grasped even less, future generations on Earth in the very near future will finally grasp these teachings.

TEACHINGS ON CERTAINTY OF FAITH

On a preaching tour through Galilee, at the village of Ramah, Jesus had a memorable discussion with an aged Greek philosopher who was teaching that science and philosophy were sufficient to satisfy the needs of human experience. Jesus listened patiently and with sympathy to this Greek teacher, acknowledging the truth of many things he said. And when the man was through with his teachings, Jesus advised him that he had failed in his discussion of human existence to explain where, why, and how, and added: "Where you leave off my dear friend, we begin. Religion is a revelation to man's soul dealing with spirituality which the mind alone can never discover or fully understand.

Intellectual discussions and exercises may reveal the facts of life, but the gospel of the new way unfolds the truths of living. You have discussed the material shadows of truth. Will you now listen while I tell you about the eternal and spiritual things which cast these transient shadows of the material facts of mortal existence?" For more than an hour thereafter Jesus taught this Greek philosopher the saving truths of the new gospel. The old philosopher was open to the Master's mode of teaching, and being sincerely honest of heart, he quickly believed this gospel of salvation.

The Apostles were a bit disturbed by the open manner of the Master's agreement to many of the Greek's propositions, but Jesus afterward privately said to them: "My children, marvel not that I was tolerant of the Greek philosophy. True and genuine certainty of what you believe in does not in the least fear outward analysis, nor does truth resent honest criticism. You should never forget that intolerance is the mask covering up secret doubts as to the trueness of one's belief. No man will at any time be disturbed by his neighbor's attitude if he has perfect confidence in the truth of that which he wholeheartedly believes. Courage ensues from the confidence of sincere honesty about those things which one professes to believe. Sincere men are unafraid of the critical examination of their true convictions and noble ideals."

TEACHINGS ON MERCY AND WORSHIP

While on a preaching tour at Jotapa in Galilee, Nathaniel became confused in his mind about his Master's teachings regarding mercy and worship. In response to his questions Jesus spoke at great length in further explanation of the meaning of his teachings. This is a brief excerpt of that discourse in modern language:

"The conscious and persistent regard for iniquity in the heart of man will gradually destroy the prayer connection of the human soul with the spiritual communication between man and God. Naturally, God hears the petition of his child, but when the human heart deliberately and persistently harbors the concepts of iniquity, there gradually ensues the loss of personal communion between the Earth child and his Heavenly Father.

A prayer which is inconsistent with the known and established laws of God is an abomination to the Heavenly Host. If man will not listen to the gods as they speak to their creation in the laws of spirit, mind, and matter, the very act of such deliberate and conscious disdain by the creature turns the ears of spirit personalities away from hearing the personal petitions of such lawless and disobedient mortals."

Jesus quoted to his Apostles from the Prophet Zechariah: "But they refused to listen and pulled away to the shoulder and stopped their ears that they should not hear. Yes, they made their hearts adamant like a stone, lest they should hear my law and the words which I sent by my spirit through the prophets. Therefore, the results of their evil thinking came as a great wrath upon their guilty heads. So it came to pass that they cried for mercy, but there was no ear open to hear." Then Jesus quoted the proverb of the wise man who said: "He who turns away his ear from hearing the divine laws, even his prayer shall be an abomination."

By opening the human end of the channel of the God-to-man communication, mortals can make immediately available the ever-flowing stream of divine ministry to the humans of the world. When man hears God's spirit speak within the human heart, inherent in such an experience is the fact that God simultaneously hears the man's prayers. Even the forgiveness of sin operates in this same unerring fashion. The Father in Heaven has forgiven you even before you have thought to ask him, but such forgiveness is not available in your personal religious experience until such a time as you can forgive your fellow man. God's forgiveness in fact is not conditioned upon your forgiving your fellows, but in experience it is exactly so conditioned.

There is a basic law of justice in the universe which mercy is powerless to circumvent. The unselfish glories of Heaven are not possible of reception by a selfish creature of the realms of time and space. Even the infinite love of God cannot force the salvation of eternal survival upon any mortal creature who does not choose to survive. Mercy has great latitude of bestowal, but, after all, there are mandates of justice which even love combined with mercy cannot effectively abrogate."

Jesus then quoted to the disciples from the Scriptures: "I have called, and you refused to hear. I stretched out my hand, but no man regarded. You have refused my counsel, and you have rejected my advice, and because of this rebellious attitude it becomes inevitable that you shall call upon me and fail to receive an answer. Having rejected the way of life, you may seek me diligently in your times of suffering, but you will not find me."

Then Jesus said: "They who would receive mercy must show mercy. Judge not that you are not judged. With the spirit with which you judge others you also shall someday be judged. In the end it will prove true: whosoever stops his ears from hearing the cry of the poor, shall someday also cry for help, and no one will hear him. The sincerity of any prayer is the assurance of its being heard. The spiritual wisdom of any petition is the determiner of the time, manner, and the degree of the answer. A wise father does not literally answer the foolish prayers of his ignorant and inexperienced children, albeit the children may derive much pleasure and real soul satisfaction from the making of such absurd petitions.

When you have become wholly dedicated to the doing of the will of the Father in Heaven, the answer to all your petitions will be forthcoming because your prayers will be in full accordance with the Father's will, and the Father's will is ever manifest throughout his vast universe. What the true son desires, the infinite Father will grant.

Such a prayer cannot remain unanswered, and no other sort of petition can possibly be fully answered.

The cry of the righteous is the act of the child of God which opens the door of the Father's storehouse of goodness, truth and mercy, and these good gifts have long been in waiting for the son's approach and personal appropriation. Prayer does not change the divine attitude toward man, but it does change man's attitude toward the changeless Father. The motive of the prayer gives it right of way to the Divine ear, not the social, economic, or outward religious status of the one who prays.

Prayer must not be employed to avoid the delays of time or to overcome the handicaps of space. Prayer was never meant to be a technique for exalting self or for gaining an unfair advantage over one's fellows. A thoroughly selfish soul cannot pray in the true sense of the word. Let your greatest delight be in the character of God, and he shall surely give you the sincere desires of your heart. Commit your life to the Father. Trust in him, and he will act. For the Father hears the cry of the needy, and he will regard the prayer of the destitute.

I have come forth from the Father. If, therefore, you are ever in doubt as to what you would ask of the Father, ask in my name, and I will present your petition in accordance with your real needs and desires and in accordance with my Father's will. Guard against the great danger of becoming self-centered in your prayers. Avoid praying much for yourself. Pray more for the spiritual progress of your brothers. Avoid materialistic praying. Pray in the spirit and for the abundance of the gifts of the spirit.

When you pray for the sick and afflicted, do not expect that your petitions will take the place of loving and intelligent ministry to the necessities of these afflicted ones. Pray for the welfare of your families, friends, and fellows, but especially pray for those who curse you, and make loving petitions for those who persecute you. When to pray, I will not say. Only the spirit that dwells within you may move you to the utterance of those petitions which are expressive of your inner relationship with the Father of spirits.

Many resort to prayer only when in trouble. Such a practice is thoughtless and misleading. True, you do well to pray when harassed, but you should also be mindful to speak as a son to your Father even when all goes well with your soul. Let your real petitions always be secret. Do not let men hear your personal prayers. Prayers of thanksgiving are appropriate for groups of worshipers, but the prayer of the soul is a personal matter. There is but one form of prayer which is appropriate for all God's children, and that is: Not mine, but thine Will be done, Father.

All believers in the gospel should pray sincerely for the extension of the kingdom of Heaven."

Of all the prayers of the Hebrew scriptures, Jesus commented most approvingly on the petition of the Psalmist: "Create in me a clean heart, O Father, and renew a right spirit within me. Purge me from secret sins and keep back your servant from presumptuous transgressions." Jesus commented at great length on the relation of prayer to careless and offending speech, quoting: "Set a watch,

0 Father, before my mouth. Keep the door of my lips. The human tongue is a member which few men can tame, but the spirit within can transform this unruly member into a kindly voice of tolerance and an inspiring minister of mercy."

Jesus taught that the prayer for divine guidance over the pathway of earthly life was next in importance to the petition for knowledge of the Father's will. In reality this means a prayer for divine wisdom.

Jesus never taught that human knowledge and special skill could be gained by prayer. But he did teach that prayer is a factor in the enlargement of one's capacity to receive the presence of the divine spirit. When Jesus taught his associates to pray in the spirit and in truth, he explained that he referred to praying sincerely and in accordance with one's enlightenment, rather than to praying wholeheartedly and intelligently, earnestly and steadfastly.

Jesus warned his followers against thinking that their prayers would be rendered more effective by ornate repetitions, eloquent phraseology, fasting, penance, or sacrifices. But he did urge his believers to employ prayer as a means of leading up through thanksgiving to true worship. Jesus deplored that so little of the spirit of thanksgiving was to be found in the prayers and worship of his followers. He quoted to his disciples from the Scriptures: "It is a good thing to give thanks to the Father and to sing praises to the name of the most high, to acknowledge his loving kindness every morning and his faithfulness every night, for God has made me glad through his work. In everything I will give thanks according to the Will of God."

He said to them, "Be not constantly over-anxious about your common needs. Be not apprehensive concerning the problems of your earthly existence, but in all these things by prayer and supplication, with the spirit of sincere thanksgiving, let your needs be spread out before your Father who is in Heaven." Then he quoted from the Scriptures: "I will praise the name of God with a song and will magnify him with thanksgiving. This will please the Father better than the sacrifice of an ox or bullock with horns and hoofs."

Jesus taught his followers that, after they made their prayers to the Father, they should remain for a time in silent receptivity to afford the spirit the better opportunity to speak to the listening soul. The spirit of the Father speaks best to man when the human mind is in an attitude of true worship. We worship God by the aid of the Father's indwelling spirit and by the illumination of the human mind through the ministry of truth. Jesus taught that worship makes one increasingly like the being who is worshipped. Worship is a transforming experience whereby the finite gradually approaches and ultimately reaches the presence of the infinite.

TEACHINGS ON THE WILL OF THE FATHER IN HEAVEN

On one of the many teaching tours, Jesus and his disciples worked their way up into Galilee as they moved from village to village north from Jerusalem, preaching through Samaria and into Galilee.

They finally arrived back in Capernaum for an extended stay. The very next Sabbath, at the afternoon service in the synagogue, Jesus preached his sermon on "The Will of the Father in Heaven". That morning Simon Peter had preached a Sermon on "The Kingdom." At the Thursday evening meeting of the synagogue,

Andrew had taught on "The New Way." After hearing these wonderful discourses, more people believed in Jesus in Capernaum, at this point in time, than in any other city on Earth.

As Jesus taught in the synagogue this Sabbath afternoon, according to custom he took the first text from the law, reading from the Book of Exodus: "You shall serve the Father, your God, and he shall bless your bread and your water, and all sickness shall be taken away from you." He chose the second text from the Prophets, reading from Isaiah: "Arise and shine, for your light has come, and the glory of the Father has risen upon you. Darkness may cover the Earth and gross darkness the people, but the spirit of the Father shall arise upon you, and the Divine glory shall be seen with you. Even the Gentiles shall come to this light, and many great minds shall surrender to the brightness of this light."

This sermon was an effort on Jesus' part to make clear the fact that religion is a personal experience. Among other things, the Master said:

"You well know that, while a kindhearted Father loves his family as a whole, he so regards them as a group because of his strong affection for each individual member of that family. No longer must you approach the Father in Heaven as a child of Judea but as a child of God. As a group, you are indeed the children of Judea, but as individuals, each one of you is a child of God. I have come, not to reveal the Father to the children of Judea, but rather to bring this knowledge of God and the revelation of his love and mercy to all individual believers as a genuine personal experience. The prophets have all taught you that Yahweh cares for his people, that God loves the Hebrew people, but I have come among you to teach you a greater truth, one which many of the later prophets also grasped, that God loves you - every one of you - as individuals. All these past generations you have had a national or racial religion. Now I have come to give you a personal religion.

But even this is not a new idea. Many of the spiritually minded among you have known this truth, inasmuch as some of the prophets have instructed you. Have you read in the Scriptures where the prophet Jeremiah said: 'The fathers have eaten sour grapes and the children's teeth are set on edge. Every man shall die for his own iniquity. Every man who eats sour grapes, his teeth shall be set on edge. Behold, the days shall come when I will make a new covenant with my people, not according to the covenant which I made with their father when I brought them out of the land of Egypt, but according to the new way. I will even write my law in their hearts. I will be their God, and they shall be my people.'

In that day they shall not say, one man to his neighbor, do you know the Father? No, for they shall all know me personally, from the least to the greatest.

Have you read these promises? Do you believe in the scriptures? Do you understand that the prophet's words are fulfilled in what you behold this very day? Did not Jeremiah exhort you to make religion an affair of the heart, to relate yourselves to God as individuals? Did not the prophet tell you that the God of Heaven would search your individual hearts? Were you not warned that the natural human heart is deceitful above all things and often times desperately wicked?

Have you read also where Ezekiel taught even your fathers that religion must become real in your individual experiences? No more shall you use the proverb which says, 'The fathers have eaten sour grapes and the children's teeth are set on edge. As I live, says the Father, behold all souls are mine. As the soul of the Father, so also the soul of the son. Only the soul that sins shall die.' Then Ezekiel foresaw even this day when he spoke on behalf of God, saying: 'A new heart also, will I give you, and a new spirit will I put within it to you.'

You should no longer fear that God will punish a nation for the sins of an individual. Neither will the Father in Heaven punish one of his believing children for the sins of a nation, albeit the individual member of any family must often suffer the material consequences of family mistakes and group transgressions. Do you realize that the hope of a better nation, or a better world, is bound up in the progress and enlightenment of the individual?"

Then the Master explained that the Father in Heaven, after man recognizes spiritual freedom, will order that his children on Earth should begin the journey to find the Creator, to know God and to seek to become like him.

The Apostles were greatly helped by this sermon. All of them realized more fully that the new gospel is a message directed to the individual, not to the nation.

Even though the people of Capernaum were familiar with Jesus' teachings they were astonished at his sermon on this Sabbath day. He taught, indeed, as one having authority and not as the scribes.

Just as Jesus finished speaking, a young man in the congregation who had been much agitated by his words was seized with a violent epileptic attack and loudly cried out. At the end of the seizure, when recovering consciousness, he spoke in a dreamy state, saying: "What have we to do with you, Jesus of Nazareth? You are the holy one of God. Have you come to destroy us?" Jesus bade the people be quiet and, taking the young man by the hand, said, "Come out of it." and the boy immediately awoke.

This young man was not possessed of an evil spirit or demon. He was a victim of ordinary epilepsy. But he had been taught that his affliction was due to possession by an evil spirit. He believed this teaching and behaved accordingly in all that he thought or said concerning his ailment. The people all believed that such phenomena were directly caused by the presence of unclean spirits. Accordingly, they believed that Jesus had cast a demon out of this man. Long after the day of Pentecost the Apostle John, who was the last to write of Jesus' doings, avoided all reference to these so-called acts of casting out devils, and this he did in view of the fact that such cases of demon possession never occurred after Pentecost.

As a result of this commonplace incident the report was rapidly spread through Capernaum that Jesus had cast a demon out of a man and miraculously healed him in the synagogue at the conclusion of his afternoon sermon. The Sabbath was just the time for the rapid and effective spreading of such a startling rumor. This report was also carried to all the smaller settlements around Capernaum, and many of the people believed it.

The cooking and the housework at the large Zebedee home, where Jesus and the twelve made their headquarters, was for the most part done by Simon Peter's wife and her mother. Peter's home was near that of the Zebedee home. Jesus and his friends stopped there on the way from the synagogue because Peter's mother-in-law had for several days been sick with chills and fever. Now it chanced that, at about the time Jesus stood over this sick woman, holding her hand, smoothing her brow, and speaking words of comfort and encouragement, the fever left her. Jesus had not yet had time to explain to his Apostles that no miracle had been performed at the synagogue. With this incident so fresh and vivid in their minds, and recalling the water and the wine at Cana, they seized upon this coincidence as another miracle, and some of them rushed out to spread the news abroad throughout the city.

These cases are typical of the manner in which a wonder-seeking generation and a miracle minded people unfailingly seized upon all such coincidences as the pretext for proclaiming that another miracle had been performed by Jesus.

Teachings on the Rule of Living

On one evening of a Sabbath, during a short trip to Jerusalem, Jesus and the twelve were assembled around the fire in Lazarus' garden in Bethany. Nathaniel asked Jesus this question: "Master, although you have taught us the positive version of the old rule of life, instructing us that we should do to others as we wish them to do to us, I do not fully understand how we can always abide by such an injunction. Let me illustrate my argument by giving the example of a lustful man who thus wickedly looks upon his intended consort in sin. How can we teach that this evil-intending man should do to others as he would want them to do to him?"

When Jesus heard Nathaniel's question, he immediately stood upon his feet and, pointing his finger at the Apostle, said: "Nathaniel, Nathaniel! What manner of thinking is going on in your heart? Do you not receive my teachings as one who has been born of the spirit? Do you not hear the truth as a man of wisdom and spiritual understanding? When I admonished you to do to others as you would have them do to you, I spoke of men of high ideals, not of those who would be tempted to distort my teachings into a license for the encouragement of evil doing."

When the Master had spoken, Nathaniel stood up and said: "But Master, you should not think that I approve of such an interpretation of your teaching. I asked the question because I thought that many such men might thus misjudge your admonitions, and I hoped you would give us further instruction regarding these matters." Then when Nathaniel had sat down, Jesus continued speaking: "I well know, Nathaniel, that no such idea of evil is approved in your mind, but I am disappointed that you all so often fail to put a genuinely spiritual interpretation upon all my commonplace teachings, instructions which must be given you in human language and as men must speak. Let me now teach you concerning the differing levels of meaning attached to the interpretation of this rule of living, this admonition to do to others that which you desire others to do to you. Jesus said:

1. "The level of the flesh - such a purely selfish and lustful interpretation would be well exemplified by your question.
2. The level of the feelings - this plane is one level higher than that of the flesh and implies that sympathy and pity would enhance one's interpretation of this rule of living.
3. The level of the mind - now come into action the reason of mind and the intelligence of experience. Good judgment dictates that such a rule of living should be interpreted in accordance with the highest idealism embodied in the nobility of self-respect.

4. The level of brotherly love - still higher is discovered the level of unselfish devotion to the welfare of one's brothers. On this higher plane of wholehearted social service growing out of the consciousness of the Fatherhood of God and the ensuing recognition of the brotherhood of man, there is discovered a new and far more beautiful interpretation of this basic rule of life.

5. The moral level - then when you reach true philosophic levels of interpretation, when you have real insight into the rightness and wrongness of things of this world, when you perceive the eternal fitness of human relationships, you will begin to view such a problem of interpretation as you would imagine a high minded, idealistic, wise, and impartial third person would so view and interpret such an injunction as applied to your personal problems of adjustment to your life situation.

6. The spiritual level - then last, but greatest of all, we reach the level of spiritual insight and spiritual interpretation which urges us to recognize in this rule of life the divine command to treat all men as we conceive God would treat them. This is the ideal of human relationships. This should be your attitude toward all such problems when your highest desire is ever to follow the Father's will. I would, therefore, urge that you should treat all men the way that I would treat them."

TEACHINGS ON THE JOURNEY TO THE FATHER

One evening around the campfire in Capernaum, as Jesus was teaching his Apostles, he made the long-to-be-remembered address regarding the value of status with God and progress in the eternal journey to Heaven. These are the words of Jesus from that evening: "My children, if there exists a true and living connection between the child and the father, the child will progress continuously toward the father's ideals. While it is true that the child may at first make slow progress, the progress is none the less sure. The important thing to remember is not the speed of your progress but rather its certainty.

Your actual achievement is not so important as the fact that the direction of your progress is towards God. What you are becoming day by day is of infinitely more importance than what you are today.

The transformed woman whom some of you saw at Simon's house today is, at this moment, living on a level which is vastly below that of Simon and his associates. But while these Pharisees are occupied with the false progress of meaningless ceremonial services, this woman has, in complete earnest, started out on the long and eventful search for God, and her path toward Heaven is not blocked by spiritual pride or moral self-satisfaction. The woman is, humanly speaking, much farther away from God than Simon right now, but her soul is in progressive motion. She is on the way toward an eternal goal. There are present in this woman tremendous spiritual possibilities for the future. It is better by far to have a small but living and growing faith than to be possessed of a great intellect with its dead stores of worldly wisdom and spiritual ignorance."

But Jesus also earnestly warned his Apostles against the foolishness of the child of God who presumes upon the Father's love. He declared that the Heavenly Father is not a lax, loose, or foolishly indulgent parent who is ever ready to condone sin and forgive recklessness. He cautioned his disciples not to mistakenly apply his illustrations of father and son so as to make it appear that God is like some overindulgent and unwise parents on Earth who foolishly engage in the moral undoing of their thoughtless children, and who are thereby certainly and directly contributing to the delinquency and early demoralization of their own offspring. Said Jesus, "My Father does not indulgently condone those acts and practices of his children which are self-destructive and suicidal to all moral growth and spiritual progress. Such sinful practices are an abomination in the sight of God."

TEACHINGS ON SPIRITUAL GOODNESS

One night, long after the masses had departed from a full day of preaching, around the campfire Jesus continued to teach his Apostles far into the night. He began this special instruction by quoting from the Prophet Isaiah thus: "Why have you fasted? For what reason do you afflict your souls while you continue to find pleasure in oppressing your brothers and taking delight in injustice against your own people?

Behold, you fast for the sake of strife and contention and to smite with the fist of wickedness. But you shall not fast in this way to make your voices heard in Heaven."

Is this the fast that I have chosen, a day for a man to afflict his soul? Is it to bow down his head like a bulrush, to grovel in sackcloth and ashes? Will you dare to call this a fast and an acceptable day in the sight of the Father? Is this the fast that I should choose instead: to loose the bonds of wickedness, to undo the knots of heavy burdens, to let the oppressed go free, and to break every yoke? Is it not my duty to share my bread with the hungry and to bring those who are homeless and poor to my house? When I see those who are naked, I will clothe them."

Then shall your light break forth as the morning while your health springs forth speedily. Your righteousness shall go before you while the glory of the Father shall be your rear guard. Then will you come upon the Father, and he shall answer. You will cry out, and he shall say: 'Here I am.' All this he will do if you refrain from oppression, condemnation, and vanity. The Father desires that you draw out your heart to the hungry, and that you minister to the afflicted of your brothers. Then shall your light shine forth from obscurity, and even your darkness shall be as the noonday. Then shall the Father guide you continually, satisfying your soul and renewing your strength. You shall become like a watered garden, like a spring whose waters fail not. They who do these things shall restore the wasted glories. They shall raise up the foundations of many generations. They shall be called the rebuilders of broken walls, the restorers of safe paths in which to dwell."

Then long into the night Jesus explained to his Apostles the truth that it was their faith that made them secure in the kingdom of Heaven, and not their affliction of soul nor fasting of body. He challenged the Apostles to live up to the ideas of the prophets of old and expressed the hope that they would progress far beyond even the ideals of Isaiah and the older prophets. His last words of the night were: "Grow in grace by means of that living faith which grasps the fact that you are the sons of God while at the same time it recognizes every man as a brother."

Teachings on Sin and Evil

Most of the lessons that Jesus taught the Apostles occurred in the garden of Zebedee's home in Capernaum, after supper, around the campfire. Jesus and the Apostles gathered around the fire and talked long into the night. At one of these sessions, Thomas asked the Master: "Why is it necessary for men to be born of the spirit in order to enter the Father's kingdom? Is rebirth necessary to escape the control of evil? What is evil?" When Jesus heard these questions, he taught the following lessons:

"Evil is the unconscious or unintended transgression of the divine law, the Father's will. Evil is likewise the measure of the imperfectness of obedience to the Father's will.

Sin is the conscious, knowing, and deliberate transgression of the divine law, the Father's will. Sin is the measure of unwillingness to be divinely led and spiritually directed.

Iniquity is the willful, determined, and persistent transgression of the divine law, the Father's will. Iniquity is the measure of the continued rejection of the Father's loving plan of spiritual growth.

By nature, mortal man is subject to inherent evil tendencies, but such natural imperfections of behavior are neither sin nor iniquity.

Mortal man is just beginning his long journey to the finding of the Father in Heaven. To be imperfect or partial in natural endowment is not sinful. Man is indeed subject to evil, but he is in no way the child of the evil one unless he has knowingly and deliberately chosen the paths of sin and the life of iniquity. Evil is inherent in the natural order of this world, but sin is an attitude of conscious rebellion.

You are confused, Thomas, by the doctrines of the Greeks and the errors of the Persians and the teachings of the Jews. You do not understand the relationship between evil and sin because you view mankind as beginning on Earth with a perfect Adam and rapidly degenerating, through sin, to man's present deplorable state. But why do you refuse to comprehend the meaning of the record which discloses how Cain, the son of Adam, went over into the land of Nod and there got himself a wife? Adam was not the first man, and he did not bring evil and ruin upon mankind. Those are merely stories from long ago which had a purpose in those days to teach the children about good and evil.

Men are indeed, by nature potentially evil, but not necessarily sinful. The new birth, the baptism of the spirit, is essential to deliverance from evil and necessary for entrance into the kingdom of Heaven, but none of this detracts from the fact that man is the son of God. Neither does this inherent presence of potential evil mean that man is in some mysterious way separate from the Father in Heaven so that, as an alien, foreigner, or stepchild, he must in some manner seek for legal adoption by the Father. All such notions are born, first, of your misunderstanding of the Father and, second, of your ignorance of the origin, nature, and destiny of man.

The Greeks teach that man is descending from Godly perfection steadily down toward oblivion or destruction. I have come to show that man, by entrance into the Heavenly way, is ascending certainly and surely up to God and divine perfection. Any being who in any manner falls short of the divine and spiritual ideals of the eternal Father's will is potentially evil, but such beings are in no way sinful, much less iniquitous.

Thomas, have you read in the Scriptures, where it is written: 'You are the children of the Father your God. I will be his Father and he shall be my son. I have chosen him to be my son. I will be his Father. Bring my sons from far and my daughters from the ends of the Earth. Even everyone who is called by my name, for I have created them for my glory.' You, my Apostles, are the sons of the Living God.

They who have the spirit of God within them are indeed the sons of God. While there is a material part of the human father in each natural child, there is a spiritual part of the Heavenly Father in every faithful son."

All this and much more Jesus taught to Thomas and the others that evening around the fire. Much of it the Apostles comprehended, but much of it was beyond their ability to absorb.

Teachings on Human Suffering

At another of the evening sessions around the fire in the back yard of Zebedee's home, Nathaniel asked Jesus: "Master, though I am beginning to understand why you refuse to practice healing indiscriminately, I am still at a loss to understand why the loving Father in Heaven permits so many of his children on Earth to suffer so many afflictions." The Master answered Nathaniel, saying:

"Nathaniel, you and many others are perplexed because you do not comprehend how the natural order of this world has been so many times upset by the sinful adventures of certain rebellious traitors to the Father's will. I have come to make a beginning of setting these things in order. But many ages will be required to restore this world to former paths and thus release the children of men from the extra burdens of sin and rebellion. The presence of evil alone is a sufficient test for the ascension of man - sin is not essential to survival.

But, my son, you should know that the Father does not purposely afflict his children. Man brings down upon himself unnecessary afflictions as a result of his persistent refusal to walk in the better ways of the Divine Will. Most of the time affliction has its basis in evil, but much of affliction has been produced by sin and iniquity.

Many unusual events have transpired on this world, and it is not strange that all thinking men should be perplexed by the scenes of suffering and affliction which they witness. But of one thing you may be sure: the Father does not send affliction as an arbitrary punishment for wrongdoing. The imperfections and handicaps of evil are inherent. The penalties of sin are inevitable. Man should not blame God for those afflictions which are the natural result of the life which he chooses to live. Neither should man complain of those experiences which are a part of life as it is lived on this world. It is the Father's will that mortal man should work persistently and consistently toward the betterment of his estate on Earth. Intelligent living would enable man to overcome much of his earthly misery.

Nathaniel, it is our mission to help men solve their spiritual problems and, in this way, to quicken their minds so that they may be the better prepared and inspired to go about solving their many material problems. I know of your confusion as you have read the Scriptures.

All too often there has prevailed a tendency to ascribe to God the responsibility for everything which ignorant man fails to understand. The Father is not personally responsible for all you may fail to comprehend. Do not doubt the love of the Father just because some just and wise law of the universe chances to afflict you because you have innocently or deliberately transgressed such a divine ordinance.

"But, Nathaniel, there is much in the Scriptures which would have instructed you if you had only read with understanding. Do you not remember that it is written: 'My son, despise not the chastening of the Father. Neither be weary of his correction, for whom the Father loves he corrects, even as the Father corrects the son in whom he takes delight. The Father does not afflict willingly. Before I was afflicted, I went astray, but now I keep the law. Affliction was good for me that I might thereby learn the divine statutes. I know your sorrow. The eternal God is your refuge, while underneath are the everlasting arms. The Father also is a refuge for the oppressed, a haven of rest in times of trouble. The Father will strengthen him upon the bed of affliction. The Father will not forget the sick. As a father shows compassion for his children, so is the Father compassionate to those who fear him. He knows your body. He remembers that you are dust. He heals the brokenhearted and binds up their wounds. He is the hope of the poor, the strength of the needy in his distress, a refuge from the storm, and a shadow from the devastating heat. He gives power to the faint, and to them who have no might he increases strength. A bruised reed he shall not break, and the smoking flax he will not quench. When you pass through the waters of affliction, he will be with you, and when the rivers of adversity overflow you, he will not forsake you.' He sent me to bind up the brokenhearted, to proclaim liberty to the captives, and to comfort all who mourn. There is correction in suffering. Affliction does not spring forth from the dust."

TEACHINGS ON THE STORY OF JOB

One evening at Bethsaida as Jesus and his Apostles sat around the fire, John asked Jesus why so many apparently innocent people suffered from so many diseases and experienced so many afflictions. In answering John's questions, among many other things, the Master said:

"My son, you do not comprehend the meaning of adversity or the mission of suffering. Have you read that masterpiece of Semitic literature, the scripture story of the afflictions of Job? Do you recall how this wonderful parable begins with the recital of the material prosperity of Job, the Fathers' servant? You well remember that Job was blessed with children, wealth, dignity, position, health, and everything else which men value in this material life. According to the time-honored teachings of the children of Abraham such material prosperity was all-sufficient evidence of divine favor.

But such material possessions and such earthly prosperity do not indicate God's favor.

My Father in Heaven loves the poor just as much as the rich. He does not favor one man over another.

Although transgression of divine law is sooner or later followed by the harvest of punishment, while men eventually do reap what they sow, still you should know that human suffering is not always a punishment for prior sin. Both Job and his friends failed to find the true answer to their perplexities. With the light you now enjoy you would hardly assign to either Satan or God the parts they play in this unique parable. While Job did not, through suffering, find the resolution of his intellectual troubles or the solution of his philosophical difficulties, he did achieve great victories. Even in the very face of the breakdown of his theological defenses he ascended to those spiritual heights where he could sincerely say: 'I abhor myself.' Then had there granted him the salvation of a vision of God. So even through misunderstood suffering, Job ascended to the higher plane of moral understanding and spiritual insight. When the suffering servant obtains a vision of God, there follows a peace within the soul which surpasses all human understanding.

The first of Job's friends, Eliphaz, encouraged the sufferer to exhibit in his afflictions the same strength he had prescribed for others during the days of his prosperity. Said this false comforter to Job: 'Trust in your religion, Job. Remember that it is the wicked and not the righteous who suffer. You deserve this punishment; else you would not be afflicted. You well know that no man can be righteous in God's sight. You know that the wicked never really prosper. Anyway, man seems predestined to trouble, and perhaps the Father is only chastising you for your own good.' No wonder poor Job failed to get much comfort from such an interpretation of the problem of human suffering.

But the counsel of his second friend, Bildad, was even more depressing, notwithstanding its soundness from the standpoint of the then accepted theology. Bildad said: 'God cannot be unjust. Your children must have been sinners since they perished. You must be in error; else you would not be so afflicted. If you are really righteous, God will certainly deliver you from your afflictions. You should learn from the history of God's dealings with man that the almighty destroys only the wicked.'

Then remember how Job replied to his friends, saying: 'I well know that God does not hear my cry for help. How can God be just and at the same time so utterly disregard my innocence? I am learning that I can get no satisfaction from appealing to the almighty. Can't you understand that God tolerates the persecution of the good by the wicked? Since man is so weak, what chance has he for consideration at the hands of an omnipotent God? God has made me as I am, and when he thus turns upon me, I am defenseless. Why did God ever create me just to suffer in this miserable fashion?' Who can challenge the attitude of Job in view of the counsel of his friends and the erroneous ideas of God which occupied his own mind? Do you see how Job longed for a human God, that he hungered to commune with a divine being who knows man's mortal estate and understands that the just must often suffer in innocence as a part of this material life in a long journey to the Father? This is precisely why the son of God has come forth from the Father to live such a life in the flesh that he will be able to comfort all those who must henceforth be called upon to endure the afflictions of Job?

Job's third friend, Zophar, then spoke still less comforting words when he said: 'You are foolish to claim to be righteous, seeing that you are thus afflicted. But I admit that it is impossible to comprehend God's ways. Perhaps there is some hidden purpose in all your miseries.' When Job had listened to all three of his friends, he appealed directly to God for help, pleading the fact that man, born of woman, is few of days and full of trouble.

Then began the second session with his friends. Eliphaz grew more stern, accusing and sarcastic. Bildad became indignant at Job's contempt for his friends. Zophar reiterated his melancholy advice. Job by this time had become disgusted with his friends and appealed again to God, and now he appealed to a just God against the God of injustice embodied in the philosophy of his friends and enshrined even in his own religious attitude. Next Job took refuge in the consolation of a future life in which the iniquities of mortal existence may be more justly rectified. Failure to receive help from man drives Job to God. Then ensues the great struggle in his heart between faith and doubt. Finally, the human sufferer begins to see the light of life. His tortured soul ascends to new heights of hope and courage. He may suffer on and even die, but his enlightened soul now utters that cry of triumph: 'My vindicator lives.'

Job was altogether right when he challenged the belief that God afflicts children in order to punish their parents. Job was ready to admit that God is righteous, but he longed for some soul-satisfying revelation of the personal character of the Father. That is our mission on Earth. No more shall suffering mortals be denied the comfort of knowing the love of God and understanding the mercy of the Father in Heaven. While the speech of God spoken from the whirlwind was a majestic concept for the day of its utterance, you have already learned that the Father does not thus reveal himself, but rather that he speaks within the human heart as a still, small voice, saying: 'This is the way.

Walk therein.' Do you comprehend that God dwells within you, that he has become what you are that he may make you what he is."

Then Jesus made this final statement: "The Father in Heaven does not willingly afflict the children of men. Man suffers, first, from the accidents of time and the imperfections of an immature physical existence. Next, he suffers the consequences of sin, the transgression of the laws of life and light. Finally, man reaps the harvest of his own rebellion against the righteous rule of Heaven on Earth. But man's miseries are not a personal visitation of divine judgment. Man can, and will, do much to lessen his temporal sufferings. One day he will even be delivered from the superstition that God afflicts man at the behest of the evil one. Study the Book of Job if for no other reason than to just discover how many wrong ideas of God even good men can honestly entertain. Then note how even the painfully afflicted Job found the God of comfort and salvation in spite of such erroneous teachings. At last, his faith pierced the clouds of suffering to discern the light of life pouring forth from the Father as healing mercy and everlasting righteousness."

John pondered these sayings in his heart for many days. The rest of his life was markedly changed as a result of this conversation with the Master in the garden, and he did much, in later times, to cause the other Apostles to change their viewpoints regarding the source, nature, and purpose of commonplace human afflictions.

TEACHINGS ON CONTENTMENT

At one of the evening sessions around the fire, Simon Zelotes asked the Master, "Why are some people so much more happy and contented than others? Is contentment a matter of religious experience?" Jesus answered thus:

"Simon, some people are naturally more happy than others.

Much, very much, depends upon the willingness of man to be led and directed by the Father's spirit which lives within him. Have you read in the scriptures the words of the wise man who said: 'The spirit of man is the candle of the Father, searching all the inward parts.' And remember the words that such spirit-led mortals say: 'The lines are fallen to me in pleasant places. Yes, I have a Godly heritage. A little that a righteous man has is better than the riches of many wicked, for a good man shall be satisfied from within himself. A merry heart makes a cheerful countenance and is a continual feast. Better is a little reverence of the Father than great treasure and trouble therewith. Better is a dinner of herbs where love is than a fatted ox and hatred therewith. Better is a little with righteousness than great wealth without rectitude. A merry heart does good like medicine. Better is a handful with composure than a superabundance with sorrow and vexation of spirit.'

Much of man's sorrow is born of the disappointment of his ambitions and the wounding of his pride. Although men owe a duty to themselves to make the best of their lives on Earth, having thus overly exerted themselves, they should cheerfully accept their lot and exercise ingenuity in making the most of that which has fallen to their hands.

All too many of man's troubles take origin in the fear of his own natural heart. The wicked flee when no man pursues. The wicked are like the troubled sea, for it cannot rest, but its waters cast up mire and dirt. 'There is no peace' says God, 'for the wicked.'

Seek not, then, for false peace and transient joy but rather for the assurance of faith and the comfort of divine sonship which yield composure, contentment, and utter joy in the spirit.

Jesus hardly regarded this world as a "vale of tears." He instead looked upon it as the birth sphere of the eternal and immortal spirits of Heaven, the "vale of soul making."

TEACHINGS ON FEAR OF GOD

During one of their evening teaching sessions, at Gamala, Philip asked Jesus: "Why is it, Master, that the scriptures instruct us to fear God, while you would have us look to the Father in Heaven without fear? How are we to harmonize these teachings?" Jesus replied:

"My children, I am not surprised that you ask such questions. In the beginning it was only through fear that man could learn reverence, but I have come to reveal the Father's love so that you will be attracted to the worship of the Father by a son's affectionate recognition and return of the Father's profound and perfect love. I have come to deliver you from the bondage of driving yourselves through slavish fear to the loathsome service of a jealous and wrathful king-god. I have come to instruct you in the father-son relationship of God and man so that you may be joyfully led into the free worship of a loving, just, and merciful Father God.

The fear of the Father has had many different meanings in successive ages, coming up from fear, through anguish and dread, to awe and reverence. Now from reverence I will lead you up, through recognition, realization, and appreciation, to love. When man recognizes only the works of God, he is led to fear the Father. But when man begins to understand and experience the personality and character of the living God, he is led increasingly to love such a good and perfect, universal and eternal Father. It is just this changing of the relation of man to God that constitutes the mission of the Son of God on Earth.

Intelligent children do not fear their father in order that they may receive good gifts from his hand. But having already received the abundance of good things bestowed by the father's affection for his sons and daughters, these much-loved children are led to love their father in response and in recognition of such grand benevolence. The recognition of the goodness of God leads to repentance from wrongdoing. The recognition of the benevolence of God leads to unselfish service. The recognition of the mercy of God leads to salvation. While the love of God leads to intelligent and freehearted worship.

Your forefathers feared God because they had created a God who was mighty, mysterious and angry. You must now learn to love God because he is magnificent in love, charitable in mercy, and glorious in truth. The power of God engenders fear in the heart of man, but the nobility and righteousness of his personality instills reverence, love, and willing worship. A dutiful and affectionate son does not fear or dread even a mighty and noble Father. I have come into the world to put love in the place of fear, joy in the place of sorrow, confidence in the place of dread, and loving service in the place of slavish bondage to meaningless ceremonies. But it is still true of those who sit in darkness that the fear of the Father is the beginning of wisdom. When the light has more fully come, those sons of God will be led to praise the infinite for what he is rather than to fear him for what they perceive he does.

When children are young and unthinking, they must necessarily be admonished to honor their parents. But when they grow older and become somewhat more appreciative of the benefits of the parental ministry and protection, they are led up, through understanding respect and increasing affection, to that level of experience where they actually love their parents for what they are more than for what they have done. The father naturally loves his child, but the child must develop his love for the father from the fear of what the father can do, through awe, dread, dependence, reverence, and finally to the appreciative and affectionate regard of love.

You have been taught that you should fear God and keep his commandments, for that is the whole duty of man. But I have come to give you a new and higher commandment. I will teach you to love God and learn to do his will, for that is the highest privilege of man. Your fathers were taught to fear God - the almighty king. I have come to teach you to love God, the all merciful Father.

In the kingdom of Heaven, which I have come to declare, there is no high and mighty king. This brotherhood is a divine family. The universally recognized head of this far-flung brotherhood of intelligent beings in all inhabited worlds, is my Father and your Father. I am his son, and you are also his sons. Therefore, it is eternally true that you and I are brothers in the Heavenly estate, and all the more so since we have become brothers in the flesh of this earthly life. Cease, then, to fear God as a king or serve him as a master. Learn to reverence him as the creator. Honor him as the father of your spirit. Love him as a merciful defender, and ultimately worship him as the loving and all- wise Father of your more mature spiritual life.

Out of your erroneous concepts of the Father in Heaven grow your false ideas of humility. From this fallacy also springs much of your hypocrisy. Man may be a worm of the dust by nature and origin, but when he became indwelt by my Father's spirit, that man became divine in his destiny. The spirit that my Father bestowed on you will eventually return to the divine source of origin, and the human soul of mortal man which shall have become the child of this indwelling spirit shall also ascend with the divine spirit to the very presence of the eternal Father.

Humble indeed becomes mortal man who receives all these gifts from the Father in Heaven, although there is a divine dignity attached to all such candidates for the eternal ascent to the Heavenly realms.

The meaningless practices of a false humility are incompatible with the appreciation of the source of your grace and the recognition of the destiny of your souls. Humility before God is altogether appropriate to the depths of your hearts. Meekness before men is commendable, but the hypocrisy of self-conscious and attention-craving humility is childish and unworthy of the enlightened sons of Heaven."

You do well to be meek before God and self-controlled before men, but let your meekness be of spiritual origin and not the self- deceptive display of a sense of self-righteous superiority. The prophet spoke wisely when he said: 'Walk humbly with God, for, while the Father in Heaven is the infinite and the eternal, he also dwells with him who is of contrite mind and a humble spirit.' My Father dislikes pride, loathes hypocrisy, and abhors iniquity. It was to emphasize the value of sincerity and perfect trust in the loving support and faithful guidance of the Heavenly Father that I have so often referred to the example of the little child as illustrative of the attitude of mind and the response of the spirit which are essential to the entrance of mortal man into the kingdom of Heaven.

The Prophet Jeremiah described very well many mortals when he said: 'You are near God in your mouth but far from him in your heart.' Have you not also read that warning of the prophet who said: 'The priests teach for hire, and the prophets divine for money at the same time they profess piety and proclaim that the Father is with them.' Have you not been well warned against those who speak peace to their neighbors when mischief is in their hearts, those who flatter with their lips while the heart is given to double-dealing. Of all the sorrows of a trusting man, none is so terrible as to be wounded in the house of a trusted friend.

TEACHINGS ON SALVATION

One evening after supper, around the fire, at Shunem, the Master was engaged in the teaching of a group of young evangelists together with some women from the women's corp. Rachel asked this question, "Master, what shall we answer when women ask us: 'What must I do to be saved?'" Jesus answered:

"When men and women ask you what they shall do to be saved, you shall answer them saying: Believe the gospel of the Father. Accept divine forgiveness. By faith recognize the indwelling spirit of God, whose acceptance makes you a son or daughter of God. Have you not read in the scriptures where it says: 'In the Father I find righteousness and strength.' Also, where the Father says: 'My righteousness is near.

My salvation has gone forth, and my arms shall enfold my people.'

Also remember the words of the prophet who said: 'My soul shall be joyful in the love of my God, for he has clothed me with the garments of salvation and has covered me with the robe of his righteousness.' Have you not also read these words: 'Take away the filthy rags of self- righteousness and clothe my son with the robe of divine righteousness and eternal salvation.' It is forever true that the just shall live by faith alone. Entrance into the Father's realm is wholly free, but progress, growth in grace, is essential to continuance therein.

Salvation is the gift of the Father and is revealed by his sons and daughters. Acceptance by faith on your part makes you a partner of the divine nature, a son or a daughter of God. By faith you are justified. By faith you are saved. By this same faith you are advancing in the way of progressive and divine perfection. By faith, Abraham was made aware of salvation by the teachings of Melchizedek. All down through the ages this same faith has saved the sons of men, but now a son has come forth from the Father to make salvation more real and acceptable."

When Jesus had finished speaking, there was great rejoicing among those who had heard these gracious words, and they all went on in the days that followed proclaiming the gospel of the new religion with new power and with renewed energy and enthusiasm. The women rejoiced all the more to know they were included in these plans for the establishment of the new religion on Earth.

In summing up his remarks, Jesus said, "You cannot buy salvation. You cannot earn righteousness. Salvation is the gift of God, and righteousness is the natural fruit of being a child of the Father.

You will not be saved just because you live a righteous life. Rather is it that you will live a righteous life because you have already been saved, because you have recognized sonship as the gift of God and service in the new religion as the ultimate delight of life on Earth.

When men believe this gospel, which is a revelation of the goodness of God, they will be led to voluntary repentance of all known sin and wrongdoing. The realization of sonship is incompatible with the desire to sin. Kingdom believers hunger for righteousness and thirst for divine perfection."

THE WOMEN'S CORPS

Of all the daring things which Jesus did in connection with his earthly career, the most amazing was his sudden announcement that he was setting apart ten women as the beginning of a women's corps for the work of ministering to women. At the beginning of a two-week period during which the Apostles and other evangelists were absent from Bethsaida on their furlough, Jesus requested David Zebedee to dispatch messengers calling to Bethsaida ten devout women who had already served in the administration of the former encampments and the tented infirmaries. These women had all been present and listened to the instructions given the young evangelists who had been recruited, but it had never occurred to either themselves or their teachers that Jesus would dare to commission women to teach the gospel and minister to the sick. These ten women selected and commissioned by Jesus were: Susanna, the daughter of the former Chazzan of the Nazareth synagogue; Joanna, the wife of Chuza, the chief steward of Herod Antipas; Elizabeth, the daughter of a wealthy Jew of Tiberias and Sepphoris; Martha, the elder sister of Andrew and Peter; Rachel, the sister-in-law of Jude, the brother of Jesus; Nasanta, the daughter of Elman, a Syrian physician; Milcha, a cousin of the Apostle Thomas; Ruth, the eldest daughter of Matthew Levi; Celta, the daughter of a Roman centurion; and Agaman, a widow from Damascus. Subsequent to this, Jesus added two other women to this group, Mary Magdalene, and Rebecca, the daughter of Joseph of Arimathea.

Jesus called the ten together and authorized these women to create their own organization and directed Judas to provide funds for their equipment and for pack animals. The ten elected Susanna as their chief and Joanna as their treasurer. From this time on they furnished their own funds. Never again did they draw upon Judas for support.

It was the most astounding event of that day, when women were not even allowed on the main floor of the synagogue, to behold them being recognized as authorized teachers of the new gospel. In those days in the Jewish religion and ceremonies, women were relegated to the women's gallery. The charge which Jesus gave these ten women as he set them apart for gospel teaching and ministry was the emancipation proclamation which set all women free for all time. No more was man to look upon woman as his spiritual inferior. This was a decided shock to even the twelve Apostles. Notwithstanding they had many times heard the Master say: "In the kingdom of Heaven there is neither rich nor poor, free nor bond, male nor female, all are equally the sons and daughters of God." They were stunned when he proposed formally to commission these ten women as religious teachers and even to permit their traveling about with them. The whole country was stirred up by this proceeding, the enemies of Jesus made great issue out of this move, but everywhere the women believers in the good news stood solidly behind their chosen sisters and voiced a loud approval of this tardy acknowledgment of woman's place in religious work. This liberation of women, giving them due recognition, was practiced by the Apostles immediately after the Master's departure, although they fell back to the olden customs in subsequent generations. Throughout the early days of the Christian church women teachers and ministers were called Deaconesses and were accorded general recognition. They are referred to in the Bible as "the Holy Women." Paul, despite the fact that he conceded all this in theory, never incorporated it into his own attitude and personally found it difficult to carry out in practice.

Women were left out of his organization of the early church.

As the apostolic party journeyed from Bethsaida on another preaching tour, the Women's Corps traveled alongside. During the conference time they always sat in a group in front and to the right of the speaker. Increasingly, women had become believers in the new gospel. Before this time, it had been a source of much difficulty and no end of embarrassment when they had desired to hold personal conversation with Jesus or one of the Apostles but could not get an audience with them. Now all this was changed. When any of the women believers desired to see the Master or confer with the Apostles, they went to Susanna, and in company with one of the twelve women evangelists, they would go at once into the presence of the Master or one of his Apostles.

It was during the first preaching tour for these women, at Magdala, that the women first demonstrated their usefulness and vindicated the wisdom of their choosing. Andrew had imposed very strict rules upon his associates about doing personal work with women especially with those of ill repute. When the party entered Magdala, these ten women evangelists were free to enter the houses of ill repute and preach the glad tidings directly to all their inmates. As the result of the ministry of these ten women at this place, Mary Magdalene was won for the new gospel. Through a succession of misfortunes, and in consequence of the attitude of a reputable society toward women who commit such errors of judgment, this woman had found herself in one of the resorts of Magdala. It was Martha and Rachel who made it plain to Mary that the doors of Heaven were open to even such as her. Mary believed the good news and was baptized by Peter the next day.

Mary Magdalene became the most effective teacher of the gospel among this group of twelve women evangelists. She was set apart for such service, together with Rebecca, at Jotapata about four weeks after her conversion. Mary and Rebecca, with the others of this group, went on through the remainder of Jesus' life on Earth, laboring faithfully and effectively for the enlightenment and uplifting of their downtrodden sisters. When the last and tragic episode in the drama of Jesus' life was being enacted, when

JESUS OF NAZARETH 317

the Apostles all fled but one, these twelve women were all present, and not one of them either denied him or betrayed him.

TEACHINGS ON MAGIC AND SUPERSTITION

Late one evening, while on a preaching tour of Tiberias, Jesus gave the assembled group a memorable talk on magic and superstition. In those days the appearance of a bright and supposedly new star in the heavens was regarded as a token indicating that a great man had been born on Earth. Such a star having then recently been observed, Andrew asked Jesus if these beliefs had any merit. In the long answer to Andrew's question the Master entered upon a thorough discussion of the whole subject of human superstition. The statements which Jesus made at this time may be summarized in modern terminology as follows:

"1) The courses of the stars in the heavens have nothing whatever to do with the events of human life on Earth. Astronomy is a proper pursuit of science, but astrology is a superstitious error which has no place in the new gospel.

2) The examination of the internal organs of an animal recently killed can reveal nothing about weather, future events, or the outcome of human affairs.

3) The spirits of the dead do not come back to communicate with their families or their onetime friends among the living.

4) Charms and relics are impotent to heal diseases, ward off disaster, or influence evil spirits. The belief in all such

material means of influencing the spiritual world is nothing but gross superstition.

5) Casting lots, while it may be a convenient way of settling many minor difficulties, is not a method designed to disclose the divine will. Such outcomes are purely matters of material chance. The only means of communion with the spirit world is through the spirit of the Father that dwells within you, together with the outpoured spirit of the son, the Spirit of Truth, and the omnipresent influence of the infinite spirit, that which you call the Holy Spirit.

6) Divination, sorcery, and witchcraft are superstitions of ignorant minds, as also are the delusions of magic. The belief in magic numbers, omens of good luck, and harbingers of bad luck, is pure and unfounded superstition.

7) The interpretation of dreams is largely a superstition and groundless system of ignorance and fantastic speculation. The new gospel must have nothing in common with the soothsayer priests of primitive religions.

8) The spirits of good or evil cannot dwell within idols of clay, wood, or metal. Idols are nothing more than the material of which they are made.

9) The practices of the enchanters, the wizards, the magicians, and the sorcerers, were derived from the superstitions of the Egyptians, the Assyrians, the Babylonians, and your own forefathers, the Hebrews. Amulets and all sorts of incantations are futile either to win the protection of good spirits or to ward off supposed evil spirits."

Jesus, at this time, also identified and denounced the Jewish beliefs in spells, ordeals, bewitching, cursing, signs, mandrakes, knotted cords, and many other forms of ignorant and enslaving superstitions practiced in Palestine in those days.

THE EPOCHAL ADDRESS

As the Master traveled and preached through Northern Palestine, he saw the political winds blowing and knew that the time was rapidly approaching when the religious and political leaders of Jerusalem would declare open warfare on him, and he elected boldly to assume the offensive. After the feeding of the five thousand from a basket of bread and a basket of fish, he openly challenged the Jewish ideas of the Messiah. Now he chose again openly to attack their concept of the Jewish deliverer. This crisis, which began with the feeding of the five thousand, and which culminated with this epochal sermon on a Sabbath afternoon at the synagogue in Jerusalem, was the outward turning of the tide of popular fame and acclaim. Henceforth, the work of the new religion was to be increasingly concerned with the more important task of winning lasting spiritual converts for the truly religious brotherhood of mankind. This sermon marked the crisis in the transition from the period of discussion about the new religion, to that of open warfare with the Jewish religious and political leaders, and final public acceptance or rejection.

The Master well knew that many of his followers were slowly but surely preparing their minds finally to reject him. He likewise knew that many of his disciples were slowly but certainly passing through that training of mind and that discipline of soul which would enable them to triumph over doubt and courageously assert their full-fledged faith in the new gospel. Jesus fully understood how men prepare themselves for the decisions of a crisis and the performance of sudden deeds of courage by choosing between the recurring situations of good and evil. He subjected his chosen messengers to repeated rehearsals in disappointment and provided them with frequent and testing opportunities for choosing between the right and the wrong way of meeting spiritual trials. He knew he could depend on his followers, when they met the final test, to make their vital decisions in accordance with prior and habitual mental attitudes and spiritual reactions.

This was the most spiritually profound crisis in Jesus' Earth life.

It began with the feeding of the five thousand and ended with this sermon in the synagogue in Jerusalem. The crisis came about because of the belief by the masses that he was truly the Jewish Messiah after they witnessed him feeding five thousand people with a few loaves of bread and a basket of fish. He had to make a direct and concerted attack on this belief. In the process of doing this he had to dash the hopes and dreams of many of his followers who truly believed that he was the long-awaited temporal deliverer of the Jewish people. The major crisis in the lives of the Apostles began with this sermon in the synagogue and continued for an entire year, ending only with the Master's trial and crucifixion. It was a trial for them because they had to come face to face with the realization that their concept of the Jewish Messiah was an erroneous concept, and that many of the things that they had believed in for their entire lives were false.

As they sat there in the synagogue that afternoon waiting for Jesus to begin to speak, there was just one great mystery, just one huge question in the minds of all those assembled. Both his friends and his enemies pondered just one thought, and that was: "Why did he himself so deliberately and effectively turn back the tide of popular enthusiasm about the Messiah?" It was immediately before and immediately after this sermon that the doubts and disappointments of his disgruntled followers grew into unconscious opposition and eventually turned into actual hatred. It was after this sermon in the synagogue that Judas Iscariot entertained his first conscious thought of deserting, but he did, for the time being, effectively master all such inclinations.

Everyone was in a state of perplexity. Jesus had left them dumfounded and confounded. He had recently engaged in the greatest demonstration of supernatural power to characterize his whole career. The feeding of the five thousand was the one event of his Earth life which made the greatest appeal to the Jewish concept of the expected Messiah. But this extraordinary event was immediately and unexplainably offset by his prompt and unequivocal refusal to be made king or to be called the Jewish Messiah.

On Friday evening, and again on Sabbath morning, the Jerusalem leaders had labored long and earnestly with Jairus to prevent Jesus' speaking in the synagogue, but it was of no avail. Jairus' only reply to all this pleading was: "I have granted this request, and I will not violate my word."

Jesus stood and addressed the assembled. He introduced his sermon by reading from Deuteronomy: "But it shall come to pass, if this people will not listen to the voice of Yahweh, that the curses of transgression shall surely overtake them. Yahweh shall cause you to be beaten by your enemies. You shall be removed into all the kingdoms of the Earth. Yahweh shall bring you, and the king you have set up over you, into the hands of a strange nation. You shall become an astonishment, a proverb, and a byword among all nations. Your sons and your daughters shall go into captivity. The strongest among you shall rise high in authority while you, as a people, are brought very low. These things shall be upon you and your seed forever because you would not listen to the word of Yahweh. Therefore, shall you serve your enemies who shall come against you. You shall endure hunger and thirst and wear an alien yoke of iron. Yahweh shall bring against you a nation from afar, from the ends of the Earth, a nation whose tongue you shall not understand, a nation of fierce countenance, a nation which will have little regard for you. They shall besiege you in all your towns until the high fortified walls wherein you have trusted come down. All the land shall fall into their hands. It shall come to pass that you will be driven to eat the fruit of your own bodies, the flesh of your sons and daughters, during this time of siege, because of the straightness wherewith your enemies shall oppress you."

When Jesus had finished this reading, he turned to the Prophets and began reading from Jeremiah: "If you will not listen to the words of my servants, the Prophets, whom I have sent you, then will I make this house like Shiloh, and I will make this city a curse to all the nations of the Earth."

Then Jesus said, "The priests and the teachers heard Jeremiah speak these words in the house of the Father. It came to pass that, when Jeremiah had made an end of speaking all that the Father had commanded him to speak to all the people, the priests and teachers laid hold of him saying, 'You shall surely die.' All the people crowded around Jeremiah in the house of the Father, and when the princes of Judah heard these things, they sat in judgment on Jeremiah. Then spoke the priests and the teachers to the princes and to all the people, saying: 'This man is worthy to die, for he has prophesied against our city, and you have heard him with your own ears.'

Then spoke Jeremiah to all the princes and the people: 'The Father sent me to prophesy against this house and against this city all the words which you have heard. Now, therefore, amend your ways and reform your doings and obey the voice of the Father, your God, so that you may escape the evil which has been pronounced against you. As for me, I am in your hands. Do with me as seems good and right in your eyes. But know you for certain that, if you put me to death, you shall bring innocent blood upon yourselves and upon this people. It is the truth that the Father has sent me to speak all these words in your ears.'

The priests and teachers of that day sought to kill Jeremiah, but the judges would not consent. Instead, the judges ordered that he be lowered by ropes into a filthy dungeon until he sank in mire up to his armpits. That is what this Jewish people did to the prophet Jeremiah when he obeyed the Father's command to warn his brothers of their impending political downfall. Today, I desire to ask you: What will the chief priests and religious leaders of this people do with the man who dares to warn them of the day of their spiritual doom? Will you also seek to put to death the teacher who dares to proclaim the word of the Father, and who fears not to point out wherein you refuse to walk in the way of light which leads to the entrance to the kingdom of Heaven?

What is it you seek as evidence of my mission on Earth? We have left you undisturbed in your positions of influence and power while we preached the Good News to the poor and the outcast. We have made no hostile attack upon that which you hold in reverence. But we have instead proclaimed new liberty for man's fear-ridden soul. I came into the world to reveal my Father and to establish on Earth the spiritual brotherhood of the sons of God, the kingdom of Heaven.

Notwithstanding that, I have so many times reminded you that my realm is not of this world. Still has my Father granted you many manifestations of material wonders in addition to more outward spiritual transformations and regenerations.

What new sign is it that you seek at my hands? I declare that you already have sufficient evidence to enable you to make your decision. Strongly I state to all those seated before me today, you are confronted with the necessity of choosing which way you will go. I say to you, as Joshua said to your forefathers, choose you this day whom you will serve. Today many of you stand at the parting of the ways.

Some of you, when you could not find me after feasting on the other side of the sea, hired the Tiberias fishing fleet, which a week before had taken shelter nearby during a storm, to go in pursuit of me, and what for? Not for truth and righteousness or that you might the better know how to serve and minister to your fellow men. No, but rather that you might have more bread for which you had not labored. You did not go in search of me to fill your souls with the word of life, but rather to fill your bellies with the bread of ease. Long have you been taught that the Messiah, when he should come, would work those wonders which would make life pleasant and easy for all the chosen people. It is not strange, then, that you who have been thus taught should long for the easy loaves and the fishes. But I declare to you that such is not the mission of the Son of God. I am not your Messiah. I have come to proclaim spiritual liberty, teach eternal truth, and foster living faith.

My brothers do not seek after the meat which perishes but rather seek the spiritual food that nourishes even to eternal life. This is the bread of life which the son gives to all who will take it and eat, for the Father has given the son this life without measure. When you asked me, 'What must we do to perform the work of God?' I plainly told you: this is the work of God, that you believe him whom he has sent."

Then said Jesus, pointing up to a pot of manna which decorated the lintel of the synagogue, and which was embellished with grape clusters: "You have thought that your forefathers in the wilderness ate manna, the bread of Heaven, but I say to you that this was the bread of Earth. While Moses did not give your forefathers bread from Heaven, my Father now stands ready to give you the true bread of life. The bread of Heaven is that which comes down from God and gives eternal life to the men of the world. When you say to me, 'Give us this living bread!', I will answer I am the living bread. He who comes to me shall not hunger, while he who believes in me shall never thirst. You have seen me, lived with me, and beheld my works, yet you do not believe that I came forth from the Father. But to those who do believe, fear is not. All those who believe in my Father shall come to me, and he who comes to me shall never be cast out.

Now let me declare to you once and for all time, that I have come down to Earth, not to do my own will, but the will of him who sent me. This is the will of him who sent me, that of all those he has given me I should not lose one. This is the will of the Father, that everyone who beholds the son and who believes in him shall have eternal life. Only yesterday did I feed you bread for your bodies. Today I offer you the bread of life for your hungry souls. Will you now take the bread of the spirit as you then so willingly ate the bread of this world?"

As Jesus paused for a moment to look over the congregation, one of the members of the Sanhedrin rose up and asked: "Do I understand you to say that you are the bread which comes down from Heaven, and that the manna which Moses gave to our fathers in the wilderness did not come from Heaven?" Jesus answered the Pharisee: "You understand right." Then said the Pharisee: "But are you not Jesus of Nazareth, the son of Joseph, the carpenter? Are not your father and mother, as well as your brothers and sisters well known to us all? How then is it that you appear here in God's house and declare that you have come down from Heaven?"

By this time there was much murmuring in the synagogue, and such a tumult was threatened that Jesus stood up and said: "Let us be patient. The truth never suffers from honest examination. I am all that you say and more. The Father in Heaven has sent me. The son does only what the Father teaches him while all those who are given to the son by the Father, the son will receive to himself. You have read where it is written in the Prophets, 'You shall all be taught by God', and also that, 'Those whom the Father teaches will hear also his son.'

Everyone who yields to the teaching of the Father's indwelling spirit will eventually come to me. Not that any man has seen the Father, but the Father's spirit does live within man, and the spiritual man is aware of this. The son who came down from Heaven has surely seen the Father. Those who truly believe this son already have eternal life.

I am this bread of life. Your fathers ate manna in the wilderness and are dead. But if man eats the bread which comes down from God, he shall never die in spirit. I repeat to you that I am this living bread, and every soul who understands the united nature of God and man shall live forever. This bread of life which I give to all who will receive is my own living and combined nature. The Father in the son and the son one with the father, which is my life-giving revelation to the world and my saving gift to all nations."

When Jesus had finished speaking, the rulers of the synagogue dismissed the congregation, but the people would not depart. They crowded up around Jesus to ask more questions while others murmured and disputed among themselves. This state of affairs continued for more than three hours. It was well into evening time when the crowd finally dispersed.

Jesus departed from Jerusalem that evening under cover. He knew that his life was in danger. His followers passed word that he had departed for Capernaum, and the Pharisees and their armed assistants quickly followed, spending almost a week searching for him throughout Capernaum and its environs. Jesus had slipped quietly to the Phoenician coast and from this moment on to the end, subterfuge was used to confound the enemy and ensure that the Son of God would not be captured until his message was complete.

Teachings on the Wrath of God

After fleeing from Jerusalem, Jesus and the Apostles found themselves once again preaching through northern Galilee. At one of the nighttime teaching sessions around the campfire, Jesus said to those assembled: "You shall all recall how the Psalmist spoke of these times, saying, 'Why do the heathen rage and the people plot in vain? The rulers of the people take counsel together, against the Father and against his anointed one, saying, let us break the bonds of mercy asunder and let us cast away the cords of love.'

Today you see these words fulfilled before your very eyes. But you shall not see the remainder of the Psalmist's prophecy fulfilled, for he had erroneous ideas about the Son of God's mission on Earth. My new religion is founded on love, proclaimed in mercy, and established by unselfish service. My Father does not sit in Heaven laughing in derision at the heathen. He is not wrathful in his great displeasure.

True is his promise that the son shall have these heathen for an inheritance. All this loving kindness shall be shown the so-called heathen, notwithstanding the unfortunate declaration of the record which states that the triumphant son, 'Shall break them with a rod of iron and dash them to pieces like a potter's vessel.' The Psalmist urged you to serve the Father with fear. I have come to teach you to enter into the high privileges of divine sonship by faith alone. The Psalmist commanded you to rejoice with trembling. I bid you rejoice with love and assurance. The Psalmist said, 'Kill the son, lest he be angry, and you perish when his wrath is kindled.' But you who have lived with me well know that anger and wrath are not a part of the establishment of the kingdom of Heaven in the hearts of men. But the Psalmist did glimpse the true light when, in finishing this exhortation, he said: 'Blessed are they who put their trust in this son.'

Jesus continued to teach the group saying, "The heathen are not without excuse when they rage at us. Because their outlook is small and narrow, they are able to concentrate their energies enthusiastically.

Their goal is near and more or less visible. Therefore, do they strive with valiant and effective execution. You who have professed entrance into the kingdom of Heaven are altogether too vacillating and indefinite in your teaching conduct. The heathen strikes directly for their objectives. You are guilty of too much chronic yearning. If you desire to enter the kingdom, why do you not take it by spiritual assault even as the heathen take a city they lay siege? You are hardly worthy of the new religion when your service consists so largely in an attitude of regretting the past, whining over the present, and vainly hoping for the future. Why do the heathen rage? Because they do not know the truth. Why do you languish in futile yearning? Because you do not obey the truth. Cease your useless yearning and go forth bravely doing that which concerns the establishment of the new gospel.

In all that you do, do not become one-sided and over-specialized.

The Pharisees who seek our destruction sincerely think they are doing God's service. They have become so narrowed by tradition that they are blinded by prejudice and hardened by fear. Consider the Greeks, who have a science without religion, while the Jews have a religion without science. When men become thus misled into accepting a narrow and confused disintegration of truth, their only hope of salvation is to become converted into the truths of the Father.

Let me emphatically state this eternal truth: If you, by the conversion of truth, learn to exemplify in your lives this beautiful wholeness of righteousness, your fellow men will then seek after you so that they may learn from you what you have so acquired. The measure whereby truth seekers are drawn to you represents the measure of your righteousness as seen by them. The extent to which you, yourself, have to go with your message to the people, rather than they are seeking for you, will be the measure of your failure to live the righteous life."

TEACHINGS ON TRUE RELIGION

While pausing for lunch under the shadow of an overhanging ledge of rock on the way to Sidon, Jesus delivered one of the most remarkable addresses which his Apostles ever listened to throughout all their years of association with him. No sooner had they sat down to break bread this noontime when Simon Peter asked Jesus: "Master, since the Father in Heaven knows all things, and since his spirit is our support in the establishment of the kingdom of Heaven on Earth, why is it that we flee from the threats of our enemies? Why do we refuse to confront the foes of truth?" But before the Master had begun to answer, Thomas broke in, asking: "Master, I should really like to know just what is wrong with the religion of our enemies in Jerusalem. What is the real difference between their religion and ours? Why is it we are at such diversity of belief when we all profess to serve the same God?"

When Thomas had finished, Jesus said: "While I would not ignore Peter's question, knowing full well how easy it would be to misunderstand my reasons for avoiding an open clash with the rulers of the Jews at just this time, it will prove more helpful to all of you if I choose instead to answer Thomas' question. This I will proceed to do when you have finished your lunch."

This memorable discourse on religion, summarized and restated in modern terminology, gave expression to the following truths:

"While the religions of the world have a double origin, natural and revelatory, at any one time and among any one people there are to be found three distinct forms of religious devotion. These three manifestations of the religious urge are:

1. Primitive Religions - the natural and instinctive urge to fear mysterious energies and worship superior forces, chiefly religions of the physical nature, the religions of fear.

2. The Religions of Civilization - the advancing religious concepts and practices of the civilizing races, the religions of the mind, the intellectual theology of the authority of established religious tradition.

3. True Religion - the religion of revelation. A glimpse of the goodness and beauty of the infinite character of the Father in Heaven, the religion of the spirit as demonstrated in human experience."

The Master refused to belittle the religions of the physical senses and the superstitious fears of natural man though he deplored the fact that so much of this primitive form of worship should persist in the religious ceremonies of the more intelligent races of mankind. Jesus made it clear that the great difference between the religions of the mind and the religion of the spirit is that, while the former are upheld by ecclesiastical authority, the latter are wholly based on human experience.

Then the Master, in one hour of teaching, went on to make clear these truths paraphrased in modern language: "Until the races become highly intelligent and more fully civilized, there will persist many of those childlike and superstitious ceremonies which are so characteristic of the evolutionary religious practices of primitive and backward peoples. Until the human races progress to the level of a higher and more general recognition of the truths of spiritual experience, large numbers of men and women will continue to show a personal preference for those religions of authority which require only intellectual agreement, in contrast to the religion of the spirit, which requires active participation of mind and soul in grappling with the tough tests of human experience.

The acceptance of a religion of authority presents the easy way out for man's urge to seek satisfaction for the longings of his spiritual nature. The settled, crystallized, and established religions of authority afford a ready refuge to which the distracted and distraught soul of man may flee when harassed by fear and tormented by uncertainty.

Such a religion requires of its followers, as the price to be paid for its satisfactions and assurances, only a passive and purely intellectual commitment.

For a very long time yet there will live on Earth those timid, fearful, and hesitant individuals who will prefer thus to secure their religious consolations, even though, in so casting their lot with the religions of authority, they will give up the freedom of personality, debase the dignity of self-respect, and utterly surrender their right to participate in that most thrilling and inspiring of all possible human experiences: the personal quest for truth, the exhilaration of facing the perils of intellectual discovery, the determination to explore personal religious experiences, and the satisfaction of experiencing the triumph of spiritual faith over intellectual doubt, the ultimate adventure of all human existence, man seeking God and finding him.

The religion of the spirit means effort, struggle, conflict, faith, determination, love, loyalty, and progress. The religions of the mind, the theology of authority, require little or none of these exertions from its believers. Tradition is a safe refuge, and the easy way out, for those fearful and halfhearted souls who instinctively shun the spirit struggles and mental uncertainties associated with those faith voyages of daring adventure out upon the high seas of unexplored truth in search for the farthest shores of spiritual truths as they can be discovered by the human mind and experienced by the evolving human soul.

At Jerusalem, the religious leaders have formulated the various doctrines of their teachers and prophets into an established system of intellectual beliefs. They have created a religion of authority. The appeal of all such religions is largely to the mind. Now we are about to enter upon a deadly conflict with such a religion since we will shortly begin the bold proclamation of a new religion, a religion which is not a religion in the present-day meaning of that word, a religion that makes its chief appeal to the divine spirit of my Father which resides in the mind of each man, a religion which shall derive its authority from the fruits of its acceptance.

Now, which one of you would prefer to travel the easy path of conformity to an established and fossilized religion, as defended by the Pharisees at Jerusalem, rather than to suffer the difficulties and persecutions attendant upon the mission of proclaiming a better way of salvation to men while you realize the satisfaction of discovering for yourselves the beauties of the living kingdom of Heaven? Are you fearful, soft, and ease-seeking? Are you afraid to trust your future in the hands of the God of truth, whose sons you are? Are you distrustful of the Father, whose children you are? Will you go back to the easy path of the certainty and intellectual settledness of the religion of traditional authority, or will you bind yourselves to go forward with me into that uncertain and troubled future of proclaiming the new truths of the religion of the spirit, the kingdom of Heaven in the hearts of men?"

All those gathered rose to their feet immediately, intending to signify their united and loyal response to this, one of the few emotional appeals which Jesus ever made to them, but he raised his hand and stopped them, saying: "Go now by yourselves, each man alone with the Father, and there find the unemotional answer to my questions, and having found such a true and sincere attitude of soul, speak that answer freely and boldly to my Father and your Father, whose infinite love is the very heart and soul of the religion that we proclaim."

The evangelists and Apostles went apart by themselves for a short time. Their spirits were uplifted, their minds were inspired, and their emotions mightily stirred by what Jesus had said. But when Andrew called them together, the Master said only: "Let us

resume our journey. We are going into Phoenicia to preach for a
season, and all of you should pray for the Father to transform your
emotions of mind and body into the higher loyalties of mind and
the more satisfying experiences of the spirit."

As they journeyed down the road, all were silent, but presently
they began to talk to one another, and by midafternoon they could
not go further. They came to a halt, and Peter, going up to Jesus,
said: "Master, you have spoken to us the words of life and truth.
We would like to hear more. We ask you to speak to us further
concerning these matters." While they paused in the shade of the
hillside, Jesus continued to teach them regarding the religion of
the spirit saying:

"You have all come out from among those of your fellows who
chose to remain satisfied with a religion of the mind, who crave
security and prefer conformity. You have elected to exchange your
feelings of authoritative certainty for the assurances of the spirit
of adventurous and progressive faith. You have dared to protest
against the grueling bondage of institutional religion and to reject
the authority of the traditions of record which are now regarded
as the word of God. Our Father did indeed speak through Moses,
Elijah, Isaiah, Amos, Hosea and many others, but he did not cease
to minister words of truth to the world when these prophets of old
made an end of their utterances. My father does not favor one race
or generation over another in that the word of truth is not uttered
to one generation and withheld from another. Do not commit the
folly of calling something divine which is totally human, and do
not fail to understand the words of truth which do not always come
through the traditional oracles of supposed inspiration.

I have called upon you to be born again, to be born of the spirit. I have called you out of the darkness of authority and tradition into the bright light of the possibility of making for yourselves the greatest discovery possible for the human soul to make, the wonderful experience of finding God for yourself, in yourself, and of yourself, and of doing all this as your own personal experience. So may you pass from death to life, from the authority of tradition to the experience of knowing God. Thus, will you pass from darkness to light, from an inherited racial faith to a personal faith achieved by actual experience. Thereby will you progress from a theology of mind handed down by your ancestors to a true religion of spirit which shall be built up on your souls as an eternal endowment.

Your religion shall change from the mere intellectual belief in traditional authority to the actual experience of living faith which is able to grasp the realness of God and all that relates to the divine spirit of the Father. Your old religion of the mind ties you hopelessly to the past. Your new religion of the spirit consists in understanding the divine truths of the universe and will beckon you on toward higher and holier achievements in spiritual ideals.

While the religions of authority may give you a present feeling of settled security, you pay for such a temporary satisfaction the price of the loss of your spiritual freedom and religious liberty. My Father does not require of you as the price of entering the kingdom of Heaven that you should force yourself to agree to a belief in things which are spiritually repugnant, unholy, and untruthful. It is not required of you that your own sense of mercy, justice, and truth should be outraged by submission to an outworn system of religious forms and ceremonies.

The religion of the spirit will leave you forever free to follow the truth wherever the leadings of the spirit may take you.

Shame on those false religious teachers who would drag hungry souls back into the dark and distant past and there leave them. These unfortunate people are doomed to become frightened by every new discovery, while they are bothered by every new revelation of truth.

The Prophet who said, 'He will be kept in perfect peace whose mind is stayed on God!', was not a mere intellectual believer in authoritative theology. This truth-knowing human had discovered God. He was not merely talking about God.

I admonish you to give up the practice of always quoting the prophets of old and praising the heroes of the Jews, and instead aspire to become living prophets of the Father, and spiritual heroes of the kingdom of Heaven. To honor the prophets of the past may indeed be worthwhile, but why, in so doing, should you sacrifice the greatest goal of human existence: finding God for yourselves and knowing him in your own souls?

Every race of man has its own mental outlook on human existence. Therefore, must the religion of the mind ever run true to these various racial viewpoints. Never will the religions of authority come to unification. Human unity and mortal brotherhood can be achieved only by the religion of the spirit. Racial minds may differ, but all mankind is indwelt by the same divine and eternal spirit. The hope of human brotherhood will only be realized when the many religions of authority become overshadowed by the unifying and ennobling religion of the spirit, the religion of personal spiritual experience.

The religions of authority can only divide men and set them in conscientious array against each other. The religion of the spirit will progressively draw men together and cause them to become understandingly sympathetic with one another. The religions of authority require of men uniformity in belief, but this is impossible in the present state of the world. The religion of the spirit requires only unity of experience, uniformity of destiny, making full allowance of diversity of belief. The religion of the spirit requires only uniformity of insight, not uniformity of viewpoint. The religion of the spirit does not demand uniformity of intellectual views, only unity of spiritual feelings. The religions of authority crystallize into lifeless creeds. The religion of the spirit grows into the joy and liberty of noble deeds of loving service and merciful ministrations to your fellow man.

But watch, lest any of you look with disdain upon the children of the Jews because they have fallen on these evil days of traditional barrenness. Our forefathers gave themselves up to the persistent and passionate search for God, and they found him as no other whole race of men have ever known him. My Father has not failed to mark the long and untiring struggle of the Hebrews, ever since the days of Moses, to find God and to know God. For weary generations the Jews have not ceased to toil, sweat, groan, travail, and endure the sufferings and experience the sorrows of a misunderstood and despised people, all in order that they might come a little nearer the discovery of the truth about God. Notwithstanding all the failures and faltering of the Jews, our fathers progressively, from Moses to the time of Amos and Hosea, did reveal increasingly to the whole world an ever clearer and more truthful picture of the eternal God. So was the way prepared for the still greater revelation of the Father which you have been called to share.

Never forget there is only one adventure which is more satisfying and thrilling than the attempt to discover the will of the living God, and that is the experience of honestly trying to do the divine will.

Remember that the will of God can be done in any earthly occupation. Some callings are not holy and others secular. All things are sacred in the lives of those who are spirit led, that is, subordinated to truth, ennobled by love, dominated by mercy, and restrained by fairness and justice. The spirit which my Father and I shall send into the world after I depart is not only the spirit of truth but also the spirit of beauty.

You must cease to seek for the word of God only on the pages of the olden records of theological authority. Those who are born of the spirit of God shall henceforth understand the word of God regardless of where it appears to take origin. Divine truth must not be discounted just because the source of its origin is apparently human. The divine spirit that resides within you is entirely capable of speaking through you. That is how your Father in Heaven speaks through you.

Many of your brothers have minds which accept the theory of God while they spiritually fail to realize the presence of God. That is just the reason why I have so often taught you that the kingdom of Heaven can best be realized by acquiring the spiritual attitude of a sincere child. It is not the mental immaturity of the child that I recommend to you but rather the spiritual simplicity of such a believing and trusting little one. It is not so important that you should know about the fact of God as that you should increasingly grow in the ability to feel the presence of God.

When you once begin to find God in your soul, presently you will begin to discover him in other men's souls and eventually in all the creatures and creations of a mighty universe. But what chance does the Father have to appear as a God of loyalties and divine ideals in the souls of men who give little or no time to the thoughtful contemplation of such eternal realities? While the mind is not the seat of spiritual nature, it is indeed the gateway into it.

Do not make the mistake of trying to prove to other men that you have found God. You cannot consciously produce such valid proof, although there are two positive and powerful demonstrations of the fact that you know God. These are:

1) The fruits of the spirit of God showing forth in your daily life.
2) The fact that your entire life furnishes positive proof that you have risked everything you are and have in the pursuit of the hope of finding the God of eternity, whose presence you have forecasted in time.

My Father will ever respond to the faintest flicker of faith. He takes note of the physical and superstitious emotions of primitive man. With those honest but fearful souls whose faith is so weak that it amounts to little more than a passive attitude of agreement to religions of authority, the Father is ever alert to honor and foster even all such feeble attempts to reach out for him. But you who have been called out of darkness into the light are expected to believe with a whole heart.

Your faith shall dominate the combined attitudes of body, mind, and spirit.

You are my Apostles, and to you religion shall not become a theological shelter to which you may flee in fear of facing the rugged truths of spiritual progress and idealistic adventure, but rather shall your religion become the fact of real experience which testifies that God has found you, idealized, ennobled, and spiritualized you, and that you have enlisted in the eternal adventure of finding the God who has thus found you."

When Jesus had finished, he beckoned Andrew and told him it was time to get on their journey to the Phoenician coast.

TEACHINGS ON FREEDOM FROM TEMPTATION

One evening, while at Sidon, Nathaniel asked: "Master, why do we pray that God will lead us not into temptation when we well know from your revelation of the Father that he never does such things?" Jesus answered:

"It is not strange that you should ask such a question seeing that you are beginning to know the Father as I know him, and not as the Jews of today and the early Hebrew Prophets so dimly saw him. You well know how our forefathers, millenniums before the times of the Hebrews, were disposed to see God in almost everything that happened.

They looked for the hand of God in all natural occurrences and in every unusual episode of human experience. They connected God with both good and evil. Man was in the habit of accounting for these unusual emotions by remarking: 'The Father spoke to me saying, 'Do thus and so.', or 'Go here and there'. Accordingly, since men so often and so violently ran into temptation, it became the habit of our forefathers to believe that God led them into those situations for testing, punishing, or strengthening. But you, indeed, now know better. You know that men are all too often led into temptation by the urge of their own selfishness and by the impulses of their animal natures. When you are in this way tempted, I admonish you that, while you recognize temptation honestly and sincerely for what it is, you intelligently redirect the energies of spirit, mind, and body, which are seeking expression, into higher channels and toward more idealistic goals. In this way you may transform your temptations into the highest types of uplifting mortal actions while you almost wholly avoid these wasteful and weakening conflicts between your animal and spiritual natures.

But let me warn you against the folly of trying to surmount temptations by the effort of replacing one desire by another, and supposedly superior, desire through the mere force of the human will. If you would be truly triumphant over the temptations of your lower nature, you must come to that place of spiritual advantage where you have really and truly developed an actual interest in, and love for, those higher and more idealistic forms of conduct which your mind is desirous of substituting for these lower habits of behavior that you recognize as temptations. You will, in this way, be delivered through spiritual transformation rather than be increasingly overburdened with the deceptive suppression of mortal desires. The old and the inferior will be forgotten in the love for the new and the superior. Beauty is always triumphant over ugliness in the hearts of all who are illumined by the love of truth. There is mighty power in the energy of a new and sincere spiritual affection. Again, I say to you, be not overcome by evil but rather overcome evil with good."

Long into the night the Apostles and evangelists continued to ask questions, and from the many answers here are some of the thoughts, restated in modern terminology:

"Forceful ambition, intelligent judgment, and seasoned wisdom are the essentials of material success. Leadership is dependent on natural ability, discretion, will power, and determination. But spiritual success is dependent on faith, love, and devotion to truth, hunger and thirst for righteousness, the wholehearted desire to find God and to be like him."

"Do not become discouraged by the discovery that you are human. Human nature may tend toward evil, but it is not inherently sinful. Do not be downcast by your failure wholly to forget some of your regrettable experiences. The mistakes which you fail to forget in time will be forgotten in eternity. Lighten the burdens of your soul by speedily acquiring a long-distance view of your destiny."

"Do not make the mistake of estimating the soul's worth by the imperfections of the mind or by the appetites of the body. Do not judge the soul nor evaluate its destiny by the standards of a single unfortunate human episode. Your spiritual destiny is conditioned only by your spiritual longings and purposes."

"True religion is the spiritual experience of the evolving soul of the God-knowing man. But moral power and spiritual energy are mighty forces which may be utilized in dealing with difficult social situations and in solving intricate economic problems. These moral and spiritual endowments make all levels of human living richer and more meaningful."

"You are destined to live a very narrow and mean life if you learn to love only those who love you. Human love may indeed be reciprocal, but divine love is outgoing in all its endeavors. The less love in any creature's nature, the greater the need for love, and the more does divine love seeks to satisfy such a need. Love is never self-seeking, and it cannot be self-bestowed. Divine love cannot be self-contained. It must be unselfishly given."

"Believers in God the Father should possess an implicit faith, a belief in the certain triumph of righteousness. Kingdom builders must not doubt the truth of the gospel of eternal salvation. Believers must increasingly learn how to step aside from the rush of life, escape the harassments of material existence, and refresh the soul, inspire the mind and renew the spirit by worshipful communion."

"God-knowing individuals must not be discouraged by misfortune or downcast by disappointment. Believers must be immune to the depressions consequent upon purely material upheavals. Those who live in the spirit must not be perturbed by the episodes of the material world. Candidates for eternal life must be practitioners of an invigorating and constructive technique for meeting all of the vicissitudes and harassments of mortal living. Every day a true believer lives, he shall find it easier to do the right thing."

"Spiritual living mightily increases true self-respect. But self-respect is not self-admiration. Self-respect is always related to the love and service of one's fellows. It is not possible to respect yourself more than if you love your neighbor. The one is the measure of the capacity for the other."

"As the days pass, every true believer becomes more skillful in leading his fellows into the love of eternal truth. Are you more resourceful in revealing goodness to humanity today than you were yesterday? Are you a better recommender of righteousness this year than you were last year? Are you becoming increasingly artistic in your technique of leading hungry souls into the new religion?"

"Are your ideals high enough to ensure your eternal salvation while your ideas are so practical as to render you a useful citizen to function on Earth in service to your mortal fellows? In the spirit, your citizenship is in Heaven. In the flesh, you are still citizens of the kingdoms of Earth. Render to the Caesars the things which are material and render to God those which are spiritual."

"The measure of your spiritual capacity is your faith in divine truths and your love for man, but the measure of your human strength of character is your ability to resist the holding of grudges and your capacity to overcome brooding in the face of deep sorrow. Defeat is the mirror in which you may honestly view your real self."

"As you grow older in years and more experienced in the affairs of the new gospel, you must become more tactful in dealing with troublesome mortals and more tolerant in living with stubborn associates. Tact is the fulcrum of social leverage, and tolerance is the mark of a great soul. If you possess these rare and charming gifts, as the days pass you will become more alert and expert in your efforts to avoid all unnecessary social misunderstandings. Such wise souls are able to avoid much of the trouble which is certain to be the portion of all who suffer from lack of emotional adjustment, those who refuse to grow up, and those who refuse to grow old gracefully."

"Avoid dishonesty and unfairness in all your efforts to preach truth and proclaim the gospel. Seek no unearned recognition and crave no undeserved sympathy. Receive love freely from both divine and human sources regardless of whether you deserve it and love freely in return. But in all other things related to honor and position, seek only that which honestly belongs to you."

"The man who is conscious of God is certain of salvation. He is unafraid of life. He is honest and consistent. He knows how bravely to endure unavoidable suffering. He is uncomplaining when faced by inescapable hardship."

"The true believer does not grow weary in doing good deeds just because he is thwarted. Difficulty whets the appetite of the truth lover and obstacles only challenge the efforts of the truth seeker."

Teachings on Forgiveness

One evening, at Hippos, the Master gave a memorable lesson on forgiveness. Said the Master:

"If a kindhearted man has a hundred sheep and one of them goes astray, does he not immediately leave the ninety-nine and go out in search of the one that has gone astray? If he is a good shepherd, will he not keep up his quest for the lost sheep until he finds it? Then, when the shepherd has found his lost sheep, he lays it over his shoulder and, going home rejoicing, calls to his friends and neighbors saying: Rejoice with me, for I have found my sheep that was lost. I tell you that there is more joy in Heaven over one sinner who repents than over ninety-nine righteous persons who need no repentance. Even so, it is not the will of my Father in Heaven that one of these little ones should go astray, much less that they should perish. In your Jewish religion you have been taught that God may receive repentant sinners. In the true workings of Heaven, the Father goes forth to find them even before they have seriously thought of repentance.

The Father in Heaven loves his children, and therefore should you learn to love one another. The Father in Heaven forgives you for your sins. Therefore, you should learn to forgive one another. If your brother sins against you, go to him and with tact and patience show him his fault. Do all this between you and him alone. If he will listen to you, then you have won your brother. But if your brother will not hear you, if he persists in the error of his way, go again to him, taking with you one or two mutual friends that you may thus have two or even three witnesses to confirm your testimony and establish the fact that you have dealt justly and mercifully with your offending brother. Now if he refuses to hear your brothers, you may tell the whole story to the community, and then, if he refuses to hear the brotherhood, let them take such action as they deem wise. Let such an unruly member become an outcast from the new religion. While you cannot pretend to sit in judgment on the souls of your fellows, and while you may not forgive sins or otherwise presume to take over the prerogatives of the Father in Heaven, at the same time, it has been committed to your hands that you should maintain order in the new religion. So, in all these matters connected with the discipline of the brotherhood, whatsoever you shall decree on Earth, shall be recognized in Heaven.

Although you cannot determine the eternal fate of the individual, you may legislate regarding the conduct of the group, for where two or three of you agree concerning any of these things and ask of me, it shall be done for you if your petition is not inconsistent with the will of my Father in Heaven. All this is true, for where two or three believers are gathered together, there shall I be in the midst of them."

Peter was the Apostle in charge of the workers at Hippos, and when he heard Jesus speak, he asked: "Master, how often shall my brother sin against me that I have to forgive him? Until seven times?"

The Master answered: "Not only seven times but even seventy times and seven. Therefore, may the kingdom of Heaven be likened to a certain king who ordered a financial reckoning with his stewards.

When they had begun to conduct this examination of accounts, one of his chief retainers was brought before him confessing that he owed his king ten thousand talents. Now this officer of the king's court pleaded that hard times had come upon him, and that he did not have the funds to pay this obligation. So, the king commanded that his property be confiscated, and that his children be sold to pay his debt. When this chief steward heard this stern decree, he fell down on his face before the king and implored him to have mercy and grant him more time, saying: 'Have a little more patience with me, and I will pay you all of it.' When the king looked upon this negligent servant and his family, he was moved with compassion. He ordered that he should be released, and that the loan should be wholly forgiven.

This chief steward, having thus received mercy and forgiveness at the hands of the king, went about his business, and finding one of his subordinate stewards who owed him a mere hundred denari, laid upon him and, taking him by the throat, said: 'Pay me all you owe.' Then did this fellow steward fall down before the chief steward and, beseeching him, said: 'Only have patience with me, and I will presently be able to pay you.' But the chief steward would not show mercy to his fellow steward but rather had him cast in prison until he would pay his debt. When his fellow servants saw what had happened, they were so distressed that they went and told the king. When the king heard of the doings of his chief steward, he called this ungrateful and unforgiving man before him and said: 'You are a wicked and unworthy steward.

When you sought compassion, I freely forgave you your entire debt. Why did you not also show mercy to your fellow steward, even as I showed mercy to you?' The king was so very angry that he delivered. his ungrateful chief steward to the jailers so that they might hold him until he had paid all that was due.

Even so shall my Heavenly Father show the more abundant mercy to those who freely show mercy to their fellows. How can you come to God asking consideration for your shortcomings when you persist in chastising your brothers for being guilty of these same human frailties which you have committed? I say to all of you: freely you have received the good things of the new gospel, therefore freely give these blessings to your fellows on Earth."

TEACHINGS ON THE STRANGE PREACHER

The Master went over to Gamala to visit John and those who were working with him at that place evangelizing. That evening, after the session of questions and answers, John said to Jesus; "Master, yesterday I went over to Ashtaroth to see a man who was teaching in your name and even claiming to be able to cast out devils. Now this fellow had never been with us, neither did he follow after us.

Therefore, I forbade him to do such things."

Jesus answered: "Forbid him not, John. Do you not realize that this new gospel shall soon be proclaimed in all the world? How can you expect that all who will believe the gospel shall be subject to your direction? Rejoice that already our teaching has begun to manifest itself beyond the borders of our personal influence. Do you not see, John, that those who profess to do great works in my name must eventually support our cause? They certainly will not be quick to speak evil of me. My son, in matters of this sort it would be better for you to reckon that he who is not against us is with us. In the generations to come many who are not wholly worthy will do many strange things in my name, but I will not forbid them. I tell you that, even when a cup of cold water is given to a thirsty soul in the Father's name, the Father's messengers shall ever make record of such a service of love."

This instruction greatly perplexed John because on a previous occasion he had heard the Master say, "He who is not with me is against me." He could not perceive that in this case Jesus was referring to man's personal relation to the spiritual teachings of the new gospel, while in the other case he was referring to the outward and far-flung social relations of believers regarding the questions of administrative control and the jurisdiction of one group of believers over the work of other groups which would eventually compose the forthcoming world- wide brotherhood.

But John oftentimes recounted this experience in connection with his subsequent labors on behalf of the new religion. Nevertheless, many times the Apostles did take offense at those who taught in the Master's name. To them it always seemed inappropriate that those who had never sat at Jesus' feet should dare to teach in his name.

The man whom John forbade to teach and work in Jesus' name did not heed the Apostle's injunction. He went right on with his efforts and raised up a considerable company of believers at the village of Kanata before going on into Mesopotamia preaching as he went. This man had been led to believe in Jesus through the remarkable testimony of a man who had been healed of a lifelong illness at the hands of the Master.

TEACHING TO TEACHERS

At Edrei, where Thomas and his associates labored, Jesus spent a day and a night in one memorable visit. In the course of the evening's discussion, he explained the principles which should guide those who preach truth, and which should activate all who teach the new gospel.

Summarized and restated in modern terminology, the Master taught: "Always respect the personality of man. Never promote a righteous cause by force. Spiritual victories can be won only by spiritual power. This injunction against the employment of material influences refers to psychic force as well as to physical force.

Overpowering arguments and mental superiority are not to be employed to coerce men and women into the new religion. Man's mind is not to be crushed by the mere weight of logic or overawed by shrewd eloquence. While emotion as a factor in human decisions cannot be totally eliminated, it should not be directly appealed to in the teachings of those who want to advance the cause of the new gospel. Make your appeals directly to the divine spirit that dwells within the minds of men. Do not appeal to fear, pity, or mere sentiment. In appealing to men, be fair. Exercise self-control and exhibit due restraint. Show proper respect for the personalities of your pupils. Remember that I have taught you: Behold, I stand at the door and knock, and if any man opens, I will come in.

In bringing men into the new religion, do not lessen or destroy their self-respect. While too much self-respect may destroy humility and end in pride, conceit, and arrogance, the loss of self-respect often ends in paralysis of the will. It is the purpose of this gospel to restore self-respect to those who have lost it and to restrain it in those who have it. Do not make the mistake of only condemning the wrongs in the lives of your pupils. Remember also to accord generous recognition for the most praiseworthy things in their lives. Never forget that I will stop at nothing to restore self-respect to those who have lost it, and who really desire to regain it.

Take care that you do not wound the self-respect of timid and fearful souls. Do not indulge in sarcasm at the expense of my simple- minded children. Do not be cynical with my fearful children. Idleness is destructive of self-respect, therefore encourage your brothers to keep busy with their chosen tasks and put forth every effort to secure work for those who find themselves without employment. Never be guilty of such unworthy tactics as trying to frighten men and women into the new religion. A loving father does not frighten his children into yielding obedience to his requirements.

Someday the children of the new gospel will realize that strong feelings of emotion are not equivalent to the leadings of the divine spirit. To be strongly influenced to do something or to go to a certain place, does not necessarily mean that such impulses are the leading of the indwelling spirit.

Forewarn all believers regarding the conflict which must be experienced by all who pass from this life as it is lived in the flesh to the higher life as it is lived in the spirit. To those who live totally within either realm, there is little conflict or confusion, but all are doomed to experience uncertainty during the times of transition between the two levels of living. In entering the new way, you cannot escape its responsibilities or avoid its obligations, but remember, the yoke of the new gospel is easy, and the burden of truth is light.

The world is filled with hungry souls who hunger in the very presence of the bread of life. Men die searching for the very God who lives within them. Men travel to the ends of the Earth seeking for the treasures of the new gospel with yearning hearts and weary feet when they are all within the immediate grasp of living faith. Faith is to religion what sails are to a ship. It is an addition of power, not an added burden of life. There is but one struggle for those who enter the new way, and that is to fight the good fight for faith. The believer has only one battle, and that is against doubt.

In preaching the gospel of the new religion, you are simply teaching friendship with God. This fellowship will appeal alike to men and women in that both will find that which most truly satisfies their characteristic longings and ideals. Tell my children that I am not only tender with their feelings and patient with their frailties, but that I am also ruthless with sin and intolerant of iniquity. I am indeed meek and humble in the presence of my Father, but I am equally and relentlessly indignant where there is deliberate evildoing and sinful rebellion against the will of my Father in Heaven.

You shall not portray your teacher as a man of sorrows. Future generations shall know also the radiance of our joy, the buoyancy of our good will, and the inspiration of our good humor. We proclaim a message of good news which is infectious in its transforming power.

Our religion is throbbing with new life and new meanings. Those who accept this teaching will be filled with joy, and in their hearts will be constrained to rejoice evermore. Increasing happiness is always the experience of all who are certain about God.

Teach all believers to avoid leaning upon the insecurities of false sympathy. You cannot develop strong characters out of the indulgence of self-pity. Honestly endeavor to avoid the deceptive influence of mere fellowship in misery. Extend sympathy to the brave souls while you withhold pity from those cowardly souls who only halfheartedly stand up before the trials of living. Do not offer consolation to those who surrender to their troubles without a struggle. Do not sympathize with your fellows merely so that they may sympathize with you in return.

When my children become self-conscious of the assurance of the divine spirit within them, such a faith will expand the mind, ennoble the soul, reinforce the personality, and enhance the power to love and be loved.

Teach all believers that those who enter the new way will not thereby be rendered immune to the accidents of time or to the ordinary catastrophes of nature. Believing the gospel will not prevent you from getting into trouble, but it will ensure that you shall be unafraid when trouble does overtake you. If you dare to believe in me and wholeheartedly proceed to follow after me, you shall most certainly enter upon the pathway to trouble in these times that we live in. I will not promise to deliver you from the waters of adversity, but I will promise to go with you through all of them."

TEACHING ON THE SCRIPTURES

Then Jesus went over to Abila, where Nathaniel and a group of evangelists were laboring. Nathaniel was much bothered by some of Jesus' pronouncements which seemed to detract from the authority of the recognized Hebrew scriptures. Accordingly, on this night, after the usual period of questions and answers, Nathaniel took Jesus away from the others and asked: "Master, could you trust me to know the truth about the scriptures? I observe that you teach us only a portion of the sacred writings, the best as I view it, and I infer from what you say that you reject the rabbi's teachings that the words of the law are the very words of God, having been with God in Heaven even before the times of Abraham and Moses. What is the truth about the scriptures?" When Jesus heard the questions of his bewildered Apostle, he answered:

"Nathaniel, you have understood me correctly. I do not regard the scriptures as do the rabbis. I will talk with you about this matter on condition that you do not relate these things to your brothers, who are not all prepared to receive this teaching. The words of the law of Moses and the teachings of the scriptures were not in existence before Abraham. Only in recent times have the scriptures that you know been gathered together as we now have them. While they contain some of the best of the thoughts and longings of the Hebrew, Egyptian, Mesopotamian and other peoples also contain much that is far from being representative of the character and teachings of the Father in Heaven. Wherefore must I choose from among the better teachings those truths which are to be gleaned for the new gospel.

These writings which you call sacred are the work of men, some of them holy men, others not very holy. The teachings of these books represent the views and extent of enlightenment of the times in which they were written. As a revelation of truth, the more recent ones are more dependable than the older records. The scriptures are faulty and altogether human in origin, but they do constitute the best collection of religious wisdom and spiritual truth to be found in all the world at this time.

Many of these books were not written by the people whose names they bear, but that in no way detracts from the value of the truths which they contain. If the story of Jonah were not to be a fact, even if Jonah had never lived, still would the profound truths of this narrative, the love of God for Ninevah and the so-called heathen, be none the less precious in the eyes of all those who love their fellow men. The scriptures are sacred because they present the thoughts and acts of men who were searching for God, and who in these writings left on record their highest concepts of righteousness, truth, and holiness. The scriptures contain much that is true, very much, but in the light of your present teaching, you know that these writings also contain much that is false and misrepresentative of the Father in Heaven, the loving God I have come to reveal to all the worlds.

Nathaniel, never permit yourself for one moment to believe the scripture records which tell you that the God of love directed your forefathers to go forth in battle to slay all their enemies, men, women, and children. Such records are the words of men, confused and wicked men. They are not the words of God. The scriptures always have, and always will, reflect the intellectual, moral and spiritual status of those who created them. Have you not noticed that the concepts of Yahweh grow in beauty and glory as the prophets made their records from Samuel to Isaiah? You should remember that the scriptures are intended for religious instruction and spiritual guidance. They are not the works of either historians or philosophers.

The thing most deplorable is not merely this erroneous idea of the absolute perfection of the scripture records and the infallibility of its teachings, but rather the confusing misinterpretation of these writings by the tradition enslaved Scribes and Pharisees at Jerusalem. Now they will employ both the doctrine of the inspiration of the scriptures and their misinterpretations of them in their determined effort to attack our new teachings of the gospel. Nathaniel, never forget, the Father does not limit the revelation of truth to any one generation or to any one people. Many earnest seekers after the truth have been, and will continue to be, confused and disheartened by the Jewish doctrines of the perfection of the scriptures.

The authority of truth is the very spirit that dwells within its living manifestations, and not the dead words of the less illuminated and supposedly inspired men of another generation. Even if these holy men of old lived inspired and spirit filled lives, which does not mean that their words were similarly spiritually inspired. Today I make no record of the teachings of this gospel lest, when I have gone, you speedily become divided up into sundry groups of truth contenders as a result of the diversity of your interpretation of my teachings. For this generation it is best that we live out these truths daily while we shun the making of records.

Mark well my words, Nathaniel, nothing which human nature has touched can be regarded as infallible. Through the mind of man divine truth may indeed shine forth, but always of relative purity and partial divinity. The creature may crave infallibility, but only the creator possesses it.

The greatest error of the teachings about the scriptures is the doctrine that they are sealed books of mystery and wisdom which only the wise minds of the nation dare to interpret. My dear fellow, the revelations of divine truth are not sealed except by human ignorance, bigotry, and narrow-minded intolerance. The light of the scriptures is only dimmed by prejudice and darkened by superstition. A false fear of sacredness has prevented religion from being safeguarded by common sense.

The fear of the authority of the sacred writings of the past effectively prevents the honest souls of today from accepting the new light of the gospel, the light which these very God-knowing men of another generation so intensely longed to see.

The saddest thing about all this is the fact that some of the teachers of the sanctity of this traditionalism know this very truth. They more or less fully understand the limitations of the scriptures, but they are intellectually dishonest cowards. They know the truth regarding the sacred writings, but they prefer to withhold such disturbing facts from the people. Thus, do they pervert and distort the scriptures, making them the guide to enslave daily life and an authority in things nonspiritual, instead of treating the sacred writings as the repository of the moral wisdom, religious inspiration, and the spiritual teaching of the God-knowing men of other generations."

Nathaniel was enlightened and shocked by the Master's pronouncements. For the rest of his life, he pondered this talk in the depths of his soul, but he told no man concerning this personal conference.

TEACHING ON THE GOSPEL OF THE KINGDOM

During a visit to Philadelphia, where James labored with a group of evangelists, Jesus taught the disciples about the positive nature of the new gospel. In the course of his remarks, he suggested that some parts of the scriptures were more truth-containing than others and he admonished his hearers to feed their souls upon the best of spiritual food. James interrupted the Master, asking: "Master, would you be good enough to suggest to us how we may choose the better passages out of the scriptures for our personal edification?"

Jesus replied: "Yes, James, when you read the scriptures look for those eternally true and divinely beautiful teachings, such as:

Create in me a clean heart, O Father.

The Father is my shepherd. I shall not want.

You should love your neighbor as much as yourself.

For I, the Father your God, will hold your right hand, saying, fear not, I will help you.

Neither shall the nations learn war anymore."

This is illustrative of the way Jesus, day by day, selected the cream of the Hebrew scriptures for the instruction of his followers and for inclusion in the teachings of the new gospel. Other religions had suggested the thought of the nearness of God to man, but Jesus made the care of God for man like the relationship of a loving Father for the welfare of his dependent children. Then he made this teaching the cornerstone of his religion. Thus did the doctrine of the fatherhood of God bring forth the practice of the brotherhood of man. The worship of God and the service of man became the sum and substance of his religion. Jesus took the best of the Jewish religion and translated it to a worthy setting in the new teachings of the new gospel.

Jesus put the spirit of positive action into the passive doctrines of the Jewish religion. In the place of negative compliance with ceremonial requirements, Jesus urged the positive doing of that which his new religion required of those who accepted it. Jesus' religion consisted not merely in believing, but in actually doing, those things which the gospel required. He did not teach that the essence of his religion consisted in social service, but rather that social service was one of the visible effects of the possession of the spirit of true religion.

Jesus did not hesitate to choose the better half of a scripture while he rejected the lesser portion. His great commandment, "Love your neighbor as yourself," he took from the scripture which reads: "You shall not take vengeance against the children of your people, but you shall love your neighbor as yourself." Jesus appropriated the positive portion of this scripture while rejecting the negative part. He even opposed negative or purely passive nonresistance. Said he often: "When an enemy hits you on one cheek, do not stand there dumb and passive, but in positive attitude turn the other. Do the best thing possible to actively lead your brother in error away from the evil paths into the better ways of righteous living." Jesus required his followers to react positively and aggressively to every life situation. The turning of the other cheek, or whatever act that may typify, demands initiative, necessitates vigorous, active and courageous expression of the believer's personality.

Jesus did not teach negative submission as the response to the indignities purposely imposed upon the practitioners of nonresistance to evil. Instead, he taught his followers that they should be wise and alert in a quick and positive reaction of good to evil, with the purpose that they might effectively overcome evil with good. Do not forget, in the universe we live in, the truly good is invariably more powerful than the most malignant of evil. The Master taught a positive standard of righteousness: "Whosoever wishes to be my disciple, let him disregard himself and take up the full measure of his responsibilities daily to follow me." He lived this out himself in that he went about always doing good for someone. This aspect of the gospel was well illustrated by many parables which he later spoke to his followers. He never urged his followers patiently to bear their obligations but rather with energy. and enthusiasm to live up to the full measure of their human responsibilities and divine privileges.

When Jesus instructed his Apostles that they should, when one unjustly took away the coat, offer the other garment, he referred not so much to a literal second coat as to the idea of doing something positive to save the wrongdoer in the place of the olden advice to retaliate: "An eye for an eye". Jesus rejected the idea either of retaliation or of becoming just a passive sufferer or victim of injustice. On this occasion he taught them the three ways of contending with, and resisting, evil:

1) to return evil for evil - the positive but unrighteous method
2) to suffer evil without complaint and without resistance - the purely negative method.
3) to return good for evil, to assert the will so as to become master of the situation, to overcome evil with good, the positive and righteous method.

One of the Apostles once asked: "Master, what should I do if a stranger forced me to carry his pack for a mile?" Jesus answered: "Do not sit down and beg for relief while you berate the stranger under your breath. Righteousness does not come from such passive attitudes. If you can think of nothing more positive to do, you can at least carry the pack a second mile. That will certainly challenge the unrighteous and ungodly stranger."

The Jews had heard of a God who would forgive repentant sinners and forget their misdeeds, but not until Jesus came did men hear about a God who went in search of lost sheep, who took the initiative in looking for sinners, and who rejoiced when he found them willing to return to the Father's house. This positive note in religion, Jesus extended even to his prayers. He converted the negative golden rule into a positive rule of human fairness.

In all his teachings Jesus unfailingly avoided distracting details.

He shunned flowery language and avoided the mere poetic imagery of a play upon words. He habitually put large meanings into small expressions. For purposes of illustration Jesus reversed the current meanings of many terms, such as salt, leaven, fishing, and little children. He most effectively employed the antithesis, comparing the minute to the infinite and so on. His pictures were striking, such as, "The blind leading the blind." But the greatest strength to be found in his illustrative teachings was their naturalness. Jesus brought the philosophy of religion from Heaven down to Earth. He portrayed the basic needs of the soul with a new insight and a new bestowal of affection.

Teaching at the Feast of Tabernacles

The following Feast of Tabernacles found Jesus back in Jerusalem preaching to the multitudes who gathered from all parts of the Roman Empire. The leaders of the Jews were greatly astonished when he appeared in the temple courts and began publicly to teach, and the Jewish authorities were surprised beyond expression when it was reported that he was teaching in the temple itself.

Although his disciples had not expected Jesus to attend the feast, the vast majority of the pilgrims from afar who had heard of him entertained the hope that they might see him in Jerusalem. Indeed, many came just for the purpose of listening to him preach. They were not disappointed, for on several occasions he taught on Solomon's porch and elsewhere in the temple courts. These teachings were really the official or formal announcement of the divinity of Jesus to the Jewish people and to the whole world.

The multitudes who listened to the Master's teachings were divided in their opinions. Some said he was a good man. Some said he was a prophet. Some said that he was truly the Messiah, while others said he was nothing more than a mischievous meddler, that he was leading the people astray with his strange doctrines. His enemies hesitated to denounce him openly for fear of his friendly believers, while his friends feared to acknowledge him openly for fear of the Jewish leaders, knowing that the Sanhedrin was already determined to put him to death. But even his enemies marveled at his teachings, knowing that he had not been instructed in the schools of the rabbis.

Every time Jesus went to Jerusalem, his Apostles were filled with terror. They were the more afraid as, from day to day, they listened to his increasingly bold pronouncements regarding the nature of his mission on Earth. They were unaccustomed to hearing Jesus make such positive claims and such amazing assertions even when preaching among his friends.

One afternoon during this visit, Jesus taught in the temple. A considerable company sat listening to his words depicting the liberty of the new gospel and the joy of those who believe the good news, when a curious listener interrupted him to ask: "Teacher, how is it you can quote the scriptures and teach the people so fluently when I am told that you are untaught in the learning of the rabbis?"

Jesus replied: "No man has taught me the truths which I declare to you. This teaching is not mine but his who sent me. If any man really desires to do my Father's will, he shall certainly know about my teaching, whether it be God's or whether I speak for myself. He who speaks for himself seeks his own glory, but when I declare the words of the Father, I thereby seek the glory of him who sent me. But before you try to enter into the new light, should you not rather follow the light you already have? Moses gave you the law, yet how many of you honestly seek to fulfill its demands? Moses in this law enjoins you, saying: 'You shall not kill'. Notwithstanding this command there are some here who seek to kill the Son of God."

When the crowd heard these words, they began to wrangle among themselves. Some said he was mad. Some that he had a devil in him. Others said this was indeed the prophet of Galilee whom the Scribes and Pharisees had long sought to kill. Some said the religious authorities were afraid to molest him. Others thought that the authorities would not lay hands on him because they had become believers in him.

After considerable debate one of the crowd stepped forward and asked Jesus: "Why do the rulers seek to kill you?" Jesus replied: "The rulers seek to kill me because they resent my teaching about the good news of the kingdom, a gospel that sets men free from the burdensome traditions of a formal religion of ceremonies which your rabbis are determined to uphold at any cost. They circumcise in accordance with the law on the Sabbath day, but they have threatened to kill me because I once on the Sabbath day set free a man held in the bondage of affliction. They follow after me on the Sabbath to spy on me, but they seek to kill me because on another occasion I chose to make a grievously stricken man completely well on the Sabbath day.

They seek to kill me because they well know that, if you honestly believe and dare to accept my teachings, their system of traditional religion will be overthrown, forever destroyed. Thus, will they be deprived of authority over that to which they have devoted their lives since they steadfastly refuse to accept this new and more glorious gospel of the kingdom of God. Now do I appeal to every one of you: judge not according to outward appearances but rather judge by the true spirit of these teachings. Judge righteously."

Then another inquirer stood up and asked: "Yes, teacher, we do look for the Messiah, but when he comes, we know that his appearance will be a mystery. We know where you came from. You have been among your brothers from the beginning. The deliverer will come in power to restore the throne of David's kingdom. Do you really claim to be the Messiah?"

Jesus replied: "You claim to know me and to know who I am. I wish your claims were true, for indeed then you would find abundant life in that knowledge. But I declare that I have not come to you for myself. I have been sent by the Father, and he who sent me is true and faithful. By refusing to hear me, you are refusing to receive him who sent me. You, if you will receive this gospel, shall come to know him who sent me. I know the Father, for I have come from the Father to declare and reveal him to you."

The agents of the Scribes wanted to lay hands on him right then and there, but they feared the multitude, for many believed in him.

Jesus' work since his baptism had become well known to all Palestine, and as many of these people recounted these things, they said among themselves: "Even though this teacher is from Galilee, and even though he does not meet all of our expectations of the Messiah, we wonder if the deliverer, when he does come, will really do anything more wonderful than this Jesus of Nazareth has already done."

When the Pharisees and their agents heard the people talking this way, they took counsel with their leaders and decided that something should be done forthwith to put a stop to these public appearances of Jesus in the temple courts. The leaders of the Jews, in general, were disposed to avoid a clash with Jesus, believing that the Roman authorities had promised him immunity. They could not otherwise account for his boldness in coming at this time to Jerusalem. But the officers of the Sanhedrin did not wholly believe this rumor. They reasoned that the Roman rulers would not do such a thing secretly and without the knowledge of the highest governing body of the Jewish nation.

Accordingly, Eber, the chief officer of the Sanhedrin, with two assistants was dispatched to arrest Jesus. As Eber made his way toward Jesus, the Master said: "Fear not to approach me. Draw near while you listen to my teachings. I know you have been sent to apprehend me, but you should understand that nothing will befall the Son of God until his hour comes. You are not arrayed against me. You come only to do the bidding of your masters, and even these rulers of the Jews think they are doing God's service when they secretly seek my destruction.

I bear none of you ill will. The Father loves you, and therefore do I long for your deliverance from the bondage of prejudice and the darkness of tradition. I offer you the liberty of life and the joy of salvation. I proclaim the new and living way, the deliverance from evil and the breaking of the bondage of sin. I have come that you might have life and have it eternally. You seek to be rid of me and my disquieting teachings. If you could only realize that I am to be with you only a little while longer. In just a short time I go to him who sent me into this world. Then will many of you diligently seek me, but you shall not discover my presence, for where I am about to go you cannot come. But all who truly seek me shall sometime find the life that leads to my Father's presence."

Some of the scoffers said among themselves: "Where will this man go that we cannot find him? Will he go to live among the

Greeks? Will he destroy himself? What can he mean when he declares that soon he will depart from us, and that we cannot go where he goes?"

Eber and his assistants refused to arrest Jesus. They returned to their meeting place without him. When the chief priests and the Pharisees admonished Eber and his assistants because they had not brought Jesus with them, Eber replied: "We feared to arrest him in the midst of the multitude because many believe in him. Besides, we never heard a man speak like this man. There is something out of the ordinary about this teacher. You would all do well to go over to hear him." When the chief rulers heard these words, they were astonished and spoke tauntingly to Eber: "Are you also led astray? Are you about to believe in this deceiver? Have you heard that any of our learned men or any of the rulers have believed in him? Have any of the Scribes or the Pharisees been deceived by his clever teachings? How does it come that you are influenced by the behavior of this ignorant multitude who know not the law or the prophets? Do you not know that such untaught people are accursed?" Then answered Eber: "Even so, my masters, this man speaks to the multitudes words of mercy and hope. He cheers the downhearted, and his words were comforting even to my own ears.

What can there be wrong in these teachings even though he may not be the Messiah of the scriptures? Even then does not our law require fairness? Do we condemn a man before we hear him?" The chief of the Sanhedrin was livid with Eber by this time and, turning upon him, said: "Have you gone mad? Are you by any chance also from Galilee?

Search the scriptures man, and you will discover that out of Galilee arises no prophet, much less the Messiah."

TEACHING ON THE WATER OF LIFE

The presence of people from all the known world, from Spain to India made the Feast of Tabernacles an ideal occasion for Jesus for the first time publicly to proclaim his full gospel in Jerusalem. At this feast the people lived much in the open air, in leafy booths. It was the feast of the harvest gathering, and coming, as it did, in the cool of the Autumn months, it was more generally attended by the Jews of the world than was the Passover at the end of the winter or Pentecost at the beginning of summer. The Apostles at last beheld their Master making the bold announcement of his mission on Earth before all the world.

This was the feast of feasts, since any sacrifice not made at the other festivals could be made at this time. This was the occasion of the reception of the temple offerings. It was a combination of vacation pleasures with the solemn rites of religious worship. Here was a time of racial rejoicing, mingled with sacrifices, Levitical chants, and the solemn blasts of the silvery trumpets of the priests. At night the impressive spectacle of the temple and its pilgrim throngs was brilliantly illuminated by the great candelabras which burned brightly in the court of the women as well as by the glare of scores of torches standing about the temple courts. The entire city was gaily decorated except the Roman castle of Antonia, which looked down in grim contrast upon this festive and worshipful scene. How the Jews did hate this ever-present reminder of the Roman yoke around their necks.

Seventy bullocks were sacrificed during the feast, the symbolic killing of the seventy nations of heathendom to the Jews. The ceremony of the outpouring of the water symbolized the outpouring of God's spirit. This ceremony of the water followed the sunrise procession of the priests and Levites. The worshippers passed down the steps leading from the Court of Judea to the Court of the Women while successive blasts were blown upon the silvery trumpets. Then the faithful marched on toward the beautiful gate, which opened upon the Court of the Gentiles. Here they turned about to face westward, to repeat their chants, and to continue their march for the symbolic water.

On the last day of the feast almost four hundred and fifty priests with a corresponding number of Levites officiated. At daybreak the pilgrims assembled from all parts of the city, each carrying in the right hand a sheaf of myrtle, willow, and palm branches, while in the left hand each one carried a branch of the paradise apple, the Citron, or the "Forbidden Fruit." These pilgrims divided into three groups for this early morning ceremony. One band remained at the temple to attend the morning sacrifices. Another group marched down below Jerusalem to near Maza to cut the willow branches for the adornment of the sacrificial altar, while the third group formed a procession to march from the temple behind the water priest, who, to the sound of the silvery trumpets, bore the golden pitcher which was to contain the symbolic water, out through Ophel to near Siloam, where was located the fountain gate.

After the golden pitcher had been filled at the pool of Siloam, the procession marched back to the temple, entering by way of the water gate and going directly to the court of the priests, where the priest bearing the water pitcher was joined by the priest bearing the wine for the drink offering. These two priests then moved to the silver funnels leading to the base of the altar and poured the contents of the pitchers therein. The execution of this rite of pouring the wine and the water was the signal for the assembled pilgrims to begin the chanting of the Psalms from 113 to 118 inclusive, in alternation with the Levites. As they repeated these lines, they would wave their sheaves at the altar.

Then followed the killing of the sacrificial animals for the day, associated with the repeating of the Psalm for the day, the Psalm for the last day of the feast being the 82nd, beginning with the fifth verse.

On the evening of the next to last day of the feast, when the scene was brilliantly illuminated by the lights of the candelabras and the torches, Jesus stood up in the midst of the assembled throng and said:

"I am the light of the world. He who follows me shall not walk in darkness but shall have the light of life. Presuming to place me on trial and assuming to sit as my judges, you declare that, if I bear witness of myself, my witness cannot be true. But never can the creature sit in judgment on the creator. Even if I do bear witness about myself, my witness is everlastingly true, for I know from where I came, who I am, and where I shall go. You who would kill the Son of God know not from where I came, who I am, or where I go. You judge only by the appearance of the flesh. You do not perceive the realities of the spirit. I judge no man, not even my archenemies. But if I should choose to judge, my judgment would be true and righteous, for I would judge not alone but in association with my Father, who sent me into the world, and who is the source of all true judgment. Jewish law allows that the witness of two reliable persons may be accepted, well then, I bear witness of these truths, so also does my Father in Heaven. We are your two legal witnesses. When I told you this yesterday, in your darkness you asked me: 'Where is your Father?' Truly, you know neither me nor my Father, for if you had known me, you would also have known the Father.

I have already told you that I am going away, and that you will seek me and not find me, for where I am going you cannot come. You who would reject this light live in darkness. I am from the light above. You who prefer to sit in darkness are of this world. I am not of this world, and I live in the eternal light of the Father of lights. You all have had abundant opportunity to learn who I am, but you shall have still other evidence confirming the identity of the Son of God. I am the light of life, and everyone who deliberately and with understanding rejects this saving light shall die in his sins. Much I have to tell you, but you are unable to accept my words. However, he who sent me is true and faithful. My Father loves even his erring children. All that my Father has spoken I also proclaim to the world.

When the Son of God is lifted up, then shall you all know that I am he, and that I have done nothing of myself but only as the Father has taught me. I speak these words to you and to your children. He who sent me is even now with me. He has not left me alone, for I do always that which is pleasing in his sight."

The next day, on the last day of the feast, as the procession from the pool of Siloam passed through the temple courts, and just after the water and the wine had been poured down upon the altar by the priests, Jesus, standing among the pilgrims, said "If any man thirst, let him come to me and drink. From the Father above I bring to this world the water of life. He who believes me shall be filled with the spirit which this water represents, for even the scriptures have said: 'Out of him shall flow rivers of living waters.' When the Son of God has finished his work on Earth, there shall be poured out upon all flesh the living spirit of Truth. Those who receive this spirit shall never know spiritual thirst."

Jesus did not interrupt the service to speak these words. He addressed the worshippers immediately after the chanting of the Hallel, the responsive reading of the Psalms accompanied by waving of the branches before the altar. There was a pause while the sacrifices were being prepared, and it was at this time that the pilgrims heard the fascinating voice of the Master declare that he was the giver of living water to every thirsty soul.

At the conclusion of this early morning service Jesus continued to teach the multitude out in the courtyard, saying: "Have you not read in the scriptures the words: 'Behold, as the waters are poured out upon the dry ground and spread over the parched soil, so will I give the Spirit of Holiness to be poured out upon your children for a blessing even to your children's children.' Why will you thirst for the ministry of the spirit while you seek to water your souls with the traditions of men, poured from the broken pitchers of ceremonial service? That which you see going on about this temple is the way in which your Father sought to symbolize the bestowal of the divine spirit upon the children of faith, and you have done well to perpetuate these symbols, even down to this day. But now has been given to this generation, the revelation of the Father of spirits through the bestowal of his Son. All of this will be followed by the bestowal of the Spirit of the Father and the Son upon the children of men. To everyone who has faith shall this bestowal of the spirit become the true teacher of the way which leads to life everlasting, to the true waters of life in the kingdom of Heaven on Earth and in the Father's paradise beyond."

Jesus continued to answer the questions of both the multitude and the Pharisees. Some thought he was a prophet. Some believed him to be the Messiah. Others said he could not be the Messiah since he came from Galilee. Still, they dared not arrest him.

On the afternoon of the last day of the feast, and after the Apostles had failed in their efforts to persuade him to flee from Jerusalem, Jesus again went into the temple to teach. Finding a large company of believers assembled in Solomon's porch, he spoke to them saying:

"If my words abide in you and you are minded doing the will of my Father, then are you truly my disciples. You shall know the truth, and the truth shall make you free. I know how you will answer me: 'We are the children of Abraham, and we are in bondage to none.

How then shall we be made free?' Even so, I do not speak of outward subjection to another's rule. I refer to the liberties of the soul. Verily, Verily, I say to you, everyone who commits sin is the servant of sin.

You know that the servant is not likely to abide forever in the Master's house. You also know that the son does remain in his Father's house. If, therefore, the Son shall make you free, shall make you sons of the Father, you shall be free indeed.

Your leaders seek to kill me because my word has not been allowed to have its transforming influence in their hearts. Their souls are sealed by prejudice and blinded by the pride of revenge. I declare to you the truth which the eternal Father shows me, while these deluded teachers seek to do the things which they have learned only from their temporal fathers. When you reply that Abraham is your father, then do I tell you that, if you were the children of Abraham, you would do the works of Abraham. Some of you believe my teaching, but others seek to destroy me because I have told you the truth which I received from God. But Abraham did not so treat the truth of God. I perceive that some among you are determined to do the works of evil. If God were your Father, you would know me and love the truth which I reveal. Will you not see that I come forth from the Father, that I am sent by God, that I am not doing this work of myself? Why do you not understand my words? Is it because you have chosen to become the children of evil? If you are the children of darkness, you will hardly walk in the light of the truth which I reveal. The children of evil follow only in the ways of their father, who was a deceiver and stood not for the truth because there came to be no truth in him. But now comes the Son of God speaking and living the truth, and many of you refuse to believe.

Which of you would convict me of sin? If I, then, proclaim and live the truth shown to me by the Father, why do you not believe? He who is of God hears gladly the words of God. For this cause many of you do not hear my words, because you are not of God. Your teachers have even presumed to say that I do my work by the power of the prince of the devils. One nearby has just said that I have a devil in me, that I am a child of the devil. But all of you who deal honestly with your own souls know full well that I am not a devil. You know that I honor the Father even while you would dishonor me. I seek not my own glory, only the glory of my Father in Paradise. I do not judge you, for there is one who judges me.

Verily, verily, I say to you who believe the gospel that, if a man will keep this word of truth alive in his heart, he shall never taste death. Now just at my side I heard a scribe say this statement proves that I have a devil, seeing that Abraham and the prophets are dead. He asked: 'Are you so much greater than Abraham and the prophets that you dare to stand here and say that whosoever keeps your word shall not taste death? Who do you claim to be that you dare to utter such blasphemies?' I say in answer to that, if I glorify myself, my glory is as nothing. But it is the Father who shall glorify me, even the same Father whom you call God. But you have failed to know that your God is my Father. I have come to bring you together, to show you how to become truly the sons of God. Though you do not know the Father, I truly know him. Even Abraham rejoiced to see my day, and by faith he saw it and was glad."

When the unbelieving Jews and the agents of the Sanhedrin who had gathered about by this time heard these words, they raised a tumult, shouting, "You are not fifty years old, and yet you talk about seeing Abraham. You are a child of the devil." Many of them rushed forth for stones to cast at him, and as they did Jesus made his way through the crowds of the temple corridors and escaped to Bethany.

FAREWELL COMMISSION TO THE SEVENTY

Aside from the Apostles and other close disciples that followed Jesus everywhere, there was recruited a corps of 70 believers who were to go out and preach the good news of the kingdom. At Magadan, Jesus gave these 70 their commission. It was a stirring time around the Magadan camp the day the seventy went forth on their first mission. Early that morning, in his last talk with the seventy, Jesus placed emphasis on the following:

1. The gospel of the kingdom must be proclaimed to all the world, to Gentile as well as to Jew.

2. While ministering to the sick, refrain from teaching the expectation of miracles.

3. Proclaim a spiritual brotherhood of the sons of God, not an outward kingdom of worldly power and material glory.

4. Avoid loss of time through overly social visiting and other trivialities which might detract from wholehearted devotion to preaching the gospel.

5. If the first house to be selected for a headquarters proves to be a worthy home, abide there throughout the sojourn in that city.

6. Make clear to all faithful believers that the time for an open break with the religious leaders of the Jews at Jerusalem has now come.

7. Teach that man's whole duty is summed up in this one commandment: Love the Father your God with all your mind and soul and love your neighbor as yourself.

When Jesus had talked to the seventy in the presence of all the Apostles and disciples, Peter took them off by themselves and preached to them their ordination sermon, which was an elaboration of the Master's charge to the twelve Apostles given at the time he laid his hands upon them and set them apart as messengers of the kingdom.

Peter exhorted the seventy to cherish in their experience the following virtues:

1. Consecrated Devotion - to pray always for more laborers to be sent forth into the gospel harvest. He explained that, when one prays, he will the more likely say, "Here I am Father, send me." He admonished them not to neglect their daily worship.

2. True Courage - he warned them that they would encounter hostility and be certain to meet with persecution. Peter told them their mission was no undertaking for cowards and advised them that anyone who was afraid could step out before they started. But none withdrew.

3. Faith and Trust - they must go forth on this short mission wholly unprovided for. They must trust the Father for food and shelter and all other things needful.

4. Zeal and Initiative - they must be possessed with zeal and intelligent enthusiasm. They must attend strictly to their Master's business. Oriental salutation was a lengthy and elaborate ceremony, therefore had they been instructed to "salute no man by the way" which was a common method of exhorting one to go about his business without the waste of time. It had nothing to do with the matter of friendly greetings.

5. Kindness and Courtesy - the Master had instructed them to avoid unnecessary wasting of time in social ceremonies, but he enjoined courtesy toward all with whom they should come in contact. They were to show every kindness to those who might entertain them in their homes. They were strictly warned against leaving a modest home to be entertained in a more comfortable or influential one.

6. Minister to the sick - the seventy were charged by Peter to search out the sick in mind and body and to do everything in their power to bring about the alleviation or cure of their maladies.

When they had thus been charged and instructed, they started out, two by two, on their mission through Galilee, Samaria and Judea.

TEACHING ON THE GOOD SHEPHERD

A company of over three hundred people from Jerusalem, including some Pharisees, had followed Jesus north to the Pella encampment when he hastened away from the jurisdiction of the Jewish rulers in Jerusalem at the end of the Feast of Tabernacles. It was in the presence of these Jewish teachers and leaders, as well as within the hearing of the twelve Apostles, that Jesus preached the Sermon on the Good Shepherd. After half an hour of informal discussion, speaking to a group of about one hundred, Jesus stood up and addressed all assembled, saying:

"On this night I have much to tell you, and since many of you are my disciples and some of you are my bitter enemies, I will present my teachings in a parable, so that you may each take for yourself that which finds a reception in your heart.

Tonight, here before me are men who would be willing to die for me and for this gospel of the kingdom, and some of them will so offer themselves in the years to come. Here also are some of you, slaves of tradition, who have followed me up from Jerusalem, and who, with your darkened and deluded leaders, seek to kill the

Son of God. The life which I now live in the flesh shall judge both of you, the true shepherds and the false shepherds. If the false shepherd were blind, he would have no sin, but you claim that you see. You profess to be teachers of the word of God. Therefore, does your sin remain with you. The true shepherd gathers his flock into the fold for the night in times of danger. When the morning has come, he enters into the fold by the door, and when he calls, the sheep knows his voice. Every shepherd who gains entrance to the sheepfold by any other means than by the door is a thief and a robber. The true shepherd enters the fold after the porter has opened the door for him, and his sheep, knowing his voice, come out at his word. When they that are his are thus brought forth, the true shepherd goes before them. He leads the way, and the sheep follow him. His sheep follow him because they know his voice. They will not follow a stranger. They will flee from the stranger because they don't know his voice. This multitude which is gathered about us here are like sheep without a shepherd, but when we speak to them, they know the shepherd's voice and they will follow after us. At least, those who hunger for truth and thirst for righteousness do. Some of you are not of my fold. You don't know my voice, and you do not follow me. Because you are false shepherds, the sheep know not your voice and will not follow you."

When Jesus had spoken this parable, no one dared asked him a question. After a time, he began again to speak and went on to discuss the parable:

"You who would be the shepherds of my Father's flocks must not only be worthy leaders, but you must also feed the flock with good food. You are not true shepherds unless you lead your flocks into green pastures and beside still waters.

Now, lest some of you too easily comprehend this parable, I will declare that I am both the door to the Father's sheepfold and at the same time the true shepherd of my Father's flocks. Every shepherd who seeks to enter the fold without me shall fail, and the sheep will not hear his voice. I, with those who minister with me, am the door. Every soul who enters upon the eternal way by the means I have created and ordained shall be saved and will be able to go on to the finding of the eternal pastures of Paradise.

But I also am the true shepherd who is willing even to lay down his life for the sheep. The thief breaks into the fold only to steal, and to kill, and to destroy. But I have come that you all may have life and have it more abundantly. He who is a hireling, when danger arises, will flee and allow the sheep to be scattered and destroyed. But the true shepherd will not flee when the wolf comes. He will protect his flock and, if necessary, lay down his life for his sheep. Verily, verily, I say to you, friends and enemies. I am the true shepherd. I know my own and my own knows me. I will not flee in the face of danger. I will finish this service of the completion of my Father's will, and I will not forsake the flock which the Father has entrusted to my keeping.

But I have many other sheep not of this fold, and these words are true not only of this world. These other sheep also hear and know my voice, and I have promised the Father that they shall all be brought into one-fold, one brotherhood of the sons of God. Then shall you all know the voice of one shepherd, the true shepherd, and shall all acknowledge the Fatherhood of God.

So shall you know why the Father loves me and has put all of his flocks in this domain in my hands for keeping. It is because the Father knows that I will not falter in the safeguarding of the sheepfold, that I will not desert my sheep, and that, if it shall be required, I will not hesitate to lay down my life in the service of his flocks. But mind you, if I lay down my life, I will take it up again. No man nor any other creature can take away my life. I have the right and the power to lay down my life, and I have the same power and right to take it up again.

You cannot understand this, but I received such authority from my Father even before this world was created."

When they heard these words, his Apostles were confused, his disciples were amazed, while the Pharisees from Jerusalem went out into the night, saying: "He is either mad or has a devil inside of him." But even some of the Jerusalem teachers said: "He speaks like one having authority. Besides, who ever saw one having a devil open the eyes of a man born blind and do all of the wonderful things which this man has done."

By next morning, half of the visitors from Jerusalem professed belief in Jesus, the other half returned home in utter dismay.

Teaching on Trust and Spiritual Preparedness

By the following January, the Sabbath-afternoon multitudes had grown to almost three thousand. One Sabbath, Jesus preached the memorable Sermon on Trust and Spiritual Preparedness. After a preliminary introduction by Peter, the Master said:

"What I have many times said to my Apostles and to my disciples, I now declare to this multitude: Beware of the leaven of the Pharisees which is hypocrisy, born of prejudice and nurtured in traditional bondage, albeit many of these Pharisees are honest of heart and some of them now abide here as my disciples. All of you shall understand my teachings, for there is nothing now covered that shall not be revealed. That which is now hid from you shall all be made known when the Son of God has completed his mission on Earth and in the flesh.

Soon, very soon, will the things which our enemies now plan in secrecy and in darkness be brought out into the light and be proclaimed from the housetops. But I say to you, my friends, when they seek to destroy the Son of God, be not afraid of them. Fear not those who, although they may be able to kill the body, after that have no more power over you. I admonish you to fear none, in Heaven or on Earth, but to rejoice in the knowledge of him who has power to deliver you from all unrighteousness-- and to present you blameless before the judgment seat of a universe.

Are not five sparrows sold for two pennies? Yet, when these birds flit about in quest of their sustenance, not one of them exists without the knowledge of the Father, the source of all life. To the Seraphic guardians the very hairs of your head are numbered. If all of this is true, why should you live in fear of the many trifles which come upon your daily lives? I say to you: Fear not, you are of much more value than many sparrows.

All of you who have had the courage to confess faith in my gospel before men I will presently acknowledge before the Angels of Heaven. But he who shall knowingly deny the truth of my teachings before men shall be denied by his guardian of destiny even before the Angels of Heaven.

Say what you will about the Son of God, and it shall be forgiven you. But before other high authorities, be not concerned about what you should say and be not anxious as to how you should answer their questions, for the spirit that dwells within you shall certainly teach you in that very hour what you should say in honor of the gospel of the kingdom.

How long will you wait in the valley of decisions? Why do you halt between two opinions? Why should Jew or Gentile hesitate to accept the good news that he is a son of the eternal God? How long will it take us to persuade you to enter joyfully into your spiritual inheritance? I came into this world to reveal the Father to you and to lead you to the Father. The first I have done, but the last I may not do without your consent. The Father never compels any man to enter the kingdom. The invitation ever has been and always will be: Whosoever will, let him come and freely partake of the water of life."

Teaching on the Trial

Teaching on the trials of life, Jesus said: "In the time of testing, a man's soul is revealed. Trial discloses what really is in the heart. When the servant is tested and proved, then may the Father of the house set such a servant over his household and safely trust this faithful steward to see that his children are fed and nurtured. Likewise, will I soon know who can be trusted with the welfare of my children when I return to the Father. As the Father of the household shall set the true and tried servant over the affairs of his family, so will I exalt those who endure the trials of this hour in the affairs of my kingdom.

But if the servant is slothful and begins to say in his heart, 'My master delays his coming,' and begins to mistreat his fellow servants and to eat and drink until drunken, then the Master of that servant will come at a time when he looks not for him and, finding him unfaithful, will cast him out in disgrace. Therefore, you do well to prepare yourselves for that day when you will be visited suddenly and in an unexpected manner. Remember, much has been given to you.

Therefore, will much be required of you. Fiery trials are drawing near you. You preach peace on Earth, but my mission will not bring peace in the material affairs of men - not for a time, at least. Division can only be the result where two members of a family believe in me, and three members reject me. Friends, relatives, and loved ones are destined to be set against each other by the gospel you preach. True, each of these believers shall have great and lasting peace in his own heart, but peace on Earth will not come until all are willing to believe and enter into their glorious inheritance of sonship with God. Nevertheless, go into all the world proclaiming this gospel to all nations, to every man, woman and child."

TEACHING ON ACCIDENTS

It was the custom of Jesus and the Apostles, when on a journey, to pause at midday for rest and refreshment. It was at such a noontime stop on the way to Philadelphia that Thomas asked Jesus: "Master, from hearing your remarks as we journeyed this morning, I would like to inquire whether spiritual beings are concerned in the production of strange and extraordinary events in the material world and, further, to ask whether the Angels and other spirit beings are able to prevent accidents."

In answer to Thomas, Jesus said: "Have I been so long with you, Thomas, yet you continue to ask me such questions? Have you failed to observe how the Son of God lives as one with you and consistently refuses to employ the forces of Heaven for his personal assistance? Do we not all live by the same means whereby all men exist? Do you see the power of the spiritual world manifested in the material life of this world, save for the revelation of the Father and the sometime healing of his afflicted children?

All too long have your forefathers believed that prosperity was the token of divine approval, and that diversity was the proof of God's wrath. I declare that such beliefs are superstitions. Do you not observe that far greater numbers of the poor joyfully receive the gospel and immediately enter the kingdom? If material riches are evidence of divine favor, why do the rich so many times refuse to believe this good news from Heaven?

The Father causes his rain to fall on the just and the unjust. The sun likewise shines on the righteous as well as on the unrighteous. You know about those Galileans whose blood Pilate mingled with the sacrifices, but I tell you these Galileans were not in any manner sinners above all their fellows just because this happened to them. You also know about the eighteen men upon whom the Tower of Siloam fell, killing them. Think not that these men who were thus destroyed were offenders above all their brothers in Jerusalem. These folks were simply innocent victims of one of the accidents of time.

There are three groups of events which may occur in your lives:

1. You may share in those normal happenings which are a part of the life you and your fellows live on the face of the Earth.

2. You may chance to fall victim to one of the accidents of nature, one of the mischances of men, knowing full well that such occurrences are in no way prearranged or otherwise produced by the spiritual forces of the realm.
3. You may reap the harvest from your direct efforts to comply with the natural laws governing the world.

There was a certain man who planted a fig tree in his yard, and when he had many times sought fruit thereon and found none, he called the vinedressers before him and said: 'Here have I come these three seasons looking for fruit on this fig tree and have found none. Cut down this barren tree. Why should it encumber the ground?' But the head gardener answered his master: 'Let it alone for one more year so that I may dig around it and put on fertilizer, and then next year, if it bears no fruit, it shall be cut down.' When they had thus complied with the laws of fruitfulness, since the tree was living and good, they were rewarded with an abundant yield.

In the matter of sickness and health, you should know that these bodily states are the result of material causes. Health is not the smile of Heaven, neither is affliction the frown of God.

The Father's human children have equal capacity for the reception of material blessings. Therefore, does he bestow things physical upon the children of men without discrimination. When it comes to the bestowal of spiritual gifts, the Father is limited by man's capacity for receiving these divine endowments. Although the Father does not favor one man over another, in the bestowal of spiritual gifts, he is limited by man's faith and by his willingness always to abide by the Father's will."

CHAPTER 7

The Last Week

PALM SUNDAY

T HE FEAST OF THE PASSOVER WAS UPON THE LAND ONCE AGAIN, but this time the Master determined that the time had come for him to go into Jerusalem for the final time. He felt that his mission was accomplished, the journey was at an end. He gathered his Apostles together and told them that they must go down into the city for the Passover, and that this trip would end in his death and departure for his Father's kingdom.

They arrived at Bethany in midafternoon Friday, March 31, AD 30 by your current calendar. Lazarus, his sisters, and their friends were expecting them. Since so many people came every day to talk with Lazarus about his resurrection, Jesus was informed that arrangements had been made for him to stay with a neighboring believer, one Simon, the leading citizen of the little village since the death of Lazarus' father.

That evening, Jesus received many visitors, and the common folks of Bethany and Bethpage did their best to make him feel welcome.

Although many thought Jesus was now going into Jerusalem, in utter defiance of the Sanhedrin's decree of death, to proclaim himself king of the Jews, the Bethany family, Lazarus, Martha, and Mary, more fully realized that the Master was not that kind of a king. They dimly felt that this might be his last visit to Jerusalem and Bethany.

The chief priests were informed that Jesus lodged at Bethany, but they thought best not to attempt to seize him among his friends. They decided to wait for his coming on into Jerusalem. Jesus knew about all this, but he was majestically calm. His friends had never seen him more composed and congenial. Even the Apostles were astounded that he should be so unconcerned when the Sanhedrin had appealed to all Jewry to deliver him into their hands. While the Master slept that night, the Apostles watched over him by twos, and many of them were armed with swords. Early the next morning they were awakened by hundreds of pilgrims who came out from Jerusalem to see Jesus and Lazarus, whom he had raised from the dead.

Pilgrims from outside of Judea, as well as the Jewish authorities, had all been asking: "What do you think? Will Jesus come up to the feast?" Therefore, when the people heard that Jesus was at Bethany, they were glad, but the chief priests and Pharisees were perplexed.

They were pleased to have him under their jurisdiction, but they were a bit troubled by his boldness. They remembered that on his previous visit to Bethany, Lazarus had been raised from the dead, and Lazarus was becoming a big problem to the enemies of Jesus.

Six days before the Passover, on the evening after the Sabbath, all Bethany and Bethpage joined in celebrating the arrival of Jesus by a public banquet at the home of Simon. This supper was in honor of both Jesus and Lazarus. It was tendered in defiance of the Sanhedrin.

Martha directed the serving of the food. Her sister Mary was among the women onlookers as it was against the custom of the Jews for a woman to sit at a public banquet. The agents of the Sanhedrin were present, but they feared to apprehend Jesus in the midst of his friends.

Jesus talked with Simon about Joshua of old, whose namesake he was, and recited how Joshua and the Israelites had come up to Jerusalem through Jericho. In commenting on the legend of the walls of Jericho falling down, Jesus said: "I am not concerned with such walls of brick and stone, but I would cause the walls of prejudice, self- righteousness, and hate to crumble at the preaching of the Father's love for all men."

The banquet went along in a very cheerful and normal manner except that all the Apostles were unusually sober. Jesus was exceptionally cheerful and had been playing with the children up to the time of coming to the table.

Nothing out of the ordinary happened until near the close of the feasting when Mary the sister of Lazarus stepped forward from among the group of women onlookers and, going up to where Jesus reclined as the guest of honor, proceeded to open a large alabaster vase of very rare and costly ointment. After anointing the Master's head, she began to pour it upon his feet as she took down her hair and wiped them with it. The whole house became filled with the odor of the ointment, and everybody present was amazed at what Mary had done. Lazarus said nothing, but when some of the people murmured, showing indignation that so costly an ointment should be thus used, Judas Iscariot stepped over to where Andrew reclined and said: "Why was this ointment not sold and the money bestowed to feed the poor? You should speak to the Master that he refuse such waste."

Jesus, knowing what they thought and hearing what they said, put his hand upon Mary's head as she knelt by his side and, with a kindly expression upon his face, said: "Leave her alone, every one of you. Why do you trouble her about this, seeing that she has done a good thing in her heart? To you who murmur and say that this ointment should have been sold and the money given to the poor, let me say that you have the poor always with you so that you may minister to them at any time it seems good to you. But I shall not always be with you. I shall go soon to my Father. This woman has long saved this ointment for my body at its burial, and now that it has seemed good to her to make this anointing in anticipation of my death, she shall not be denied such satisfaction. In the doing of this, Mary has surpassed all of you in that by this act she demonstrates faith in what I have said about my death and ascension to my Father in Heaven. This woman shall not be criticized for that which she has this night done. Rather do I say to you that in the ages to come, wherever this gospel shall be preached throughout the whole world, what she has done will be spoken of in memory of her."

It was because of this rebuff, which he took as a personal admonishment, that Judas Iscariot finally made up his mind to

seek revenge for his hurt feelings. Many times, he had entertained
such ideas subconsciously, but now he dared to think such wicked
thoughts in his open and conscious mind. Many others encouraged
him in this attitude since the cost of this ointment was a sum equal
to the earnings of one man for one year, enough to provide bread
for five thousand persons. But Mary loved Jesus. She had provided
this precious ointment with which to embalm his body in death,
for she believed his words when he forewarned them that he must
die, and it was not to be denied her if she changed her mind and
chose to bestow this offering upon the Master while he yet lived.
Both Lazarus and Martha knew that Mary had long saved the
money to buy this cruse of ointment, and they heartily approved
of her doing as her heart desired in such a matter, for they were
well-to-do and could easily afford to make such an offering.

When the chief priests heard of this dinner in Bethany for
Jesus and Lazarus, they began to take counsel among themselves
as to what should be done with Lazarus. Presently they decided
that Lazarus must also die. They rightly concluded that it would
be useless to put Jesus to death if they permitted Lazarus, whom
he had raised from the dead, to live.

On Sunday morning, in Simon's beautiful garden, the Master
called his twelve Apostles around him and gave them their final
instructions preparatory to entering Jerusalem. He told them that
he would probably deliver many addresses and teach many lessons
this week before returning to the Father but advised the Apostles
to refrain from doing any public work during this Passover sojourn
in Jerusalem. He instructed them to remain near him and to watch
and pray. Jesus knew that many of his Apostles and immediate

followers even then carried swords concealed on their persons, but he made no reference to this fact.

This morning's instructions embraced a brief review of their ministry from the day of their ordination near Capernaum down to this day when they were preparing to enter Jerusalem. The Apostles listened in silence. They asked no questions.

Early that morning David Zebedee had turned over to Judas the funds realized from the sale of the equipment of the Pella encampment, and Judas, in turn, had placed the greater part of this money in the hands of Simon, their host, for safekeeping in anticipation of the necessities of their entry into Jerusalem.

After the conference with the Apostles Jesus conversed with Lazarus and instructed him to avoid the sacrifice of his life to the vengefulness of the Sanhedrin. It was in obedience to this admonition that Lazarus, a few days later, fled to Philadelphia when the officers of the Sanhedrin sent men to arrest him.

In a way, all of Jesus' followers sensed the impending crisis, but they were prevented from fully realizing its seriousness by the unusual cheerfulness and exceptional good humor of the Master.

Bethany was about two miles from the temple, and it was half past one that Sunday afternoon when Jesus made ready to start for Jerusalem. He had feelings of profound affection for Bethany and its simple people. Nazareth, Capernaum, and Jerusalem had rejected him, but Bethany had accepted him, had believed in him. It was in this small village, where almost every man, woman, and child were believers, that he chose to perform the mightiest work of his Earth bestowal, the resurrection of Lazarus. He did not raise Lazarus so that the villagers might believe, but rather because they already believed.

All morning Jesus had thought about his entry into Jerusalem.

Before this time, he had always endeavored to suppress all public belief in him as the Messiah, but it was different now. He was nearing the end of his career in the flesh. His death had been decreed by the Sanhedrin, and no harm could come from allowing his disciples to give free expression to their feelings, just as might occur if he elected to make a formal and public entry into the city.

Jesus did not decide to make this public entrance into Jerusalem as a last bid for popular favor nor as a final grasp for power. Neither did he do it to satisfy the human longings of his disciples and Apostles. Jesus entertained none of the illusions of a fantastic dreamer. He well knew what was to be the outcome of this visit.

Having decided upon making a public entrance into Jerusalem, the Master was confronted with the necessity of choosing a proper method of executing such an entrance. Jesus thought over all of the many more or less contradictory so-called Messianic prophesies, but there seemed to be only one which was at all appropriate for him to follow. Most of these prophetic utterances depicted a king, the son and successor of David, a bold and aggressive temporal deliverer of all Judea from the yoke of foreign domination. But there was one Scripture that had sometimes been associated with the Messiah by those who held more to the spiritual concept of his mission, which Jesus thought might consistently be taken as a guide for his projected entry into Jerusalem. This Scripture was found in Zechariah, and it said: "Rejoice greatly, 0 daughter of Zion; shout, 0 daughter of Jerusalem.

Behold, your king comes to you. He is just and he brings salvation. He comes as the lowly one, riding upon a colt, the foal of a donkey."

A warrior king always entered a city riding upon a horse; a king on a mission of peace and friendship always entered riding upon a donkey. Jesus would not enter Jerusalem as a man on horseback, but he was willing to enter peacefully and with good will as the Son of God on a donkey.

Jesus had long tried by direct teaching to impress upon his Apostles and his disciples that his kingdom was not of this world, that it was a purely spiritual matter, but he had not succeeded in this effort.

Now, what he had failed to do by plain and personal teaching, he would attempt to accomplish by a symbolic appeal. Accordingly, right after the noon lunch, Jesus called Peter and John, and after directing them to go over to Bethpage, a neighboring village a little off the main road and a short distance northwest of Bethany, he further said: "Go to Bethpage, and when you come to the junction of the roads, you will find the colt of a donkey tied there. Loose the colt and bring it back with you. If anyone asks you why you do this, merely say, 'The Master has need of him." When the two Apostles had gone into Bethpage as the Master had directed, they found the colt tied near his mother in the open street and close to a house on the corner. As Peter began to untie the colt, the owner came over and asked why they did this, and when Peter answered him as Jesus had directed, the man said: "If your Master is Jesus from Galilee, let him have the colt." So, they returned bringing the colt with them.

By this time several hundred pilgrims had gathered around Jesus and his Apostles. Since midmorning the visitors passing by on their way to Passover had waited. Meanwhile, David Zebedee and some of his former messenger associates took it upon themselves to hasten on down to Jerusalem, where they effectively spread the report among the throngs of visiting pilgrims around the temple that Jesus of Nazareth was making a triumphal entry into the city. Accordingly, several thousand of these visitors flocked forth to greet this much talked of prophet and wonderworker, whom some believed to be the Messiah.

This multitude, coming out from Jerusalem, met Jesus and the crowd going into the city just after they had passed over the brow of Olivet and had begun the descent into the city.

As the procession started out from Bethany, there was great enthusiasm among the festive crowd of disciples, believers, and visiting pilgrims, many hailing from Galilee and Perea. Just before they started, the twelve women of the original women's corps, accompanied by some of their associates, arrived on the scene and joined this unique procession as it moved on joyously toward the city.

Before they started, the Alpheus twins put their cloaks on the donkey and held him while the Master got on. As the procession moved toward the summit of Olivet, the festive crowd threw their garments on the ground and brought branches from the nearby trees in order to make a carpet of honor for the donkey bearing the royal Son, the promised Messiah. As the merry crowd moved on toward Jerusalem, they began to sing, or rather to shout in unison, the Psalm, "Hosanna to the son of David. Blessed is he who comes in the name of the Lord.

Hosanna in the highest. Blessed be the kingdom that comes down from Heaven."

Jesus was lighthearted and cheerful as they moved along until he came to the brow of Olivet, where the city and the temple towers came into full view. There the Master stopped the procession, and a great silence came upon all as they beheld him weeping. Looking down upon the vast multitude coming forth from the city to greet him, the Master, with much emotion and with tearful voice, said: "O Jerusalem, if you had only known the things which belong to your peace, and which you could so freely have had. But now are these glories about to be hidden from your eyes. You are about to reject the Son of Peace and turn your backs upon the gospel of salvation. The days will soon come upon you where your enemies will cast a trench around you and lay siege to you on every side. They shall utterly destroy you, insomuch that not one stone shall be left upon another. All this shall befall you because you know not the time of your divine visitation. You are about to reject the gift of God, and all men will reject you."

When he had finished speaking, they began the descent of Olivet and presently were joined by the multitude of visitors who had come from Jerusalem waving palm branches, shouting hosannas, and otherwise expressing gleefulness and good fellowship. The Master had not planned that these crowds should come out from Jerusalem to meet them. That was the work of others. He never premeditated anything which was dramatic.

Along with the multitude which poured out to welcome the Master, there came also many of the Pharisees and his other enemies.

They were so perturbed by this sudden and unexpected outburst of popular acclaim that they feared to arrest him lest such action precipitate an open revolt of the populace. They greatly feared the attitude of the large numbers of visitors, who had heard much of Jesus, and who, many of them, believed in him.

As they neared Jerusalem, the crowd became more demonstrative, so much so that some of the Pharisees made their way up alongside Jesus and said: "Teacher, you should reprimand your disciples and order them to behave more seemly." Jesus answered: "It is only fitting that these children should welcome the Son of Peace, whom the chief priests have rejected. It would be useless to stop them unless in their stead these stones by the roadside cry out."

The Pharisees hurried on ahead of the procession to rejoin the Sanhedrin, which was then in session at the temple, and they reported to their associates: "Behold, all that we do is of no avail. We are confounded by this Galilean. The people have gone mad over him. If we do not stop these ignorant ones, all the world will go after him."

There really was no deep significance to be attached to this superficial and spontaneous outburst of popular enthusiasm. This welcome, although it was joyous and sincere, did not signify any real or deep-seated conviction in the hearts of this festive multitude. These same crowds were equally as willing quickly to reject Jesus later on this week when the Sanhedrin once took a firm and decided stand against him, and when they became disillusioned when they realized that Jesus was not going to establish the kingdom in accordance with their long- cherished expectations.

But the whole city was mightily stirred up, insomuch that everyone asked, "Who is this man?" The multitude answered, "This is the prophet of Galilee, Jesus of Nazareth."

While the Alpheus twins returned the donkey to its owner, Jesus and the other ten Apostles detached themselves from their immediate associates and strolled about the temple, viewing the preparations for the Passover. No attempt was made to apprehend Jesus as the Sanhedrin greatly feared the people, and that was, after all, one of the reasons Jesus had for allowing the multitude thus to acclaim him. The Apostles did not understand that this was the only human procedure which could have been effective in preventing Jesus' immediate arrest upon entering the city. The Master desired to give the inhabitants of Jerusalem, high and low, as well as the tens of thousands of Passover visitors, this one more and last chance to hear the gospel and receive, if they would, the Son of Peace.

Now, as the evening drew on and the crowds went in quest of nourishment, Jesus and his immediate followers were left alone. What a strange day it had been! The Apostles were thoughtful, but speechless. Never, in their years of association with Jesus, had they seen such a day. For a moment they sat down by the treasury, watching the people drop in their contributions: the rich putting much in the receiving box and all giving something in accordance with the extent of their possessions. At last, there came along a poor widow, scantily attired, and they observed as she cast two mites (small coppers) into the trumpet. Then said Jesus, calling the attention of the Apostles to the widow: "Heed well what you have just seen. This poor widow cast in more than all the others, for all these others, from their excess, cast in some trifle as a gift, but this poor woman, even though she is in want, gave all that she had, even her living."

As the evening drew on, they walked around the temple courts in silence, and after Jesus had surveyed these familiar scenes once more, recalling his emotions in connection with previous visits, he said, "Let us go up to Bethany for our rest." Jesus, with Peter and John, went to the home of Simon, while the other Apostles lodged among their friends in Bethany and Bethpage.

MONDAY

Early on this Monday morning, by prearrangement, Jesus and the Apostles assembled at the home of Simon in Bethany, and after a brief conference they set out for Jerusalem. The twelve were strangely silent as they journeyed on toward the temple. They had not recovered from the experience of the preceding day. They were expectant, fearful, and profoundly affected by a certain feeling of detachment growing out of the Master's sudden change of tactics, coupled with his instruction that they were to engage in no public teaching throughout this Passover week.

As this group journeyed down Mount Olivet, Jesus led the way, the Apostles following closely behind in meditative silence. There was just one thought uppermost in the minds of all save Judas Iscariot, and that was: "What will the Master do today?" The one absorbing thought of Judas was: "What shall I do? Shall I go on with Jesus and my associates, or shall I withdraw? If I am going to quit, how shall I break off?"

It was about nine o'clock on this beautiful morning when these men arrived at the temple. They went at once to the large court where Jesus so often taught, and after greeting the believers who were awaiting him, Jesus mounted one of the teaching platforms and began to address the gathering crowd. The Apostles withdrew for a short distance and awaited developments.

A huge commercial traffic had grown up in association with the services and ceremonies of temple worship. There was the business of providing suitable animals for all the sacrifices. Though it was permissible for a worshipper to provide his own sacrifice, the fact remained that this animal must be free from all blemishes in the meaning of the Levitical law and as interpreted by official inspectors of the temple. Many a worshipper had experienced the humiliation of having his supposedly perfect animal rejected by the temple examiners. It therefore became the more general practice to purchase sacrificial animals at the temple, and although there were several stations near Olivet where they could be bought, it had become the vogue to buy these animals directly from the temple pens. Gradually there had grown up this custom of selling all kinds of sacrificial animals in the temple courts. An extensive business, in which enormous profits were made, had thus been brought into existence. Part of these gains was reserved for the temple treasury, but the larger part went indirectly into the hands of the ruling high-priestly families.

This sale of animals in the temple prospered because, when the worshiper purchased such an animal, although the price might be somewhat high, no more fees had to be paid, and he could be sure the intended sacrifice would not be rejected on the ground of possessing real or technical blemishes.

At one time or other systems of exorbitant overcharge were practiced upon the common people, especially during the great national feasts. At one time the greedy priests went so far as to demand the equivalent of the value of a week's labor for a pair of doves which should have been sold to the poor for a few pennies. The Sons of Annas had already begun to establish their bazaars in the temple precincts, those very merchandise marts which persisted to the time of their final overthrow by a mob three years before the destruction of the temple itself.

But traffic in sacrificial animals and miscellaneous merchandise was not the only way in which the courts of the temple were profaned. At this time there had grown an extensive system of banking and commercial exchange which was carried on right within the temple precincts. This all came about in the following manner: During the Asmonean dynasty the Jews coined their own silver money, and it had become the practice to require the temple dues of one-half shekel and all other temple fees to be paid with this Jewish coin. This regulation necessitated that moneychangers be licensed to exchange the many sorts of currency in circulation throughout Palestine and other provinces of the Roman Empire for this orthodox shekel of Jewish coining. The temple head tax, payable by all except women, slaves, and minors, was one-half shekel, a coin about the size of a ten-cent piece but twice as thick. By the times of Jesus, the priests had also been exempted from the payment of temple dues.

Accordingly, from the 15th to the 25th of the month preceding the Passover, accredited moneychangers erected their booths in the principal cities of Palestine for the purpose of providing the Jewish people with proper money to meet the temple dues after they had reached Jerusalem. After this ten-day period these moneychangers moved on to Jerusalem and proceeded to set up their exchange tables in the courts of the temple. They were permitted to charge the equivalent of from three to four cents commission for the exchange of a coin valued at about ten cents, and in case a coin of larger value was offered for exchange, they were allowed to collect double. Likewise did these temple bankers profit from the exchange of all money intended for the purchase of sacrificial animals and for the payment of vows and the making of offerings.

These temple moneychangers not only conducted a regular banking business for profit in the exchange of more than twenty sorts of money which the visiting pilgrims would periodically bring to Jerusalem, but they also engaged in all other kinds of transactions pertaining to the banking business. Both the temple treasury and the temple rulers profited tremendously from these commercial activities.

It was not uncommon for the temple treasury to hold upwards of ten million dollars while the common people languished in poverty and continued to pay these unjust levies.

In the midst of this noisy aggregation of moneychangers, merchandisers, and animal sellers, Jesus, on this Monday morning, attempted to teach the Sermon on the Heavenly kingdom. He was not alone in resenting this profanation of the temple. The common people, especially the Jewish visitors from foreign provinces, also heartily resented this profiteering desecration of their national house of worship. At this time the Sanhedrin itself held its regular meetings in a chamber surrounded by all this babble and confusion of trade and barter.

As Jesus was about to begin his address, two things happened to get his attention. At the money table of a near-by exchanger a violent and heated argument had arisen over the alleged overcharging of a Jew from Alexandria, while at the same moment there arose a bellowing from a drove of some one hundred bullocks which were being driven from one section of the animal pens to another. As Jesus paused, silently but thoughtfully contemplating this scene of commerce and confusion, close by he beheld a simple-minded Galilean, a man he had once talked with in Iron, being ridiculed and jostled about by sarcastic and would-be superior Judeans. All of this combined to produce one of those strange and periodic uprisings of indignant emotion in the soul of Jesus.

To the amazement of his Apostles, standing near at hand, who refrained from participation in what so soon followed, Jesus stepped down from the teaching platform and, going over to the lad who was driving the cattle through the court, took from him his whip of cords and swiftly drove the animals from the temple. But that was not all. He strode majestically before the wondering gaze of the thousands assembled in the temple court to the farthest cattle pen and proceeded to open the gates of every stall and to drive out the imprisoned animals. By this time the assembled pilgrims were electrified, and with uproarious shouting they moved toward the bazaars and began to overturn the tables of the moneychangers. In less than five minutes all commerce had been swept from the temple. By the time the nearby Roman guards had appeared on the scene, all was quiet, and the crowds had become orderly. Jesus, returning to the speaker's stand, spoke to the multitude: "You have this day witnessed that which is written in the Scriptures: 'My house shall be called a house of prayer for all nations, but you have made it a den of thieves.'"

But before he could utter other words, the great assembly broke out in hosannas of praise, and presently a throng of youths stepped out from the crowd to sing grateful hymns of appreciation that the profane and profiteering merchandisers had been ejected from the sacred temple. By this time some of the priests had arrived on the scene, and one of them said to Jesus, "Do you not hear what the children of the Levites say?" The Master replied, "Have you never read, 'Out of the mouths of babes and sucklings has praise been perfected?'" And all the rest of that day while Jesus taught, guards set by the people stood watch at every archway, and they would not permit anyone to carry even an empty vessel across the temple courts.

When the chief priests and the scribes heard about these happenings, they were dumfounded. All the more they feared the Master, and all the more they were determined to destroy him. But they were confused. They did not know how to accomplish his death, for they greatly feared the multitudes, who were now so outspoken in their approval of his overthrow of the profane profiteers. All this day, a day of quiet and peace in the temple courts, the people heard Jesus' teaching and literally hung on his words. This surprising act of Jesus was beyond the comprehension of his Apostles.

They were so surprised by this sudden and unexpected move of their Master that they remained throughout the whole episode huddled together near the speaker's stand. They never lifted a hand to further this cleansing of the temple. If this spectacular event had occurred the day before, at the time of Jesus' triumphal arrival at the temple at the termination of his tumultuous procession through the gates of the city, all the while loudly acclaimed by the multitude, they would have been ready for it, but coming as it did, they were wholly unprepared to participate.

This cleansing of the temple discloses the Master's attitude toward commercializing the practices of religion as well as his strong dislike of all forms of unfairness and profiteering at the expense of the poor and the unlearned. This episode also demonstrates that Jesus did not look with approval upon the refusal to employ force to protect the majority of any given human group against the unfair and enslaving practices of unjust minorities who may be able to entrench themselves behind political, financial, or ecclesiastical power. Shrewd, wicked, and designing men are not to be permitted to organize themselves for the exploitation and oppression of those who, because of their idealism, are not disposed to resort to force for self-protection or for the furtherance of their worthwhile life projects.

On Sunday the triumphal entry into Jerusalem so overawed the Jewish leaders that they refrained from placing Jesus under arrest.

Today, this spectacular cleansing of the temple likewise effectively postponed the Master's apprehension. Day by day the rulers of the Jews were becoming more and more determined to destroy him, but they were overcome by two fears, which conspired to delay the hour of striking. The chief priests and the scribes were unwilling to arrest Jesus in public for fear the multitude might turn upon them in a fury of resentment. They also dreaded the possibility of the Roman guards being called upon to quell a popular uprising.

At the noon session of the Sanhedrin, it was unanimously agreed that Jesus must be speedily destroyed, inasmuch as no friend of the Master attended this meeting. But they could not agree as to when and how he should be taken into custody. Finally, they agreed upon appointing five groups to go out among the people and seek to entangle him in his teaching or otherwise to discredit him in the sight of those who listened to his instruction. Accordingly, about two o'clock, when Jesus had just begun his discourse on the liberty of being a Son of God, a group of these elders of Israel made their way up near Jesus and, interrupting him in the customary manner, asked this question: "By what authority do you do these things? Who gave you this authority?"

It was altogether proper that the temple rulers and the officers of the Jewish Sanhedrin should ask this question of anyone who presumed to teach and perform in the extraordinary manner which had been characteristic of Jesus, especially as concerned his recent conduct in clearing the temple of all commerce. These traders and moneychangers all operated by direct license from the highest rulers, and a percentage of their gains was supposed to go directly into the temple treasury. Do not forget that authority was the watchword of all Jewry. The prophets were always stirring up trouble because they so boldly presumed to teach without authority, without having been duly instructed in the rabbinical academies and subsequently ordained by the Sanhedrin.

The lack of this authority in open public teaching was looked upon as indicating either ignorant presumption or open rebellion. At this time only the Sanhedrin could ordain an elder or teacher, and such a ceremony had to take place in the presence of at least three persons who had previously been so ordained. Such an ordination conferred the title of rabbi upon the teacher and also qualified him to act as a judge, binding and loosing such matters as might be brought to him for adjudication.

The rulers of the temple came before Jesus at this afternoon hour challenging not only his teaching but his acts. Jesus well knew that these very men had long publicly taught that his authority for teaching was Satanic, and that all his mighty works had been created by the power of the prince of devils. Therefore, did the Master began his answer to their question by asking them a counter question. Said Jesus: "I would also like to ask you one question which, if you will answer me, I likewise will tell you by what authority I do these works. The baptism of John, where did it come from? Did John get his authority from Heaven or from men?"

When his questioners heard this, they withdrew to one side to take counsel among themselves as to what answer they might give. They had thought to embarrass Jesus before the multitude, but now they found themselves much confused before all who were assembled at that time in the temple court. Their discomfort and confusion were all the more apparent when they returned to Jesus, saying: "Concerning the baptism of John, we cannot answer. We do not know." They so answered the Master because they had reasoned among themselves: "If we shall say that he got his authority from Heaven, then he will say, 'Why did you not believe him', and then he will add that he received his authority from John. If we shall say that he got his authority from men, then he will say that John was never ordained by men, and then might the multitude turn upon us, for most of them hold that John was a prophet." Thus, they were compelled to come before Jesus and the people confessing that they, the religious teachers and leaders of the Jews could not (or would not) express an opinion about John's mission. When they had spoken, Jesus, looking down upon them, said, "Neither will I tell you by what authority I do these things."

Jesus never intended to appeal to John for his authority. John had never been ordained by the Sanhedrin. Jesus' authority was in himself and in his Father's eternal supremacy. In employing this method of dealing with his adversaries, Jesus did not mean to dodge the question. At first it may seem that he was guilty of a masterly evasion, but it was not so. Jesus was never disposed to take unfair advantage of even his enemies. In this apparent evasion he really supplied all his hearers with the answer to the Pharisees' question as to the authority behind his mission. They had asserted that he performed by authority of the prince of devils. Jesus had repeatedly asserted that all his teaching and works were by the power and authority of his Father in Heaven. This, the Jewish leaders refused to accept and were seeking to comer him into admitting that he was an irregular teacher since he had never been approved by the Sanhedrin. In answering them as he did, while not claiming authority from John, he so satisfied the people with the inference that the effort of his enemies to ensnare him was effectively turned upon themselves and was much to their discredit in the eyes of all present.

It was this genius of the Master for dealing with his adversaries that made them so afraid of him. They attempted no more questions that day. They retired to take further counsel among themselves. But the people were not slow to notice the dishonesty and insincerity in these questions asked by the Jewish rulers. Even the common folk could not fail to distinguish between the moral majesty of the Master and the designing hypocrisy of his enemies. But the cleansing of the temple had brought the Sadducees over to the side of the Pharisees in perfecting the plan to destroy Jesus. The Sadducees at this time represented a majority of the Sanhedrin.

TUESDAY

On Tuesday afternoon of Passover Week, Jesus, accompanied by eleven Apostles, Joseph of Arimathea, thirty Greek followers, and other disciples, arrived at the temple and began the delivery of his last public address. This discourse was intended to be his last appeal to the Jewish people and the final indictment of his bitter enemies and would-be destroyers, the Scribes, Pharisees, Sadducees, and the other chief rulers of Palestine.

As the Master began to speak, the temple court was quiet and orderly. The moneychangers and the merchandisers had not dared again to enter the temple since Jesus and the aroused multitude had driven them out the previous day. Before beginning the discourse, Jesus tenderly looked down upon this audience, including his enemies, which were so soon to hear his farewell public address of mercy to mankind coupled with his last denunciation of the false teachers and the bigoted rulers of the Jews. He began his address:

"A long time have I been with you, going up and down this land proclaiming my Father's love for the children of men. Many have seen the light and, by faith, have entered into the kingdom of Heaven. In connection with this teaching and preaching my Father has done many wonderful works, even to the resurrection of the dead. Many sick and afflicted have been made whole because they believed. But all of this proclamation of truth and healing of disease has not opened the eyes of those who refuse to see light, those who are determined to reject this new gospel of the kingdom.

In every manner consistent with doing my Father's will, I and my Apostles have done our utmost to live in peace with our brothers, to conform with the reasonable requirements of the laws of Moses and the traditions of Judea. We have persistently sought peace, but the leaders of Judea will not have it. By rejecting the truth of God and the light of Heaven, they are aligning themselves on the side of error and darkness. There cannot be peace between light and darkness, between life and death, between truth and error.

Many of you have dared to believe my teachings and have already entered into the joy and liberty of the consciousness of sonship with God. You will bear me witness that I have offered this same sonship with God to all the Jewish nation, even to these very men here present who seek my destruction. Even now would my Father receive these blinded teachers and these hypocritical leaders if they would only turn to him and accept his loving mercy. Even now it is not too late for this people to receive the word of Heaven and to welcome the Son of God.

My Father has long dealt in mercy with this people. Generation after generation has, he sent his prophets to teach and warn them, and generation after generation have, they killed these Heaven-sent teachers. Now do your sinful high priests and corrupt rulers go right on doing this same thing. As Herod brought about the death of John, you likewise now make ready to kill the Son of God.

As long as there is a chance that the Jews will turn to my Father and seek salvation, the God of Abraham, Isaac, and Jacob will keep his hands of mercy outstretched toward you. But when you have once filled up your cup of impenitence, and when once you have finally rejected my Father's mercy, this nation will be left to its own counsels, and it shall speedily come to an inglorious end. This people was given the opportunity to become the light of the world, to show forth the spiritual glory of a God-knowing race, but you have so far departed from the fulfillment of that divine mission that your leaders are about to commit the greatest folly of all the ages in that they are on the verge of finally rejecting the gift of God to all men and for all ages - the revelation of the love of the Father in Heaven for all his creatures on Earth.

When you do once reject this revelation of God to man, the kingdom of Heaven shall pass to other peoples, to those who will receive it with joy and gladness. In the name of the Father who sent me, I solemnly warn you that you are about to lose your position in the world as the standard-bearers of eternal truth and the custodians of the divine law. I am now offering you your last chance to come forward and repent your erroneous ways, to signify your intention to seek God with all your hearts and to enter, like little children and by sincere faith, into the security and salvation of the kingdom of Heaven.

My Father has long worked for the salvation of all men of this Earth, and I came down to live among you and personally show you the way. Many of both the Jews and the Gentiles have believed the gospel of the kingdom, but those who should be first to come forward and accept the light of Heaven have steadfastly refused to believe the revelation of the truth of God - God revealed in man and man uplifted to God.

This afternoon my Apostles stand here before you in silence, but you shall soon hear their voices ringing out with the call to salvation and with the urge to unite with the Heavenly kingdom as the sons of the living God. Now I call to witness these, my disciples and believers in the gospel of the kingdom, as well as the unseen messengers by their sides, that I have once more offered Judea and her rulers deliverance and salvation. But you all behold how the Father's mercy is slighted and how the messengers of truth are rejected. Nevertheless, I warn you that these Scribes and Pharisees still sit in Moses' seat, and therefore, until the rulers of the kingdoms of men shall finally overthrow this nation and destroy the place of these Jewish rulers, I bid you co-operate with these elders in Judea. You are not required to unite with them in their plans to destroy the Son of God, but in everything related to the peace of Judea you are to be subject to them. In all these matters do whatsoever they bid you and observe the essentials of the law but do not pattern after their evil works. Remember, this is the sign of these rulers: they say that which is good, but they do not. You well know how these leaders bind heavy burdens on your shoulders, burdens grievous to bear, and that they will not lift as much as one finger to help you bear these weighty burdens. They have oppressed you with ceremonies and enslaved you with traditions.

Furthermore, these self-centered rulers delight in doing their good works so that they will be seen by men. They broaden their phylacteries and enlarge the orders of their official robes. They crave the choicest places at the feasts and demand the chief seats in the synagogues. They covet laudatory salutations in the marketplaces and desire to be called rabbi by all men. Even while they seek all this honor from men, they secretly lay hold of widow's houses and take profit from the services of the sacred temple. For a pretense these hypocrites make long prayers in public and give alms to attract the notice of their fellows.

While you should honor your rulers and reverence your teachers, you should call no man father in the spiritual sense, for there is only one who is your father, and that is God himself. Neither should you seek to Father it over your brothers in the kingdom. Remember, I have taught you that the one who would be greatest among you should become the server of all. If you presume to exalt yourselves before God, you will certainly be humbled. But whoever truly humbles himself will surely be exalted. Seek in your daily lives, not self-glorification, but the glory of God. Intelligently subordinate your own will to the will of the Father in Heaven.

Mistake not my words. I bear no malice toward these chief priests and rulers who even now seek my destruction. I have no ill will for these Scribes and Pharisees who reject my teachings. I know that many of you believe in secrets, and I know you will openly profess your allegiance to the kingdom when my hour comes. But how will your rabbis justify themselves since they profess to talk with God and then presume to reject and destroy him who comes to reveal the Father to the world?

Woe upon you, Scribes and Pharisees, hypocrites. You would shut the doors of the kingdom of Heaven against sincere men because they happen to be unlearned in the ways of your teaching. You refuse to enter the kingdom and at the same time do everything within your power to prevent all others from entering. You stand with your backs to the doors of salvation and fight with all who would enter therein.

Woe upon you, Scribes and Pharisees, hypocrites that you are, for you do indeed travel land and sea to make one convert, and when you have succeeded, you are not content until you have made him twofold worse off spiritually than when he was a child of the heathen.

Woe upon you, chief priests and rulers, who lay hold of the property of the poor and demand heavy dues of those who would serve God as they think Moses ordained. You who refuse to show mercy, can you hope for mercy in the worlds to come?

Woe upon you, false teachers, blind guides. What can be expected of a nation when the blind lead the blind? They both shall stumble into the pit of destruction.

Woe upon you who dissimulate when you take an oath. You are tricksters since you teach that a man may swear by the temple and break his oath, but that whoever swears by the gold in the temple must remain bound. You are all fools and blind. You are not even consistent in your dishonesty, for which is the greater, the gold or the temple which has supposedly sanctified the gold? You also teach that, if a man swears by the altar, it is nothing. But that, if one swears by the gift that is upon the altar, then shall he be held as a debtor. Again, are you blind to the truth, for which is the greater, the gift or the altar which sanctifies the gift? How can you justify such hypocrisy and dishonesty in the sight of the God of Heaven?

Woe upon you, Scribes and Pharisees, and all other hypocrites who make sure that they tithe mint, anise, and cumin and at the same time disregard the weightier matters of the law, faith, mercy, and justice. You are truly blind guides and dumb teachers. You strain out the gnat and swallow the camel.

Woe upon you, Scribes and Pharisees, you hypocrites. You are scrupulous to cleanse the outside of the cup and the platter, but within there remains the filth of extortion, excesses, and deception. You are spiritually blind. Do you not recognize how much better it would be first to cleanse the inside of the cup, and then that which spills over would of itself cleanse the outside? You wicked tricksters, you make the outward performances of your religion conform with the letter of your interpretation of Moses' law while your souls are steeped in iniquity and filled with murder.

Woe upon all of you who reject truth and spurn mercy. Many of you are like white sepulchers, which outwardly appear beautiful but within are full of dead men's bones and all sorts of uncleanness. You, who knowingly reject the counsel of God, appear outwardly to men as holy and righteous, but inwardly your hearts are filled with hypocrisy and iniquity.

Woe upon you, false guides of a nation. Over yonder have you built a monument to the martyred prophets of old, the prophets that your own forefathers stoned and murdered. You garnish the tombs of the righteous and flatter yourselves that, had you lived in the days of your forefathers, you would not have killed the prophets. Then in the face of such self-righteous thinking you make ready to kill him of whom. the prophets spoke, the Son of God. Inasmuch as you do these things, you are witness to yourselves that you are the wicked sons of them who slew the prophets that my Father sent. Go on then and fill up the cup of your condemnation to the full.

Woe upon you, children of evil. John did truly call you the offspring of vipers, and I ask how can you escape the judgment that John pronounced upon you?

But even now I offer you in my Father's name mercy and forgiveness. Even now I offer the loving hand of eternal fellowship. My Father, over the past several centuries, sent you the wise men and the prophets. Some you persecuted and others you murdered. Then appeared John proclaiming the coming of the Son of God, and him you destroyed after many had believed his teachings. Now you are ready to shed more innocent blood. Do you not comprehend that a terrible day of reckoning will come when the judge of all the Earth shall require of this people an accounting for the way they have rejected, persecuted, and destroyed these messengers of Heaven? Do you not understand that you must account for all of this blood, from the first prophet killed down to the times of Zechariah, who was slain at the very altar? If you go on in your evil ways, this accounting may be required of this very generation.

O Jerusalem, you who have stoned the prophets and killed the teachers that were sent to you, even now would I gather your children together as a hen gathers her chicks under her wings.

Now I take leave of you. You have heard my message and have made your decision. Those who have believed my gospel are even now safe within the kingdom of God. To you who have chosen to reject the gift of God, I say that you will no longer see me teaching in the temple. My work for you is done. Behold, I now go forth with my children, and your house is left to you desolate."

After this discourse, the crowds were speechless. Jesus, along with his Apostles conducted many discussions around the temple the rest of the day and then departed for Bethany to rest for the night.

WEDNESDAY

When the work of teaching the people did not press them, it was the custom of Jesus and his Apostles to rest from their labors each Wednesday. On this particular Wednesday they ate breakfast somewhat later than usual, and the camp was permeated with an ominous silence. Little was said during the first half of this morning meal. At last Jesus spoke: "I desire that you rest today. Take time to think over all that has happened since we came to

Jerusalem and meditate on what is just ahead, of which I have plainly told you. Make sure that the truth lives in your hearts, and that you daily grow in grace."

After breakfast the Master informed Andrew that he intended to be absent for the day and suggested that the Apostles be permitted to spend the time in accordance with their own choosing, except that under no circumstances should they go within the gates of Jerusalem. When Jesus made ready to go into the hills alone, David Zebedee accosted him, saying: "You well know, Master, that the Pharisees and rulers seek to destroy you, and yet you make ready to go alone into the hills. To do this is folly. I will therefore send three men with you well prepared to see that no harm befalls you." Jesus looked over the three well-armed and stalwart Galileans and said to David: "You mean well, but you err in that you fail to understand that the Son of God needs no one to defend him. No man will lay hands on me until that hour when I am ready to lay down my life in conformity to my Father's will. These men may not accompany me. I desire to go alone, that I may commune with the Father."

Upon hearing these words, David and his armed guards withdrew. But as Jesus started off alone the lad, John Mark, came forward with a small basket containing food and water and suggested that, if he intended to be away all day, he might find himself hungry.

The Master smiled at John and reached down to take the basket.

As Jesus was about to take the lunch basket from John's hand, the young lad ventured to say: "But, Master, you may set the basket down while you turn aside to pray and go on without it. Besides, if I should go along to carry the lunch, you would be more free to worship, and I will surely be silent. I will ask no questions and will stay by the basket when you go apart by yourself to pray."

While making this speech, the brazenness of which astonished some of the nearby listeners, John kept a firm hold on the basket.

There they stood, both John and Jesus holding the basket. Presently the Master let go and, looking down on the lad, said: "Since with all your heart you desire to go with me, it shall not be denied you. We will go off by ourselves and have a good visit. You may ask me any question that arises in your heart, and we will comfort and console each other. You may start out carrying lunch, and when you grow weary, I will help you. Follow on with me."

Jesus did not return to the camp that evening until after sunset.

The Master spent this last day of quiet on Earth visiting with this truth- hungry fourteen-year-old boy and talking with his Paradise Father.

This event has become known in the Heavenly Realms as "the day which a young man spent with God in the hills." Forever this occasion exemplifies the willingness of the Creator to commune with the creature. Even a youth, if the desire of the heart is really great, can command the attention and enjoy the loving companionship of the God of a universe, actually experience the unforgettable ecstasy of being alone with God in the hills, and for a whole day. Such was the unique experience of this young boy named John Mark on this Wednesday in the hills of Judea.

Jesus visited much with John, talking freely about the affairs of this world and the next. John told Jesus how much he regretted that he had not been old enough to be one of the Apostles and expressed his great appreciation that he had been permitted to follow on with them since their first preaching at the Jordan ford near Jericho, except for the trip to Phoenicia. Jesus warned the lad not to become discouraged by impending events and assured him he would live to become a mighty messenger of the kingdom.

John Mark was thrilled for the rest of his life by the memory of this day with Jesus in the hills, but he never forgot the Master's final admonition, spoken just as they were about to return to the Gethsemane camp, when he said: "Well, John, we have had a good visit, a real day of rest, but see to it that you tell no man the things which I told you." John Mark never did reveal anything that transpired on this day which he spent with Jesus in the hills.

Throughout the few remaining hours of Jesus' Earth life, John Mark never permitted the Master for long, to get out of his sight.

Always was the lad in hiding nearby. He slept only when Jesus slept.

In the course of this day's visiting with John Mark, Jesus spent considerable time comparing their early childhood and later boyhood experiences. Although John's parents possessed more of this world's goods than had Jesus' parents, there was much experience in their boyhood which was very similar. Jesus said many things which helped John better to understand his parents and other members of his family. When the lad asked the Master how he could know that he would turn out to be a "mighty messenger of the kingdom," Jesus said: "I know you will prove loyal to the gospel of the kingdom because I can depend upon your present faith and love when these qualities are grounded upon such an early training as has been your upbringing at home. You are the product of a home where the parents bear each other a sincere affection, and therefore you have not been over loved so as injuriously exalt your concept of self-importance. Neither has your personality suffered distortion which occurs when parents indulge in loveless maneuvering for your confidence and loyalty, one against the other. You have enjoyed that parental love which ensures self-confidence, and which fosters normal feelings of security. But you have also been fortunate in that your parents possessed wisdom as well as love; and it was wisdom which led them to withhold most forms of indulgence and many luxuries which wealth can buy while they sent you to the synagogue school along with your neighborhood playfellows, and they also encouraged you to learn how to live in this world by permitting you to have original experiences.

You came over to the Jordan, where we preached and John's disciples baptized, with your young friend Amos. Both of you wanted to go with us. When you returned to Jerusalem, your parents consented. Amos' parents refused. They loved their son so much that they denied him the blessed experience which you have had, even such as you this day enjoy. By running away from home, Amos could have joined us, but in so doing he would have wounded the love he has for his parents and sacrificed his loyalty to them. Even if such a course had been wise, it would have been a terrible price to pay for experience, independence, and liberty. Wise parents, such as yours, see to it that their children do not have to wound love or stifle loyalty in order to develop independence and enjoy invigorating liberty when they have grown up to your age.

Love, John, is the greatest gift of the universe when bestowed by all wise beings, but it is a dangerous and oftentimes semi-selfish trait as it is exhibited by mortal parents. When you get married and have children of your own to raise, make sure that your love is tempered by wisdom and guided by intelligence.

Your young friend, Amos, believes this gospel of the kingdom just as much as you, but I cannot fully depend upon him. I am not certain about what he will do in the years to come. His early home life was not such as would produce a wholly dependable person. Amos is too much like one of the Apostles who failed to enjoy a normal, loving, and wise home training. Your whole afterlife will be more happy and dependable because you spent your first eight years in a normal and well-regulated home. You possess a strong and well-knit character because you grew up in a home where love prevailed, and wisdom reigned. Such a childhood training produces a type of loyalty which assures me that you will go through with the course you have begun."

For more than an hour Jesus and John continued this discussion of home life. The Master went on to explain to John how a child is wholly dependent on his parents and the associated home life for all his early concepts of everything intellectual, social, moral, and even spiritual since the family represents to the young child all that he can first know of either human or divine relationships. The child must derive his first impressions of the universe from the mother's care. He is wholly dependent on the earthly father for his first ideas of the Heavenly Father. The child's subsequent life is made happy or unhappy, easy or difficult, in accordance with his early mental and emotional life, conditioned by these social and spiritual relationships of the home. A human being's entire afterlife is enormously influenced by what happens during the first few years of existence.

The Apostles spent most of this day walking around on Mount Olivet and visiting with the disciples who were encamped with them, but early in the afternoon they strongly desired to see Jesus return. As the day wore on, they grew increasingly anxious about his safety. They felt inexpressibly lonely without him. There was much debating throughout the day as to whether the Master should have been allowed to go off by himself in the hills, accompanied only by an errand boy.

Though no man openly so expressed his thoughts, there was not one of them, save Judas Iscariot, who did not wish himself in John Mark's place.

It was around midafternoon when Nathaniel made his speech on "Ultimate Desire" to about half a dozen of the Apostles and as many disciples, the ending of which was: "What is wrong with most of us is that we are only halfhearted. We fail to love the Master as he loves us. If we had all wanted to go with him as much as John Mark did, he would surely have taken us all. We stood by while the lad approached the Master and offered him the basket, but when the Master took hold of it, the lad would not let go. So, the Master left us here while he went off to the hills with basket, boy, and all."

About four o'clock this afternoon, runners came to David Zebedee bringing him word from his mother at Bethsaida and from Jesus' mother. Several days previously David had made up his mind that the chief priests and rulers were going to kill Jesus. David knew they were determined to destroy the Master, and he was about convinced that Jesus would neither exert his divine power to save himself nor permit his followers to employ force in his defense. Having reached these conclusions, he lost no time in dispatching a messenger to his mother, urging her to come at once to Jerusalem and to bring Mary the mother of Jesus and every member of his family.

David's mother did as her son requested, and now the runners came back to David bringing him word that his mother and Jesus' entire family were on the way to Jerusalem and should arrive sometime late on the following day or very early the next morning. Since David did this on his own initiative, he thought it wise to keep the matter to himself. He told no one, therefore, that Jesus' family was on the way to Jerusalem.

Shortly after noon, more than twenty of the Greeks who had met with Jesus and the twelve at the home of Joseph of Arimathea arrived at the camp, and Peter and John spent several hours in conference with them. These Greeks, at least some of them, were well advanced in the knowledge of the kingdom, having been instructed at Alexandria.

That evening, after returning to the camp, Jesus visited with the Greeks, and had it not been that such a course would have greatly disturbed his Apostles and many of his leading disciples, he would have ordained these twenty Greeks, even as he had ordained the seventy.

While all of this was going on at the camp, in Jerusalem the chief priests and elders were amazed that Jesus did not return to address the multitudes. True, the day before, when he left the temple, he had said, "I leave your house to you desolate." But they could not understand why he would be willing to forget the great advantage which he had built up in the friendly attitude of the crowds. While they feared he would stir up tumult among the people, the Master's last words to the multitude had been an exhortation to conform in every reasonable manner with the authority of those "who sit in Moses' seat." But it was a busy day in the city as they simultaneously prepared for the Passover and perfected their plans for destroying Jesus.

Not many people came to the camp due to its establishment had been kept a well-guarded secret by all who knew that Jesus was expecting to stay there in place of going out to Bethany every night.

Shortly after Jesus and John Mark left the camp, Judas Iscariot disappeared from among his brothers, not returning until late in the afternoon. This confused and discontented Apostle, notwithstanding his Master's specific request to refrain from entering Jerusalem, went in haste to keep his appointment with Jesus' enemies at the home of Caiaphas, the high priest. This was an informal meeting of the Sanhedrin and had been arranged for midmorning. This meeting was called to discuss the nature of the charges which should be lodged against Jesus and to decide upon the procedure to be employed in bringing him before the Roman authorities for the purpose of securing the necessary civil confirmation of the death sentence which they had already passed upon him.

On the preceding day Judas had disclosed to some of his relatives and to certain Sadduccean friends of his father's family that he had reached the conclusion that, while Jesus was a well-meaning dreamer and idealist, he was not the expected deliverer of the Jews. Judas stated that he would very much like to find some way of withdrawing gracefully from the whole movement. His friends flatteringly assured him that his withdrawal would be hailed by the Jewish rulers as a great event, and that nothing would be too good for him. They led him to believe that he would forthwith receive high honors from the Sanhedrin, and that he would at last be in a position to erase the stigma of his well-meant but "unfortunate association with untaught Galileans." Judas was now fully convinced that Jesus would not exert his power in self-aggrandizement. He was at last convinced that Jesus would allow himself to be destroyed by the Jewish rulers, and he could not endure the humiliating thought of being identified with a movement of defeat. He refused to entertain the idea of apparent failure. He thoroughly understood the sturdy character of his Master and the keenness of that majestic and merciful mind, yet he derived pleasure from even the partial entertainment of the suggestion of one of his relatives that Jesus, while he was a well-meaning fanatic, was probably not really sound of mind, that he had always appeared to be a strange and misunderstood person.

Now, as never before, Judas found himself becoming strangely resentful that Jesus had never assigned him a position of greater honor. All along he had appreciated the honor of being the apostolic treasurer, but now he began to feel that he was not appreciated, that his abilities were unrecognized. He was suddenly overcome with indignation that Peter, James, and John should have been honored with close association with Jesus, and at this time, when he was on the way to the high priest's home, he was bent on getting even with Peter, James, and John more than he was concerned with any thought of betraying Jesus. But over and above all, just then, a new and dominating thought began to occupy the forefront of his conscious mind - he had set out to get honor for himself, and if this could be secured simultaneously with getting even with those who had contributed to the greatest disappointment of his life, all the better. He was seized with a terrible conspiracy of confusion, pride, desperation, and determination. So, it must be plain that it was not for money that Judas was then on his way to the home of Caiaphas to arrange for the betrayal of Jesus.

As Judas approached the home of Caiaphas, he arrived at the final decision to abandon Jesus and his fellow Apostles. Having thus made up his mind to desert the cause of the kingdom of Heaven, he was determined to secure for himself as much as possible of that honor and glory which he had thought would sometime be his when he first identified himself with Jesus and the new gospel of the kingdom. All of the Apostles once shared this ambition with Judas, but as time passed, they learned to admire truth and to love Jesus, at least more than did Judas.

The traitor was presented to Caiaphas and the Jewish rulers by his cousin, who explained that Judas, having discovered his mistake in allowing himself to be misled by the subtle teaching of Jesus, had arrived at the place where he wished to make public and formal renunciation of his association with the Galilean and at the same time to ask for reinstatement in the confidence and fellowship of his Judean brothers. This spokesman for Judas went on to explain that Judas recognized it would be best for the peace of Judea if Jesus should be taken into custody, and that, as evidence of his sorrow in having participated in such a movement of error and as proof of his sincerity in now returning to the teachings of Moses, he had come to offer himself to the Sanhedrin as one who could so arrange with the captain holding the orders for Jesus' arrest that he could be taken into custody quietly, thus avoiding any danger of stirring up the multitudes or the necessity of postponing his arrest until after the Passover.

When his cousin had finished speaking, he presented Judas, who, stepping forward near the high priest, said: "All that my cousin has promised, I will do, but what are you willing to give me for this service?" Judas did not seem to notice the look of disdain and even disgust that came over the face of the hardhearted and vainglorious Caiaphas. His heart was set on self-glory and the craving for the satisfaction of self-exaltation.

Then Caiaphas looked down upon the betrayer while he said: "Judas, you go to the captain of the guard and arrange with that officer to bring your Master to us either tonight or tomorrow night, and when he has been delivered by you into our hands, you shall receive your reward for this service." When Judas heard this, he went forth from the presence of the chief priests and rulers and took counsel with the captain of the temple guards as to the manner in which Jesus was to be apprehended. Judas knew that Jesus was then absent from the camp and had no idea when he would return that evening, and so they agreed among themselves to arrest Jesus the next evening (Thursday) after the people of Jerusalem and all of the visiting pilgrims had retired for the night.

Judas returned to his associates at the camp intoxicated with thoughts of grandeur and glory such as he had not had for many a day. He had enlisted with Jesus hoping someday to become a great man in the new kingdom. He at last realized that there was to be no new kingdom such as he had anticipated. But he rejoiced in being so sagacious as to trade off his disappointment in failing to achieve glory in an anticipated new kingdom for the immediate realization of honor and reward in the old order, which he now believed would survive, and which he was certain would destroy Jesus and all that he stood for. In its last motive of conscious intention, Judas' betrayal of Jesus was the cowardly act of a selfish deserter whose only thought was his own safety and glorification, no matter what the results of his conduct upon his Master might be and upon his former associates.

But it was ever just that way. Judas had long been engaged in this deliberate, persistent, selfish, and vengeful consciousness of progressively building up in his mind, and entertaining in his heart, these hateful and evil desires of revenge and disloyalty. Jesus loved and trusted Judas even as he loved and trusted the other Apostles, but Judas failed to develop loyal trust and to experience wholehearted love in return. How dangerous ambition can become when it is joined with selfishness and motivated by vengeance. What a crushing thing disappointment is in the lives of those foolish persons who fasten their gaze on the shadowy allurements of this material world, while they become blinded to the higher and more exquisite achievements of finding the eternal worlds of divine love and true spirituality. Judas craved worldly honor in his mind and grew to love this desire with his whole heart. The other Apostles likewise craved this same worldly honor in their minds, but with their hearts they loved Jesus and were doing their best to learn to love the truths which he taught them.

Judas did not realize it at this time, but he had been a subconscious critic of Jesus ever since John the Baptizer was beheaded by Herod. Deep down in his heart Judas always resented the fact that Jesus did not save John. You should not forget that Judas had been a disciple of John before he became a follower of Jesus. All these accumulations of human resentment and bitter disappointment which Judas had piled in his soul in layers of hate were now well organized in his subconscious mind and ready to spring up to engulf him when he once dared to separate himself from the supporting influence of his brothers. Every time Judas allowed his hopes to soar high and Jesus would do or say something to dash them to pieces, there was always left in Judas' heart a scar of bitter resentment. As these scars multiplied, presently that heart, so often wounded, lost all real affection for the one who had inflicted this distasteful experience upon a well-intentioned but cowardly and self-centered personality. Judas did not realize it, but he was a coward. Accordingly, he was always inclined to assign to Jesus cowardice as the reason why he refused to grasp for power or glory when they were apparently within his easy reach. Every mortal man knows full well how love, even when once genuine, can, through disappointment, jealousy, and long-continued resentment, be eventually turned into actual hate.

At last, the chief priests and elders could breathe easily for a few hours. They would not have to arrest Jesus in public, and the securing of Judas as a traitorous ally insured that Jesus would not escape from their jurisdiction as he had so many times in the past.

Since it was Wednesday, this evening at the camp was a social hour. The Master tried his best to cheer his downcast Apostles, but that was almost impossible. They were all beginning to realize that troublesome and crushing events were coming near. They could not be cheerful, even when the Master recounted their years of eventful and loving association. Jesus made careful inquiry about the families of all of the Apostles and, looking over toward David Zebedee, asked if anyone had heard recently from his mother, his youngest sister, or other members of his family. David looked down at his feet. He was afraid to answer. This was the occasion of Jesus' warning his followers to beware of the support of the multitude. He recounted their experiences in Galilee when time and again great throngs of people enthusiastically followed them around and then just as quickly turned against them and returned to their former ways of believing and living. And then he said: "So you must not allow yourselves to be deceived by the great crowds who heard us in the temple, and who seemed to believe our teachings. These multitudes listen to the truth and believe it superficially with their minds, but few of them permit the word of truth to strike down into the heart with living roots. Those who know the gospel only in the mind, and who have not experienced it in the heart, cannot be depended upon for support when real trouble comes. When the rulers of the Jews reach an agreement to destroy the Son of God, and when they strike with one accord, you will see the multitude either flee in dismay or else stand by in silent amazement while these maddened and blinded rulers lead the teachers of the gospel of truth to their death."

"Then, when adversity and persecution descend upon you, still others who you think love the truth will be scattered, and some will renounce the gospel and desert you. Some who have been very close to us have already made up their minds to desert. You have rested today in preparation for those times which are now upon us. Watch, therefore, and pray that on the morrow you may be strengthened for the days that are just ahead."

The atmosphere of the camp was charged with an inexplicable tension. Silent messengers came and went, communicating only with David Zebedee. Before the evening had passed, Jesus and the Apostles were notified that Lazarus had taken hasty flight from Bethany. John Mark was ominously silent after returning to camp, notwithstanding that he had spent the whole day in the Master's company. Every effort to persuade him to talk only indicated clearly that Jesus had told him not to talk.

Even the Master's good cheer and his unusual sociability frightened them. They all sensed the impending isolation which they realized was about to descend with crashing suddenness and inescapable terror. They vaguely sensed what was coming, and none felt prepared to face the test. The Master had been away all day. They had missed him tremendously.

This Wednesday evening was the low-water mark of their spiritual status up to the actual hour of the Master's death. Although the next day was one more day nearer the tragic Friday, still, he was with them, and they passed through their anxious hours more gracefully.

It was just before midnight when Jesus, knowing this would be the last night he would ever sleep through with his chosen family on Earth, said, as he dispersed them for the night: "Go to your sleep, my brothers, and peace be upon you till we rise on the morrow, one more day to do the Father's will and experience the joy of knowing that we are his sons."

THURSDAY

Jesus planned to spend this Thursday, his last free day on Earth as a divine Son incarnated in the flesh, with his Apostles and a few loyal and devoted disciples. Soon after the breakfast hour on this beautiful morning, the Master led them to a secluded spot a short distance above their camp and there taught them many new truths.

Although Jesus delivered other discourses to the Apostles during the early evening hours of this day, this talk of Thursday morning was his farewell address to the combined camp group of Apostles and chosen disciples, both Jews and Gentiles. All the Apostles were present except for Judas. Peter and several of the Apostles commented about his absence, and some of them thought Jesus had sent him into the city to attend to some matter, probably to arrange the details of their forthcoming celebration of the Passover. Judas did not return to the camp until midafternoon, a short time before Jesus led the twelve into Jerusalem to partake of the Last Supper.

Jesus talked to about fifty of his trusted followers for almost two hours and answered a score of questions regarding the relation of the kingdom of Heaven to the kingdoms of this world, the relation of sonship with God to citizenship in earthly governments. This discourse, together with his answers to questions, is summarized and restated in modern language as follows:

"The kingdoms of this world, being material, may often find it necessary to employ physical force in the execution of their laws and for the maintenance of order. In the kingdom of Heaven true believers do not resort to the employment of physical force. The kingdom of Heaven, being a spiritual brotherhood of the Sons of God, is carried out only by the power of the spirit. This distinction of procedure refers to the relations of the kingdom of believers to the kingdoms of secular government and does not take away the right of social groups of believers to maintain order in their ranks and administer discipline upon unruly and unworthy members.

There is nothing incompatible between sonship in the spiritual kingdom and citizenship in the secular or civil government. It is the believer's duty to render to Caesar the things which are Caesar's and to render to God the things which are God's. There cannot be any disagreement between these two requirements, the one being material and the other spiritual, unless it should happen that a Caesar presumes to usurp the prerogatives of God and demand that spiritual homage and worship be rendered to him. In such a case, you shall worship only God while you seek to enlighten such misguided earthly rulers and, in this way, lead them also to the recognition of the Father in Heaven. You shall not render spiritual worship to earthly rulers. Neither should you employ the physical forces of earthly governments, whose rulers may sometime become believers, in the work of furthering the mission of the spiritual kingdom.

Citizenship in the Father's kingdom, from the standpoint of advancing civilization, should assist you in becoming the ideal citizens of the kingdoms of this world since brotherhood and service are the cornerstones of the gospel of the kingdom. The love calls of the spiritual kingdom should prove to be the effective destroyer of the hate urge of the unbelieving and war-minded citizens of these earthly kingdoms.

But these material-minded people in darkness will never know of your spiritual light of truth unless you draw very near them and through unselfish social service show them the better way for them to follow. By your actions will they come to know what the kingdom of Heaven is about.

As mortal men, you are indeed citizens of the earthly kingdoms, and you should be good citizens, all the better for having become reborn sons of the Heavenly kingdom. As faith-enlightened and spirit- liberated sons of the kingdom of Heaven, you face a double responsibility of duty to man and duty to God while you voluntarily assume a third and sacred obligation: service to the brotherhood of God-knowing believers.

You may not worship your temporal rulers, and you should not employ temporal power in the furtherance of the spiritual kingdom, but you should always manifest your ministry of loving service to believers and unbelievers alike. In the gospel of the kingdom there resides the mighty Spirit of Truth, and presently I will pour out this same spirit upon all flesh. The fruits of this spirit will be your sincere and loving service. These qualities are the mighty social lever to uplift the races, and this Spirit of Truth will become your power-multiplying fulcrum.

This Spirit of Truth I will bestow upon the world and all its peoples when I am once more with my Father in the Heavenly realms.

Display wisdom and exhibit sagacity in your dealings with unbelieving civil rulers. By discretion show yourselves to be expert in ironing out minor disagreements and adjusting trifling misunderstandings. In every possible way in everything short of your spiritual allegiance to the rulers of this world, seek to live peaceably with all men. Be you always as wise as serpents but as harmless as doves.

You shall be made all the better citizens of the secular governments as a result of becoming enlightened sons of the kingdom. So shall the rulers of earthly governments become all the better rulers in civil affairs as a result of believing this gospel of the Heavenly kingdom. The attitude of unselfish service of man and intelligent worship of God shall make all kingdom believers better world citizens.

So long as the rulers of earthly governments seek to exercise the authority of religious dictators, you who believe this gospel can expect only trouble, persecution, and even death. But the very light which you bear to the world, and even the very manner in which you will suffer and die for this gospel of the kingdom, will, in themselves, eventually enlighten the whole world and result in the gradual separation of politics and religion. The persistent preaching of this gospel will someday bring to all nations a new and unbelievable liberation, intellectual freedom, and religious liberty.

Under the persecutions that will be brought against you by those who hate this gospel of joy and liberty, you will thrive, and the kingdom will prosper. But you will stand in grave danger in subsequent times when most men speak well of kingdom believers and many in high places nominally accept the gospel of the Heavenly kingdom. Learn to be faithful to the kingdom even in times of peace and prosperity.

Complacency will become your enemy. Tempt not the angels of your supervision to lead you in troublesome ways as a loving discipline designed to save your ease-drifting souls.

Remember that you are commissioned to preach this gospel of the kingdom, the desire to do the Father's will together with the joy of being a son of God. You must not allow anything to divert your devotion to this one duty. Let all mankind benefit from the overflow of your loving spiritual ministry, enlightening intellectual communion, and uplifting social service. But none of these humanitarian labors, nor all of them, should be permitted to take the place of wholeheartedly proclaiming the gospel.

You must not seek to carry out spiritual truths nor to establish righteousness by the power of civil governments or by the action of secular laws. You must always labor to persuade men's minds, but you must never dare to compel them. You must not forget the great law of human fairness which I have taught you in positive form: Whatsoever you would that men should do to you, do even so to them.

When a kingdom believer is called upon to serve the civil government, let him render such service as an earthly citizen of such a government, although such a believer should display in his civil service all of the ordinary traits of citizenship as these have been enhanced by the spiritual enlightenment of the association of the mind of mortal man with the indwelling spirit of the eternal God. If an unbeliever can qualify better than you as a superior civil servant, you should seriously question whether the roots of truth in your heart have not died from your lack of spiritual communion and social service. The consciousness of being a son or daughter of God should quicken the entire life service of every man, woman, and child who has become the possessor of such a mighty stimulus to human personality.

You must not allow yourselves to become passive mystics or colorless ascetics. You must not become dreamers and drifters, supinely trusting in a fictitious providence to provide even the necessities of life. You must indeed be gentle in your dealings with erring mortals, patient in your intercourse with ignorant men, and forbearing under provocation, but you must also be valiant in defense of righteousness, mighty in the carrying out of truth, and aggressive in the preaching of this gospel of the kingdom, even to the ends of the Earth.

This gospel of the kingdom is a living truth. I have told you it is like the leaven in the dough, like the grain of mustard seed. Now I declare that it is like the seed of the living being, which, from generation to generation, while it remains the same living seed, unfailingly unfolds itself in new manifestations and grows in channels of new adaptation to the peculiar needs and conditions of each successive generation. The revelation I have made to you is a living revelation, and I desire that it shall bear appropriate fruits in each individual and in each generation in accordance with the laws of spiritual growth. From generation to generation this gospel must show increasing vitality and exhibit greater depth of spiritual power. It must not be permitted to become merely a sacred memory, a mere tradition about me and the times in which we now live.

Forget not: we have made no direct attack upon the people or upon the authority of those who sit in Moses' seat. We only offered them the new light, which they have so vigorously rejected. We have attacked them only by the denunciation of their spiritual disloyalty to the very truths which they profess to teach and safeguard. We clashed with these established leaders and recognized rulers only when they threw themselves directly in the way of the preaching of the gospel of the kingdom to the sons of men. Even now, it is not we who attack them, but they who seek our destruction. Do not forget that you are commissioned to go forth preaching only the good news. You are not to attack the old ways. You are skillfully putting the new truths in the midst of the old beliefs. Let the Spirit of Truth do his own work when it comes upon you. Let controversy come only when they who despise the truth force it upon you. But when the willful unbeliever attacks you, do not hesitate to stand in vigorous defense of the truth which has saved and sanctified you.

Throughout the vicissitudes of life, remember always to love one another. Do not strive with men, even with unbelievers. Show mercy even to those who spitefully abuse you. Show yourselves to be loyal citizens, upright artisans, praiseworthy neighbors, devoted kinsmen, understanding parents, and sincere believers in the brotherhood of the Father's kingdom. My spirit shall be upon you, now and even to the end of the world."

When Jesus had concluded this teaching, it was almost one o'clock, and they immediately went back to the camp, where David and his associates had lunch ready for them.

Not many of the Master's hearers were able to understand even a part of his morning address. Of all who heard him, the Greeks comprehended most. Even the eleven Apostles were bewildered by his allusions to future political kingdoms and to successive generations of kingdom believers. Jesus' most devoted followers could not reconcile the impending end of his earthly ministry with these references to an extended future of gospel activities. Some of these Jewish believers were beginning to sense that Earth's greatest tragedy was about to take place, but they could not reconcile such an impending disaster with either the Master's cheerfully indifferent personal attitude or his morning discourse, wherein he repeatedly alluded to the future transactions of the Heavenly kingdom, extending over vast stretches of time and embracing relations with many and successive temporal kingdoms on Earth.

By noon of this day all the Apostles and disciples had learned about the hasty flight of Lazarus from Bethany. They began to sense the grim determination of the Jewish rulers to exterminate Jesus and his teachings.

David Zebedee, through the work of his secret agents in Jerusalem, was fully advised concerning the progress of the plan to arrest and kill Jesus. He knew all about the part of Judas in this plot, but he never disclosed this knowledge to the other Apostles nor to any of the disciples. Shortly after lunch he did lead Jesus aside and asked him whether he knew. But he never got further with his question. The Master, holding up his hand, stopped him, saying: "Yes, David, I know all about it, and I know that you know, but see to it that you tell no man. Only doubt not in your own heart that the will of God will prevail in the end."

This conversation with David was interrupted by the arrival of a messenger from Philadelphia bringing word that Abner had heard of the plot to kill Jesus and asking if he should depart for Jerusalem. This runner hastened off for Philadelphia with this message for Abner: "Go on with your work. If I depart from you in the flesh, it is only that I may return in the spirit. I will not forsake you. I will be with you to the end."

About this time Philip came to the Master and asked: "Master, seeing that the time of Passover draws near, where would you have us prepare to eat it?" When Jesus heard Philip's question, he answered: "Go and bring Peter and John, and I will give you directions concerning the supper we will eat together this night. As for Passover, that you will have to consider after we have first done this."

When Judas heard the Master speaking with Philip about these matters, he drew closer that he might overhear their conversation. But David Zebedee, who was standing near, stepped up and engaged Judas in conversation while Philip, Peter, and John went to one side to talk with the Master.

Jesus said to the three: "Go immediately into Jerusalem, and as you enter the gate, you will meet a man bearing a water pitcher. He will speak to you, and then you shall follow him. When he leads you to a certain house, go in after him and ask of the good man of that house: Where is the guest chamber wherein the Master is to eat supper with his Apostles? When you have thus inquired, this householder will show you a large upper room all furnished and ready for us."

When the Apostles reached the city, they met the man with the water pitcher near the gate and followed on after him to the home of John Mark, where the lad's father met them and showed them the upper room in readiness for the evening meal.

All of this came to pass as the result of an understanding arrived at between the Master and John Mark during the afternoon of the preceding day when they were alone in the hills. Jesus wanted to be sure he would have this one last meal undisturbed with his Apostles, and believing if Judas knew beforehand of their place of meeting, he might arrange with his enemies to take him during this supper. In this way Judas did not learn of their place of meeting until later on when he arrived there in company with Jesus and the other Apostles.

David Zebedee had much business to transact with Judas so that he was easily prevented from following Peter, John, and Philip, as he so much desired to do. When Judas gave David a certain sum of money for provisions, David said to him: "Judas, might it not be well, under the circumstances, to provide me with a little money in advance of my actual needs?" After Judas had reflected for a moment, he answered: "Yes, David, I think it would be wise. In fact, in view of the disturbed conditions in Jerusalem, I think it would be best for me to turn over all the money to you. They plot against the Master, and in case anything should happen to me, you would not be hampered." David received all the apostolic cash funds and receipts for all money on deposit.

It was about half past four o'clock when the three Apostles returned and informed Jesus that everything was in readiness for the supper. The Master immediately prepared to lead his twelve Apostles over the trail to the Bethany road and on into Jerusalem. This was the last journey he ever made with all twelve of them.

Seeking again to avoid the crowds passing through the Kidron valley back and forth between Gethsemane Park and Jerusalem, Jesus and the twelve walked over the western brow of Mount Olivet to meet the road leading from Bethany down to the city. As they drew near the place where Jesus had waited momentarily the previous evening to discuss on the destruction of Jerusalem, they unconsciously paused while they stood and looked down in silence upon the city. As they were a little early, and since Jesus did not wish to pass through the city until after sunset, he said to his associates: "Sit down and rest yourselves while I talk with you about what must shortly come to pass. All these years have I lived with you as brothers, and I have taught you the truth concerning the kingdom of Heaven and have revealed to you the mysteries thereof. My Father has indeed done many wonderful works in connection with my mission on Earth. You have been witnesses of all this and participants in the experience of being laborers together with God. You will bear me witness that I have for some time warned you that I must presently return to the work the

Father has given me to do. I have plainly told you that I must leave you in the world to carry on the work of the kingdom. It was for this purpose that I set you apart, in the hills of Capernaum. The experience you have had with me, you must now make ready to share with others. As the Father sent me into this world, so am I about to send you forth to represent me and finish the work I have begun.

You look down on yonder city in sorrow, for you have heard my words telling of the end of Jerusalem. I have forewarned you lest you should perish along with her destruction and so delay the proclamation of the gospel of the kingdom. Likewise, do I warn you to take heed lest you needlessly expose yourselves to peril when they come to take the Son of God. I must go, but you are to remain to witness to this gospel when I have gone, even as I directed that Lazarus flee from the wrath of man that he might live to make known the glory of God. If it is the Father's will that I depart, nothing you may do can frustrate the divine plan. Take heed to yourselves lest they kill you also. Let your souls be valiant in defense of the gospel by spirit power but be not misled into any foolish attempt to defend the Son of God by the sword. I need no defense by the hand of man. The armies of Heaven are even now near at hand, but I am determined to follow the will of my Father in Heaven, and therefore must we submit to that which is so soon to come upon us.

When you see this city destroyed, forget not that you have entered already the eternal life of endless service in the ever-advancing kingdom of Heaven. You should know that in my Father's universe and in mine are many mansions, and that there waits for the children of light the revelation of cities whose builder is God and worlds whose habit of life is righteousness and joy in the truth. I have brought the kingdom of Heaven to you here on this Earth, but I declare that all of you who by faith enter therein and remain therein by the living service of truth, shall surely ascend to the worlds on high and sit with me in the spiritual kingdom of our Father. But first you must strengthen yourselves and complete the work which you have begun with me. You must first pass through much tribulation and endure many sorrows and these trials are even now upon us. When you have finished your work on Earth, you shall come to me, even as I have finished my Father's work on Earth and am about to return to his embrace."

When the Master had thus spoken, he arose, and they all followed him down Olivet and into the city. None of the Apostles, save three, knew where they were going as they made their way along the narrow streets in the approaching darkness. The crowds jostled them, but no one recognized them nor knew that the Son of God was passing by on his way to the last mortal rendezvous with his chosen ambassadors of the kingdom. Neither did the Apostles know that one of their own number had already entered into a conspiracy to betray the Master into the hands of his enemies.

John Mark had followed them all the way into the city, and after they had entered the gate, he hurried on to another street so that he was waiting to welcome them to his father's home when they arrived.

During the afternoon of this Thursday, when Philip reminded the Master about the approaching Passover and inquired concerning his plans for its celebration, he had in mind the Passover supper which was due to be eaten on the evening of the next day, Friday. It was the custom to begin the preparations for the celebration of

Passover no later than noon of the preceding day. Since the Jews reckoned the day as beginning at sunset, this meant that Saturday's Passover supper would be eaten on Friday night, sometime before the midnight hour.

The Apostles were, therefore, entirely at a loss to understand the Master's announcement that they would celebrate the Passover one day early. They thought, at least some of them did, that he knew he would be placed under arrest before the time of the Passover supper on Friday night and was therefore calling them together for a special supper on this Thursday evening. Others thought that this was merely a special occasion which was to precede the regular Passover celebration.

The Apostles knew that Jesus had celebrated other Passovers without the lamb. They knew that he did not personally participate in any sacrificial service of the Jewish system. He had many times partaken of the paschal lamb as a guest, but always, when he was the host, no lamb was served. It would not have been a great surprise to the Apostles to have seen the lamb omitted even on Passover night, and since this supper was given one day earlier, they thought nothing of its absence.

After receiving the greetings of welcome extended by the father and mother of John Mark, the Apostles went immediately to the upper chamber while Jesus lingered behind to talk with the Mark family. It had been understood beforehand that the Master was to celebrate this occasion alone with his twelve Apostles, therefore no servants were provided to wait upon them.

When the Apostles had been shown upstairs by John Mark, they beheld a large and commodious chamber, which was completely furnished for the supper, and observed that the bread, wine, water, and herbs were all in readiness on one end of the table. Except for the end on which rested the bread and wine, this long table was surrounded by thirteen reclining couches, just such as would be provided for the celebration of the Passover in a well-to-do Jewish household.

As the twelve entered this upper chamber, they noticed, just inside the door, the pitchers of water, the basins, and towels for washing their dusty feet. Since no servant had been provided to render this service, the Apostles began to look at one another as soon as John Mark had left them. Each began to think within himself: "Who shall wash our feet?" Each likewise thought that it would not be he who would thus seem to act as the servant of the others.

As they stood there, debating in their hearts, they surveyed the seating arrangement of the table, taking note of the higher divan of the host with one couch on the right and eleven arranged around the table on up to opposite this second seat of honor on the host's right.

They expected the Master to arrive any moment, but they were in a quandary as to whether they should seat themselves or await his coming and depend on him to assign them their places. While they hesitated, Judas stepped over to the seat of honor, at the left of the host, and signified that he intended there to recline as the preferred guest.

This act of Judas immediately stirred up a heated dispute among the other Apostles. Judas had no sooner seized the seat of honor than John Zebedee laid claim to the next preferred seat, the one on the right of the host. Simon Peter was so enraged at this assumption of choice positions by Judas and John that, as the other angry Apostles looked on, he marched clear around the table and took his place on the lowest couch, the end of the seating order and just opposite to that chosen by John Zebedee. Since others had seized the high seats, Peter thought to choose the lowest, and he did this, not merely in protest against the unseemly pride of his brothers, but with the hope that Jesus, when he should come and see him in the place of least honor, would call him up to a higher one, thus displacing, one who had presumed to honor himself.

With the highest and the lowest positions thus occupied, the rest of the Apostles chose places, some near Judas and some near Peter, until all were located. They were seated around the U-shaped table on these reclining divans in the following order: on the right of the Master, John; on the left, Judas, Simon Zelotes, Matthew, James Zebedee, Andrew, the Alpheus twins, Philip, Nathaniel, Thomas, and Simon Peter.

They are gathered together to celebrate, at least in spirit, an event which preceded even Moses and referred to the times when their forefathers were slaves in Egypt. This supper will be their last rendezvous with Jesus, and even in such a solemn setting, under the leadership of Judas, the Apostles are led once more to give way to their old predisposition for honor, preference, and personal exaltation.

They were still engaged in voicing angry recriminations when the Master appeared in the doorway, where he hesitated a moment as a look of disappointment slowly crept over his face. Without comment he went to his place, and he did not disturb their seating arrangement.

They were now ready to begin the supper, except that their feet were still unwashed, and they were in anything but a pleasant frame of mind. When the Master arrived, they were still engaged in making uncomplimentary remarks about one another, to say nothing of the thoughts of some who had sufficient emotional control to refrain from publicly expressing their feelings.

For a few moments after the Master had gone to his place, not a word was spoken. Jesus looked them all over and, relieving the tension with a smile, said: "I have greatly desired to eat this Passover with you. I wanted to eat with you once more before I suffered, and realizing that my hour has come, I arranged to have this supper with you tonight, for, as concerns the morrow, we are all in the hands of the Father, whose will I have come to carry out. I shall not again eat with you until you sit down with me in the kingdom which my Father will give me when I have finished that for which he sent me into this world."

After the wine and the water had been mixed, they brought the cup to Jesus, who when he had received it from the hand of Thaddeus, held it while he offered thanks. When he had finished offering thanks, he said: "Take this cup and divide it among yourselves and, when you partake of it, realize that I shall not again drink with you the fruit of the vine since this is our last supper. When we sit down again in this manner, it will be in the kingdom of Heaven."

Jesus began thus to talk to his Apostles because he knew that his hour had come. He understood that the time had come when he was to return to the Father, and that his work on Earth was almost finished. The Master knew he had revealed the Father's love on Earth and had shown forth his mercy to mankind, and that he had completed that for which he came into the world, even to the receiving of all power and authority in Heaven and on Earth.

Likewise, he knew Judas Iscariot had fully made up his mind to deliver him that night into the hands of his enemies. He fully realized that this traitorous betrayal was the sole work of Judas. But he feared none of those who sought his spiritual overthrow any more than he feared those who sought to accomplish his physical death. The Master had but one anxiety, and that was for the safety and salvation of his chosen followers. With the full knowledge that the Father had put all things under his authority, the Master now prepared to enact the parable of brotherly love.

After drinking the first cup of the Passover, it was the Jewish custom for the host to arise from the table and wash his hands. Later on, in the meal and after the second cup, all of the guests likewise rose up and washed their hands. Since the Apostles knew that their Master never observed these rites of ceremonial hand washing, they were very curious to know what he intended to do when, after they had partaken of this first cup, he arose from the table and silently made his way over to near the door, where the water pitchers, basins, and towels had been placed. Their curiosity grew into astonishment as they saw the Master remove his outer garment, arm himself with a towel, and begin to pour water into one of the foot basins. Imagine the amazement of these twelve men, who had so recently refused to wash one another's feet, and who had engaged in such unseemly disputes about positions of honor at the table, when they saw him make his way around the unoccupied end of the table to the lowest seat of the feast, where Simon Peter reclined, and, kneeling down in the attitude of a servant, make ready to wash Simon's feet. As the Master knelt, all twelve arose as one man to their feet. Even the traitorous Judas forgot his infamy for a moment and arose with his fellow Apostles in this expression of surprise, respect, and utter amazement.

There stood Simon Peter, looking down into the upturned face of his Master. Jesus said nothing. It was not necessary that he should speak. His attitude plainly revealed that he was minded to wash Simon Peter's feet. Notwithstanding his frailties of the flesh, Peter loved the Master. This Galilean fisherman was the first human being wholeheartedly to believe in the divinity of Jesus and to make full and public confession of that belief. Peter had never since really doubted the divine nature of the Master. Since Peter so revered and honored Jesus in his heart, it was not strange that his soul resented the thought of Jesus' kneeling there before him in the attitude of a menial servant and proposing to wash his feet as would a slave. When Peter presently collected his wits sufficiently to address the Master, he spoke the heart feelings of all his fellow Apostles.

After a few moments of this great embarrassment, Peter said, "Master, do you really mean to wash my feet? " Then, looking up into Peter's face, Jesus said: "You may not fully understand what I am about to do, but hereafter you will know the meaning of all these things." Then Simon Peter, drawing a long breath, said, "Master, you shall never wash my feet!" Each of the Apostles nodded their approval of Peter's firm declaration of refusal to allow Jesus thus to humble himself before them. The dramatic appeal of this unusual scene at first touched the heart of even Judas Iscariot. But when his vainglorious intellect passed judgment upon the spectacle, he concluded that this gesture of humility was just one more episode which conclusively proved that Jesus would never qualify as the deliverer of the Jews, and that he had made no mistake in the decision to desert the Master's cause.

As they all stood there in breathless amazement, Jesus said: "Peter, I declare that, if I do not wash your feet, you will have no part with me in that which I am about to perform." When Peter heard this declaration, coupled with the fact that Jesus continued kneeling there at his feet, he made one of those decisions of blind acquiescence in compliance with the wish of one whom he respected and loved. As it began to dawn on Simon Peter that there was attached to this proposed enactment of service some signification that determined one's future connection with the Master's work, he not only became reconciled to the thought of allowing Jesus to wash his feet but, in his characteristic and impetuous manner, said: "Then, Master, wash not my feet only but also my hands and my head."

As the Master made ready to begin washing Peter's feet, he said: "He who is already clean needs only to have his feet washed. You who sit with me tonight are clean, but not completely. The dust of your feet should have been washed away before you sat down to eat with me.

Besides, I am performing this service for you as a parable to illustrate the meaning of a new commandment which I will presently give you." In like manner the Master went around the table, in silence, washing the feet of his twelve Apostles, not even passing by Judas. When Jesus had finished washing the feet of the twelve, he donned his cloak, returned to his place as host, and after looking over his bewildered Apostles, said: "Do you really understand what I have done to you? You call me Master, and you say well, for so I am. If then, the Master has washed your feet, why was it that you were unwilling to wash one another's feet? What lesson should you learn from this parable in which the Master so willingly does that service which his brothers were unwilling to do for one another? With a whole heart I say to you: A servant is not greater than his master; neither is one who is sent greater than he who sends him. You have seen the way of service in my life among you, and blessed are you who will have the gracious courage to serve. But why are you so slow to learn that the secret of greatness in the spiritual kingdom is not like the methods of power in the material world?

When I came into this chamber tonight, you were not content proudly to refuse to wash one another's feet, but you must also fall to disputing among yourselves as to who should have the places of honor at my table. Such honors the Pharisees and the people of this world seek, but it should not be so among the ambassadors of the Heavenly kingdom. Do you not know that there can be no place of honor at my table? Do you not understand that I love each of you as I do the others? Do you not know that the place nearest me, as men regard such honors, can mean nothing concerning your standing in the kingdom of Heaven? You know that the kings have dominion over their subjects, while those who exercise this authority are sometimes called benefactors. But it shall not be so in the kingdom of Heaven. He who would be great among you, let him become as the younger, while he who would be chief, let him become as one who serves. Who is the greater, he who sits to eat, or he who serves? Is it not commonly regarded that he who sits to eat is the greater? But you will observe that I am among you as one who serves. If you are willing to become fellow servants with me in doing the Father's will, in the kingdom to come you shall sit with me in power, still doing the Father's will in future glory." When Jesus had finished speaking, the Alpheus twins brought on the bread and wine, with the bitter herbs and the paste of dried fruits for the next course of the Last Supper.

For some minutes the Apostles ate in silence, but under the influence of the Master's cheerful demeanor they were soon drawn into conversation, and before long the meal was proceeding as if nothing out of the ordinary had occurred to interfere with the good cheer and social accord of this extraordinary occasion. After some time had elapsed, in about the middle of this second course of the meal, Jesus, looking them over, said: "I have told you how much I desired to have this supper with you, and knowing how the evil forces of darkness have conspired to bring about the death of the Son of God, I determined to eat this supper with you in this secret chamber and a day in advance of the Passover since I will not be with you by this time tomorrow night. I have repeatedly told you that I must return to the Father. Now has my hour come, but it was not required that one of you should betray me into the hands of my enemies."

When the twelve heard this, having already been robbed of much of their self-assertiveness and self-confidence by the parable of the feet washing and the Master's subsequent discourse, they began to look at one another while in concerned tones they hesitatingly inquired, "Is it I?" When they had all so inquired, Jesus said: "While it is necessary that I go to the Father, it was not required that one of you should become a traitor to fulfill the Father's will. This is the coming to fruit of the concealed evil in the heart of one who failed to love the truth with his whole soul. How deceitful is the intellectual pride that precedes the spiritual downfall of my friend of many years, who even now eats my bread. He will be willing to betray me, even as he now dips his hand with me in the dish."

When Jesus had thus spoken, they all began again to ask, "Is it I?" As Judas, sitting on the left of his Master, again asked, "Is it I?" Jesus, dipping the bread in the dish of herbs, handed it to Judas, saying, "You have said." But the others did not hear Jesus speak to Judas.

John, who reclined on Jesus' right hand, leaned over and asked the Master: "Who is it? We should know who it is that has proved untrue to his trust." Jesus answered: "Already have I told you, even he to whom I gave the bread." But it was so natural for the host to give a piece of bread to the one who sat next to him on the left that none of them took notice of this, even though the Master had so plainly spoken. But Judas was painfully conscious of the meaning of the Master's words associated with his act, and he became fearful lest his brothers were likewise now aware that he was the betrayer.

Peter was highly excited by what had been said, and leaning forward over the table, he addressed John, "Ask him who it is, or if he has told you, tell me who is the betrayer." Jesus brought their whisperings to an end by saying: "I sorrow that this evil should have come to pass and hoped even up to this hour that the power of truth might triumph over the deceptions of evil, but such victories are not won without the faith of the sincere love of truth. I would not have told you about these things at this, our last supper, but I desire to warn you of these sorrows and to prepare you for what is now upon us. I have told you of this because I desire that you should recall, after I have gone, that I knew about all these evil plotting, and that I forewarned you of my betrayal. I do all this so that you may be strengthened for the temptations and trials which are just ahead."

When Jesus had thus spoken, leaning over toward Judas, he said: "What you have decided to do, do quickly." When Judas heard these words, he arose from the table and hastily left the room, going out into the night to do what he had set his mind to accomplish. When the other Apostles saw Judas hasten off after Jesus had spoken to him, they thought he had gone to procure something additional for the supper or to do some other errand for the Master since they supposed he still carried the bag.

Jesus now knew that nothing could be done to keep Judas from turning traitor. He started at twelve, now he had eleven. He chose six of these Apostles, and though Judas was among those nominated by his first-chosen Apostles, still the Master accepted him and had, up to this very hour, done everything possible to sanctify and save him, even as he had strived for the peace and salvation of the others.

This supper, with its tender episodes and softening touches, was Jesus' last appeal to the deserting Judas, but it was of no avail.

Warnings, even when administered in the most tactful manner and conveyed in the most kindly spirit, as a rule, only intensify hatred and fire the evil determination to carry out to the full one's own selfish projects, when love is once really dead.

As they brought Jesus the third cup of wine, the "cup of blessing," he arose from the couch and, taking the cup in his hands, blessed it, saying: "Take this cup, all of you, and drink of it. This shall be the cup of my remembrance. This is the cup of the blessing of a new outpouring of grace and truth. This shall be to you the emblem of the bestowal and ministry of the divine Spirit of Truth. And I will not again drink this cup with you until I drink it in new form with you in the Father's eternal kingdom."

The Apostles all sensed that something out of the ordinary was transpiring as they drank of this cup of blessing in profound reverence and perfect silence. The old Passover commemorated the emergence of their fathers from a state of racial slavery into individual freedom; now the Master was instituting a new remembrance supper as a symbol of the new dispensation wherein the enslaved individual emerges from the bondage of ceremonialism and selfishness into the spiritual joy of the brotherhood and fellowship of the liberated sons of the living God.

When they had finished drinking this new cup of remembrance, the Master took up the bread and, after giving thanks, broke it in pieces and, directing them to pass it around, said: "Take this bread of remembrance and eat it. I have told you that I am the bread of life.

This bread of life is the united life of the Father and the Son in one gift. The word of the Father, as revealed in the Son, is indeed the bread of life." When they had eaten of the bread of remembrance, the symbol of the living word of truth incarnated in the likeness of mortal flesh, they all sat down.

In instituting this remembrance supper, the Master, as was always his habit, resorted to parables and symbols. He employed symbols because he wanted to teach certain great spiritual truths in such a manner as to make it difficult for his successors to attach precise interpretations and definite meanings to his words. In this way he sought to prevent successive generations from crystallizing his teaching and binding down his spiritual meanings by the dead chains of tradition and dogma. In the establishment of the only ceremony or sacrament associated with his whole life mission, Jesus took great pains to suggest his meanings rather than to commit himself to precise definitions. He did not wish to destroy the individual's concept of divine communion by establishing a precise form. Neither did he desire to limit the believer's spiritual imagination by formally cramping it. Instead, he sought to set man's soul free upon the joyous wings of a new and living spiritual liberty.

Notwithstanding the Master's effort thus to establish this new sacrament of the remembrance, those who followed after him in the intervening centuries saw to it that his express desire was effectively thwarted in that his simple spiritual symbolism of that last night in the flesh has been reduced to precise interpretations and subjected to the almost mathematical precision of a set formula. Of all Jesus' teachings none have become more tradition standardized.

This supper of remembrance, when it is celebrated by those who are believers in God, does not need to have associated with its symbolism any of man's misinterpretations regarding the meaning of the divine presence, for upon all such occasions the Master is really present. The remembrance supper is the believer's symbolic acknowledgment and recommitment, together with Jesus, to honor the Father. When you become thus spirit-conscious, the Son is actually present, and his spirit communes with the indwelling fragment of his Father which resides within you.

After they had engaged in meditation for a few moments, Jesus continued speaking: "When you do these things, recall the life I have lived on Earth among you and be glad that I am to continue to live on Earth with you and to serve through you. As individuals, argue not among yourselves as to who shall be greatest. Be you all as brothers. When the kingdom grows to embrace large groups of believers, likewise should you refrain from fighting for greatness or seeking preferment between such groups."

This mighty occasion took place in the upper chamber of a friend. There was nothing of sacred form or of ceremonial consecration about either the supper or the building. The remembrance supper was established without ecclesiastical sanction. When Jesus had thus established the supper of the remembrance, he said to the Apostles: "As often as you do this, do it in remembrance of me. When you do remember me, first look back upon my life in the flesh, recall that I was once with you, and then, by faith, discern that you shall all sometime sit with me at the dinner table in the Father's eternal kingdom. This is the new Passover which I leave with you: the memory of my life with you, the word of eternal truth which I have spoken to you, my love for you, and the outpouring of my Spirit of Truth upon all flesh when I am gone to my Father."

They ended this celebration of the old but bloodless Passover in connection with the inauguration of the new supper of the remembrance, by singing, all together, the one hundred and eighteenth Psalm.

After singing the Psalm at the conclusion of the Last Supper, the Apostles thought that Jesus intended to return immediately to the camp, but he indicated that they should sit down. Said the Master: "You well remember when I sent you forth without purse or wallet and even advised that you take with you no extra clothes. You will all recall that you lacked nothing. But now have you come upon troublesome times. No longer can you depend upon the good will of the multitudes. Henceforth, he who has a purse, let him take it with him. When you go out into the world to proclaim this gospel, make such provision for your support as seems best. I have come to bring peace, but it will not appear for a time.

The time has now come for the Son of God to be glorified, and the Father shall be glorified in me. My friends, I am to be with you only a little longer. Soon you will seek me, but you will not find me, for I am going to a place to which you cannot yet come. But when you have finished your work on Earth as I have now finished mine, you shall then come to me even as I now prepare to go to my Father. In just a short time I am going to leave you, you will see me no more on Earth, but you shall all see me in the age to come when you ascend to the kingdom which my Father has given to me."

After a few moments of informal conversation, Jesus stood up and said: "When I enacted for you a parable indicating how you should be willing to serve one another, I said that I desired to give you a new commandment, and I would do this now as I am about to leave you.

You well know the commandment which directs that you love one another, that you love your neighbor even as yourself. But I am not wholly satisfied with even that sincere devotion on the part of my children. I will ask you to perform still greater acts of love in the kingdom of the believing brotherhood. So, I give you this new commandment: That you love one another even as I have loved you. By this will all men know that you are my disciples if you thus love one another.

When I give you this new commandment, I do not place any new burden upon your souls. Rather do I bring you new joy in making it possible for you to give the full measure of your heart's affection upon your fellow man. I am about to experience the greatest joy of this lifetime, even as I endure outward sorrow, in the giving of my wholehearted love to you and your fellow mortals for all time.

As I encourage you to love one another, even as I have loved you, I hold up before you the highest measure of true affection. Greater love can no man have than this: that he will lay down his life for his friends. You are my friends. You will continue to be my friend if you are but willing to do what I have taught you. You have called me Master, but I do not call you servants. If you will only love one another as I have loved you, you shall be my friends, and I will ever speak to you of that which the Father reveals to me.

You have not merely chosen me, but I have also chosen you, and I have ordained you to go forth into the world to yield the fruit of loving service to your fellows even as I have lived among you and revealed the Father to you. The Father and I will both work with you, and you shall experience the divine fullness of joy if you will only obey my command to love one another, even as I have loved you.

If you would like to share the Master's joy, you must share his love. To share his love means that you have shared his service. Such an experience of love will not deliver you from the difficulties of this world. It will not create a new world, but it most certainly will make the old world new. Keep in mind that it is loyalty, not sacrifice, that God demands. If you perform your deeds as a sacrifice, it implies the absence of that wholehearted affection which would have made such a loving service a great joy. The idea of performing your service as a duty signifies that you are small-minded and hence are missing the exhilarating thrill of doing your service as a friend and for a friend.

The impulse of friendship surpasses all convictions of duty, and the service of a friend for a friend can never be called a sacrifice."

The Master taught the Apostles that they are the sons of God. He called them brothers, and now, before he leaves, he calls them his friends.

Then Jesus stood up again and continued teaching his Apostles: "I am the true vine, and my Father is the vintner. I am the vine, and you are the branches. The Father requires of me only that you shall bear much fruit. The vine is pruned only to increase the fruitfulness of its branches. Every branch coming out of me which bears no fruit, the Father will take away. Every branch which bears fruit, the Father will cleanse so that it may bear more fruit. Already are you clean through the word I have spoken, but you must continue to be clean. You must abide in me, and I in you. The branch will die if it is separated from the vine. As the branch cannot bear fruit except it abides in the vine, so neither can you yield the fruits of loving service except you abide in me.

Remember, I am the real vine, and you are the living branches.

He who lives in me, and I in him, will bear much fruit of the spirit. If you maintain this living spiritual connection with me, you will bear abundant fruit. If you abide in me and my words live in you, you will be able to commune freely with me, and then can my living spirit so energize you that you may ask whatsoever of my spirit with the assurance that the Father will grant us our petition. If the Father is to be glorified, the vine must have many living branches, and every branch must bear much fruit. When the world sees these fruit-bearing branches, my friends in action, all men will know that you are truly my disciples.

As the Father has loved me, so have I loved you. Live in my love even as I live in the Father's love. If you do as I have taught you, you shall abide in my love even as I have kept the Father's word and evermore abide in his love."

The Jews had long taught that the Messiah would be "a stem arising out of the vine" of David's ancestors, and in commemoration of this olden teaching a large emblem of the grape and its attached vine decorated the entrance to Herod's temple. The Apostles all recalled these things as the Master spoke to them this night about the vine and the branches. This lesson made sense to them.

But Jesus' teachings regarding prayer in his name has become the subject of great confusion in later times. There would have been little difficulty with these teachings if his exact words had been remembered and subsequently truthfully recorded. But as the record was made, believers eventually regarded prayer in Jesus' name as a sort of magic, thinking that they would receive from the Father anything they asked for if they only prayed in Jesus' name. For centuries honest souls have continued to crash their faith against this stumbling block. How long will it take the world of believers to understand that prayer is not a process of getting your way but rather a program of taking God's path, an experience of learning how to recognize and execute the Father's will? It is entirely true that, when your will has been truly aligned with his, you can ask anything conceived by that will, and it will be granted. Such a will is affected by and through Jesus even as the life of the vine flows into and through the living branches.

The eleven had scarcely ceased their discussions of the teaching on the vine and the branches when the Master, indicating that he was desirous of speaking to them further and knowing that his time was short, said: "When I have left you, be not discouraged by the hate of the world. Be not downcast even when faint-hearted believers turn against you and join hands with the enemies of the kingdom. If the world shall hate you, you should recall that it hated me even before it hated you. If you were of this world, then would the world love its own, but because you are not, the world refuses to love you. You are in this world, but your lives are not to be world like. I have chosen you out of the world to represent the spirit of another world even to this world from which you have been chosen. But always remember the words I have spoken to you: The servant is not greater than his master. If they dare to persecute me, they will also persecute you. If my words offend the unbelievers, so also will your words offend the ungodly. All of this will they do to you because they believe not in me nor in Him who sent me. So will you suffer many things for the sake of my gospel. But when you endure these tribulations, you should recall that I also suffered before you for the sake of this gospel of the Heavenly kingdom.

Many of those who will attack you are ignorant of the light of Heaven, but this is not true of some who now persecute us. If we had not taught them the truth, they might do many strange things without falling under condemnation, but now, since they have known the light and presumed to reject it, they have no excuse for their attitude. He who hates me hates my Father. It cannot be otherwise. The light which would save you if accepted can only condemn you if it is knowingly rejected. What have I done to these men that they should hate me with such a terrible hatred? Nothing, save to offer them fellowship on Earth and salvation in Heaven. Have you not read in the Scripture the saying: 'And they hated me without a cause'? But I will not leave you alone in the world. Very soon, after I have gone, I will send you a spirit helper. You shall have with you one who will take my place among you, one who will continue to teach you the way of truth, who will even comfort you.

Let your hearts not be troubled. You believe in God. Continue to believe also in me. Even though I must leave you, I will not be far from you. I have already told you that in my Father's universe there are many mansions. If this were not true, I would not have repeatedly told you about them. I am going to return to those worlds of light, stations in Father's Heaven to which you shall some time ascend.

From those places I came into this world, and the hour is now at hand when I must return to my Father's work in the spheres on high.

If I thus go before you into the Father's Heavenly kingdom, so will I surely send for you that you may be with me in the places that were prepared for the mortal sons of God before this world was. Even though I must leave you, I will be present with you in spirit, and eventually you shall be with me in person when you have ascended to me in my universe even as I am about to ascend to my Father in his greater universe. What I have told you is true and everlasting, even though you may not fully understand it at this time. I go to the Father, and though you cannot now follow me, you shall certainly follow me in the ages to come."

When Jesus sat down, Thomas arose and said: "Master, we do not know where you are going, so of course we do not know the way. But we will follow you this very night if you show us the way."

When Jesus heard Thomas, he answered: "Thomas, I am the way, the truth, and the life. No man goes to the Father except through me. All who find the Father, first find me. If you know me, you know the way to the Father. You do know me, for you have lived with me all these years and you now see me."

But this teaching was too deep for many of the Apostles, especially for Philip, who, after speaking a few words with Nathaniel, arose and said: "Master, show us the Father, and everything you have said will be made plain."

When Philip had spoken, Jesus said: "Philip, have I been so long with you and yet you do not even now know me? Again, do I declare he who has seen me has seen the Father. How can you now say, show us the Father? Do you not believe that the Father is in me? Have I not taught you that the words which I speak are not my words but the words of the Father? I speak for the Father and not for myself. I am in this world to do the Father's will, and that I have done. My Father abides in me and works through me. Believe me when I say that the Father is in me, or else believe me for the sake of the very life I have lived for the work's sake."

As the Master went aside to refresh himself with water, the eleven engaged in a spirited discussion of these teachings, and Peter was beginning to deliver himself of an extended speech when Jesus returned and beckoned them to be seated.

Jesus continued to teach, saying: "When I have gone to the Father, and after he has fully accepted the work I have done for you on Earth, I shall say to my Father: Having left my children alone on Earth, it is in accordance with my promise to send them another teacher.

When the Father shall approve, I will pour out the Spirit of Truth upon all flesh. Already is my Father's spirit in your hearts, and when that day shall come, you will also have me with you even as you now have the Father. This new gift is the spirit of living truth. The unbelievers will not at first listen to the teachings of this spirit, but the sons of light will all receive him gladly and with a whole heart. You shall know this spirit when he comes even as you have known me, and you will receive this gift in your hearts, and he will abide with you. I am not going to leave you without help and guidance. I will not leave you desolate.

Today I can be with you only in person. In the times to come I will be with you and all other men who desire my presence, wherever you may be, and with each of you at the same time. Do you understand now that it is better for me to go away, that I leave you in the flesh so that I may the better and more fully be with you in the spirit?

In just a few hours the world will see me no more, but you will continue to know me in your hearts even until I send you this new teacher, the Spirit of Truth. As I have lived with you in person, then shall I live in you in spirit. When this has come to pass, you shall surely know that I am in the Father, and that I am also in you. I have loved the Father and have kept his word. You have loved me, and you will keep my word. As my Father has given me of his spirit, so will I give you of my spirit. This Spirit of Truth which I will bestow upon you shall guide and comfort you and shall eventually lead you into all truth.

I am telling you these things while I am still with you that you may be better prepared to endure those trials which are even now right upon us. When this new day comes, you will be indwelt by a spirit from the Son as well as a spirit from the Father. These gifts of Heaven will ever work the one with the other even as the Father and I have created on Earth and before your very eyes as one person, the Son of God. This spirit friend will bring to your remembrance everything I have taught you."

As the Master paused for a moment, Judas Alpheus asked one of the few questions which either he or his brother ever addressed to Jesus in public. Said Judas: "Master, you have always lived among us as a friend. How shall we know you when you no longer manifest yourself to us save by this spirit? If the world sees you not, how shall we be certain about you? How will you show yourself to us?"

Jesus looked down upon them all, smiled, and said: "My little children, I am going away, going back to my Father. In a little while you will not see me as you do here, as flesh and blood. In a very short time, I am going to send you my spirit, just like me except for this material body. This new teacher is the Spirit of Truth who will live with each one of you, in your hearts and so will all the children of light be made one and be drawn toward one another. In this very manner will my Father and I be able to live in the souls of each one of you and also in the hearts of all other men who love us and make that love real in their experiences by loving one another, even as I am now loving you."

Judas Alpheus did not fully understand what the Master said, but he grasped the promise of the new teacher, and from the expression on Andrew's face, he perceived that his question had been satisfactorily answered.

The new helper which Jesus promised to send into the hearts of believers, to pour out upon all flesh, is the Spirit of Truth. This divine gift is not the letter or law of truth, neither does it function as the form or expression of truth. The new teacher is the conviction of truth, the consciousness and assurance of true meanings on real spiritual levels.

This new teacher is the spirit of living and growing truth, expanding, unfolding, and adaptive truth.

The true child of God looks for the living Spirit of Truth in every wise saying. The God-knowing individual is constantly elevating wisdom to the living-truth levels of divine understanding. The spiritually unprogressive soul is all the while dragging the living truth down to the dead levels of wisdom and to the domain of mere exalted knowledge.

The golden rule, when separated from the spiritual insight of the Spirit of Truth, becomes nothing more than a rule of high ethical conduct. The golden rule, when literally interpreted, can become an instrument of great offense to one's fellows. Without a spiritual understanding of the golden rule of wisdom you might reason that, since you desire that all men speak the full and frank truth of their minds to you, you should therefore fully and frankly speak the full thought of your mind to your fellow beings. Such an unspiritual interpretation of the golden rule might result in untold unhappiness and no end to sorrow.

Some people understand and interpret the golden rule as a purely intellectual affirmation of human fraternity. Others experience this expression of human relationship as an emotional gratification of the tender feelings of the human personality. Another mortal recognizes this same golden rule as the yardstick for measuring all social relations, the standard of social conduct. Still others look upon it as being the positive injunction of a great moral teacher who embodied in this statement the highest concept of moral obligation as regards all fraternal relationships. In the lives of such God-seeking beings the golden rule becomes the wise center and circumference of all their philosophy.

In the brotherhood of God's children, the golden rule takes on living qualities of spirituality which cause the mortal sons of God to view this injunction of the Master as requiring them to relate themselves to their fellows so that they will receive the highest possible good as a result of contact with their fellows. This is the essence of true religion: that you love your neighbor as yourself.

But the highest thought and the best interpretation of the golden rule consists in the realization that the Spirit of Truth is a part of, and is what energizes, this divine declaration. The true meaning of this rule of universal relationships is revealed only in its spiritual concept, in the interpretation of the law of conduct by the spirit of the Son together with the spirit of the Father, both of which dwell in the soul of mortal man. When spirit-led mortals realize the true meaning of this golden rule, they will be filled to overflowing with the sense of connectivity to a friendly universe, and their ideals of spirit will be satisfied only when they love their fellows as Jesus loved us all, and that is the final realization of the love of God.

This same philosophy of the adaptability of divine truth to the individual daily requirements of every son of God, must be understood before you can hope adequately to understand the

Master's teaching and practice of nonresistance to evil. The Master's teaching is basically a spiritual pronouncement. Even the material implications of his philosophy cannot be adequately considered separate from their spiritual correlations. The spirit of the Master's injunction consists in the nonresistance of all selfish reaction to the universe, coupled with the aggressive seeking out of true spirit values, i.e. divine beauty, infinite goodness, and eternal truth, to know God and to become increasingly like him.

Therefore, we must clearly understand that neither the golden rule nor the teaching of nonresistance can ever be properly understood as dogmas or precepts. They can only be comprehended by living them in our heart, and by finding out their meanings in the living interpretation of the Spirit of Truth, who directs the loving contact of one human being with another.

All this clearly shows the difference between the old religion and the new one which the Master was trying to teach to the world. The old religion taught self-sacrifice. The new religion teaches only self-forgetfulness, enlarged and enlightened social service towards our brothers, and together with our brothers. The old religion was motivated by fear of God. The new gospel of the kingdom is dominated by love, the spirit of eternal and universal truth. No amount of piety or loyalty can compensate for the absence, in the life of God believers, of that spontaneous, generous, and sincere affection and friendliness which becomes the characteristic of the sons and daughters of the living God. Neither tradition nor a ceremonial system of formal worship can compensate for the lack of genuine compassion for one's fellows.

After Peter, James, John, and Matthew had asked the Master numerous questions, he continued his farewell discourse by saying:

"I am telling you about all this before I leave you in order that you may be so prepared for what is coming upon you that you will not stumble into serious error. The authorities will not be content with merely putting you out of the synagogues. I warn you the hour draws near when they who will try to kill you will think they are doing a service to God. All of these things they will do to you and to those whom you lead into the kingdom of Heaven because they do not know the Father. They have refused to know the Father by refusing to receive me, and they refuse to receive me when they reject you, provided you have kept my new commandment that you love one another even as I have loved you. I am telling you in advance about these things so that, when your hour comes, as mine now has, you may be strengthened in the knowledge that all was known to me, and that my spirit shall be with you in all your sufferings for my sake. It was for this purpose that I have been talking so plainly to you from the very beginning. I have even warned you that a man's foes may be those of his own household. Although this gospel of the kingdom never fails to bring great peace to the soul of the individual believer, it will not bring peace on Earth until man is willing to believe my teaching wholeheartedly and to establish the practice of doing the Father's will as the chief purpose in living the mortal life.

Now that I am leaving you, seeing that the hour has come when I am about to go to the Father, I am surprised that none of you have asked me, 'why do you leave us'? Nevertheless, I know that you ask such questions in your hearts. I will speak to you plainly, as one friend to another. It is really profitable for you that I go away. If I do not go away, the new teacher cannot come into your hearts. I must leave behind this mortal body and be restored to my place in Heaven before I can send this spirit teacher to live in your souls and lead your spirits into the truth. When my spirit comes to dwell in your heart, he will illuminate the difference between sin and righteousness and will enable you to judge wisely in your heart concerning them.

I have much to say to you, but you cannot stand any more just now. Although, when he, the Spirit of Truth, comes, he shall eventually guide you into all truth as you pass through the many abodes in my Father's universe. This spirit will not speak of himself, but he will declare to you that which the Father has revealed to the Son, and he will even show you things to come. He will glorify me even as I have glorified my Father. This spirit comes forth from me, and he will reveal my truth to you. Everything which the Father has in this domain is now mine, wherefore did I say that this new teacher would take care of that which is mine and reveal it to you. In just a little while I will leave you for a short time. Afterward, when you again see me, I shall already be on my way to the Father so that even then you will not see me for long."

While he paused for a moment, the Apostles began to talk with each other: "What is this that he tells us? In just a little while I will leave you, and when you see me again it will not be for long, for I will be on my way to the Father? What can he mean when he says in a little while and not for long? We cannot understand what he is telling us."

Since Jesus knew they asked these questions, he said: "Do you inquire among yourselves about what I meant when I said that in a little while I would not be with you, and that, when you would see me again, I would be on my way to the Father? I have plainly told you that the Son of God must die, but that he will rise again.

Can you not then understand the meaning of my words? You will first be made sorrowful, but later on you will rejoice with many who will understand these things after they have come to pass. A woman is indeed sorrowful in the hour of her childbearing, but when she is once delivered of her child, she immediately forgets her anguish in the joy that a child has been born into the world. So are you about to sorrow over my departure, but I will soon see you again, and then will your sorrow be turned into rejoicing, and there shall come to you a new revelation of the salvation of God which no man can ever take away from you. All the worlds will be blessed in this same revelation of life in effecting the overthrow of death. Up to this time have you made all your requests in my Father's name. After you see me again, you may also ask in my name, and I will listen to you.

Down here I have taught you proverbs and spoken to you in parables. I did so because you were only children in the spirit, but the time is coming when I will talk to you plainly concerning the Father and his kingdom. I shall do this because the Father himself loves you and desires to be more fully revealed to you. Mortal man cannot see the spirit Father, therefore have I come into the world to show the Father to your limited vision. But when you have become perfected in spiritual growth, you too shall see the Father himself."

When the eleven had heard him speak, they said to each other: "Behold, he does speak plainly to us. Surely the Master did come forth from God. But why does he say he must return to the Father?" Jesus saw that they did not even yet comprehend him. These eleven men could not overcome their long-nourished ideas of the Jewish concept of the Messiah. The more fully they believed in Jesus as the Messiah, the more troublesome became these deep-rooted notions regarding the glorious material triumph of the kingdom on Earth.

After the conclusion of the farewell address to the eleven, Jesus visited informally with them and recounted many experiences which concerned them as a group and as individuals. At last, it was beginning to dawn upon these Galileans that their friend and teacher was going to leave them, and their hope grasped at the promise that, after a little while, he would again be with them, but they were prone to forget that this return visit was also for a little while. Many of the Apostles and the leading disciples really thought that this promise to return for a short season indicated that Jesus was just going away for a brief visit with his Father, after which he would return to establish the kingdom. Such an interpretation of his teachings conformed both with their preconceived beliefs and with their ardent hopes. Since their lifelong beliefs and hopes of wish fulfillment were thus agreed, it was not difficult for them to find an interpretation of the Master's words which would justify their intense longings. After the farewell address had been discussed and had begun to settle down in their minds, Jesus again called the Apostles to order and began the delivery of his final admonitions and warnings.

When the eleven had taken their seats, Jesus stood and addressed them: "As long as I am with you in the flesh, I can be but one individual in your midst or in the entire world. But when I have been delivered from this mortal nature, I will be able to return as a spirit to dwell within each of you and of all other believers in this gospel of the kingdom. In this way the Son of God will become a spiritual incarnation in the souls of all true believers.

When I have returned to live in you and work through you, I can better lead you on through this life and guide you through the many mansions in the future life in Heaven. Life in the Father's eternal creation is not an endless rest of idleness and selfish ease but rather a ceaseless progression in grace, truth, and glory. Each of the many, many stations in my Father's house is a stopping place, a life designed to prepare you for the next one ahead. So will the children of light go on from glory to glory until they reach the divine estate wherein, they are spiritually perfected even as the Father is perfect in all things.

If you desire to follow after me when I leave you, put forth your earnest efforts to live in accordance with the spirit of my teachings and with the ideal of my life, the doing of my Father's will. Do this instead of trying to imitate my natural life in the flesh as I have been required to live it on this world.

The Father sent me into this world, but only a few of you have chosen fully to receive me. I will pour out my spirit upon all flesh, but all men will not choose to receive this new teacher as the guide and counselor of the soul. But all those who gladly receive the Spirit of Truth shall be enlightened, cleansed, and comforted. This Spirit of Truth will become in them a well of living water springing up into eternal life.

Now, as I am about to leave you, I want to speak words of comfort to you. Peace, I leave with you. My peace I give to you. I make these gifts not as the world gives, in portions. I give each of you all that you can receive. Let not your heart be troubled, neither let it be afraid. I have overcome the world, and in me you shall all triumph through faith. I have warned you that the Son of God will be killed, but I assure you I will come back before I go to the Father, even though it be for only a little while. After I have ascended to the Father, I will surely send the new teacher to be with you and to live in your very hearts.

When you see all this come to pass, be not afraid, but rather believe, inasmuch as you knew it all beforehand. I have loved you with great affection, and I would not leave you, but it is the Father's will. My hour has come.

Doubt not any of these truths even after you are scattered abroad by persecution and are downcast by many sorrows. When you feel that you are alone in the world, I will know of your isolation even as tonight, when you are leaving the Son of God in the hands of his enemies, you will know of my isolation. But I am never alone. Always is the Father with me. Even at such a time I will pray for you. All of these things have I told you that you might have peace and have it more abundantly. In this world you will have tribulation but be of good cheer. I have triumphed in the world and shown you the way to eternal joy and everlasting service."

Jesus faced trouble on Earth. He has even been falsely called the "man of sorrows," but throughout all of these experiences he enjoyed the comfort of that confidence which ever empowered him to proceed with his life purpose in the full assurance that he was achieving the Father's will. Jesus was determined, persistent, and thoroughly devoted to the accomplishment of his mission, but he was not an unfeeling and callused stoic. He ever sought for the cheerful aspects of his life experiences, but he was not a blind and self-deceived optimist.

The Master knew all that was to happen to him, and he was unafraid. After he had bestowed this peace upon each of his followers, he could consistently say, "Let not your heart be troubled, neither let it be afraid."

The peace of Jesus is the peace and assurance of a son who fully believes that his career for time and eternity is safely and wholly in the care and keeping of an all-wise, all-loving, and all-powerful spirit Father. This is, indeed, a peace which passes the understanding of mortal mind, but which can be enjoyed to the full by the believing human heart.

The Master had finished giving his farewell instructions and imparting his final admonitions to the Apostles as a group. He then addressed himself to saying good-bye individually and to giving each a word of personal advice, together with his parting blessing. The Apostles were still seated about the table as when they first sat down to partake of the Last Supper, and as the Master went around the table talking to them, each man rose to his feet when Jesus addressed him.

To John, Jesus said: "You, John, are the youngest of my brothers. You have been very near me, and while I love you all with the same love which a father bestows upon his sons, you were designated by Andrew as one of the three who should always be near me. Besides this, you have acted for me and must continue to act in many matters concerning my Earth family. I go to the Father, John, having full confidence that you will continue to watch over those who are mine in the flesh. See to it that their present confusion regarding my mission does not in any way prevent your extending to them all sympathy, counsel, and help even as you know I would if I were to remain in the flesh. When they all come to see the light and enter fully into the kingdom, while you all will welcome them joyously, I depend upon you, John, to welcome them for me.

Now, as I enter upon the closing hours of my earthly career, remain near at hand that I may leave any message with you regarding my family. As concerns the work put in my hands by the Father, it is now finished except for my death in the flesh, and I am ready to drink this last cup. But as for the responsibilities left to me by my earthly father, Joseph, while I have attended to these during my life, I must now depend upon you to act in my stead in all these matters. I have chosen you to do this for me, John, because you are the youngest and will therefore very likely outlive these other Apostles.

Once we called you and your brother Sons of Thunder. You started out with us strong-minded and intolerant, but you have changed much since you wanted me to call fire down upon the heads of ignorant and thoughtless unbelievers. You must change yet more. You should become the Apostle of the new commandment which I have this night given you. Dedicate your life to teaching your brothers how to love one another, even as I have loved you."

As John Zebedee stood there in the upper chamber, the tears rolling down his cheeks, he looked into the Master's face and said: "So I will, my Master, but how can I learn to love my brothers more?" Then answered Jesus: "You will learn to love your brothers more when you first learn to love their Father in Heaven more, and after you have become truly more interested in their welfare in time and in eternity. All such human interest is fostered by understanding sympathy, unselfish service, and unstinted forgiveness. No man should despise your youth, but I remind you always to give due consideration to the fact that age often times represents experience, and that nothing in human affairs can take the place of actual experience. Strive to live peaceably with all men, especially your friends in the brotherhood of the Heavenly kingdom. John, always remember, strive not with the souls you would win for the kingdom."

Then the Master, passing around his own seat, paused a moment by the side of the place of Judas Iscariot. The Apostles were rather surprised that Judas had not returned before this, and they were very curious to know the significance of Jesus' sad countenance as he stood by the betrayer's vacant seat. But none of them, except possibly Andrew, entertained even the slightest thought that their treasurer had gone out to betray his Master, as Jesus had intimated to them earlier in the evening and during the supper. So much had been going on that, for the time being, they had quite forgotten about the Master's announcement that one of them would betray him.

Jesus now went over to Simon Zelotes, who stood up and listened to this admonition: "You are a true son of Abraham, but what a time I have had trying to make you a son of this Heavenly kingdom. I love you and so do all of your brothers. I know that you love me, Simon, and that you also love the kingdom, but you are still set on making this kingdom according to your liking. I know full well that you will eventually grasp the spiritual nature and meaning of my gospel, and that you will do valiant work in its proclamation, but I am distressed about what may happen to you when I depart. I would rejoice to know that you would not falter. I would be made happy if I could know that, after I go to the Father, you would not cease to be my Apostle, and that you would acceptably conduct yourself as an ambassador of the Heavenly kingdom."

Jesus had hardly ceased speaking to Simon Zelotes when the fiery patriot, drying his eyes, replied: "Master, have no fears for my loyalty. I have turned my back upon everything so that I might dedicate my life to the establishment of your kingdom on Earth. I will not falter. I have survived every disappointment so far, and I will not forsake you."

Then, laying his hand on Simon's shoulder, Jesus said: "It is indeed refreshing to hear you talk like that, especially at such a time as this, but, my good friend, you still do not know what you are talking about. Not for one moment would I doubt your loyalty, your devotion. I know you would not hesitate to go forth in battle and die for me, as all these others would, but that will not be required of you. I have repeatedly told you that my kingdom is not of this world, and that my disciples will not fight physically to affect its establishment. I have told you this many times, Simon, but you refuse to face the truth. I am not concerned with your loyalty to me and to the kingdom, but what will you do when I go away and you at last wake up to the realization that you have failed to grasp the meaning of my teaching, and that you must adjust your misconceptions to the reality of another and spiritual order of affairs in the kingdom?"

Simon wanted to speak further, but Jesus raised his hand and, stopping him, went on to say: "None of my Apostles are more sincere and honest at heart than you, but not one of them will be so upset and disheartened as you, after my departure. In all of your discouragement, my spirit shall abide with you, and these, your brothers, will not forsake you. Do not forget what I have taught you regarding the relation of citizenship on Earth to sonship in the Father's spiritual kingdom.

Ponder well all that I have said to you about rendering to Caesar the things which are Caesar's and to God that which is God's. Dedicate your life, Simon, to showing how acceptably mortal man can fulfill my injunction concerning the simultaneous recognition of temporal duty to civil powers and spiritual service in the brotherhood of the kingdom. If you will be taught by the Spirit of Truth, never will there be conflict between the requirements of citizenship on Earth and sonship in Heaven unless the temporal rulers presume to require of you the homage and worship which belong only to God.

Now, Simon, when you do finally see all of this, and after you have shaken off your depression and have gone forth proclaiming this gospel in great power, never forget that I was with you even through all of your seasons of discouragement, and that I will go on with you to the very end. You shall always be my Apostle, and after you become willing to see by the eye of the spirit and more fully to yield your will to the will of the Father in Heaven, then will you return to labor as my ambassador, and no one shall take away from you the authority which I have conferred upon you. Thus, Simon, once more I warn you that they who fight with the sword perish with the sword, while they who labor in the spirit achieve life everlasting in the kingdom to come with joy and peace in the kingdom which now is. When the work given into your hands is finished on Earth, you, Simon, shall sit down with me in my kingdom over there. You shall really see the kingdom you have longed for, but not in this life. Continue to believe in me and in that which I have revealed to you, and you shall receive the gift of eternal life."

When Jesus had finished speaking to Simon Zelotes, he stepped over to Matthew Levi and said: "No longer will it be your responsibility to provide for the treasury of the apostolic group. Soon, very soon, you will all be scattered. You will not be permitted to enjoy the comforting and sustaining association of even one of your brothers. As you go onward preaching this gospel of the kingdom, you will have to find for yourselves new associates. I have sent you forth two and two during the times of your training, but now that I am leaving you, after you have recovered from the shock, you will go out alone, and to the ends of the Earth, proclaiming this good news: That faith-endowed mortals are the sons of God."

Then spoke Matthew: "But, Master, who will send us, and how shall we know where to go? Will Andrew show us the way?" Jesus answered: "No, Matthew, Andrew will no longer direct you in the proclamation of the gospel. He will, indeed, continue as your friend and counselor until that day whereon the new teacher comes, and then shall the Spirit of Truth lead each of you abroad to labor for the extension of the kingdom. Many changes have come over you since that day at the customhouse when you first set out to follow me. But many more must come before you will be able to see the vision of a brotherhood in which Gentile sits alongside Jew in fraternal association. But go on with your urge to win your Jewish brothers until you are fully satisfied and then turn with power to the Gentiles. One thing you may be certain of, Levi: You have won the confidence and affection of your brothers. They all love you."

"Matthew, I know much about your anxieties, sacrifices, and labors to keep the treasury replenished which your brothers do not know, and I am rejoiced that, though he who carried the bag is absent, the publican ambassador is here at my farewell gathering with the messengers of the kingdom. I pray that you may understand the meaning of my teaching with the eyes of the spirit. When the new teacher comes into your heart, follow on as he will lead you and let your brothers see, even all the world, what the Father can do for a hated tax gatherer who dared to follow the Son of God and to believe the gospel of the kingdom. Even from the first, Matthew, I loved you as I did these other Galileans. Knowing then so well that neither the Father nor the Son exalts one person over another, see to it that you make no such distinctions among those who become believers in the gospel through your ministry. So, Matthew, dedicate your whole future life service to showing all men that God does not favor one man over another, that in the sight of God and in the fellowship of the kingdom, all men are equal, all believers are the sons of God."

Jesus then stepped over to James Zebedee, who stood in silence as the Master addressed him, saying: "James, when you and your younger brother once came to me seeking preferential treatment in the honors of the kingdom, and I told you such honors were for the Father to bestow, I asked if you were able to drink my cup, and both of you answered that you were. Even if you were not then able, and if you are not now able, you will soon be prepared for such a service by the experience you are about to pass through. By such behavior you angered your brothers at that time. If they have not already fully forgiven you, they will when they see you drink my cup. Whether your ministry is long or short, possess your soul in patience. When the new teacher comes let him teach you the poise of compassion and that sympathetic tolerance which is born of sincere confidence in me and of perfect submission to the Father's will. Dedicate your life to the demonstration of that combined human affection and divine dignity of the God-knowing and Son- believing disciple. All who thus live will reveal the gospel even in the manner of their death. You and your brother John will go different ways, and one of you may sit down with me in the eternal kingdom long before the other. It would help you much if you would learn that true wisdom embraces discretion as well as courage. You should learn sagacity to go along with your aggressiveness. There will come those trying moments when my disciples will not hesitate to lay down their lives for this gospel, but in all ordinary circumstances it would be far better to temper the wrath of unbelievers that you might live and continue to preach the Good News of the Kingdom. As far as lies in your power, live long on the Earth that your life of many years may be fruitful in souls won for the Heavenly kingdom."

When the Master had finished speaking to James Zebedee, he stepped around to the end of the table where Andrew sat and, looking his faithful helper in the eyes, said: "Andrew, you have faithfully represented me as acting head of the ambassadors of the Heavenly kingdom. Although you have sometimes doubted and at other times manifested dangerous timidity, still, you have always been sincerely just and eminently fair in dealing with your associates. Ever since the ordination of you and your brothers as messengers of the kingdom, you have been self-governing in all group administrative affairs except that I designated you as the acting head of these chosen ones. In no other temporal matter have I acted to direct or to influence your decisions.

This I did in order to provide for leadership in the direction of all your subsequent group deliberations. In my universe and in my Father's universe of universes, our brothers are dealt with as individuals in all their spiritual relations, but in all group relationships we unfailingly provide for definite leadership. Our kingdom is a realm of order, and where two or more creatures act in cooperation, there is always provided the authority of leadership.

Now, Andrew, since you are the chief of your brothers by authority of my appointment, and since you have thus served as my personal representative, and as I am about to leave you and go to my Father, I release you from all responsibility as regards these temporal and administrative affairs. From now on you may exercise no jurisdiction over your brothers except that which you have earned in your capacity as spiritual leader, and which your brothers therefore freely recognize. From this hour you may exercise no authority over your brothers unless they restore such jurisdiction to you by their definite action after I shall have gone to the Father. But this release from responsibility as the administrative head of this group does not in any manner lessen your moral responsibility to do everything in your power to hold your brothers together with a firm and loving hand during the trying times just ahead, those days which must intervene between my departure in the flesh and the sending of the new teacher who will live in your hearts, and who ultimately will lead you into all truth. As I prepare to leave you, I would liberate you from all administrative responsibility which had its inception and authority in my presence as one among you. Henceforth I shall exercise only spiritual authority over you and among you.

If your brothers desire to retain you as their counselor, I direct that you should, in all matters temporal and spiritual, do your utmost to promote peace and harmony among the various groups of sincere gospel believers. Dedicate the remainder of your life to promoting the practical aspects of brotherly love among your brothers. Be kind to my brothers in the flesh when they come fully to believe this gospel.

Manifest loving and impartial devotion to the Greeks in the West and to Abner and his followers in the East. Although these, my Apostles, are soon going to be scattered to the four corners of the Earth, there to proclaim the good news of the salvation of sonship with God, you are to hold them together during the trying time just ahead, that season of intense testing during which you must learn to believe this gospel without my personal presence while you patiently await the arrival of the new teacher, the Spirit of Truth. So, Andrew, though it may not fall to you to do the great works as seen by men, be content to be the teacher and counselor of those who do such things. Go on with your work on Earth to the end, and then shall you continue this ministry in the eternal kingdom, for have I not many times told you that I have other sheep not of this flock?"

Jesus then went over to the Alpheus twins and, standing between them, said: "My little children, you are one of the three groups of brothers who chose to follow after me. All six of you have done well to work in peace with your own flesh and blood, but none have done better than you. Hard times are ahead of us. You may not understand all that will befall you and your brothers, but never doubt that you were once called to the work of the kingdom. For some time, there will be no multitudes to manage, but do not become discouraged. When your lifework is finished, I will receive you on high, where in glory you shall tell of your salvation to seraphic hosts and to multitudes of the high Sons of God. Dedicate your lives to the enhancement of commonplace toil. Show all men on Earth and the angels of Heaven how cheerfully and courageously mortal man can, after having been called to work for a season in the special service of God, return to the labors of former days. If, for the time being, your work in the outward affairs of the kingdom should be completed, you should go back to your former labors with the new enlightenment of the experience of sonship with God and with the exalted realization that, to him who is God- knowing, there is no such thing as common labor or secular toil. To you who have worked with me, all things have become sacred, and all earthly labor has become a service even to God the Father. When you hear the news of the doings of your former apostolic associates, rejoice with them and continue your daily work as those who wait upon God and serve while they wait. You have been my Apostles, and you always shall be, and I will remember you in the kingdom to come."

Then Jesus went over to Philip, who, standing up, heard this message from his Master: "Philip, you have asked me many foolish questions, but I have done my utmost to answer every one, and now would I answer the last of such questionings which have arisen in your most honest but unspiritual mind. All the time I have been coming around toward you, have you been saying to yourself, 'What shall I ever do if the Master goes away and leaves us alone in the world?' You of little faith! Yet you have almost as much as many of your brothers.

You have been a good steward, Philip. You failed us only a few times, and one of those failures we utilized to manifest the Father's glory.

Your office of stewardship is about over. You must soon more fully do the work you were called to do, the preaching of this gospel of the kingdom. Philip, you have always wanted to be shown, and very soon shall you see great things. Far better that you should have seen all this by faith, but since you were sincere even in your material sightedness, you will live to see my words fulfilled. Then, when you are blessed with spiritual vision, go forth to your work, dedicating your life to the cause of leading mankind to search for God and to seek eternal realities with the eye of spiritual faith and not with the eyes of the material mind.

Remember, Philip, you have a great mission on Earth, for the world is filled with those who look at life just as you have tended to. You have a great work to do, and when it is finished in faith, you shall come to me in my kingdom, and I will take great pleasure in showing you which eye has not seen, ear heard, nor the mortal mind conceived. In the meantime, become as a little child in the kingdom of the spirit and permit me, as the spirit of the new teacher, to lead you forward in the spiritual kingdom. In this way will I be able to do much for you which I was not able to accomplish when I lived with you as a mortal of the realm. Always remember, Philip, he who has seen me has seen the Father."

Then went the Master over to Nathaniel. As Nathaniel stood up, Jesus bade him be seated and, sitting down by his side, said: "Nathaniel, you have learned to live above prejudice and to practice increased tolerance since you became my Apostle. But there is much more for you to learn. You have been a blessing to your fellows in that they have always been admonished by your consistent sincerity. When I have gone, it may be that your frankness will interfere with your getting along well with your brothers, both old and new. You should learn that the expression of even a good thought must be modulated in accordance with the intellectual status and spiritual development of the hearer. Sincerity is most serviceable in the work of the kingdom when it is wedded to discretion.

If you would learn to work with your brothers, you might accomplish more permanent things, but if you find yourself going off in quest of those who think as you do, in that event dedicate your life to proving that the God-knowing disciple can become a kingdom builder even when alone in the world and wholly isolated from his fellow believers. I know you will be faithful to the end, and I will someday welcome you to the service of my kingdom on high."

Then Nathaniel spoke, asking Jesus this question: "I have listened to your teachings ever since you first called me to the service of this kingdom, but I honestly cannot understand the full meaning of all you tell us. I do not know what to expect next, and I think most of my brothers are likewise perplexed, but they hesitate to confess their confusion. Can you help me?" Jesus, putting his hand on Nathaniel's shoulder, said: "My friend, it is not strange that you should encounter perplexity in your attempt to grasp the meaning of my spiritual teachings since you are so handicapped by your preconceptions of Jewish tradition and so confused by your persistent tendency to interpret my gospel in accordance with the teachings of the Scribes and Pharisees."

I have taught you much by word of mouth, and I have lived my life among you. I have done all that can be done to enlighten your mind and liberate your souls, and what you have not been able to get from my teachings and my life, you must now prepare to acquire at the hand of that master of all teachers, actual experience. In all of this new experience which now awaits you, I will go before you and the Spirit of Truth shall be with you. Fear not, that which you now fail to comprehend, the new teacher, when he has come, will reveal to you throughout the remainder of your life on Earth and on through your training in the eternal ages."

Then the Master, turning to all of them, said: "Be not dismayed that you fail to grasp the full meaning of the gospel. You are but finite, mortal men, and that which I have taught you is infinite, divine, and eternal. Be patient and of good courage since you have the eternal ages before you in which to continue your progressive achievement of the experience of becoming perfect, even as your Father in Paradise is perfect."

Then Jesus went over to Thomas, who, standing up, heard him say: "Thomas, you have often lacked faith. However, when you have had your seasons with doubt, you have never lacked courage. I know well that the false prophets and spurious teachers will not deceive you. After I have gone, your brothers will the more appreciate your critical way of viewing new teachings. When you all are scattered to the ends of the Earth in the times to come, remember that you are still my ambassadors. Thomas, I am glad you joined us, and I know, after a short period of perplexity, you will go on in the service of the kingdom. Your doubts have perplexed your brothers, but they have never troubled me. I have confidence in you, and I will go before you even to the uttermost parts of the Earth."

Then the Master went over to Simon Peter, who stood up as Jesus addressed him: "Peter, I know you love me, and that you will dedicate your life to the public proclamation of this gospel of the kingdom to Jew and Gentile, but I am distressed that your years of such close association with me have not done more to help you think before you speak. What experience must you pass through before you will learn to set a guard upon your lips? How much trouble have you made for us by your thoughtless speaking, by your presumptuous self-confidence. You are destined to make much more trouble for yourself if you do not master this frailty. You know that your brothers love you in spite of this weakness, and you should also understand that this shortcoming in no way impairs my affection for you, but it lessens your usefulness and never ceases to make trouble for you. But you will undoubtedly receive great help from the experience you will pass through this very night.

What I now say to you, Simon Peter, I likewise say to all your brothers here assembled: This night you will all be in great danger of stumbling over me. You know it is written, 'The shepherd will be smitten, and the sheep will be scattered abroad.' When I am absent, there is great danger that some of you will succumb to doubts and stumble because of what befalls me. But I promise you now that I will come back to you for a little while, and that I will then go before you into Galilee."

Then said Peter, placing his hand on Jesus' shoulder: "No matter if all my brothers should succumb to doubts because of you,

I promise that I will not stumble over anything you may do. I will go with you and, if need be, die for you."

As Peter stood there before his Master, trembling with intense emotion and overflowing with genuine love for him, Jesus looked straight into his moistened eyes as he said: "Peter, verily, verily, I say to you, this night the cock will not crow until you have denied me three times. Thus, what you have failed to learn from peaceful association with me, you will learn through much trouble and many sorrows. After you have really learned this needful lesson, you should strengthen your brothers and go on living a life dedicated to preaching this gospel, though you may fall into prison and, perhaps, follow me in paying the ultimate price of loving service in the building of the Father's kingdom.

But remember my promise: When I am raised up, I will remain with you for a season before I go to the Father. Even to this night will I pray to the Father that he strengthens each of you for that which you must now so soon pass through. I love you all with the same love that the Father loves me, and therefore should you henceforth love one another, even as I have loved you."

Then Jesus invited them all to sing a hymn with him. After they had sung the hymn, they departed for the camp on the Mount of Olives.

It was about ten o'clock this Thursday night when Jesus led the eleven Apostles from the home of Elijah and Mary Mark on their way back to the Gethsemane camp. Ever since that day in the hills, John Mark had made it his business to keep a watchful eye on Jesus. John, being in need of sleep, had obtained several hours of rest while the Master had been with his Apostles in the upper room, but on hearing them coming downstairs, he arose and, quickly throwing a linen coat about himself, followed them through the city, over the brook Kidron, and on to their private encampment adjacent to Gethsemane Park.

John Mark remained so near the Master throughout this night and the next day that he witnessed everything and overheard much of what the Master said from this time on to the hour of the crucifixion.

As Jesus and the eleven made their way back to camp, the Apostles began to wonder about the meaning of Judas' prolonged absence, and they spoke to one another concerning the Master's prediction that one of them would betray him, and for the first time they suspected that all was not well with Judas Iscariot. But they did not engage in open comment about Judas until they reached the camp and observed that he was not there, waiting to receive them. When they all besieged Andrew to know what had become of Judas, their chief remarked only, "I do not know where Judas is, but I fear he has deserted us."

A few moments after arriving at camp, Jesus said to them: "My friends and brothers, my time with you is now very short, and I desire that we draw apart by ourselves while we pray to our Father in Heaven for strength to sustain us in this hour and henceforth in all the work we must do in his name."

When Jesus had thus spoken, he led the way a short distance up on Olivet, and in full view of Jerusalem he bade them kneel on a large flat rock in a circle about him as they had done on the day of their ordination. Then, as he stood there in the midst of them glorified in the mellow moonlight, he lifted up his eyes toward Heaven and prayed: "Father, my hour has come; now glorify your Son that the Son may glorify you. I know that you have given me full authority over all living creatures in my realm, and I will give eternal life to all who will become faith sons of God. This is eternal life, that my creatures should know you as the only true God and Father of all, and that they should believe in him whom you sent into the world. Father, I have exalted you on Earth and have accomplished the work which you gave me to do. I have almost finished my earth life and among the children of our own creation. There remains only for me to lay down my life in the flesh.

Now my Father, glorify me with the glory which I had with you before this world was and receive me once more at your right hand."

"I have revealed you to the men whom you chose from the world and gave to me. They are yours, as all life is in your hands. You gave them to me, and I have lived among them, teaching them the way of life, and they have believed. These men are learning that all I have comes from you, and that the life I live in the flesh is to make known my Father to the worlds. The truth which you have given to me I have revealed to them. These, my friends and ambassadors, have sincerely willed to receive your word. I have told them that I came forth from you, that you sent me into this world, and that I am about to return to you. Father, I do pray for these chosen men. I pray for them not as I would pray for the world, but as for those whom I have chosen out of the world to represent me to the world after I have returned to your work, even as I have represented you in this world during my brief life in the flesh. These men are mine. You gave them to me. But all things which are mine are ever yours, and all that which was yours you have now caused to be mine. You have been exalted in me, and

I now pray that I may be honored in these men. I can no longer be in this world. I am about to return to the work you have given me to do. I must leave these men behind to represent us and our kingdom among men. Father, keep these men faithful as I prepare to yield up my life in the flesh.

Help these, my friends, to be one in spirit, even as we are one. As long as I could be with them, I could watch over them and guide them, but now I am about to go away. Be near them, Father, until we can send the new teacher to comfort and strengthen them.

You gave me twelve men, and I have kept them all save one, the son of revenge, who would not have further fellowship with us. These men are weak and frail, but I know we can trust them. I have proved them They love me, even as they reverence you. While they must suffer much for my sake, I desire that they should also be filled with the joy of the assurance of sonship in the Heavenly kingdom. I have given these men your word and have taught them the truth. The world may hate them, even as it has hated me, but I do not ask that you take them out of the world, only that you keep them from the evil in the world.

Sanctify them in the truth. Your word is truth. As you sent me into this world, even so am I about to send these men into the world. For their sakes I have lived among men and have consecrated my life to your service that I might inspire them to be purified through the truth I have taught them and the love I have revealed to them. I well know, my Father, that there is no need for me to ask you to watch over these brothers after I have gone. I know you love them even as I, but I do this that they may the better realize the Father loves mortal men even as does the Son.

Now, my Father, I would pray not only for these eleven men but also for all others who now believe, or who may hereafter believe the gospel of the kingdom through the word of their future ministry. I want them all to be one, even as you and I are one. You are in me, and I am in you, and I desire that these believers likewise be in us so that both of our spirits may dwell in their hearts. If my children are one as we are one, and if they love one another as I have loved them, all men will then believe that I came forth from you and be willing to receive the revelation of truth and glory which I have made. The glory which you gave me I have revealed to these believers. As you have lived with me in spirit, so have I lived with them in the flesh. As you have been one with me, so have I been one with them, and so will the new teacher ever be one with them and in them. And all this have I done that my brothers in the flesh may know that the Father loves them even as does the Son, and that you love them even as you love me. Father, work with me to save these believers that they may presently come to be with me in glory and then go on to join you in the Paradise embrace. Those who serve with me in humility, I would have with me in glory so that they may see all you have given into my hands as the eternal harvest of the seed sowing of time in the likeness of mortal flesh. I long to show my earthly brothers the glory I had with you before the founding of this world. This world knows very little of you, righteous Father, but I know you, and I have made you known to these believers, and they will make known your name to other generations. Now I promise them that you will be with them in the world even as you have been with me."

The eleven remained kneeling, in this circle around Jesus for several minutes before they arose and in silence made their way back to the near-by camp.

The Master, during, the course of this final prayer with his Apostles, alluded to the fact that he had manifested the Father's name to the world. That is truly what he did by the revelation of God through his life in the flesh. The Father in Heaven had sought to reveal himself to Moses, but he could proceed no further than to cause it to be said, "I AM." When pressed for further revelation of himself, the concept grew to: "I AM that I AM." But when Jesus had finished his Earth life, the name of the Father had been so revealed that the Master could truly say of God the Father:

> I am the bread of life. I am the living water.
>
> I am the light of the world. I am the desire of all ages.
>
> I am the open door to eternal salvation. I am the reality of endless life.
>
> I am the good shepherd.
>
> I am the pathway of infinite perfection. I am the resurrection and the life.
>
> I am the secret of eternal survival.
>
> I am the way, the truth, and the life.
>
> I am the infinite Father of my finite children. I am the true vine; you are the branches.
>
> I am the hope of all who know the living truth.
>
> I am the living bridge from one world to another.
>
> I am the living link between time and eternity.

Thus did Jesus enlarge the living revelation of the name of God to all generations. As divine love reveals the nature of God, eternal truth discloses his name in ever-enlarging proportions.

The Apostles were greatly shocked when they returned to their camp and found Judas absent. While the eleven were engaged in a heated discussion of their traitorous fellow Apostle, David Zebedee and John Mark took Jesus to one side and revealed that they had kept Judas under observation for several days, and that they knew he intended to betray him into the hands of his enemies. Jesus listened to them but only said: "My friends, nothing can happen to the Son of God unless the Father in Heaven so wills. Let your hearts not be troubled. All things will work together for the glory of God and the salvation of men."

The cheerful attitude of Jesus was waning. As the hour passed, he grew more and more serious, even sorrowful. The Apostles, being much agitated, were loath to return to their tents even when requested to do so by the Master himself. Returning from his talk with David and John, he addressed his last words to all eleven, saying: "My friends, go to your rest. Prepare yourselves for the work of tomorrow. Remember, we should all submit ourselves to the will of the Father in Heaven. My peace I leave with you." Having thus spoken, he motioned them to their tents, but as they went, he called to Peter, James, and John, saying, "I desire that you remain with me for a little while."

The Apostles fell asleep only because they were literally exhausted. They had been running short on sleep ever since their arrival in Jerusalem. Before they went to their separate sleeping quarters, Simon Zelotes led them all over to his tent, where were stored the swords and other arms, and supplied each of them with this fighting equipment. All of them received these arms and armed themselves therewith except Nathaniel. Nathaniel, in refusing to arm himself, said: "My brothers, the Master has repeatedly told us that his kingdom is not of this world, and that his disciples should not fight with the sword to bring about its establishment. I believe this. I do not think the Master needs to have us employ the sword in his defense. We have all seen his mighty power and know that he could defend himself against his enemies if he so desired. If he will not resist his enemies, it must be that such a course represents his attempt to fulfill his Father's will. I will pray, but I will not wield the sword." When Andrew heard Nathaniel's speech, he handed his sword back to Simon Zelotes. So, nine of them were armed as they separated for the night.

Resentment of Judas being a traitor for the moment eclipsed everything else in the Apostles' minds. The Master's comment in reference to Judas, spoken in the course of the last prayer, opened their eyes to the fact that he had forsaken them.

After the eight Apostles had finally gone to their tents, and while Peter, James, and John were standing by to receive the Master's orders, Jesus called to David Zebedee, "Send to me your most fleet and trustworthy messenger." When David brought to the Master one Jacob, once a runner on the overnight messenger service between Jerusalem and Bethsaida, Jesus, addressing him, said: "In all haste, go to Abner at Philadelphia and say: 'The Master sends greetings of peace to you and says that the hour has come when he will be delivered into the hands of his enemies, who will put him to death, but that he will rise from the dead and appear to you shortly, before he goes to the Father, and that he will then give you guidance to the time when the new teacher shall come to live in your hearts.'" When Jacob had rehearsed this message to the Master's satisfaction, Jesus sent him on his way, saying: "Fear not what any man may do to you, Jacob, for this night an unseen messenger will run by your side."

Then Jesus turned to the chief of the visiting Greeks who were encamped with them, and said: "My brothers, be not disturbed by what is about to take place since I have already forewarned you. The Son of God will be put to death at the instigation of his enemies, the chief priests and rulers of the Jews, but I will rise to be with you a short time before I go to the Father. When you have seen all this come to pass, glorify God and strengthen your brothers."

In ordinary circumstances the Apostles would have bidden the Master a personal good night, but this evening they were so preoccupied with the sudden realization of Judas' desertion and so overcome by the unusual nature of the Master's farewell prayer that they listened to his good-bye salutation and went away in silence.

Jesus did say this to Andrew as he left his side that night: "Andrew, do what you can to keep your brothers together until I come again to you after I have drunk this cup. Strengthen your brothers, seeing that I have already told you all. Peace be with you."

None of the Apostles expected anything out of the ordinary to happen that night since it was already so late. They sought sleep so that they might rise up early in the morning and be prepared for the worst. They thought that the chief priests would seek to apprehend their Master early in the morning as no secular work was ever done after noon on the preparation day for the Passover.

Only David Zebedee and John Mark understood that the enemies of Jesus were coming with Judas that very night.

David had arranged to stand guard that night on the upper trail which led to the Bethany-Jerusalem road, while John Mark was to watch along the road coming up by the Kidron to Gethsemane. Before David went to his self-imposed task of outpost duty, he bade farewell to Jesus, saying: "Master, I have had great joy in my service with you.

My brothers are your Apostles, but I have delighted to do the lesser things as they should be done, and I shall miss you with all my heart when you are gone." Then said Jesus to David: "David, my son, others have done that which they were directed to do, but this service have you done of your own heart, and I have not been unmindful of your devotion. You, too, shall someday serve with me in the eternal kingdom."

Then, as he prepared to go on watch by the upper trail, David said to Jesus: "You know, Master, I sent for your family, and I have word by a messenger that they are tonight in Jericho. They will be here early tomorrow morning since it would be dangerous for them to come up the dangerous road by night." Jesus, looking down upon David, only said: "Let it be so David."

When David had gone up Olivet, John Mark took up his vigil near the road which ran by the brook down to Jerusalem. John would have remained at this post but for his great desire to be near Jesus and to know what was going on. Shortly after David left him, and when John Mark observed Jesus withdraw, with Peter, James, and John, into a nearby ravine, he was so overcome with combined devotion and curiosity that he forsook his sentinel post and followed after them, hiding himself in the bushes, from which place he saw and overheard all that transpired during those last moments in the garden and just before Judas and the armed guards appeared to arrest Jesus.

While all this was in progress at the Master's camp, Judas Iscariot was in conference with the captain of the temple guards, who had assembled his men preparatory to setting out, under the leadership of the betrayer, to arrest Jesus.

After all was still and quiet about the camp, Jesus, taking Peter, James, and John, went a short way up a near-by ravine where he had often before gone to pray and commune. The three Apostles could not help recognizing that he was grievously oppressed. Never before had they observed their Master to be so heavy-laden and sorrowful. When they arrived at the place of his devotion, he bade the three sit down and watch with him while he went off about a stone's throw to pray.

When he had prostrated himself on the ground, he prayed: "My Father, I came into this world to do your will, and so I have. I know that the hour has come to lay down this life in the flesh, and I do not shrink there from, but I would know that it is your will that I drink this cup.

Send me the assurance that I will please you in my death even as I have in my life."

The Master remained in a prayerful attitude for a few moments, and then, going over to the three Apostles, he found them sound asleep, for their eyes were heavy and they could not remain awake. As Jesus awoke them, he said: "Can you not watch with me even for one hour? Cannot you see that my soul is exceedingly sorrowful, even to death, and that I crave your companionship?" After the three had risen from their slumber, the Master again went apart by himself and, falling down on the ground, again prayed: "Father, I know it is possible to avoid this cup. All things are possible with you, but I have come to do your will, and while this is a bitter cup, I will drink it if it is your will." When he had thus prayed, a mighty angel came down by his side and, speaking to him, touched him and strengthened him. In the face of a horrible human death, the material mind of Jesus wavered, but the angel came and gave him strength to endure the inevitable.

When Jesus returned to speak with the three Apostles, he again found them fast asleep. He awakened them, saying: "In such an hour I need you to watch and pray with me. All the more do you need to pray that you enter not into temptation. Why do you fall asleep when I leave you?"

Then, for a third time, the Master withdrew and prayed: "Father, you see my sleeping Apostles, have mercy upon them. The spirit is indeed willing, but the flesh is weak. Now, 0 Father, if this cup may not pass, then would I drink it. Not my will, but yours, be done." When he had finished praying, he lay for a moment prostrate on the ground.

When he arose and went back to his Apostles, once more he found them asleep. He surveyed them and, with a pitying gesture, tenderly said: "Sleep on now and take your rest. The time of decision is past. The hour is now upon us wherein the Son of God will be betrayed into the hands of his enemies." As he reached down to shake them that he might awaken them, he said: "Arise, let us be going back to the camp, for he who betrays me is at hand, and the hour has come when my flock shall be scattered. But I have already told you about these things."

During the years that Jesus lived among his followers, they did, indeed, have much proof of his divine nature, but just now are they about to witness new evidence of his humanity. Just before the greatest of all the revelations of his divinity, his resurrection, must now come the greatest proofs of his mortal nature, his humiliation and crucifixion.

Each time he prayed in the garden, his humanity laid a firmer hold upon his divinity. His human will more completely became one with the divine will of his Father. Among other words spoken to him by the mighty angel was the message that the Father desired his Son to finish his Earth life by passing through the experience of death just as all mortal creatures must experience material dissolution in passing from the existence of time into the progression of eternity. This message gave Jesus much strength to go forward in grace through the final hours as he well knew that his Father was waiting and watching the final hours.

Earlier in the evening, it had not seemed so difficult to drink the cup, but as the human Jesus bade farewell to his Apostles and sent them to their rest, the trial grew more appalling. Jesus experienced that natural ebb and flow of feeling, which is common to all human experience, and just now he was weary from work, exhausted from the long hours of strenuous labor and painfully anxious concerning the safety of his Apostles. While no mortal can presume to understand the thoughts and feelings of the incarnate Son of God at such a time as this, we know that he endured great anguish and suffered untold sorrow, for the perspiration rolled off his face in great drops. He was at last convinced that the Father intended to allow natural events to take their course. He was fully determined to employ none of his sovereign power as the head-of-state of the universe to save himself.

The assembled hosts of a vast creation were now hovering over this scene under the command of Gabriel and the Divine Spirit of Jesus. The commanders of these armies of Heaven had repeatedly been warned not to interfere with these events on Earth unless Jesus himself should order them to intervene.

The experience of parting with the Apostles was a great strain on the human heart of Jesus. This sorrow of love bore down on him and made it more difficult to face such a death as he well knew awaited him. He realized how weak and how ignorant his Apostles were, and he dreaded to leave them. He well knew that the time of his departure had come, but his human heart longed to find out whether there might not possibly be some legitimate avenue of escape from this terrible plight of suffering, and sorrow. When it had thus sought escape, and failed, it was willing to drink the cup. The divine mind of Jesus knew he had done his best for the twelve Apostles, but the human heart of Jesus wished that more might have been done for them before they should be left alone in the world. Jesus' heart was being crushed. He truly loved his brothers. He was isolated from his family in the flesh. One of his chosen associates was betraying him. His father Joseph's people had rejected him. His soul was tortured by baffled love and rejected mercy. It was just one of those awful human moments when everything seems to bear down with crushing cruelty and terrible agony.

Jesus' humanity was not insensible to this situation of private loneliness, public shame, and the appearance of the failure of his cause. All these sentiments bore down on him with indescribable heaviness. In this great sorrow his mind went back to the days of his childhood in Nazareth and to his early work in Galilee. At the time of this great trial there came to his mind many of those pleasant scenes of his earthly ministry. And it was from these old memories of Nazareth, Capernaum, Mount Hermon, and of the sunrise and sunset on the shimmering Sea of Galilee, that he soothed himself as he made his human heart strong and ready to encounter the traitor who should so soon betray him.

FRIDAY - THE FINAL DAY

The hour was now past midnight, it was the beginning of Friday, the last day in the human life of Jesus of Nazareth.

Before Judas and the soldiers arrived, the Master had fully regained his customary poise. The spirit had triumphed over the flesh. Faith had asserted itself over all human tendencies to fear or entertain doubt. The ultimate test of the full realization of human nature has been met and acceptably passed. Once more the Son of God was prepared to face his enemies with dignity and in the full assurance of his invincibility as a mortal man unreservedly dedicated to the doing of his Father's will.

After Jesus had finally awakened Peter, James, and John, he suggested that they go to their tents and seek sleep in preparation for the duties of the morrow. But by this time the three Apostles were wide awake. They had been refreshed by their short naps, and besides, they were stimulated and aroused by the arrival on the scene of two excited messengers who inquired for David Zebedee and quickly went in quest of him when Peter informed them where he kept watch.

Although eight of the Apostles were sound asleep, the Greeks who were encamped alongside them were more fearful of trouble, so much so that they had posted a sentinel to give the alarm in case danger should arise. When these two messengers hurried into camp, the Greek sentinel proceeded to arouse all of his fellow countrymen, who streamed forth from their tents, fully dressed and fully armed. All the camp was now aroused except the eight Apostles. Peter desired to call his associates, but Jesus definitely forbade him. The Master mildly admonished them all to return to their tents, but they were reluctant to comply with his suggestion.

Failing to disperse his followers, the Master left them and walked down toward the olive press near the entrance to Gethsemane Park.

Although the three Apostles, the Greeks, and the other members of the camp hesitated immediately to follow him, John Mark hastened around through the olive trees and hid himself in a small shed near the olive press. Jesus withdrew from the camp and from his friends in order that his apprehenders, when they arrived, might arrest him without disturbing his Apostles. The Master feared to have his Apostles awake and present at the time of his arrest lest the spectacle of Judas' betraying him should so arouse their animosity that they would offer resistance to the soldiers and would be taken into custody with him. He feared that, if they should be arrested with him, they might also perish with him.

There is great danger of misunderstanding the meaning of numerous sayings and many events associated with the termination of the Master's career in the flesh. The cruel treatment of Jesus by the ignorant servants and the callused soldiers, the unfair conduct of his trials, and the unfeeling attitude of the professed religious leaders, must not be confused with the fact that Jesus, in patiently submitting to all this suffering, and humiliation, was truly doing the will of the Father in Paradise. It was, indeed and in truth, the will of the Father that his Son should drink to the full the cup of mortal experience, from birth to death, but the Father in Heaven had nothing whatsoever to do with the barbarous behavior of those supposedly civilized human beings who so brutally tortured the Master and so horribly heaped successive indignities upon his nonresistant person. These inhuman and shocking experiences which Jesus was called upon to endure in the final hours of his mortal life were not in any sense a part of the divine will of the Father.

The Father in Heaven desired the Son to finish his Earth career naturally, just as all mortals must finish up their lives on Earth and in the flesh. Ordinary men and women cannot expect to have their last hours on Earth and the supervening episode of death made easy by a special dispensation. Accordingly, Jesus elected to lay down his life in the flesh in the manner which was in keeping with the outworking of natural events, and he steadfastly refused to extricate himself from the cruel clutches of a wicked conspiracy of inhuman events which swept on with horrible certainty toward his unbelievable humiliation and ignominious death. Every bit of all this astounding manifestation of hatred and this unprecedented demonstration of cruelty was the work of evil men and wicked mortals. God in Heaven did not will it.

After Judas so abruptly left the table while eating the Last Supper, he went directly to the home of his cousin, and then the two went straight to the captain of the temple guards. Judas requested the captain to assemble the guards and informed him that he was ready to lead them to Jesus. Judas appeared on the scene a little before he was expected, therefore there was some delay in getting started for the Mark home, where Judas expected to find Jesus still visiting with the Apostles. The Master and the eleven left the home of Elijah Mark fully fifteen minutes before the betrayer and the guards arrived. By the time the apprehenders reached the Mark home, Jesus and the eleven were well outside the walls of the city and on their way to the Olivet camp.

Judas was much disturbed by this failure to find Jesus at the Mark residence and in the company of eleven men, only two of whom were armed for resistance. He happened to know that, in the afternoon when they had left camp, only Simon Peter and Simon Zelotes were armed with swords. Judas had hoped to take Jesus when the city was quiet, and when there was little chance of resistance. The betrayer feared that, if he waited for them to return to their camp, more than threescore of devoted disciples would be encountered, and he also knew that Simon Zelotes had an ample store of arms in his possession. Judas was becoming increasingly nervous as he meditated how the eleven loyal Apostles would detest him, and he feared they would all seek to destroy him. He was not only disloyal, but he was a real coward at heart.

When they failed to find Jesus in the upper chamber, Judas asked the captain of the guard to return to the temple. By this time the rulers had begun to assemble at the high priest's home preparatory to receiving Jesus, seeing that their bargain with the traitor called for Jesus' arrest by midnight of that day. Judas explained to his associates that they had missed Jesus at the Mark home, and that it would be necessary to go to Gethsemane to arrest him. The betrayer then went on to state that more than threescore devoted followers were encamped with him, and that they were all well-armed. The rulers of the Jews reminded Judas that Jesus had always preached nonresistance, but Judas replied that they could not depend upon all Jesus' followers obeying such teaching. He really feared for himself and therefore asked for the company of forty armed soldiers. Since the Jewish authorities had no such force of armed men under their jurisdiction, they went at once to the fortress of Antonia and requested the Roman commander to give them this guard. But when he learned that they intended to arrest Jesus, he promptly refused to agree to their request and referred them to his superior officer. In this way more than an hour was consumed in going from one authority to another until they finally were compelled to go to Pilate himself in order to obtain permission to employ the armed Roman guards. It was late when they arrived at Pilate's house, and he had retired to his private chambers with his wife. He hesitated to have anything to do with the enterprise, all the more so since his wife had asked him not to grant the request. But inasmuch as the presiding officer of the Jewish Sanhedrin was present and making personal request for this assistance, the governor thought it wise to grant the petition, thinking he could later on right any wrong they might be disposed to commit.

Accordingly, when Judas Iscariot started out from the temple, about half after eleven o'clock, he was accompanied by more than sixty men, - temple guards, Roman soldiers, and curious servants of the chief priests and rulers.

As this company of armed soldiers and guards, carrying torches and lanterns, approached the garden, Judas stepped well out in front of the band that he might be ready quickly to identify Jesus so that the apprehenders could easily lay hands on him before his associates could rally to his defense. There was yet another reason why Judas chose to be ahead of the Master's enemies. He thought it would appear that he had arrived on the scene ahead of the soldiers so that the Apostles and others gathered around Jesus might not directly connect him with the armed guards following so closely upon his heels. Judas had even thought to pose as if he had hurried out to warn them of the coming of the apprehenders, but this plan was thwarted by Jesus' outright greeting of the betrayer. Though the Master spoke to Judas kindly, he greeted him as a traitor.

As soon as Peter, James, and John, with some thirty of their fellow campers, saw the armed band with torches swing around the brow of the hill, they knew that these soldiers were coming to arrest Jesus, and they all rushed down to near the olive press where the Master was sitting in moonlit solitude. As the company of soldiers approached on one side, the three Apostles and their associates approached on the other. As Judas strode forward to accost the Master, there the two groups stood, motionless, with the Master between them and Judas making ready to impress the traitorous kiss upon his brow.

It had been the hope of the betrayer that he could, after leading the guards to Gethsemane, simply point Jesus out to the soldiers, or at most carry out the promise to greet him with a kiss, and then quickly retire from the scene. Judas greatly feared that the Apostles would all be present, and that they would concentrate their attack upon him in retribution for his daring to betray their beloved teacher. But when the Master greeted him as a betrayer, he was so confused that he made no attempt to flee.

Jesus made one last effort to save Judas from actually betraying him. Before the traitor could reach him, he stepped to one side and, addressing the foremost soldier on the left, the captain of the Romans, said, "Whom do you seek?" The captain answered, "Jesus of Nazareth." Then Jesus stepped up immediately in front of the officer and, standing there in calm majesty said, "I am he." Many of this armed band had heard Jesus teach in the temple, others had learned about his mighty works, and when they heard him thus boldly announce his identity, those in the front ranks fell suddenly backward. They were overcome with surprise at his calm and majestic announcement of identity. There was, therefore, no need for Judas to go on with his plan of betrayal. The Master had boldly revealed himself to his enemies, and they could have taken him without Judas' assistance. But the traitor had to do something to account for his presence with this armed band, and besides, he wanted to make a show of carrying out his part of the betrayal bargain with the rulers of the Jews in order to be eligible for the great reward and honors which he believed would be heaped upon him in compensation for his promise to deliver Jesus into their hands.

As the guards rallied from their first faltering at the sight of Jesus and at the sound of his unusual voice, and as the Apostles and disciples drew nearer, Judas stepped up to Jesus and, placing a kiss upon his brow, said, "Hail, Master and Teacher." As Judas thus embraced his Master, Jesus said, "Friend, is it not enough to do this! Would you even betray the Son of God with a kiss?"

The Apostles and disciples were literally stunned by what they saw. For a moment no one moved. Then Jesus, disengaging himself from the traitorous embrace of Judas, stepped up to the guards and soldiers and again asked, "Whom do you seek?" Again, the captain said, "Jesus of Nazareth." Again, answered Jesus: "I have told you that I am he. If, therefore, you seek me, let these others go their way. I am ready to go with you."

Jesus was ready to go back to Jerusalem with the guards, and the captain of the soldiers was altogether willing to allow the three Apostles and their associates to go their way in peace, but before they were able to get started, as Jesus stood there awaiting the captain's orders, one Malchus, the Syrian bodyguard of the high priest, stepped up to Jesus and attempted to bind his hands behind his back, although the Roman captain had not directed that Jesus should be thus bound. When Peter and his associates saw their Master being subjected to this indignity, they were no longer able to restrain themselves. Peter drew his sword and with the others rushed forward to smite Malchus. But before the soldiers could come to the defense of the high priest's servant, Jesus raised a forbidding hand to Peter and, speaking sternly, said: "Peter, put up your sword. They who take the sword shall perish by the sword. Do you not understand that it is the Father's will that I drink this cup? Do you not know that I could this very moment command more than twelve legions of angels who would deliver me from the hands of these few men?"

While Jesus thus effectively put a stop to this show of physical resistance by his followers, it was enough to arouse the fear of the captain of the guards, who now, with the help of his soldiers, laid heavy hands on Jesus and quickly bound him. As they tied his hands with heavy cords, Jesus said to them: "Why do you come out against me with swords and with staves as if to seize a robber?

I was daily with you in the temple, publicly teaching the people, and you made no effort to take me."

When Jesus had been bound, the captain, fearing that the followers of the Master might attempt to rescue him, gave orders that they be seized, but the soldiers were not quick enough since, having overheard the captain's orders to arrest them, Jesus' followers fled in haste back into the ravine. All this time John Mark had remained secluded in the nearby shed. When the guards started back to Jerusalem with Jesus, John Mark attempted to steal out of the shed in order to catch up with the fleeing Apostles and disciples, but just as he emerged, one of the last of the returning soldiers who had pursued the fleeing disciples was passing near and, seeing this young man in his linen coat, gave chase, almost overtaking him. The soldier got near enough to John to lay hold upon his coat, but the young man freed himself from the garment, escaping naked while the soldier held the empty coat. John Mark made his way in all haste to David Zebedee on the upper trail. When he had told David what had happened, they both hurried back to the tents of the sleeping Apostles and informed all eight of the Master's betrayal and arrest.

At about the time the eight Apostles were being awakened, those who had fled up the ravine were returning, and they all gathered together near the olive press to debate what should be done. In the meantime, Simon Peter and John Zebedee, who had hidden among the olive trees, had already gone on after the mob of soldiers, guards, and servants, who were now leading Jesus back to Jerusalem as they would have led a desperate criminal. John followed close behind the mob, but Peter followed far off. After John Mark's escape from the clutch of the soldier, he provided himself with a cloak which he found in the tent of Simon Peter and John Zebedee. He suspected the guards were going to take Jesus to the home of Annas, the high priest emeritus. So, he skirted around through the olive orchards and was there ahead of the mob, hiding near the entrance to the gate of the high priest's palace.

James Zebedee found himself separated from Simon Peter and his brother John, and so he now joined the other Apostles and their fellow campers at the olive press to deliberate on what should be done in view of the Master's arrest. Andrew had been released from all responsibility in the group management of his fellow Apostles.

Accordingly, in this greatest of all crises in their lives, he was silent.

After a short informal discussion, Simon Zelotes stood up on the stone wall of the olive press and, making an impassioned plea for loyalty to the Master and the cause of the kingdom, exhorted his fellow Apostles and the other disciples to hasten on after the mob and effect the rescue of Jesus. The majority of the company would have been disposed to follow his aggressive leadership had it not been for the advice of Nathaniel, who stood up the moment Simon had finished speaking and called their attention to Jesus' often repeated teachings regarding nonresistance. He further reminded them that Jesus had that very night instructed them that they should preserve their lives for the time when they should go forth into the world proclaiming the good news of the gospel of the Heavenly kingdom. Nathaniel was encouraged in this stand by James Zebedee, who now told how Peter and others drew their swords to defend the Master against arrest, and that Jesus bade Simon Peter, and his fellow swordsmen sheathe their blades.

Matthew and Philip also made speeches, but nothing definite came of this discussion until Thomas, calling their attention to the fact that Jesus had counseled Lazarus against exposing himself to death, pointed out that they could do nothing to save their Master inasmuch as he refused to allow his friends to defend him, and since he persisted in refraining from the use of his divine powers to frustrate his human enemies.

Thomas persuaded them to scatter, every man for himself, with the understanding that David Zebedee would remain at the camp to maintain a clearinghouse and messenger headquarters for the group. By half past two o'clock that morning the camp was deserted. Only David remained on hand with three or four messengers, the others having been dispatched to secure information as to where Jesus had been taken, and what was going to be done with him.

Five of the Apostles, Nathaniel, Matthew, Philip, and the twins, went into hiding at Bethpage and Bethany. Thomas, Andrew, James, and Simon Zelotes were hiding in the city. Simon Peter and John Zebedee followed along to the home of Annas.

Shortly after daybreak, Simon Peter wandered back to the Gethsemane camp, a dejected picture of deep despair. David sent him in charge of a messenger to join his brother, Andrew, who was at the home of Nicodemus in Jerusalem.

Until the very end of the crucifixion, John Zebedee remained, as Jesus had directed him, always near at hand, and it was he who supplied David's messengers with information from hour to hour which they carried to David at the garden camp, and which was then relayed to the hiding Apostles and to Jesus' family.

Surely, the shepherd is smitten, and the sheep are scattered! While they all vaguely realized that Jesus had forewarned them of this very situation, they were too severely shocked by the Master's sudden disappearance to be able to use their minds normally.

It was shortly after daylight and just after Peter had been sent to join his brother, that Jude, Jesus' brother in the flesh, arrived in the camp, almost breathless and in advance of the rest of Jesus' family, only to learn that the Master had already been placed under arrest. He hastened back down the Jericho road to carry this information to his mother and to his brothers and sisters. David Zebedee sent word to Jesus' family, by Jude, to gather at the house of Martha and Mary in Bethany and there await news which his messengers would regularly bring them.

This was the situation during the early morning hours of Friday as regards the Apostles, the chief disciples, and the earthly family of Jesus. All these groups and individuals were kept in touch with each other by the messenger service which David Zebedee continued to operate from his headquarters at the Gethsemane camp.

Before they started away from the garden with Jesus, a dispute arose between the Jewish captain of the temple guards and the Roman captain of the company of soldiers as to where they were to take Jesus. The captain of the temple guards gave orders that he should be taken to Caiaphas, the acting high priest. The captain of the Roman soldiers directed that Jesus be taken to the palace of Annas, the former high priest and father-in-law of Caiaphas. This he did because the Romans were in the habit of dealing directly with Annas in all matters having to do with the enforcement of the Jewish ecclesiastical laws. The orders of the Roman captain were obeyed. They took Jesus to the home of Annas for his preliminary examination.

Judas marched along near the captains, overhearing all that was said, but took no part in the dispute, for neither the Jewish captain nor the Roman officer would so much as speak to the betrayer. They held him in such contempt.

About this time John Zebedee, remembering his Master's instructions to remain always near at hand, hurried up near Jesus as he marched along between the two captains. The commander of the temple guards, seeing John come up alongside, said to his assistant:

"Take this man and bind him. He is one of this fellow's followers." But when the Roman captain heard this and, looking around, saw John, he gave orders that the Apostle should come over by him, and that no man should molest him. Then the Roman captain said to the Jewish captain: "This man is neither a traitor nor a coward. I saw him in the garden, and he did not draw a sword to resist us. He has the courage to come forward to be with his Master, and no man shall lay hands on him. The Roman law allows that any prisoner may have at least one friend to stand with him before the judgment bar, and this man shall not be prevented from standing by the side of his Master, the prisoner."

When Judas heard this, he was so ashamed and humiliated that he dropped back behind the marchers, coming up to the palace of Annas alone.

This is why John Zebedee was permitted to remain near Jesus all the way through his trying experiences. The Jews feared to say anything to John or to molest him in any way because he had something of the status of a Roman counselor designated to act as observer of the transactions of the Jewish ecclesiastical court. John's position of privilege was made all the more secure when, in turning Jesus over to the captain of the temple guards at the gate of Anna's palace, the Roman, addressing his assistant, said: "Go along with this prisoner and see that these Jews do not kill him without Pilate's consent. Watch that they do not assassinate him, and see that his friend, the Galilean, is permitted to stand by and observe all that goes on." Thus was John able to be near Jesus right on up to the time of his death on the cross, though the other ten Apostles were compelled to remain in hiding.

John was acting under Roman protection, and the Jews dared not molest him until after the Master's death.

All the way to the palace of Annas, Jesus did not say a word.

From the time of his arrest to the time of his appearance before Annas, the Son of God spoke no word. Thus, the week ended in the arrest, trial and crucifixion of the Master. This was the end of the life of the greatest man ever to walk the face of this Earth. The events of this day set the entire world into a whirlwind, a whirlwind that endures to this very day between the forces of good and evil, the choice to live the spiritual life as Jesus of Nazareth taught, or to live the selfish, self- centered life that Jesus so struggled against.

The rest of this story is well known to history, therefore it is not necessary to shine a light upon the events of this day. This book is about spirituality, and about love of God. The events that transpired the rest of this day were devoid of both spirituality and love of God therefore this is not the proper forum for that discussion.

May the Peace of the Father forever abide in your heart!

CHAPTER 8

The Ministries

J ESUS OF NAZARETH HAD WISE COUNSEL FOR ALL WHO CAME HIS way, and he would go out of his way to speak to people on the streets.

Everywhere, he would take people aside as he observed them going about their daily affairs. Here are some of the wise words he had for the man on the street paraphrased in modern terminology:

TO THE RELIGIOUS LEADER OF
THE CYNICS OF ROME

"My brother, good and evil are merely words which symbolize levels of human comprehension of the universe. If you are ethically lazy and socially indifferent, you can take as your standard of good the current social usages. If you are spiritually indolent and morally unprogressive, you may take as your standards of good the religious practices and traditions of your contemporary religions.

But the soul that survives time and emerges into eternity, is the soul that makes a living and personal choice between good and evil as they are determined by the spiritual standards established by the divine spirit which your Father in Heaven has sent to dwell within your heart. This spirit within man is the standard of spiritual life.

Goodness, like truth, is always relative and constantly compared to evil. It is the perception of these qualities of goodness and truth that enables the evolving divine spirits of men to make those personal decisions of choice which are essential to eternal life.

Goodness is always ascending toward new levels of moral self-realization and spiritual growth. This takes the form of discovery of, and identification with, the indwelling divine spirit. An experience is good when it heightens the appreciation of beauty, strengthens the moral will, enhances the discernment of truth, enlarges the capacity to love and to serve one's brothers, exalts the spiritual ideals and/or unifies the human actions with the spirit, all of which lead directly to an increased desire to do the Father's will thereby fostering the divine passion to find God and to be more like him.

As your soul develops in its journey towards God, you will find that your goodness will increase and that your tendencies towards evil will decrease in equal proportions. These two characteristics are inversely proportional to each other. But the ability to entertain error or experience evil will never be fully lost from your soul until you have reached Heaven.

Goodness is a living thing, always relative, always progressing, invariably a personal experience, and everlastingly related to the discernment of truth and beauty. Goodness is found in the recognizing of truths at the spiritual level, which must always be contrasted with the negative counterpart... the shadows of potential evil.

Until you find your way to Heaven, goodness will always be more of a quest than a possession, more of a goal than a victory achieved. But even as you hunger and thirst for a divine and moral life, you will experience a sense of satisfaction in the goodness that you will have achieved."

To A Young Greek Who Asked why God Would Not Save Him From His Oppressive Boss

"Since you seem to know the ways of kindness and you value justice, perhaps the Gods have brought this erring man near that you may lead him into a better way of living and acting. Maybe you are the salt which is to make this brother more agreeable to all other men.

That is, if you have not lost your flavor yourself. As it is, this man is your master in that his evil ways have unfavorably influenced you. You must assert your mastery over evil by virtue of the power of goodness and thus become the master of all relations between the two of you. I predict that the goodness in you can overcome the evil in him if you give it a fair and living chance. There is no adventure in the course of mortal existence that is more exciting than to become the partner of spiritual energy and divine truth in one of their triumphant struggles over evil. It is a marvelous and invigorating experience to become the channel of spiritual light to the mortal who sits in spiritual darkness."

If you are more blessed with truth than is this man, his need should challenge you. Surely you are not a coward who could stand by on the seashore and watch a fellow man drown because he could not swim. How much more of value is this man's soul floundering in darkness compared to his body drowning in water."

TO A MAN WHO ASKED WHY JESUS CALLED ALL MEN HIS BROTHERS

"No man is a stranger to one who knows God, the Father. In your adventure of searching for the Father in Heaven, you will discover that all men are your brothers. Does it seem strange to you, then, that you should enjoy the exhilaration of meeting a newly discovered brother? To become acquainted with one's brothers and sisters, to know their problems and to learn to love them, is the highest experience of living."

TO THE CHIEF MITHRAIC PRIEST IN ROME

"Truth cannot be defined with words. It can only be defined by living it out. Truth is always more than knowledge. Knowledge has to do with things observed and learned, but truth surpasses such purely material levels in that it joins with wisdom and embraces such imponderable as human experience. Knowledge originates in science, wisdom originates in true philosophy, and truth originates in the experiences of spiritual living. Knowledge deals with facts, wisdom deals with relationships and truth deals with real spiritual values.

Man tends to crystallize science, formulate philosophy and dogmatize truth because he is mentally lazy in adjusting to the progressive struggles of living, while he is also terribly afraid of the unknown. Throughout the ages evolutionary man has been slow to initiate changes in his habits of thinking and in his techniques of living.

Personally discovered truths can be the greatest delight of the human soul, but truth can never become man's possession without the exercise of faith. This is true because man's thoughts, wisdom, ethics, and ideals will never rise higher than his faith. Man's ability to find true faith is predicated on profound reflection, sincere self-criticism, and uncompromising moral consciousness."

TALKING TO STUDENTS ABOUT THE STORY OF JONAH AND THE WHALE

"My brothers, we are all Jonahs with lives to live in accordance with the Will of God. At all times when we seek to escape life by running away to far-off enticements, we put ourselves in the immediate control of those influences which are not directed by the powers of truth and the forces of righteousness. The flight from duty is the sacrifice of truth. The escape from the service of light and life can only result in distressing conflicts with the overwhelming whales of selfishness which lead eventually to darkness and death unless such God-forsaking Jonahs shall turn their hearts, even when in the very depths of despair, to seek after God and his goodness. When such disheartened and dejected souls sincerely seek for God - hunger for truth and thirst for righteousness - there is nothing that will hold them in further captivity. No matter into what great depths that men have fallen, when they seek the light with a whole heart, the spirit of the Father God of Heaven will deliver them from their captivity. The evil circumstances of life will spew them out upon dry land of fresh opportunities for renewed service and wiser living."

To A Man Who Told Jesus That He Could Not Find God

"If you truly want to find God, that desire is in itself evidence that you have already found him. Your trouble is not that you cannot find God, for the Father has already found you. Your trouble is simply that you do not know God. Have you not read in the Prophet Jeremiah where it says: 'You shall seek me and find me when you search for me with all your heart, and I will give you a heart to know me, that I am the Father, and you shall belong to my people, and I will be your God?'

The scriptures also say: 'He looks down upon men, and if any will say I have sinned and perverted that which was right, and it profited me not, then will God deliver that man's soul from darkness, and he shall see the light.'"

To A Roman Soldier

"Be brave of heart as well as of hand. Dare to do justice and be big enough to show mercy. Compel your lower nature to obey your higher nature, even as you obey your superiors. Revere goodness and exalt truth. Choose the beautiful in place of the ugly. Respect your fellows and reach out for God with a whole heart, for God is your Father in Heaven."

To A Philosophy Speaker At The Forum In Rome

"Your eloquence is pleasing, your logic is admirable, your voice is pleasant, but your teaching is hardly true. If you could only enjoy the inspiring satisfaction of knowing God as your spiritual Father, then you might employ your powers of speech to liberate your fellows from the bondage of darkness and from the slavery of ignorance."

As a result of a day spent with Jesus discussing philosophy and religion, this man became the first speaker in Rome of the Good News of Jesus. Many years later when the Apostle Paul first went to Rome, he heard this man speaking in public about the Father in Heaven, but never realized that Jesus had preceded him there and had already planted the seed that Paul was to nurture.

To The Rich Man Who Asked If Wealth Is Evil

"My brother, I detect in your demeanor that you are a sincere seeker after wisdom and an honest lover of truth. Therefore, I am minded to lay before you my view of the solution to your problems having to do with the responsibilities of wealth. I do this because you have asked for my counsel, and in giving you this advice, I am addressing the wealth of all rich men. I am offering this advice to you for your personal guidance. If you honestly desire to regard your wealth as a trust, if you really wish to become a wise and efficient steward of your accumulated wealth, then would I counsel you to make the following analysis of the sources of your riches. First, ask yourself from where this wealth came. Be honest with yourself. To help you determine from where the money came here are ten different methods of amassing wealth:

1. Inherited wealth - riches received from parents or others.
2. Discovered wealth - riches derived from the resources of Mother Earth
3. Trade wealth - riches obtained as a fair profit in the exchange of goods.
4. Unfair wealth - riches derived from the unfair exploitation or the enslavement of your brothers.
5. Interest wealth - income derived from the fair investment of capital.
6. Genius wealth - riches derived from the rewards of the creative and inventive endowments of the human mind.
7. Accidental wealth - riches derived from the generosity of one's fellows.
8. Stolen wealth - riches secured by unfairness, dishonesty, theft or fraud.
9. Trust wealth - wealth bestowed on you by a trust.
10. Earned wealth - riches derived directly from your own personal labor, the fair and just reward of your own daily efforts of mind and body.

So, my dear friend, if you would be a faithful and just steward of your large fortune, before God and in service to men, you must determine the source of your wealth and then proceed to administer each portion in accordance with the wise and honest interpretation of the laws of justice, equity, fairness, and efficiency. I advise you to follow these guidelines in relation to the ten methods that I just outlined to you:

1. As steward of inherited wealth, you should consider it's sources. You are under a moral obligation to represent the past generation in the honest transmittal of legitimate wealth to succeeding generations after subtracting a fair share for the benefit of the present generation. Any portion of your wealth which turns out to have been derived through fraud or unfairness, you may disburse in accordance with your convictions of justice, generosity, and restitution.

2. Everyone who enjoys wealth as a result of discovery should remember that one individual can live on Earth but a short season and should, therefore, make adequate provisions for the sharing of these discoveries in helpful ways to the largest possible number of his fellow men. While the discoverer should not be denied all reward for efforts of discovery, neither should he selfishly presume to lay claim to all of the advantages and blessings to be derived from the uncovering of nature's hoard of resources.

3. As long as men choose to conduct the world's business by trade and barter, they are entitled to a fair and legitimate profit. Every tradesman deserves wages for his services. The merchant is entitled to his hire. The fairness of trade

and the honest treatment accorded one's fellows in the organized business of the world create many different sorts of profit wealth, and all these sources of wealth must be judged by the highest principles of justice, honesty, and fairness. The honest trader should never hesitate to take the same profit which he would gladly accord his fellow trader in a similar transaction.

4. No man who knows God and seeks to do the divine will can stoop to engage in the suppressions of wealth. No noble man will strive to accumulate riches and amass economic power by the enslavement or unfair exploitation of his brothers in the flesh. Riches are a moral curse and a spiritual stigma when they are derived from the sweat of oppressed men. All such wealth should be restored to those who have thus been robbed or to their children and their children's children. An enduring civilization cannot be built upon the practice of defrauding the laborer of his wages.

5. Honest wealth is entitled to interest. As long as men borrow and lend, that which is fair interest may be collected provided the capital lent was legitimate wealth. First cleanse your capital before you lay claim to the interest. Do not become so small and grasping that you would stoop to the practice of usury. Never permit yourself to be so selfish as to employ economic power to gain an unfair advantage over your struggling fellows. Yield not to the temptation to take usury from your brother in financial distress.

6. If you happen to secure wealth by flights of genius, if your riches are derived from the rewards of inventive

endowment, do not lay claim to an unfair portion of such rewards. The genius owes something to both his ancestors and his progeny. Likewise, he is under obligation to the race, nation and circumstances of his inventive discoveries. He should also remember that it was as man among men that he labored and wrought out his inventions. It would be equally unjust to deprive the genius of all his increment of wealth. And it will ever be impossible for men to establish rules and regulations applicable equally to all these problems of the equitable distribution of wealth. You must first recognize man as your brother, and if you honestly desire to treat him as you would have him treat you, the commonsense dictates of justice, honesty, and fairness will guide you in the just and impartial settlement of every recurring problem of economic rewards and social justice.

7. Except for the just and legitimate fees earned in administration, no man should lay personal claim to that wealth which time and chance may cause to fall into his hands. Accidental riches should be regarded somewhat in the light of a trust to be expended for the benefit of one's social or economic group. The possessors of such wealth should be accorded the major voice in the determination of the wise and effective distribution of such unearned resources.

8. If any portion of your fortune has been knowingly derived from fraud, if some of your wealth has been accumulated by dishonest practices or unfair methods, if your riches are the product of unjust dealings with your fellows, make haste to restore all these ill-gotten gains to the rightful

owners. Make full amends and thus cleanse your fortune of all dishonest riches.

9. The trusteeship of the wealth of one person for the benefit of others is a solemn and sacred responsibility. Do not hazard or jeopardize such a trust. Take for yourself of any trust only that which all honest men would allow.

10. That part of your fortune which represents the earnings of your own mental and physical efforts - if your work has been done in fairness and equity - is truly your own. No man can deny your right to hold and use such wealth as you may see fit provided your exercise of this right does not work harm upon your fellows."

TO THE MAN BEATING HIS WIFE IN PUBLIC

"My good friend, I perceive that something terrible must have happened to you. I very much desire that you tell me what could happen to such a strong man to lead him to attack his wife, the mother of his children, and this right out here in the street before the world to see. I am sure you must feel that you have some good reason for this assault on her. What did the woman do to deserve such treatment from her husband? As I look upon you, I think I recognize in your face the love of justice if not the desire to show mercy. I venture to say that if you found me out by the wayside, attacked by robbers, you would unhesitatingly rush to my rescue. I dare say you have done many such brave things in the course of your life. Now, my friend, tell me what is the matter? Did the woman do something wrong, or did you foolishly lose your head and thoughtlessly assault her?"

It was not so much what Jesus said as the loving look and the sympathetic smile that made the man think about his actions and look at Jesus in awe. Then the man told Jesus, "My wife has done no wrong. She is a good woman, but she irritates me by the manner in which she picks at me in public, and I lose my temper at this. I am sorry for my lack of self-control, and I promise to try to live up to my former pledge to one of your brothers who taught me the better way many years ago."

Then Jesus said to the man, "My friend, always remember that man has no rightful authority over woman unless the woman has willingly and voluntarily given him such authority. Your wife has engaged to go through life with you, to help you fight its battles, and to assume the far greater share of the burden of bearing and rearing your children. In return for this special service, it is only fair that she receives from you that special protection which man can give to woman as the partner who must carry, bear, and nurture the children. The loving care and consideration which a man is willing to bestow upon his wife and their children is the measure of that man's achievement of the higher levels of spiritual development."

Jesus turned to the woman and said, "My dear woman, unless your husband does something very wrong to deserve to be humiliated in public, love your husband and treat him as you would have him treat you. Love and respect for one another at all times, whether in public or in private, will win you a lifetime of happiness together. I perceive that both of you are reasonable people and capable of loving each other for a lifetime, therefore do not waste your time in pettiness, but rather put your time together to good use in loving each other and raising your children to love you and your Father in Heaven."

Jesus walked away, and as he walked, he looked back and observed the man and woman standing in the middle of the street locked in warm embrace with tears in their eyes as they watched him go.

TO THE MAN CHASTISING TWO PROSTITUTES IN PUBLIC

"You mean well, my brother, but you should not presume thus to speak to the children of God, even though they chance to be his erring children. Who are we that we should sit in judgment of these women? Do you happen to know all of the circumstances which led them to resort to such methods of obtaining a livelihood? There lives within every human a divine spirit, the gift of the Father in Heaven. This good spirit ever strives to lead us to God, to help us to find God and to know God. But also, within mortals there are many natural physical tendencies which the Creator put there to serve the well-being of the individual and the race. Now, often times, men and women become confused in their efforts to understand themselves and to grapple with the many difficulties of making a living in a world so largely dominated by selfishness and greed. I believe that neither of these women is willfully wicked. I can tell by their faces that they have experienced much sorrow. They have suffered much at the hands of an apparently cruel fate. They have not intentionally chosen this sort of life. They have, in discouragement bordering on despair, surrendered to the pressure of the hour and accepted this distasteful means of obtaining a livelihood as the best way out of a situation that to them appeared hopeless. There are people in this world who are truly wicked at heart. They deliberately choose to do mean things, but tell me my brother, as you look into the faces of these women, do you see any evil or wickedness in them?"

To A Miller

"Grind the grains of truth in the mill of living experience so as to render the difficult things of divine life readily available to even the weak and the feeble among your brothers. Give the milk of truth to those who are babes in spiritual perception. In your living and loving ministry, serve spiritual good in attractive form and suited to the proper capacity of reception of each of your brothers."

To A Roman Centurion

"Render unto Caesar the things which are Caesar's and unto God the things which are God's. The sincere service to God and the loyal service to Caesar do not conflict unless Caesar should presume to abrogate to himself that homage which alone can be claimed by God.

Loyalty to God, if you should come to know him, would render you all the more loyal and faithful in your devotion to a worthy emperor."

To A Mithraic Priest In Corinth

"You do well to seek for a religion of eternal salvation, but your error comes in trying to find such a glorious truth among man-made mysteries and human philosophies. Do you not know that the mystery of eternal salvation dwells within your very own soul? Do you not know that the God of Heaven has sent his spirit to live within you, and that his spirit will lead all truth-loving and God-serving mortals out of this life and through the portals of death up to the eternal heights of light where God awaits to receive his children? Never forget this, they who know God are the sons of God if they truly yearn to be like him."

To An Epicurean Philosopher

"You do well to choose the best and esteem the good, but are you wise when you fail to see the great things of mortal life which are embodied in the spirit realms that are derived from the presence of God in the human heart? The greatest thing in all human experience is knowing the God whose spirit lives within you. Your God-given spirit seeks to lead you forth on that long and endless journey of discovering all the dimensions of our common Father, the God of all creation, the Father of the universes."

To A Greek Builder and Contractor

"My good friend, just as you build the material structures of men, I encourage you to build for yourself a spiritual character in the likeness of the divine spirit within your soul. Do not let your achievement as a temporal builder outdo your achievement as a spiritual son of the kingdom of Heaven. While you build the mansions of time for another, neglect not to secure your title to the mansions of eternity for yourself. Ever remember, there is a city whose foundations are righteousness and truth, and whose builder and maker is your Father in Heaven."

To A Judge in Rome

"As you judge men, remember that you yourself will also someday come to judgment before the bar of the ruler of the universe. Judge justly, even mercifully, even as you shall someday crave merciful consideration at the hands of the highest arbiter - God. Judge as you would be judged under similar circumstances, thus being guided by the spirit of the law as well as by its letter. Even as you apportion justice tempered with fairness in the light of the need of those who are brought before you, so shall you have the right to expect justice tempered by mercy when you stand before the judge of all the Earth."

To The Mistress of the Inn

"Minister your hospitality as one who entertains the children of God. Elevate the drudgery of your daily toil to the levels of a fine art through the elevated vision that you minister to God through the persons in whom his spirit dwells and in whom his spirit has descended to live within their hearts. By serving the children of God, seek to transform their minds and lead their souls to the knowledge of the Father in Heaven and of all the gifts of the divine spirit."

To a Chinese Merchant in Corinth

"Worship only God, who is your true spirit Father. Remember that the Father's spirit ever lives within you and always points the direction of your soul Heavenward. If you follow the subconscious leadings of this immortal spirit, you are certain to continue on in the uplifted way of finding God. When you do find the Father in Heaven, it will be because by seeking him you have become more and more like him. So farewell, my good friend, but only for a season, for we shall meet again in the worlds of light where the Father of spirit souls has provided many delightful stopping places for those who are bound for Paradise."

To a Traveler From the Isles of Britain

"My friend, I perceive you are seeking for truth, and I suggest that the spirit of the Father of all truth may chance to dwell within you. Did you ever sincerely endeavor to talk with the spirit that dwells within you? Such a thing is indeed difficult and seldom yields consciousness of success. But every honest attempt by the material mind of man to communicate with the indwelling spirit will meet with a certain measure of success, notwithstanding that the majority of all such magnificent human experiences must long remain as subconscious registrations in the spirits of such God searching mortals."

TO A YOUNG RUNAWAY CONTEMPLATING SUICIDE

"My sweet child, remember, there are two things you can never run away from - God and yourself. Wherever you may go, you take with you yourself and the spirit of the Heavenly Father which lives within your heart. My son, stop trying to deceive yourself. Settle down to the courageous practice of facing the facts of life. Lay firm hold on the assurances of God as your Father and of eternal life, as I have instructed you. From this day forth, make the commitment to be a real man, a man determined to face life bravely and intelligently.

No, my beautiful son, not with words but with longing looks did you appeal to my heart to help you in this distressing hour. My boy, to one who loves his fellows there is an eloquent appeal for help in your countenance of discouragement and despair. Sit down with me while I tell you of the service trails and happiness highways which lead from the sorrows of self to the joys of loving activities in the brotherhood of men and in the service of the God in Heaven.

My friend, you must pick yourself up from the dark hole you are in, not only physically, but spiritually as well. You must stand up like a man. You may be surrounded with small enemies and be retarded by many obstacles, but the big things and the real things of this world and of the universe are on your side. The sun rises every morning to salute you just as it does the most powerful and prosperous man on Earth.

Look - you have a strong body and powerful muscles - your physical equipment is better than average. Of course, it is just about useless while you sit out here on the mountainside and grieve your misfortunes, real or imagined as you contemplate ending our life. But you could do great things with your body and with your mind if you would hasten off to where great things are waiting to be done. You are trying to run away from your unhappy self, but it cannot be done. You and your problems of living are real. You cannot escape them as long as you live. But know this, your mind is clear and capable. Your strong body has an intelligent mind to direct it. Set your mind at work to solve its problems.

Teach your intellect to work for you. Refuse to be dominated any longer by fear like an unthinking animal. Your mind should be your courageous ally in the solution of your life's problems rather than you being the slave of fear, bonded to depression and defeat. Most valuable of all, your potential for real achievement is the spirit which lives within you, and which will stimulate and inspire your mind to control itself and activate your body, if only you will release it from the clutches of fear and thus enable your spiritual nature to begin your deliverance from the evils of inaction by the powerful presence of living faith. Immediately will this faith vanquish all fear by the presence of that dominating love of your fellow man which will so soon fill your soul to overflowing because of the knowledge which has been born in your heart that you are a child of God.

This day, my son, you are to be reborn, reestablished as a man of faith, courage and devoted service to man. You have been rededicated this day by the Father, who loves you as his son. And when you become so readjusted to life within yourself, you become likewise readjusted to the universe. You have been born again--born of the spirit--and from this day forth your whole life will become one of victorious accomplishments. Trouble will invigorate you.

Disappointment will spur you on. Difficulties will challenge you. Obstacles will stimulate you.

Arise, young man. Say farewell to the life of cringing fear and fleeing cowardice. Hasten back to duty and live your life in the flesh as a son of God, a mortal dedicated to the ennobling service of man on Earth and destined to the superb and eternal service of God in eternity."

To a Condemned Criminal An Hour Before Execution

"My brother, you have fallen on evil times. You lost your way. You became entangled in the meshes of crime. From talking to you, I well know that you did not mean to do the thing which is about to cost you your mortal life. But you did do this evil, and your fellows have judged you guilty. They have determined that you must die. Neither you nor I may deny the state the right to condemn you. There seems to be no way of humanly escaping the penalty of your wrongdoing. Your fellows must judge you by what you did but there is a judge in Heaven to whom you may appeal for forgiveness, and who will judge you by your real motives and better intentions. You need not fear to meet the judgment of God if your repentance is genuine and your faith sincere. The fact that your error carries with it the death penalty imposed by man does not prejudice the chance of your soul to obtain justice and enjoy mercy before the Heavenly courts."

To a Greek Mathematician/Scientist in Athens

"Scientists will someday be able to measure the energy, or evident force, of gravity and electricity, but these same scientists will never be able to tell you what these phenomena of the universe really are.

Science deals with physical energy activities. Religion deals with eternal values. True philosophy grows out of the wisdom which does its best to correlate these quantitative and qualitative observations. There will always exist the danger that the purely physical scientist may become afflicted with mathematical pride and statistical egotism as well as spiritual blindness.

Logic has validity in the material world, and mathematics is reliable when limited in its application to physical things. Neither is to be regarded as wholly dependable or infallible when applied to life problems. Life embraces problems that are not of the material world. Mathematics and logic teach you that if one man can shear a sheep in ten minutes, then ten men could shear this same sheep in one minute.

That is sound mathematics, but it is not true. The men could not do this. They would get in one another's way so badly that the task would be greatly delayed.

Mathematics also stands for the theory that if one person stands for a certain unit of intellectual and moral value, then ten persons would stand for ten times this value. But in dealing with human personality, you will find that it is nearer the truth to say that such a personality grouping is a sum equal to the square of the number of personalities concerned in the equation rather than the simple arithmetical sum. A social group of human beings, if working in harmony, stands for a force far greater than the simple sum of its parts.

Quantity may be identified as a fact, thus becoming a scientific uniformity. Quality represents an estimate of values, and must, therefore, remain an experience of the individual. When both science and religion become less dogmatic and more tolerant of criticism, philosophy will then begin to achieve unity in the intelligent comprehension of the universe.

There really is unity in the universe, if you can only see its workings in actuality. The real universe is a friend to every child of the eternal God. The real problem to comprehend is, how can the finite mind of man achieve a logical, true, and corresponding unity of thought? This universal state of mind can be had only by understanding and realizing that the quantitative fact and the qualitative value have a common causation in the Father in Heaven.

Such a concept yields a broader insight into the purposeful unity of universe phenomena. It even reveals a progressive spiritual goal.

Visible matter and unrecognized energy are both real and both exist. It is only when the energy of the universe is slowed down to the requisite degree of motion that these unrecognized energies can become mass."

To a Greek Philosopher At Ephesus

"The soul is the self-reflective and truth-discerning part of man which forever elevates the human being above the level of the animal world. Self-consciousness, in and of itself, is not the soul. Moral self- consciousness is true human understanding and constitutes the foundation of the human soul. The soul is that part of man which survives the human experience when you pass through mortal death.

Moral choice and spiritual achievement, the ability to know God and the urge to be like him, are the characteristics of the soul. The soul of man cannot exist apart from moral thinking and spiritual activity. A stagnant soul is a dying soul. But the soul of man is distinct from the divine spirit which dwells within the mind. The divine spirit arrives simultaneously with the first moral activity of the human mind. The mind of man, free will, together with the spirit which the Father gave you, create the soul of man.

All types of soul conflicts exist because of the lack of harmony between the moral, or spiritual, self-consciousness and the purely intellectual self-consciousness. The human soul, when matured, ennobled and spiritualized, approaches the Heavenly status in that it comes nearest to being an entity intervening between the material self and the divine spirit. The evolving soul of a human being is difficult to describe and even more difficult to demonstrate because it is not discoverable by the methods of either material investigation or spiritual proving. Material science cannot demonstrate the existence of a soul, neither can pure spirit-testing. Notwithstanding the failure of both material science and spiritual standards to discover the existence of the human soul, every morally conscious mortal knows and feels the existence of his soul as a real and actual personal experience."

LECTURING AT URMIA TO THIRTY RELIGIOUS LEADERS (THIS IS A BRIEF EXCERPT FROM SEVERAL DAYS OF LECTURING)

"The brotherhood of man is founded on the fatherhood of God.

The family of God is derived from the love of God - God is love, therefore, God the Father divinely loves all his children. The kingdom of Heaven is founded on the fact of divine sovereignty. God is spirit.

Since God is spirit, this kingdom is spiritual. The kingdom of Heaven is neither material nor merely intellectual. It is a spiritual relationship between man and God.

When all religions come to recognize the sovereignty of God the Father over all spirits, then will all religions be at peace. Only when one religion assumes that it is in some way superior to all others and that it possesses exclusive authority over other religions, will such a religion presume to be intolerant of other religions or dare to persecute other religious believers.

Religious peace - brotherhood - will never exist until all religions are willing to completely divest themselves of all ecclesiastical authority and fully surrender all concept of spiritual sovereignty. God alone is sovereign.

The kingdom of Heaven in the hearts of man will create religious unity because any and all religious groups composed of such religious believers will be free from all notions of ecclesiastical authority - religious sovereignty.

God is spirit, and God gives a fragment of his spirit self to dwell in the heart and mind of man. Spiritually, all men are equal. The kingdom of Heaven is free from castes, classes, social levels, and economic groups. You are all brothers, equal to each other.

The moment you lose sight of the spirit sovereignty of God the Father, one of your religions will begin to assert its superiority over other religions, and then, instead of peace on Earth and good will among men, there will start dissension, recriminations, even religious wars.

Freewill beings who regard themselves as equals sooner or later are tempted to try out their ability to gain power and authority over other people and groups. The concept of equality will never bring peace except in the mutual recognition and understanding of the sovereignty of God over all beings."

SPEAKING ABOUT SOVEREIGNTY TO POLITICAL SCIENTISTS

"Wars on Earth will never cease so long as nations cling to the illusive notions of unlimited national sovereignty. There are only two levels of sovereignty in this world: a) the individual sovereignty of each person and b) the sovereignty of all peoples on Earth, collectively.

Between these two levels are infinite and ever-changing combinations created to serve man for his welfare, well-being or progress.

Religious teachers must always remember that the spiritual sovereignty of God overrides all intervening and intermediate spiritual loyalties. Someday civil rulers will come to realize that God also rules in the kingdom of men.

This rule of God in the kingdoms of men is not for the special benefit of any favored group of men. There is no such thing as a "chosen people", or a "favored nation". The rule of God is a rule designed to foster the greatest good to the greatest number of men and for the greatest length of time.

This world will never enjoy lasting peace until the so-called sovereign nations intelligently and fully surrender their sovereign powers into the hands of the brotherhood of men - the government of mankind - one Earth, one people. Leagues of nations will be formed in the future, but they will never bring permanent peace to mankind.

World-wide confederations of nations can prevent minor wars and control the smaller nations, but they will never prevent world wars nor control the most powerful of governments. In the face of real conflicts, one of the major powers can always withdraw from a confederation and declare war on the others. You will never prevent wars as long as nations remain infected with the delusional virus of national sovereignty.

It is not a question of armament or disarmament. Neither does the question of conscription or voluntary service enter into the problem of maintaining world-wide peace. If you take every form of armament away from nations, they will fight each other with sticks and stones so long as they cling to this delusion of national sovereignty or chosen people.

War is not man's great and terrible disease. War is a symptom. The real disease is national sovereignty.

When all the peoples of this world create a world government, then and only then will they have the power and the right to make such a government sovereign over the affairs of men. When such a representative or democratic world power controls the world's land, air, and sea, peace on Earth and good will among men will prevail - but not until then."

Speaking About Law and Liberty

"If one man cherishes freedom, liberty, he must realize that all other men on the face of the Earth also cherish freedom.

Groups of freedom loving men cannot live together in peace without becoming subject to laws, rules and regulations as will grant each person the same degree of freedom while at the same time safeguarding an equal degree of freedom for all of his fellow brothers. You must realize this universal truth: If one man is absolutely free, then another man must be absolutely a slave. The relative nature of freedom is true socially, economically and politically. Freedom is the gift of civilization made possible by the enforcement of laws.

Religions make it spiritually possible to realize the brotherhood of men, but it requires mankind's governments to regulate the social, economic and political problems associated with such a goal of human happiness and efficiency."

To All People as They Departed From Him

"Peace be with you and may the blessings of our Father in Heaven forever abide in you."

CC MARTIN